Bless God and Take Courage

The Judson History and Legacy

ROSALIE HALL HUNT

God's daily blessings on you!

Rosalie Hall Hunt

JUDSON PRESS
PUBLISHERS SINCE 1824

Valley Forge, Pennsylvania

COVER IMAGES: Judson Church, Aungbinle in 1905, Adoniram Judson, Ann Hasseltine Judson, George Boardman Jr., Emily Chubbuck Judson, Abby Ann Judson, Let Ma Yoon death prison in 1824, The Caravan, Sule Pagoda are all used by permission. Except as noted in the text, photographic images are from the private collection of the author.

Library of Congress Cataloging-in-Publication Data
Hunt, Rosalie Hall.
Bless God and take courage : the Judson history and legacy / Rosalie Hall Hunt.—1st ed.
    p. cm.
Includes bibliographical references. ISBN 0-8170-1479-9 (alk. paper)
1. Judson, Adoniram, 1788-1850. 2. Missionaries—Burma—Biography. 3. Missionaries—United States—Biography. I. Title.
BV3271.J7H86 2005
266'.61'092—dc22
                                                                    2004024627

Printed in the U.S.A.

12 11 10 09 08 07 06
10 9 8 7 6 5 4 3 2

To Alice and Harold Hall,
parents who planted the heritage
in their daughter's heart;
to husband, Bob,
who bore the birth pangs of
Bless God and Take Courage
with unfailing patience;
to children, Alice, Jody, and Lori,
who originated the impetus;
and for the "Grands,"
Carl, Eric, Aidan, Gannon, and McKenna,
so they will know and cherish
the legacy and pass it on.

CONTENTS

CONTENTS

FOREWORD

TELL ME YOUR HEROES AND I WILL TELL YOU WHO YOU ARE! THE tragedy of modern American youth is that their heroes are often anti-heroes—in prison, on drugs, suicidal, living without meaning. In the 19th century, our heroes were missionaries. This book is the story of the greatest American missionary heroes of the 19th century.

In 1849, Adoniram Judson, the second most recognized name of that era, was introduced to the President of the United States as the "greatest ecclesiastical character now living." While present-day biases may associate "missionary" with insensitivity and intolerance, readers will discover that Judson was a man of great learning and sensitivity whose Bible translation and Burmese grammars are still used today. While numerous biographies of the Judsons have been written, each generation must learn anew the struggles and meaning of those lives. Rosalie Hall Hunt has done a great service to our generation by presenting the magnificent story of Judson and his amazing wives, Ann, Sarah, and Emily.

Bless God and Take Courage is not a story of paternalism or imperialism. Nor is it a pious attempt to write about heroes without taking seriously the flaws inherent in all men and women. It is a story of love; love for all people and first of all, love for Christ. Outstanding in its presentation of the role that the Judson women played in fulfilling the mission to share the gospel, this book is also distinct in that it is essentially two books: a biography of the Judsons and the story of their ongoing legacy. Readers will gain not only an appreciation of the work of the Judsons, but will also hear stories of their descendants and be brought up-to-date on the four million believers who make up the contemporary church in Myanmar.

May the younger generation rediscover these significant leaders of Christian mission to the world! Let us all recommit ourselves to the task of evangelizing the world in our own generation!

—Denton Lotz, Dr.theol.
General Secretary of the Baptist World Alliance

PREFACE

ANN AND ADONIRAM JUDSON SAILED TO THE LAND OF BURMA (NOW known as Myanmar) two hundred years ago and changed it forever. Their story is one of love and adventure, tragedy and perseverance, fame and acclaim—a story better than fiction, for it actually happened. The Judsons, America's first effort to send missionaries overseas, became *mythic* figures in nineteenth-century Christianity, but their struggles, triumphs, joys, and suffering were all too real. In New York's famous Riverside Church are stone carvings commemorating historical figures whose lives have exemplified some aspect of Christ's life. Among them, there is only one couple so honored: Ann and Adoniram Judson. (Of the sixty-three honored, only four are women and eight are Americans.)

To this new millennium the Judsons have left a living legacy, both in the United States and in Burma/Myanmar. Throughout present-day Myanmar, the intriguing trail of the Judsons can still be found. Adoniram lay fettered in prison for nearly two years; Ann's intrepidity and fortitude kept him alive. One crisis followed another, yet Ann declared, "We thank God and take courage." This spirit of determination to bless God and take courage became the hallmark of their lives. Ann saved Adoniran from execution three times, then died herself from the effects of disease and malnutrition. He lived on to give the Burmese people their first and best translation of the Bible. Judson's great personal appeal and his remarkable ability to relate to the people and preach in the Burmese language led to the establishment of the church in that land.

The Judson saga is a thrilling account of an extraordinary man who loved three equally remarkable women, each of whom made a major contribution to the foundation of Christianity among the Burmese people. Ann, with her intelligence, linguistic skills, and force of will and character, managed not only to keep Adoniram alive but also to leave behind her own translation work and the foundation of women's education. Sarah, Judson's second wife, was the widow of another young missionary, and she possessed skills and abilities that complemented Judson's. Sarah was the mother of eight children with Adoniram, but she died tragically early at age forty-one. Judson's third wife, Emily, was already a well-known writer when he met her. They married in 1846, and his last four years were rich in continued strengthening of the Burmese mission.

Many accounts of the Judsons were written in the century following their pioneer efforts, for their significance on America's missions history has been unmatched. However, the last biography of Judson was written fifty years ago, and none was written by someone who had visited Burma. All the biographies ended with Judson's death, but the *story* does not end there. Their legacy has continuing impact. *Bless God and Take Courage* travels to the land where the Judsons served to discover their footprints. The legacy lives on in that nation, for the name *Judson* is carved into the history of its people and its languages.

And in America, there are important stones of remembrance still left to the community of faith, true missions landmarks. Baptists in the United States owe their formation into a denomination to the Judsons, and the larger community of faith is able to trace in the Judsons' story the awakening of the missions consciousness of a fledgling nation. The until-now untold story of Judson descendants is also fascinating. Where did they go? What did they become, and does the line live on? This account searches for clues that shed light on this remarkable family.

This is uniquely *three* love stories, not just one. New material has been discovered, including the exquisite love letters of Adoniram and Emily. And could that copy of a portrait of a beautiful young woman found in an obscure file really be the only known likeness of Sarah Boardman Judson? Exploring the heritage left by the Judsons began as curiosity and ended as a quest. Their extraordinary legacy is very much alive; uncovering it has been the journey of a lifetime.

ACKNOWLEDGMENTS

A HOST OF PEOPLE INTERESTED IN MISSIONS HISTORY HAVE HAD A PART IN *Bless God and Take Courage*; their locations range from Burma to California, Massachusetts, and Alabama. Their enthusiasm has been contagious. The expertise, assistance, and inspiration of Iva Jewel Tucker of Birmingham, Alabama, were indispensable. Archivists have been cheerleaders, led by Betty Layton of the American Baptist Historical Society (ABHS), along with ABHS director, Dr. Deborah Van Broekhoven. Martha Mitchell (Brown University), Elizabeth Wells (Samford University), and Edie Jeter (International Mission Board) have made significant contributions. The staff at the American Baptist Samuel Colgate Historical Library in Rochester, New York, lent much assistance, as did Bob Cushing (First Baptist Church, Salem, Massachusetts), Paula Richter (Salem Peabody-Essex Museum), and Marie Harmon (Guntersville, Alabama, Public Library). Stuart Calvert, president of Alabama Woman's Missionary Union, and the outstanding state WMU staff were involved from the book's inception. WMU members across the state of Alabama were a steady source of inspiration, especially readers Peggy Gentry, Hazel Hyatt, and Mary Wells Maze. Author and friend Mr. Nguyen Dinh Huu and his family of San Jose, California, provided invaluable help.

Judson biographer Courtney Anderson gave steady inspiration. Retired missionary Russell Brown was an excellent source of information on modern Burma, as were Neil Sowards and Sam Rickard. Ron Brown lent expertise in Judson genealogy, and the computer was kept alive and functioning by Barbara Young, Paul Meigs, and Frank Duckett. Alice Hunt's technical and bibliographic expertise were indispensable. Shari Hamblin of Ohio was a special source of inspiration.

Special thanks go to the Judson Press staff: Randy Frame, Cassandra Williams, and Wendy Ronga, and to Rebecca Irwin Diehl and Laura Weller for their editorial work and indexing.

Numerous Baptist leaders in Burma gave valuable input, headed by Harriet Bain and other descendants of Ah Vong, the first Chinese-

Burmese printer. His four living granddaughters contributed personal memories of the early years in Moulmein.

Rangoon pastor Paul Johns shared valuable information. Daw Tin May, Victor Soe, Men Bah Su, and Freedom Saw Wah Htoo of Moulmeim were of significant help regarding early Baptist beginnings, along with U Win Tin in Rangoon and Silas Saw, pastor of Aungbinle's Judson Church.

Gregory Laing of Haverhill, Massachusetts, made a visit inside Ann's birthplace possible, as did Alex Corrado for Adoniram's birthplace in Malden and owner Mrs. Sproles, for Judson's boyhood home in Plymouth. Dr. George Tooze, doubtless America's leading Emily Chubbuck Judson scholar, was a lodestone of information and inspiration.

My husband, Bob, and children Alice and Jody, first suggested the need for a "new millennium" account of the Judson legacy and became an ensemble of muses. Daughter-in-law Lori entered into the spirit of research and travel with an uncanny sense of direction and unflagging enthusiasm and involvement. First Baptist Church of Guntersville, Alabama, graciously underwrote the more than 100,000 research miles that made authenticity possible and Jerry Cain, president of Judson College, Elgin, Illinois, has given lasting new meaning to the words *supporter* and *advocate*.

Judson's great-grandson, Dr. Stanley Hanna, was the manuscript's chief source of primary material and a constant inspiration, providing access to more than seven hundred original family letters and pouring a lifetime of love for Burma and his family heritage into the project, always supportive, always enthusiastic. The Judsons' legacy is a gift to all who are thankful for those who went before and set a standard of devotion without equal.

The earliest known portrait of Adoniram Judson is this 1811 miniature. Used by permission, archived collections, Board of International Ministries, American Baptist Historical Society, Valley Forge, PA.

It Began in Malden 1788–1804

The childhood shows the man as morning shows the day.
—John Milton, *Paradise Regained*

AS A NATION, AMERICA WAS BARELY A toddler that year of 1788. She did ratify a constitution in July but still had no president. Malden, Massachusetts, was a mere speck on the map, a thriving little New England town far removed from the weighty affairs of state and certainly insignificant in the grand scheme of things. Yet the birth of Adoniram Judson Jr. on August 9, 1788, was destined to place Malden forever on the map of Christian missions history. The First Congregational Church parsonage where he was born still stands, the oldest house in Malden, and a silent reminder of a powerful legacy that continues to influence lives in this century.

Little Adoniram was the joy of his gentle mother's heart and the pride of his stern father. Judson Sr. was immensely gratified by signs that his firstborn was unusually bright. An early biographer who knew Adoniram's father remarked, "He, though not...ambitious of personal distinction, appears to have coveted eminence for his children."[1] This seems a natural ambition that many fond parents experience, but in this strict clergyman it assumed an exaggerated significance.

Judson Sr. was pastor during a period when the Congregational denomination was embroiled in liberal-conservative controversy. His

1

sermons majored on the wrath and judgment of God. To the little toddler looking up to this great and solemn figure who was both adored and quite possibly feared, affection was no doubt tinged with awe. Many years later, this pastor's grandson, Edward, who was never able to meet his own grandfather, heard that eminent pastor described by an elderly man who had known him: "He was, as I remember him, a man of decidedly imposing appearance. His stature was rather above the average. His white hair, erect position, grave utterance, and somewhat taciturn manner…left one somewhat at a loss whether to class him with a patriarch of the Hebrews or a censor of the Romans. He was through life esteemed a man of inflexible integrity and uniform consistency of Christian character."[2]

Adoniram saw his father not only as an important figure in the home, but also as the central personage in the church just a hundred yards across the road. The perceptive young child realized early on that his father was the most important thing about that church. He stood up all alone in front and talked very loudly and everyone listened. And sometimes Adoniram heard his father talking to somebody the child's eyes could not see. This somebody of many names was sometimes called "our heavenly Father" or "Jehovah" or "our Lord." There is no doubt that small Adoniram based his early concept of the greatness and power of Almighty God on what he saw and experienced with his earthly father.[3]

In contrast, little is known about Adoniram's mother, Abigail. Literature of the eighteenth and nineteenth centuries seldom illuminated the lives, work, or contributions of the women of those times, particularly the great majority of women whose chief roles were as wives and mothers. Adoniram Judson's biographers, however, uniformly portray Abigail as nurturing, loving, and caring, providing for her children warmth and security. She also had very strong opinions about what was undesirable—and dirt was definitely undesirable. Dirtiness was bad, and cleanliness was highly desired. The little boy grew up to be fastidious, with a loathing of dirt that made life nearly beyond enduring when, thirty years later in a Burmese prison, he found himself in inescapable filth and stench.

The deep-seated church controversy over liberal-conservative theology was never far below the surface in the Judsons' lives. Considering the unyielding and uncompromising nature of Judson Sr., the inevitable occurred and the Malden congregation asked for his "dismission." Little Adoniram was not yet three and new baby sister Abigail (called Abby) less than two weeks old when the resolution was voted by the church that April 1791. The family, however, was allowed to remain in the parsonage a year. The search for a new pulpit was not easy, and Judson Sr. was often away from home, supplying pulpits and seeking a new pastorate. The man was anxious for the welfare of his family and what their future might be when he went for months with no success in his search for a church. It was more than a year before an acceptable call came and the Judson family moved to Wenham, Massachusetts, just north of Salem. The town and church were both smaller, but the united congregation more than compensated for less prosperous circumstances.[4]

Many children who grow to great prominence give no early clues of later distinction. This was not strictly true in young Adoniram. When still very small, he displayed an exceptionally keen and quick intellect. Once while Father was away supplying pulpits, Mother decided to prepare a surprise for him. Upon Judson Sr.'s return from a week of traveling, he settled by the fire to relax. Mother Abigail handed three-year-old Adoniram a Bible, and smiling, she gestured to him to climb onto his father's lap, whereupon the little fellow opened the Bible and read for Judson Sr. an entire chapter. Amazed, Judson held his little child and proudly said, "Son, some day you will be a great man."[5] In those formative years, Adoniram often heard his all-powerful father's assurance—you *will be* a great man. And thus did a strong determination begin to develop in the brilliant little boy.

Despite the trauma of doctrinal troubles always seething just under the surface in the Congregational denomination and in spite of several moves during their childhood years, Adoniram and little Abby enjoyed the warmth and security of a loving home. And in 1794, while in Wenham, a second son, Elnathan, was born to the Judsons.

Young Adoniram gave ample proof of self-reliance and confidence.

In later years, Abigail loved to recount how her four-year-old son would collect the neighborhood's children to "preach" to them. He always arranged to be the "pastor," while the others were the congregation. No record remains of the little preacher's sermon topics, but his mother remembered that his favorite hymn was "Go Preach My Gospel, Saith the Lord."6 And Adoniram loved puzzles, the harder the better. He had a consuming curiosity and was forever trying to figure out just how something worked. His friends, even the older ones, sometimes found themselves irritated because they never seemed able to pose a riddle he could not solve.7

An early biographer noted that there is no record of Adoniram being consistently called by a nickname, although it would seem likely, since there were two Adonirams under one roof.8 Could he have been "Addy" or "Niram" or possibly "Dom"? He *was* given an affectionate title by his schoolmates: "Old Virgil Dug Up." His phenomenal linguistic skills became apparent early as he quickly mastered both Greek and Latin. His talent in mathematics was equally profound, and he excelled just as noticeably at literature, history, and logic.

"Old Virgil" was allowed to use much of his free time as he chose, and his habits of self-dependence gave him an opportunity to greedily devour all the books he could put his hands on—some of which, like the novels of Fielding or the plays of Ben Johnson, might have surprised his Puritan father.9 Adoniram's interests were far-ranging, and when only ten, he took lessons in navigation from a Captain Cutter. What dreams that young boy must have conjured up as he learned about the sea and strolled along the wharves of nearby Salem, watching mighty ships coming from distant and exotic shores. Adoniram could often catch the scents of sandalwood and mysterious spices as a trader from the East would unload at the dock.

In a child with so many interests and abilities, it is not surprising to see strong personality traits develop. This was definitely the case with young Adoniram. He was unusually high-spirited and confident, always full of energy. His disposition, however, according to an early biographer who knew him personally, was remarkably good-natured, particularly with his family.[10] Adoniram's sister, Abby, shamelessly adored him and tried to follow him everywhere. His spirit of determination was unflagging and remained that way until the day he died. Such resolve later helped the man Adoniram Judson endure hardships most people cannot even imagine.

Adoniram Sr.'s health became precarious in 1800, and he resigned the Wenham church, although the congregation urged him to remain. The family moved yet again, to Braintree, just a few miles south of Boston. Wenham had been home for Adoniram Jr. from ages four to eleven, and now he found himself in a strange neighborhood. Being thrown on his own resources further fostered Adoniram's sense of self-reliance.

When his health improved, Judson Sr. did some itinerant work with the Massachusetts Home Missionary Society in Vermont. During this transition period, Judson Sr.'s difficulties in his own ministry made him all the more determined that his son succeed and become a man of note. Very close to where they now lived was the modest home where President John Adams had grown up. As they passed the Adams's house, Adoniram's father would comment to his son about the possibilities before him, a young fellow with as much native ability and talent as the president of the country himself.[11]

In 1802, the Congregational Church in Plymouth, Massachusetts, which had been founded by the first settlers in 1620, split. The conservative element of the membership formed the "Third Congregational Church." This new congregation built on Pleasant Street, on the slope of the hill overlooking famous Plymouth Rock in the harbor below. The congregation immediately called Judson Sr. as their pastor, and thus Plymouth became home to Adoniram when he was thirteen.

Judson Sr. purchased land on the same street as the new church. It was known as Watson's Hill, the spot on which Chief Massasoit of the Wampanoag tribe had camped the fateful spring of 1621, while he sent Squanto and Samoset as emissaries to the desperate Pilgrims. In later years, Judson bought still more land around their home and sold it for house lots. He actually became quite affluent for a minister and never again was forced to wholly depend on a pastor's salary.[12]

The family had just settled in Plymouth when young Adoniram grew dangerously ill. He was in critical condition for some time and nearly died. Previous to his illness, the teenager had not devoted a lot of time to thought. Now leisure time seemed all he had. He was forced to convalesce for more than a year. Adoniram slowly recovered to the point where he was able to read and study on his own and still had ample hours for thinking and daydreaming. He had read much about great men who had made their mark on history. Maybe he himself would become a poet or possibly a statesman. Or perhaps a great orator?

Then Adoniram's early training intruded on these solitary thoughts. He had been taught all his life that real fame must come from holiness and goodness. He mused about pulpit possibilities. Maybe he would lead a large and wealthy congregation. He could almost picture the sea of faces looking up expectantly, drinking in his every word. Then somehow he thought on the humble country pastor who labors faithfully year after year and seeks nothing for himself. This one, his heart told him, was the one with true greatness and rich reward in heaven. In later years, Adoniram was to recall that day when the words "Not unto us, not unto us, but to Thy name be the glory" rang out so clearly that he felt he had literally heard them spoken. The shock of that moment was so real that he sat almost bolt upright in his bed.[13]

Adoniram began to agonize over the stark contradiction between his personal ambition and what he knew to be genuine greatness. The easiest way of dealing with such a dichotomy was simply not to think about it, so he tamped down those disquieting thoughts. He persuaded himself he would just "think about that later." And yet the shocking insight of that single moment was so clear and stinging that he would remember it the rest of his life.[14]

As Adoniram gained strength, he began rebuilding his health and applied himself to serious study. He quickly made up the missed year of school and even more. By 1804, fifteen-year old Adoniram was ready to enter college. But what college? Although Adoniram Sr. was a Yale graduate, Yale was quite some distance from Plymouth. Harvard was nearer but far too liberal in its theology, Judson Sr. reasoned. He liked the idea of Brown University for his son. It was nominally Baptist, but Adoniram Sr. found its theology much closer to his own than that of liberals in his own Congregationalist denomination. Judson Sr. considered this college "safe" for his son.[15]

One week after his sixteenth birthday, Adoniram entered Brown University. He probably did not stand out in that matriculating class, being of medium height and slender in build. There was, however, a special warm radiance in his frequent smile and a face with clear-cut features topped by curly, dark chestnut hair. Once met, he was not forgotten.[16] Adoniram had unusually brilliant and striking hazel eyes, penetrating in their gaze. And when he opened his mouth, his voice belied his size. It was a compelling and powerful bass, drawing the ear like a magnet. So began a new era in his life. It was a different world from Plymouth, so near geographically yet so distant philosophically. Here he encountered a whole new world of thought and modern influence, some of which proved to be the despair of his loving family back home.

To Brown and Beyond 1804–1810

Judson's boyhood home in Plymouth, Mass. was built in 1802. Insert: "Missionary Woods" memorial at Phillips Academy, Andover, Mass., marks the spot where Adoniram Judson committed his life to overseas missions in 1810.

Truths that wake to
perish never.
—William Wordsworth,
Intimations of Immortality

THE FATHER ADONIRAM COULD SCARCELY RECOGNIZE THE SON
Adoniram in 1807, just three years after the youth had gone away to
college with such high hopes and ambitions. Physically there was little change other than a maturing of features and physique. The
change was in the words he spoke, words that sounded radical to his
loving parents. Brown University had seemed a good choice, a Baptist
school with more Congregationalists than Baptists and a reputation
for superior learning.[1]

Adoniram was younger than other entering students yet so academically advanced that he was placed in the second-year class. The young scholar was not only exceptional in academics but quickly made an impact on the campus with his winning smile and friendly spirit. He was equally at ease in class and in leisure time with friends and faculty. Classmates recalled in later years that Judson had never failed or even hesitated in recitation.[2]

Among his friends were those who would become leaders of government and industry, a United States senator, a Supreme Court judge, and other men of eminence. And still he excelled. Adoniram was close friends with John Bailey, later a congressman from Massachusetts. Bailey was his closest rival academically, and their friendly contest for first place added zest to Adoniram's naturally competitive tendencies. An even closer friend was Jacob Eames, slightly older, talented, witty, and a self-proclaimed Deist. He was probably the most influential friend in coloring Adoniram's thoughts about God and eternal life during those university years. The two would spend hours discussing philosophy and how they would one day achieve greatness through their own abilities. No higher power was needed. One day their goal might be the pursuit of law, another, great writing. No hint of the heresy of Deism reached the ears of Adoniram's fond parents. His father did receive a letter from Brown University president Ada Messer about the potential of his son. Messer wrote: "A uniform propriety of conduct, as well as an intense application to study, distinguished his character. Your expectations of him, however sanguine, must certainly be gratified. I must heartily congratulate you, my dear sir, on that charming prospect which you have exhibited in this very amiable and promising son."[3]

When Adoniram was ready to graduate in 1807, he wrote his father one line: "Dear Father, I have got it. Your affectionate son, A.J."[4] His parents immediately knew that their firstborn was Brown's valedictorian. Adoniram was only nineteen, unsure of what he wanted to do, but full of great ideas and energy. Since he wanted to do so much, he was not certain where to start. For this brilliant student who excelled in all he did, failure did not even cross his mind.[5]

Adoniram was always possessed with an amazing drive. After graduating from Brown, he opened a school in Plymouth, at the same time writing an English grammar textbook and a mathematics text. Yet he felt dissatisfied. These tasks seemed so ordinary and dull. Here he was, seething with ideas, yet strangely reluctant to reveal to his conservative parents how he really felt. Their way of life wasn't his, and he felt as if he were living a lie. On the other hand, Adoniram did not want to reveal his true feelings because he had no wish to hurt such a mother and father.

At first his parents were puzzled when Adoniram announced he was closing his school and traveling. First, he said, he'd go see Uncle Ephraim, who was a minister in Sheffield, about 150 miles away. Then he wanted to see something of the broad world beyond, maybe go to New York. To his staunchly conservative mother and father, it could not have been worse if he had announced he was going to Sodom and Gomorrah. They were stunned. Why on earth would he contemplate going to New York? Adoniram did not want to wound them nor feel their scorn, but somehow the truth came out. He no longer believed in a personal God and the need for a Savior—whereupon his mother burst into tears and his father tried every argument at his command. But the logic of staid Pastor Judson was no match for the scintillating skills of Brown's top debater. Adoniram could handle each verbal assault with consummate ease, but the wrenching tears of his mother haunted his thoughts and dreams for months to come.

A few days later, on his twentieth birthday, a defiant young Adoniram set out to "find himself" and sow a few wild oats. It began as a heady adventure for an ambitious man on his own at last—his own master, with an exciting world before him. Never had he been so far from family and constraints. Several days later, he left his horse with his elderly Uncle Ephraim in Sheffield and headed for the big city on the newly invented Fulton steamer.

His heart pounded with excitement as he stepped off the steamer and found himself in New York at last. Summertime in New York was the slowest time of year for the theater, but Adoniram was tenacious and managed to join a rather seedy little band of actors going from place to place, looking for opportunities. For a young minister's son from a conservative family, it was surely a wild and reckless time: looking for work, cadging off unwary landlords, and surreptitiously moving on at night without paying for room and board. Fastidious as he was and principled in spite of himself, in just a matter of weeks, Adoniram left without a word to anyone.

Fifteen years later, in the crucible of suffering, a much wiser Adoniram mentioned that early period of his life to a man who was bound and fettered with him in a Burmese death prison. His British friend recalled Judson's comments on that youthful folly: "In my early days of wildness, I joined a band of strolling players. We lived a reckless, vagabond life, finding lodgings where we could, and bilking the landlord where we found opportunity, in other words, running up a score, and then decamping without paying the reckoning. Before leaving America, when the enormity of this vicious course rested with a depressing weight on my mind, I made a second tour over the same ground, carefully making amends to all whom I had injured."[6]

But in the late summer of 1808, disillusioned and haunted by vague unformed thoughts of "What now?" Adoniram decided to return to his uncle's house, get his horse, and continue his travels west. It was a long trip back to Sheffield, and Adoniram had plenty of time for thinking as he journeyed through the countryside, aware with only a part of his mind of the late-summer sights and sounds along the way. Here was a confused young man, unable to find the answers he was seeking within his own powerful intellect. Somehow he had expected the world "out there" to be freer, more challenging, full of other bright minds eager to try something new. Tawdry actors, seedy lodgings, and never enough money were not his idea of a great adventure. New York *should* have been fascinating. Although Mother and Father were old-fashioned and rigid in their opinions, Adoniram had to admit to himself how disappointed he was with New York.

Judson arrived in Sheffield to find his uncle away and a young minister taking his place for a few weeks. He invited Adoniram to spend the night, and they talked until all hours. Adoniram noticed several things that impressed him. This was clearly a devoted young preacher who demonstrated a warmth and earnestness to which Adoniram's hungry heart responded. He was impressed that a man of God could be devout yet not overbearing or austere. The young preacher might not have lofty ambitions, but he clearly had peace. Adoniram left with a lot to think about. He himself *did* have lofty goals, but in all honesty he knew he did not have peace.[7]

The beauty of the New England countryside in September was all around him, but he scarcely noticed, so puzzling were his thoughts. How could it be that a man scarcely older than himself and showing no discernible ambitions could so clearly exhibit tranquility and contentment? Adoniram himself felt a binding sense of restlessness, when what he really desired was a clear goal, a sense of direction. He had found neither in his wanderings.

Night was falling as he came to a little village and found a small inn. The town's only innkeeper apologized because there was just one vacant room. "I'm afraid you would be disturbed, sir. It is next to the room of a young fellow who is seriously ill, maybe even dying." Adoniram, weary and wrapped up in his own uneasy thoughts, was anxious for a bed and temporary peace. He assured the landlord that a few noises wouldn't disturb him; he was a sound sleeper. After a light meal, Adoniram was ready for bed. But sleep wouldn't come. The noises coming from the adjoining room were not loud, but they were most disquieting—a groan, gasps, a moan, a voice calling, "God, God, lost." It was not the noise that bothered him, nor was it even the thought of someone dying, certainly a common enough occurrence in early nineteenth-century New England. The disturbing thing was the thought of death itself and the eerie awareness that in his own state of confusion, he was not prepared to die.

Surely his father's ideas of God's judgment and the ever-looming possibility of eternal damnation could not be true. But, the other side of his mind said, what if they *were* true? How would he face death? What if it were he who was dying? And in the night reaches, everything seemed larger than life. Certainly the grave did. Adoniram had been drilled in the importance of meticulous cleanliness. His flesh crawled with the thought of a grave, of himself lying in that cold, dark, dank place. Was this the end of humanity? Surely it couldn't be. His thoughts overwhelmed him, and sleep came only in snatches and starts. Finally, the sun rose, and Adoniram's distressing thoughts seemed to vanish in the light streaming in through the window. What a coward he had been during the night. It crossed his mind that his agnostic friend Jacob Eames would surely deride him for those night fancies, all disappearing in the clear light of day. He would be sure not to tell Jacob he had harbored such eerie thoughts.

Tired but cheerful, he ran down the stairs, prepared to pay for the night's lodging. Adoniram asked for his bill and casually inquired about the sick man: "It seems quiet now. Is he better?" The sober-faced innkeeper responded: "He is dead." "Dead?" And then Adoniram asked the obvious question, "Do you know who he was?" "Oh yes," the innkeeper responded. "Young man from the college in Providence. Name of Eames. Jacob Eames."[8]

Adoniram was stunned: Eames? Dead? His friend was gone, gone now beyond all reasoning and philosophies and lofty logic. And Adoniram had been in the very next room. Something told his astounded mind that such an occurrence could not have been simple coincidence. A higher power had to be involved. And if so, that shattered the confidence he had in his own ability to reason, to control his own destiny. Hours passed before Adoniram was coherent enough to leave the inn. Not far down the road, he reined in his horse, paused, and turned in the other direction, toward home.

Adoniram had always loved a puzzle. Surely there was none he had ever failed to solve. But *this* one required thought, soul-searching thought. Never one to procrastinate, Adoniram began going over in his mind all he knew of his parents' God and all he had himself thought about some impersonal Creator. In a state of bewilderment, he rode to his Plymouth home. It was September 22, 1808. Adoniram had been away not quite six weeks, but it had seemed more like a lifetime.

Again Providence intervened. Two eminent leaders of the conservative element of Congregationalists came to confer with Adoniram's father. Edward Griffin and Moses Stuart wanted to discuss with him the new divinity school where they were preparing to teach. Andover Seminary was north of Boston and not far from Plymouth. Adoniram not only listened to the discussions but also made an immediate impression on the new professors. He exhibited great keenness of mind yet quietly admitted that he was not a believer. Both men were drawn to him and agreed that the seminary would be glad to accept him as a special student should he wish to matriculate. Adoniram was clearly interested yet at the same time hesitant. He deferred for the moment, and the professors, sensing his tremendous potential, left their offer open. Coming to wholeheartedly accept a faith he had been firmly rejecting for some period of time would be no easy thing for one who thought as deeply as Adoniram. He was in a real quandary.

Two days later, Adoniram decided to accept a different offer—a teaching position in Boston. He went at once but took with him his doubt and apprehension about the condition of his soul. Could he really bear to remain lost—eternally lost? Who would have thought his friend Eames could suddenly die in the prime of life? What made Adoniram think that he himself would escape such a fate? Each night was endless, each hour seeming an eternity before dawn would finally break, those haunting words echoing in his mind, "God, God, lost." Scarcely had Adoniram begun teaching in Boston when he accidentally came across the book *The Fourfold State* by Thomas Boston. It was an old book, but he read it with new eyes and understanding. Ever quick to make decisions, Adoniram resigned the job he had only just begun and headed for Andover Seminary.

Two qualities were very marked in the young student when he enrolled at Andover: an enthusiasm for life and a passion for excellence. Adoniram was a fascinating conversationalist, always comfortable in social situations, quick-witted, and full of vitality. He was also marked for his kindness and a rather stately courtesy that commanded respect. And as ever, he easily made friends at Andover, never going unnoticed in a group.[9]

Just as when he had entered Brown University, so at Andover

Adoniram was admitted to the second year because of his excellent academic credentials. In no time, he was engrossed in the somewhat spartan and academic atmosphere of study, lectures, and discussions. However, he also spent much time thinking on his own, working through just who God really was and how he himself related to God. November arrived and with it colder weather, but Adoniram continued to walk alone each day in the wooded grove behind the seminary, pondering the largest of all life's puzzles. He did not see a blinding flash of light or hear a voice from heaven, but little by little, his doubts began to dissipate. December 2, 1808, was a day he never forgot, recording in his journal: "This day I made a solemn dedication of my life to God."[10] And the man who had been so full of doubts and questions never again doubted the miracle of Christ's saving grace. Twenty-year-old Adoniram Judson was a new person. The youth who in the past had been so driven by the desire to be a great man now directed his ambitions toward honoring God. Two months after his commitment to Christ, he asked himself, "How can I so order my future being as best to please God?"[11]

The skills and abilities that had been evident through all his school years were now focused. Judson had always attacked his studies with eagerness and zeal. He now had a purpose that kept him studying hard, reveling in reading sacred literature in Hebrew and Greek. In the midst of his rigorous schedule of studies, he pondered deeply on what purpose God might have for him. To study at a seminary implied the pursuit of one specific career, preparation for a pulpit. Could this be God's will for him?

As he weighed this question there surely came to his mind a vision of that long-ago afternoon at home in Plymouth when he was a sick fourteen-year-old, bedridden and daydreaming of future greatness. Would not the pastor of an obscure, little country church be greater in God's sight than the pastor of some great city church? His heart told him the answer.

Judson began looking for a sign of just what God wanted him to do. In September 1809, at the beginning of his second year at Andover, a sign appeared. It was in the form of a printed sermon by an English chaplain whose name was unknown to Adoniram. The powerful British East India Company ruled India and had been antagonistic to missionary work from the beginning. Around 1800, however, they had allowed a chaplain to join the company. The first of these was a notable minister with deep missionary interests. Upon returning to England in 1808, the chaplain preached a sermon "The Star of the East," revealing ways the Christian gospel was beginning to make an impact on the vast Indian continent. Copies of this sermon reached America, and one made its way to Andover. One cool day in September, Adoniram read this sermon and it changed his life. Precisely one year earlier, he had had a wrenching experience in a little country inn, another one of those unusual experiences that forever changed him. Now the reading of a small pamphlet transformed his plans. This transformation altered not only the future of Adoniram Judson but also the course of Christian missions history.[12]

Judson made a journal entry, "Read Buchanan's 'Star in the East,'"[13] and he began to consider the subject of missions. He read anything about the subject he could find, although precious little was available. Upon reading Michael Syme's *Embassy to Ava,* he focused on Burma, the golden land of entrenched Buddhism, and ever after that country never lost its grip on his heart and imagination. Adoniram knew of William Carey and what was happening with the handful of British Baptist missionaries in India, but there was not one foreign missionary from the United States.

On a hillside across the pond from the old seminary building at Andover stands a massive stone with a tablet marking this place in "Missionary Woods" where Adoniram Judson made his commitment. One cold February morning in 1810, the Great Commission, "Go ye therefore," came into his mind with great power and never left in all the years that followed.[14] Adoniram made his decision. How it would come about he had no idea, but he never doubted that it would become a reality. It was winter vacation, and he went home to Plymouth. Here was a quandary. His father would no doubt be shocked that his son would be willing to give up the possibility of eminence in an established pulpit and instead bury himself a world away in the midst of unknown dangers and perils. And yet Adoniram sensed that his father, especially, would hesitate to question the work of the Holy Spirit in his life. However that might be, telling Mother and Father was not a task he relished.

Adoniram's parents were delighted to have him home, and they seemed unusually animated. Adoniram Sr. broke their good news. Edward Griffin, Adoniram's professor at Andover, was soon to become pastor of Boston's prestigious Park Street Church. Best of all, Griffin wanted Adoniram to be his assistant. His mother's joy was clearly written on her face; her dear son would be so important and so near home. The parents couldn't wait to hear his excitement. Telling was ten times harder than Adoniram could have imagined. With a low and anguished voice, he shared his own news. He would never be in a pulpit near home. He was going to the Far East as a missionary. (Family tradition says that Adoniram quietly but firmly told his loving family: "I shall never live in Boston. I have much further to go.")[15] The silence was stunning. His mother's shock and his sister's grief were wrenching to watch as they wept in disbelief. There was nothing his father could say.

Returning to school in the early spring, Adoniram learned how the same Spirit so clearly at work in him was also making an impression on several of his fellow students. He discovered that, back in August 1806, at Williams College in Massachusetts, six young men had engaged in a prayer meeting in a maple grove and had taken shelter from a thunderstorm under a haystack. On that memorable afternoon, they committed themselves to consider missions. Two years later the young men formed "The Brethren." Four of them made their way to Andover, three of these being "Samuels": Samuel Nott, Samuel Newell, and Samuel Mills, plus a James Richards. Mills made himself and his impressions about missions known to Adoniram. Mills was something of an organizer and a politician, and quickly he pointed out the problem facing Adoniram. "All right, you want to be a missionary to Asia, but who will send you?" There was no foreign missionary organization anywhere in the United States. Adoniram, as impetuous as always, was simply concerned with going. *How* he would go to the mission field and who would send him were not uppermost in his mind.

The young students banded together. It was no coincidence that God had so propitiously brought each of them from various places, to the same school, with the same calling. Then another member of the original "Brethren," Gordon Hall, arrived at Andover, and with the induction of Adoniram and another student, Edward Warren, there were seven brethren. Luther Rice, who had also signed the "Brethren" constitution at Williams, came later that spring. For months the young men discussed mechanics, ways, and means. How could they implement their calling? They met with sympathetic professors and sought their advice. Impulsive as ever, Adoniram wrote to the London Missionary Society in April, inquiring about being sent out by the British.[16]

Yet even Adoniram, always eager to get on with the work at hand, had to realize that the idea was developing with remarkable speed. From being ridiculed for his enthusiasm, there were now eight friends with like commitments. Surely an opportunity would soon open up. And open it did. In June, Samuel Spring, an influential leader among Congregationalists and a true believer in missions, met with other church leaders, and they in turn invited the Andover students to present their case. The students and leaders discussed the needs, the call, the obvious problems, and the exciting possibilities. One of the council members summed up their impressions of the cause presented by those eager young men: "We had better not attempt to stop God."[17]

The timing was perfect. The council asked the students to put their proposal into writing and make it before the General Association meeting in nearby Bradford that very week. Adoniram was chosen to write and present it. None doubted the power of his compelling deep voice and persuasive skills. And with this landmark meeting would come another signal event in Adoniram's life, one entirely unforeseen but one that would change his life and bless him forever.

The Courtship 1789–1812

1811 miniature: earliest portrait of Ann Hasseltine Judson. Used by permission, archived collections, Board of International Ministries, American Baptist Historical Society, Valley Forge, PA.

But to see her was to love her.
—Robert Burns, *A Fond Kiss*

MEANWHILE, BACK WHEN ADONIRAM was a toddler, a string of events had been set in motion in another life, that was to profoundly affect his own. Christmas week 1789 the town of Bradford, Massachusetts, was covered with a blanket of soft white snow. In their snug house on Main Street, John and Rebecca Hasseltine could not have imagined what their newborn Ann would one day come to symbolize to Protestant Christianity. The delicate, chubby-cheeked little bundle with the innocent gaze knew only warmth and security. The doting parents would have been astounded had they been able to look into her future and see that it would one day be written of her: "She appears on the page of missionary history as an illuminated initial letter."[1]

Ann Hasseltine was first called Nancy. She never seemed to be overshadowed by her older siblings—Rebecca, Abigail, Mary, and John—each of whom was capable and gregarious. Two more children followed Ann: brother Joseph, when she was not quite two, and then another brother, William, lovingly known at Bille, who only lived five months. His death left a lasting impression on his six-year-old sister.

Ann shared a carefree childhood with a family who loved to entertain a houseful of young people. The little girl was especially close to her father. They proved much alike in their outgoing personalities and love of people. John Hasseltine was often quoted as saying of his Ann, "Where she is, no one can be gloomy or unhappy."[2] He just as frequently commented on her ability to devise schemes for the attainment of her wishes.[3] This same creativity and tenacity would one day be tried in the crucible of suffering thousands of miles from Bradford, and it would literally save a life—that of her own husband. Various sources refer to Ann as ardent, highly intelligent, and persevering, to say nothing of stubborn, adventurous, and impetuous—similar traits to those of the young man who later became her husband.

The Hasseltine family sporadically attended the nearby Congregational church, and the children learned the importance of moral values. The Hasseltines were subject to a certain amount of criticism in the tightly knit Bradford community, for, among other things, promoting higher education for their daughters. This was a revolutionary idea in the New England of 1800. Perhaps in later years some neighbors watched the youngest daughter travel a world away and shook their heads, saying, "That is what comes from radical learning for women!" John Hasseltine was one of the founders of Bradford Academy, and thirteen-year-old Ann was one of its first students, excelling in her studies but always finding time for parties. Her father entered into the spirit of enjoyment, even adding a "frolic room" to the house, which more puritanical neighbors sarcastically named the "Hasseltine Dance Hall."[4] Ann's mother, Rebecca, was an avid reader and, so the neighbors declared, read more books in a month than any other woman in town could read in a year. Ann learned early a love for books, even the "improving works" that were acceptable for Sunday reading. The only wide-ranging travels a female of that day could enjoy were those experienced through the pages of books. Ann read tales of exciting adventures in faraway places with strange-sounding names. She little dreamed that one day she herself would be a trailblazer for women, experiencing fascinating adventures in exotic lands and facing incredible suffering in the process.

As a happy and cherished daughter, Ann reveled in the unconditional love of her parents. Her sparkling personality made her popular among her peers. She was invited to every party and social event in the area. The promising child blossomed into a beautiful young woman, tall with a well-formed figure. With her delicate white hands, black hair, and enchanting dark eyes, Ann was a charmer. In her personal journal, Ann wrote: "During the first sixteen years of my life, I very seldom felt any serious impressions, which I think were produced by the Holy Spirit…[and] I began to attend balls and parties of pleasure, and found my mind completely occupied with what I daily heard were 'innocent amusements.' My conscience reproved me, not for engaging in these amusements, but for neglecting to say my prayers and read my Bible, on returning from them; but I finally put a stop to its remonstrances, by thinking, that, as I was old enough to attend balls, I was surely too old to say prayers."[5]

A change occurred in 1806 when Ann was sixteen. Across America there had begun the "Second Great Awakening" and spiritual change was sweeping the young nation. In Bradford, the catalyst for challenge and change came in the form of a fellow named Abraham Burham, who taught at Bradford Academy to earn money to attend seminary. Burham's influence extended beyond the classroom. He felt concern for the souls of his students and challenged them to strive for an individual redemptive experience. Under this teacher's influence, Ann became concerned about the condition of her soul, and after reading *The Pilgrim's Progress* by John Bunyan, she "resolved, from that moment, to begin a religious life." Writing in her journal, she declared, "In order to keep my resolution, I went to my chamber and prayed for divine assistance. When I had done, I felt pleased with myself, and thought I was in a fair way for heaven;…accordingly, on Monday morning, I went to school with a determination to keep my resolution and confident that I should."[6] Fun-loving Ann, however, seemed unable to hold her resolve. She was invited to a party and refused to go, but the next invitation she called a "family gathering" and convinced herself to attend. "Dancing was soon introduced, my religious plans were forgotten; I joined with the rest—was one of the gayest of the gay—and thought no more of the new life I had just begun."[7]

Yet Ann's conscience allowed her no peace. Burham helped solve her quandary. He was a frequent visitor in the Hasseltine home with its four marriageable daughters. During one visit, he discussed how Satan tempts some to "conceal their true feelings from others lest their religious convictions should increase."[8] Upon hearing this, Ann quietly left the room and, finding a spot where she could be alone, broke down in tears. With wrenching sobs, she acknowledged that she was in thrall to Satan yet hesitated to let anyone know her fears. Within a week, she and friends were visiting in a nearby village that was home to a devout aunt. Unable to maintain her composure, Ann poured out her feelings of despair and pleaded with her aunt to tell her how she had such peace of heart. The aunt immediately encouraged her to follow the promptings of her heart and not to quench the Spirit of God at work in her life. The next morning, Ann asked Burham for advice. She recorded: "He told me to pray for mercy, and submit myself to God....I began to discover a beauty in the way of salvation by Christ. He appeared to be just such a Saviour as I needed....I committed my soul into his hands, and besought him to do with me what seemed good in his sight. When I was thus enabled to commit myself into the hands of Christ, my mind was relieved from that distressing weight which had borne it down for so long a time."[9]

Ann began to read material that helped to clarify her understanding of the nature of God and found that the Lord's purity and holiness filled her soul with wonder. She recognized the difference in her own life, as did her family and friends. Ann wrote: "My chief happiness now consisted in contemplating the moral perfections of the glorious God. I longed to have all intelligent creatures love him....Sin, in myself and others, appeared as that abominable thing, which a holy God hates—and I earnestly strove to avoid sinning, not merely because I was afraid of hell, but because I feared to displease God, and grieve his Holy Spirit. I attended my studies in school, with far different feelings and different motives, from what I had ever done before."[10]

The change in Ann was both thorough and permanent. Still fun-loving and full of life, she now had purpose and abiding joy and a growing wish to be all God wanted her to be. Ann's transformation affected all of her family. A legend among the Hasseltines tells that her father, usually impatient with those he felt to be "excessively pious," came in from his fields late one evening and, glancing up, happened to see Ann through the window of her room, kneeling in prayer. He stopped abruptly at the sight and then turned away to a distant tree, where he flung himself on the ground and gave his own life to Christ. In August 1806, John and Rebecca officially joined the Bradford Congregational Church, and Ann and her older brother, John, were baptized. This much-loved brother tragically died at sea just one month later, at the age of twenty. His death had a great impact on Ann and her family. The girl so widely known for her love of good times took on a new maturity.

In the years following her graduation from Bradford Academy, Ann taught school in several nearby towns, including a period when she kept a school in the harbor city of Salem. It is likely that she boarded with her school friend Lydia Kimball during that time. Ann frequently visited the shops of Salem with all their tempting wares from lands she had only read about. She and Lydia strolled along the harbor and talked about the fabulous places the ships had visited just a few months before. The wharves always had delicious fragrances of strange spices and sandalwood, hinting of tropical scenes on distant shores.

To the average citizen of Massachusetts, distant lands were just something to read about. Women were wives and mothers. Yet Ann's personal diary gives evidence that even at nineteen, she was already being prepared for an unusual future. In 1809, she spoke of a sense of obligation to "try to be useful," and wrote several times of feeling her heart enlarged to pray not only for herself and friends but also for "the heathen world."[11] The following year, she wrote, "I have at length come to the conclusion, that if nothing in Providence appears to prevent, I must spend my days in a heathen land. I am a creature of God, and he has an undoubted right to do with me, as seemeth good in his sight. I rejoice that I am in his hands."[12] This marked the beginning of a brand-new chapter in Ann's life, for by then she had met Adoniram Judson.

Early in the morning on June 28, 1810, the seven Andover "Brethren" who had committed themselves to missions walked together the ten miles from Andover to Bradford. They were intent on their presentation to the Congregational council that very afternoon and eager to see the response of the church fathers. At noon, several of the Brethren were invited to lunch at the home of Deacon Hasseltine. Adoniram had heard of the Hasseltine daughters, particularly of the beauty and character of the youngest, Ann. Ann had also heard of the dynamic young student who had so impressed church leaders with talk of missions. This had captured her attention because of her own deep impressions about the fate of millions in distant lands. She had heard talk of Adoniram Judson's powerful voice, his forceful personality, and his magnetic hazel eyes. By no one's account was Adoniram shy, but when Ann's pastor, Parson Allen, introduced him to Ann, he was struck dumb. On the spot he decided she was the most beautiful young woman he had ever seen.

For her part, Ann was somewhat disappointed. Mr. Judson had little to say, sitting at his place scarcely looking up and only toying with the food on his plate. Little did Ann know what was preoccupying the young minister. Maybe he was preoccupied with the important presentation he was to give in a few hours. She did wish he would look up so she could get a better look at his eyes. Some months later he explained that the sight of her had rendered him speechless and he had sat through the meal composing a poem to her beauty.

Adoniram was able to calm and collect his smitten heart in time to present to council leaders the proposal for a mission-sending society. The appearance of Judson and his associates produced a profound impression on the assembly. Afterward, one who was present said, "Gray hairs were all weeping" as the students presented their plans and pleas and answered the many questions that were asked them. A committee of three, including Newburyport's pastor, Samuel Spring, and Samuel Worcester of Salem's Tabernacle Church, was appointed, and the next day the association adopted the report recommending a Board of Commissioners for Foreign Missions. The approval was unanimous but not without misgivings on the part of many.[13] Now came the hard part for the missionary candidates—making and implementing definite plans. These were untried waters. Adoniram personally doubted that the newly formed board would act quickly enough, but he himself was determined to go, whatever it took.

And he wanted Ann to go with him. Typical of his impulsiveness, he had lost no time in getting to know Ann better. Exactly one month after meeting her, he wrote her a proposal letter. Even for an impetuous personality such as Ann's, the proposal had happened with breathtaking speed, and she did not rush to an answer. Waiting about anything was not typical of Ann, so all her family knew that she was grappling with an awesome proposition. After all, this was not just any proposal. Adoniram was asking her to leave home forever and move to the other side of the world. There was no precedent that might help her make such a crucial decision. She might never again see her family, friends, hometown, or country. Only Heaven knew what perils were out there, wide oceans away. And that was the crux of it—only Heaven knew. The question confronted Ann: What did God have in mind for her? She spent countless hours in prayer, walking and thinking, searching her soul for an answer—and he who always made quick decisions had to wait this time. Judson had difficulty concentrating on advanced Hebrew and systematic theology when his heart was trying to figure out what another heart ten miles up the road might be thinking.

After several weeks, a letter finally arrived from Bradford. His heart beating rapidly, Adoniram tore it open. It was not a rejection. He felt relief, profound relief. On the other hand, the letter wasn't exactly encouraging, either. In fact, Ann had hedged by writing that her parents would have to consent before she could consider such a monumental step. It could be that she was borrowing some time in which to examine all that such a marriage would mean, time to reflect on what her heart was telling her to do.[14] In her personal journal that August, Ann speculated as to whether she could truly commit herself "entirely to God to be disposed of according to his pleasure." After asking herself several questions, she concluded that, "Yes, I feel I am willing to be placed in that situation, in which I can do most good, though it were to carry the gospel to the distant benighted heathen."[15] For several months Ann's journal revealed the quandary her heart, faced—August, September, October, and November passed by and still she pondered.

Meanwhile, Adoniram wrote a letter to John and Rebecca Hasseltine, requesting their consent. He made no attempt to varnish the facts or brighten an uncertain future: "I have now to ask, whether you can consent to part with your daughter early next spring, to see her no more in this world; whether you can consent to her departure for a heathen land, and her subjection to the hardships and sufferings of a missionary life,…to every kind of want and distress; to degradation, insult, persecution, and perhaps a violent death. Can you consent to all this…for the sake of perishing, immortal souls; for the sake of Zion, and the glory of God?"[16] Judson's letter was no romanticized view of the future. The amazing thing was John and Rebecca Hasseltine's response. They could have objected violently to such a preposterous venture. Instead, they allowed her to make up her own mind. There was nothing typical in this willingness to allow such freedom, but then their forward thinking in providing a superior education for their daughters had not been typical either.

Adoniram became a regular visitor to the Hasseltine home. Sometimes he and Ann would go walking together, an established New England courtship ritual. Other days they would gallop their horses in the beautiful fields near the Hasseltine home. By this time, Ann knew without doubt that Adoniram truly loved her and that when he made up his mind to do something, nothing would deter him from reaching for that goal. Rather tongue-in-cheek, Adoniram wrote his friend Samuel Nott about his courtship. "I have done nothing scarcely since I saw you," he wrote, "besides making a compilation of extracts for the Collection of Letters attending to this missionary business and riding about with Ann. Pretty preparation that last activity, for a missionary life, isn't it?"[17] During their long strolls, Ann learned of Adoniram's dreams about Burma. He gave her a copy of Syme's *An Account of an Embassy to the Kingdom of Ava*, which recounted intriguing stories of the king of the Burmese empire on his golden throne in Ava.

A temporary addition to the Hasseltine household during those courtship months also had an influence on Ann and her thinking about the Great Commission. Young Henry Obookiah, a convert from "Owhyhee" (Hawaii) studied at Bradford Academy and lived with the Hasseltines from late 1810 until the spring of 1811. Henry Obookiah wrote of Ann's family, "The people where I boarded at the house of Deacon H. were a most pious family."[18] This young believer was a constant reminder to Ann of the difference the knowledge of God's love could make in a life, causing her to ponder whether she might be one of the means whereby young people in some distant place could hear the Good News. Ann shared many plans with her friend Harriet Atwood. Harriet, who was just sixteen and frail of body but strong of heart, listened with awe to the stories of her friend and was thrilled to learn about her wedding plans. Neither knew that within a few months' time, Harriet would meet young Samuel Newell, who was also headed for the East, and that the two young couples would be sailing into unknown waters together.

Meanwhile, the new missionary committee was not yet doing anything about appointing any missionaries. They met but feared that not enough money could be raised anytime soon. They finally decided to consult the London Missionary Society (LMS) and agreed that Judson was the one to send to England. He was already in contact with the society, and this idea suited his adventurous spirit right to the core. So, early in January of 1811, Judson set sail on the *Packet* to inquire whether he and the other volunteers might be supported by the LMS without being wholly under that society's direction. Would it be possible for the American board to work jointly with the London board? None of this would be easy, especially since war between the United States and England seemed frighteningly imminent.

On days before sailing when he could not see Ann, Judson poured out his heart to her in beautifully written letters. On New Year's morning 1811, he wrote: "It is with the utmost sincerity, and with my whole heart, that I wish you, my love, a happy new year. May it be a year in which your walk will be close with God; your frame calm and serene....As every moment of the year will bring you nearer to the end of your pilgrimage, may it bring you nearer to God....And now, since I have begun to wish, I will go on. May this be the year in which you change your name; in which you take final leave of your relatives and native land; in which you will cross the wide ocean, and dwell on the other side of the world, among a heathen people."[19]

Judson's "adventuresome trip" turned into more of a nightmare when the *Packet* was attacked by the *L'Invincible Napoleon*, a French privateer. Judson and the other two passengers, along with officers and crew, were taken prisoner. The other passengers and officers fared quite well, because they could speak French, but no one realized Adoniram was a minister. He was thrown into the hold along with the crew. Judson abhorred dirt of any sort, and the hold of the French privateer was a distinct shock to his system. He had plenty of time in that filthy stinking spot to wonder about his calling and the tenacity of his own will in the face of appalling conditions. All around him, packed into the same hold, were violently sick men. Adoniram prayed as he had never prayed before. When there was finally a feeble bit of light available through cracks in the wall, he reached for his Hebrew Bible and kept his mind busy translating the Hebrew into Latin. The ship's doctor happened to hear Adoniram translating aloud and spoke to him in Latin. In no time, Adoniram was released from the hold, allowed the luxury of a thorough scrubbing, and then was permitted to join the officers on deck.

Upon arriving in Bayonne, France, Judson was locked in the local jail. It happened that a Philadelphian in the streets heard the young American vociferously objecting to his treatment as he was led to the prison. That night he visited the jail and bribed the guard for Judson's release. Adoniram finally reached England in May, four months after leaving Boston. His meeting with the London Missionary Society was a good one. They were willing to employ Judson and the others with the condition that the direction of the work remain in British hands. While in England, Judson was asked to read a hymn in a London church. When Adoniram finished, the minister explained that he was a prospective missionary and added, "If his faith is proportioned to his voice, he will drive the devil from all India!"[20]

In June, Judson embarked for home, and no wild adventures on the high seas interrupted this voyage. The next month he and

Samuel Nott gave a report to the annual meeting of the board. This time, the board took action and appointed Adoniram Judson, Samuel Nott, Samuel Newell, and Gordon Hall as their missionaries to work in Burma, Surat, or Penang. One help in getting definitive action was the gift of $30,000 from a Mrs. John Norris—a staggering donation in that time. Another motivation for the appointment was Judson's frank report on his England trip. He included a declaration that if the American board did not send them, they proposed to go out under the English. Judson was his usual outspoken self, and his good friend and mentor Samuel Spring reproved him. Judson was deeply affected and promised to use more tact in his approach in the future.[21]

It was fall again, and as Ann and Adoniram walked along the banks of the Merrimack, they were sobered by the realization that they would likely never again see a glorious New England autumn. The leaves of gold, green, brown, yellow, and red were riotous in their beauty, and it was easy for two young adults who had a flair for the dramatic to be caught up in the poignancy of the knowledge that the path leading to Burma was a one-way street. There would be no turning back, but they were not going blindly. Each had counted the cost. Ann wrote her friend Lydia Kimball in Salem: "I feel willing, and expect, if nothing in providence prevent, to spend my days in this world in heathen lands....My determinations are not hasty, or formed without viewing the dangers, trials, and hardships attendant on a missionary life."[22]

Now that it was settled, the couple needed to find a ship, which was no easy task in the face of looming war. There was also an ordination to be held and a wedding to be planned. Suddenly the whole undertaking was no visionary pipe dream. It was fast becoming reality. Rebecca Hasseltine never did anything by halves—her daughter was going to have an adequate and proper New England trousseau, including a dozen boots. And true to her colonial roots, Ann, who would one day soon adopt the Burmese style of dress, would never be able to bring herself to give up the sturdy half-boots and laced ankle boots she had always worn.

Adoniram paid farewell to his parents, who would not be able to attend his wedding. It was a sad time for him, knowing as he surely did that they would never again see one another. Judson had always had a horror of farewells, something Ann was soon to learn and to experience many times. One snowy morning early in February 1812, Adoniram slipped away while his parents slept. Yet the grief itself could not be avoided. Then on the morning of February 5, 1812, in the same room where he had first introduced Ann and Adoniram, Parson Allen presided over their wedding. Ann was radiant in a new white satin scoop bonnet, and Adoniram wore his familiar black velvet suit and shoes with large silver buckles. They exchanged solemn vows and enjoyed the company of a crowd of friends and relatives. Their honeymoon would be a first for a New England couple—many months at sea, headed for shores unknown and experiences beyond belief.

CHAPTER 4

The Goodbyes 1812

The time to remember, the
time for a sigh and goodbye.
—Joseph Conrad

THE WEDDING WAS IN THE
morning, followed by a long
church service that afternoon and
then goodbyes that must last a life
time. At the service, Pastor Allen bid the
newlywed Judsons and the Newells an emo-
tional farewell: "To the care of the great head of the church I now
commit you. To His grave I also resign you,…and may you all return
and come to Zion with a song and with shouts of everlasting glory."[1]
This unusual service sounded more like a funeral than a wedding day.
But then, very little was usual where Ann Hasseltine and Adoniram
Judson were concerned.

The morning after the wedding was the commissioning of
America's first foreign missionaries at America's oldest Protestant
church, the Tabernacle in Salem.[2] People came from miles around,
despite it being one of the coldest days of the year. Some arrived in
sleighs and on horseback, with many others walking long distances
through the crisp, new-fallen snow. The crowd numbered nearly two
thousand. All seats were taken, and many were standing in the aisles
and around the sides. Sitting on a narrow bench and being questioned for several hours were Adoniram Judson, Samuel Newell,

Stained-glass depiction of the *Caravan,* on which the Judsons sailed in February 1812.
Courtesy of First Baptist Church, Salem, Massachusetts.

Samuel Nott, Gordon Hall, and Luther Rice. Ann, in her wedding bonnet, sat just behind them in the aisle seat of the closest box pew. While ordination of ministers and deacons was a common practice, the setting apart of missionaries was not. The very air was electric with emotion, as one after another spoke of putting these chosen ones into God's hands. No one discounted the dangers ahead; this was untouched territory, fraught with potential peril. Then came the laying-on of hands. Five young men knelt, as did the congregation, while a minister stood before each, placing both hands on his head for the prayer of consecration. Years later, many who were present that day still remembered the emotion: "An irresistible sighing and weeping broke out. The entire congregation seemed moved as the trees of the wood are moved by a mighty wind. Pent-up emotion could no longer be restrained."[3]

The Judsons feverishly prepared to sail because war with England seemed inevitable, and was rumored to be close at hand. They needed a vessel sailing for the East before war broke out. Because of the dangers of travel on the high seas, the committee thought it best that the missionaries embark on two different ships, rather than all sail on one vessel, but the newly commissioned missionaries did not have adequate funds. They needed to go with at least a year's salary because war might cut off their supply if the mail could not get through. The bare minimum needed was $5,000. Mrs. John Norris's bequest was still hung up in court, and on ordination day, there was only $1,200 in hand. At the service, $220 was contributed, leaving more than $3,000 to be raised in just days—a daunting sum in 1812.

Luther Rice's salary for the first year was not figured in this total. He had been one of the first at Williams College to decide to be a missionary, but he did not add his name to the initial list, for he was waiting for a "yes" from his fiancée, Rebecca Eaton. She was hesitant to accept the dangers of life overseas. When she finally declined, he resolved to go on alone and at the last minute applied to the committee. Initially, the committee hesitated. They did not even have on hand half the funds needed for the other four. They finally yielded and agreed to appoint Rice, with one difficult stipulation: he had to raise the necessary funds himself in the few weeks remaining until embarkation. Rice, an intrepid young man, large of body and just as substantial in courage, got on his horse and set out to raise the money. Within six days this dynamic young speaker, with talent and personal appeal aplenty, had the funds in hand. His charismatic personality revealed a foreshadowing of how he would soon galvanize an entire denomination into responding to the Great Commission.[4]

People around Massachusetts began rallying to the call. Andover students solicited contributions and sent letters to possible donors. In two weeks, the Committee had $6,000 in hand. Many funds came anonymously, some even mysteriously. While the Judsons waited in Beverly for a ship, someone opened the door one snowy morning, said not a word, but tossed in a purse holding $50 and labeled, "For Mr. Judson's personal use."[5] Soon thereafter, they found two ships. Time was of the essence if the ships were to get under way before war broke out. The Notts, Hall, and Rice would sail from Philadelphia on the *Harmony*. The *Caravan*, with the Judsons and the Newells, would leave from Salem.

All were caught up in the excitement of embarkation and the sorrow of farewells. Adoniram continued his practice of avoiding farewell scenes, but he met his match in Deacon Hasseltine. In the early hours of a February 1812 morning, the newlyweds slipped from Ann's childhood home. Ann longed to say one last goodbye, but Adoniram was already down the stairs and to the door. Ann followed, her heart heavy with unshed tears. A heavy snow had fallen during the night, and the horses pulling their carriage had to pick their way through the crusty covering on the ground. They had scarcely reached the covered bridge over the Merrimack River when a single rider pulled up beside them. It was Ann's father. Deacon Hasseltine had stopped only long enough to throw a cloak over his nightshirt. With a will that could match his new son-in-law's, he demanded: "You'll come home and say goodbye properly." For the second time in his life, and both times due to a Hasseltine, Adoniram Judson was speechless; they returned and took a proper leave.[6]

Ann and Adoniram waited in Salem. There were no firm dates for departure and no reservation guarantees. Mother Nature was at the helm of all seagoing plans, and she was in a temper that winter. Friday, February 14, came and went. The *Caravan* could not set sail on a stormy sea. She boasted just two masts and square-rigged sails and was only ninety feet from stem to stern. Her deck was alive, not just with preparations for sailing, but with a "veritable Noah's Ark," according to Ann's journal. Scores of chicken coops and pig pens on deck made the *Caravan* sound like a barnyard. "Fresh food" was noisily accompanying the ship.[7]

The impending trip made news, for it was a one way trip for two courageous young couples who would likely never see home again. During those final days, there was an air of excitement, of being present at a moment in history. Friends, family, church leaders, and curious onlookers all wanted to be on hand for the embarkation, but few were there on the bitterly cold morning they finally sailed. Two ladies in their silk gowns sat in their warm, snug parlor in Salem enjoying a cozy gossip that day as one commented, "I heard that Miss Hasseltine is going to India!" "Why," she queried, "does she go?" Her companion answered, "Why, she thinks it her duty. Wouldn't you go if you thought it your duty?" "I," retorted her friend, "would not think it my duty!"[8]

That Wednesday morning in mid-February, four young people stood at the stern as the *Caravan* eased out to sea, the last ship to leave Salem before the War of 1812. Gazing at the shore as long as they could see the harbor, their hearts were filled with a tumult of emotions. Excitement, trepidation, joy, grief, apprehension, and resolve all warred for room in their tumbling thoughts. And then the spray and mist closed them in, and the great adventure began.[9]

Ann Judson's sensitive heart is revealed in a passage written in her diary the night before sailing: "Feb. 18: Took leave of my friends and native land and embarked on board the brig *Caravan*, for India. O America, my native land, must I leave thee? Must I leave my parents, my sisters and brother, my friends beloved, and all the scenes of my early youth? Must I leave thee, Bradford, my dear native town, where I spent the pleasant years of childhood....Yes, I must leave you all, for a heathen land, an uncongenial clime. Farewell, happy, happy scenes—but never, no, never to be forgotten."

On February 19, her journal continued: "Seasick all day, and unable to do anything. My thoughts, more than usual, fixed on divine things." By February 21, Ann recorded, "Somewhat relieved from sickness;… [I] never had a greater sense of our obligations to live devoted to God." To her mother on March 1, Ann wrote, "No daughter would ever more gladly relieve the anxieties of a mother, than I yours. The motives which induced me to go, and you to give your consent, ought now to support us, and prevent our indulging useless regret for what we cannot help. The life I now lead is much happier than I expected. Though deprived of many sources of enjoyment, I am surrounded with mercies."[10]

All four of the young missionaries were seasick. Ann was philosophical about being caught in the throes of nausea. After several days and as her stomach adjusted, she commented that she was not as sick as she had feared and in a moment of understatement said she found it "was no worse, through the whole, than if I had taken a gentle emetic [laxative]."[11] But the *Caravan* sprung a bad leak after only five days, and although everyone aboard pitched in and feverishly worked the pumps, the little brig nearly sank. All were greatly relieved when the hole was discovered and patched. With tranquil waters, newly acquired "sea legs," and warmer weather, two young couples were finally on their honeymoon.

There was more time than anything those months at sea, and when the newlyweds owned to feeling "full, heavy in the stomach," they decided it was due to a lack of exercise. A deck half full of livestock made brisk walking a little hazardous, so they hit upon the idea of jumping rope and dancing in their cabins. Within days, everyone's health and spirits had improved. Putting their supply of books to good use, Ann and Adoniram did a lot of reading. Adoniram pondered their arrival in India and how he would be able to talk to William Carey. A main theological difference between Congregationalists and Baptists was obvious. Baptists did not baptize infants, and professing believers were immersed. Judson wanted to be very clear in his understanding of what the Scriptures taught. Never one to do anything halfway, Adoniram decided to study in Greek. He had actually begun making an original translation of the New Testament in Greek while still at Andover, and he was finding that the word commonly translated *baptize* was giving him trouble.

While none of his *own* journals explain what motives Adoniram had for painstakingly exploring the issue, one hundred years later, his son Adoniram Brown Judson wrote of his father's study of baptism: "It has been intimated that he [Father] reviewed the subject of infant baptism in order to meet the arguments of the English Baptists....But he was so habitually confident of himself and his views in general that it is possible that he expected but little difficulty in convincing them of their error. If that was the case, it must have been somewhat disconcerting for him to find the more he studied on board ship the more it seemed likely that the English missionaries would be able to hold their own in a friendly discussion."[12]

Judson began examining the issue of baptism in April, and he kept at it until they reached Calcutta. He confided in Ann, admitting somewhat ruefully that it appeared the Congregationalists were wrong, that the Baptists had the right of it.[13] Adoniram was troubled, but Ann even more so. Ever practical, she quickly touched on the heart of the issue and pleaded with him just to stop thinking about the question. "I am afraid you will become a Baptist," she told him, "and what would happen to us then? And what would our dear family and friends think?"[14] At one point, she even rashly proclaimed, "If you become a Baptist I will not!"[15] But then, being incurably honest, Ann decided to make her own study and reluctantly reached the same conclusion. It was an agonizing process, and she viewed her conclusions as full of peril for their future.

The Judsons did not feel antagonistic toward Baptists. Congregationalists and Baptists were on friendly terms. In fact, Adoniram had talked with Lucius Bolles of Salem's First Baptist Church about Baptists in America following the example of British Baptists in forming a missions organization. Ann rightly pointed out that if they were immersed, it would mean that they would find themselves with no supporting body. That was a troubling dilemma for a young couple already attempting untried and treacherous waters, a dilemma that must soon be resolved. But the voyage was long, and they were by nature both buoyant and optimistic. It was their honeymoon—a final decision could be put off a little longer.

June 14 was exciting. The shout "Land ho!" from the watch had a thrilling ring that found an echo in their fast-beating hearts. Ann was entranced with their first visitors from land, two birds and a butterfly. The young couples could run across the deck now, exclaiming over one new marvel after another that they spotted on shore. All the livestock previously cluttering the deck had been consumed, and fresh food, especially milk and bread, was soon to be in their hands. Even the breezes coming from shore brought the tantalizing fragrances of unknown spices.

Ann wrote to her sister Abigail, describing some of the new wonders they were seeing: "Day before yesterday, we came in sight of land, after being out only one hundred and twelve days....The scene was truly delightful, and reminded me of the descriptions I have read of the fertile shores of India. Monday: We have been very anxious this morning to get a pilot....He has just this moment come on board, with his two servants. One of them is a Hindoo [sic]. He exactly answers the description we have had."[16]

As the sun rose, the *Caravan* carefully maneuvered between the little islands, moving up the yawning mouth of the Hooghly River, a tributary of the mighty Ganges. The eager missionaries were finally nearing the fabled Indian port of Calcutta. The river pilot and his two assistants boarded the *Caravan*, bearing some fresh treats from the great city. Ann and Harriet got their first taste of bananas, which Ann described as delicious, tasting quite like "a rich pear."

For a couple of days, Ann and Harriet were delayed on board while Adoniram and Samuel went ashore to request permission to disembark. The police clerk was not helpful in spite of assurances that they were only stopping briefly in India. They did manage to receive a certificate stating that they had abided by regulations in reporting their arrival. Information they had gleaned about Burma during their long voyage was disquieting. Evidently Syme's *Embassy to Ava* had not given an accurate description of Syme's true reception in the Golden Land. Symes had seen the Burmans as treating him as an important personage representing a great nation. The *Caravan's* Captain Heard, however, had learned from other captains that the Burman court secretly ridiculed foreigners and mocked their pompous behavior. Even if the missionaries succeeded in landing in Burma, it seemed unlikely that they would be allowed to preach. Two mission attempts in Burma by English Baptists had failed, although at that time Carey's oldest son, Felix, was hanging on precariously, tolerated only because his wife was considered part Burmese. Foreigners in Burma were at the mercy of the emperor's whims. It was a literal "off with his head" mentality, should the emperor so decide. The description of tortures and methods of execution employed by the Burman court filled the young couples with horror. And yet the Judsons could not shake Burma out of their hearts.

At the moment, they faced a more immediate problem. Ever since its founding in the 1600s, the British East India Company had opposed missionaries. Dr. William Carey was tolerated because of his great linguistic skills, which the British needed to help train their own men, and also because of the tremendous respect and stature Carey had attained among the Indian population.

That first day in port, Judson and Newell called on Carey. Adoniram had heard so much about the brilliant pioneer. In person he was quiet and unpretentious, an older man who was small and unassuming, but one whose spirit and intellect drew great respect and admiration from the young missionaries. Carey's translation of the Gospel into Bengali was a major achievement, and his contributions in diverse areas influenced an entire nation. Judson and Newell felt honored to meet the man and gain his wise counsel. About one thing Carey was emphatic: Don't consider Burma. It would be next to impossible to establish a ministry there, no matter how desperately Burmans needed the Bible in their own tongue. Meanwhile, Carey and the Indian Baptist Mission would help them in any way they could. Carey hoped they would be able to stay in India as long as they needed to, certainly until their fellow missionaries arrived on the *Harmony*. But times were precarious; England and America declared war on each other that same month, essentially making a bad situation worse.

Within two days, the two couples were allowed to temporarily disembark, and they spent their first night in the new land in William Carey's large white house in Calcutta. At first, Ann found the cacophony of noise in the streets, the masses, the dirt, the confusion, and crowds almost overwhelming. She found herself alone and being carried in a covered chair supported on poles resting on the bearers' shoulders, quickly borne through the din of the city. No wonder she had heard that European ladies did not go "strolling" in the streets of Calcutta. Adoniram was walking, but Ann's bearers soon left him behind, and Ann had a frightening sense of isolation, a feeling close to panic. However, she was soon put down before the porticoes of William Carey's home and looked about in amazement at all that was new and unusual to her eyes.

The next day they were invited to Serampore to stay at the Baptist Mission until their fellow missionaries reached India. Everything looked strange, and one question led to another. Ann was especially impressed with Dr. Carey's garden in Serampore. She was a farmer's daughter and knowledgeable about plants, but she had seen nothing in all her twenty-three years to compare with this. Ann had not realized that Carey was recognized as one of the worlds' preeminent botanists, just one more of his brilliant accomplishments. The Serampore Mission welcomed the Judsons and Newells with genuine warmth. It was balm to their somewhat bewildered hearts. The past months had been so full of changes: goodbyes, tumultuous emotions, confusion, and even moments of danger at sea. They needed a respite and found it at Serampore, greeted by people with the same goals they themselves held dear. These were mature and settled missionaries who welcomed them with open arms. It felt good.

The respite was all too short, for two serious dilemmas faced Ann and Adoniram. The first issue was where to go. They couldn't stay in India. Burma sounded out of the question. China as well seemed impossible; Robert Morrison was an interpreter in Macau and known only as a translator because anything else meant death there. The Judsons thought of the Isle of France (Mauritius), but no ships were sailing there. Then they considered places from Arabia and Persia to Turkey, but Moslem control made those unfeasible.

Judson was presented with the possibility of a professorship at Fort William College where William Carey was teaching. This appealed to his scholarly bent, but his calling was to preach, and he immediately turned down the offer.[17] Friends in Calcutta, where the Judsons had returned to wait for the arrival of the *Harmony*, even suggested that they give up and return to the United States, where they could be missionaries in the West, but this they did not even consider an option. God had not led them this far to reverse his calling now.[18]

Marshman, one of the famous "Serampore Trio" of Carey, Marshman, and Ward, tried to find a way for them to embark for some needy country. The East India Company was becoming increasingly strident in their demands that the four Americans leave India immediately, whether for England or America, it mattered not. Then, late in July, Marshman came with good news. An official had "unofficially" told him that permission might be given to the *Caravan* to leave without them if they promised to leave by some other ship. Poor Captain Heard of the *Caravan* had not been given clearance until he was willing to take the young Americans back aboard.

The *Colonel Gillespie* was to sail for the Isle of France on August 1, but the captain would not take passengers. What to do? The next morning word came. The captain of the *Gillespie* agreed to take two passengers; he would sail in three days. This left little time for a decision. Clearly the Newells should be chosen; Harriet was expecting a baby within months and desperately needed to be settled before the baby arrived. On August 1, the Newells said goodbye to their closest friends and departed, for just what reception, they had no idea.[19]

Four days later, the *Harmony* arrived in Calcutta, bringing Gordon Hall, the Notts, and Luther Rice. And once again the Judsons faced their two ever present dilemmas. where to go and what to do about baptism. Within three hours of their reunion, Adoniram had told the others of his deep misgivings about infant baptism and the conclusion to which he was coming. As his friends discussed the issue, it appeared they must go separate ways and form different mission stations. This had been Ann's great fear, that they would be alone with no one to share their hearts and work. Yet honesty compelled Ann and Adoniram to follow their convictions.

Ann's journal gives a clear sense of the struggle through which they both were going. With time on their hands while in Calcutta, and staying with the Rolt family, he a merchant married to the widow of an English Baptist missionary, the Judsons had time to delve once more into the issue of baptism. Mrs. Rolt had made her late husband's considerable library available to the Judsons, and they read numerous books on baptism. Ann wrote a friend in Massachusetts explaining their struggle, beginning with Adoniram's Scripture search while on their voyage.

"The more he examined," Ann wrote, "the more his doubts increased; and unwilling as he was to admit it, he was afraid the Baptists were right and he wrong. After we arrived at Calcutta...he again renewed the subject. I felt afraid he would become a Baptist, and frequently urged the unhappy consequences if he should. But he said duty compelled him to satisfy his own mind....I always took the Pedobaptist [infant baptism] side in reasoning with him, even after I was as doubtful of the truth of that system as he. We left Serampore to reside in Calcutta a week or so...and as we had nothing in particular to occupy our attention, we confined it exclusively to this subject. We procured the best authors on both sides, compared them with the Scriptures...and were finally compelled, from a conviction of truth, to embrace those of the former."

"My dear Nancy," Ann continued in her letter, "we are confirmed Baptists, not because we wished to be, but because truth compelled us to be....the most trying circumstance attending this change...is the separation which must take place between us and our dear missionary associates....These things, my dear Nancy, have caused us to weep and pour out our hearts in prayer....We feel that we are alone in the world, with no real friend but each other, no one on whom we can depend but God."[20] Ann was frank about the inner struggle such a move cost her. She dragged her feet far longer than did Adoniram, not because she was not clear in her convictions, but because of the inevitable separations and loss of support that would result.

It was an agonizing time for Adoniram because of their deep friendships and close ties to the Congregational board that had organized in large part because of the powerful persuasiveness of Judson himself. It was painful for him, on September 1, to write them: "My change of sentiments on the subject of baptism is considered by my missionary brethren as incompatible with my continuing their fellow-laborer in the mission which they contemplate....The Board will, undoubtedly, feel as unwilling to support a Baptist missionary as I feel to comply with their instructions, which particularly direct us to baptize 'credible believers with their households.' The dissolution of my connection with the Board of Commissioners, and a separation from my dear missionary brethren, I consider most distressing consequences of my late change of sentiments....I have now the prospect before me of going alone to some distant island, unconnected with any society at present existing, from which I might be furnished with... pecuniary support. Whether the Baptist churches in America will compassionate my situation, I know not. I hope...that while my friends condemn what they deem a departure from the truth, they will at least pity me and pray for me."[21]

Judson also wrote to Baptists, addressing the letter to Lucius Bolles, with whom he had discussed Baptists and missions just the winter before. He explained what had happened and ended by saying: "Under these circumstances, I look to you. Alone, in this foreign heathen land, I make my appeal to those whom, with their permission, I will call my Baptist brethren in the United States."[22] Adoniram also wrote Thomas Baldwin, pastor of Boston's Second Baptist Church saying, "Should there be formed a Baptist Society for the support of a missionary in these parts, I shall be ready to consider myself their missionary."[23]

Joshua Marshman also corresponded with Baptists in America, stating that it seemed "as though Providence itself were raising up their young man....I would wish then, that you should share in the glorious work, by supporting him....After God has given you a man of your own nation, faith and order without the help or knowledge of man, let me entreat you...humbly to accept the gift."[24] And William Carey, powerfully influential in the United States, wrote Baptist leaders in America, urging them to consider the Judsons as their missionaries and make a plan to support them. Carey generously offered to loan the Judsons sufficient funds until such time as Baptists in America would adopt them as their own. In the same letter, Carey referred to Judson's sermon at Lal Bazaar Baptist church in October as "the best sermon on baptism I have ever heard."[25]

On September 6, 1812, Ann and Adoniram Judson were baptized by William Ward at Lal Bazaar Church in Calcutta. The die was cast. Now they were Baptists. They were Baptists thousands of miles from home, however, with no supporting board. Still facing them was that other urgent question as well: Where on earth, literally, will we go?

CHAPTER 5

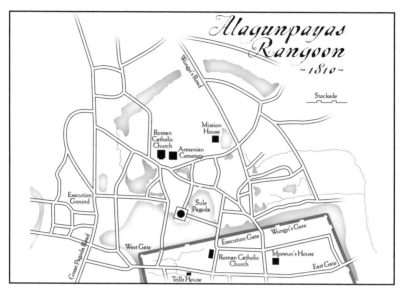

No Place to Call Their Own
1812–1814

The night is dark and I am far from home.
—Cardinal Newman, *Lead Kindly Light*

NOW WHAT? EACH MORNING ANN AND ADONIRAM WOKE UP WITH THAT gnawing thought uppermost in their minds. They had examined their options exhaustively, and most of them varied from dangerous to virtually impossible. By October 1812, Adoniram was making daily efforts to find passage somewhere. Nearly anywhere seemed preferable to being forced ignominiously into sailing for England or

The only known early map pinpointing the location of the first mission house in Rangoon was drawn by British Historian B. R. Pearn. From *History of Rangoon* by B. R. Pearn (Rangoon: Baptist Press, 1939).

America. Luther Rice shared their dilemma, because he too had been baptized at Lal Bazaar Church and now found himself a missionary without a sponsoring board.

In mid-November came a terse order from the East India Company; they were to be sent to England; they were not permitted to leave their place of residence, and their names were placed in the newspaper as passengers on a Company ship. What now indeed? The two young men slipped out of the house that night, still desperately searching for a ship that would accept them as passengers. This time they had a measure of success. *La Belle Creole* was sailing in two days for the Isle of France, where the Newells had gone. Judson and Rice took their story to the captain, pleading with him to take them even though they had no official pass. The captain, who had no love for the East India Company, agreed: "There is my ship. Do as you like."[1]

But how could they get themselves and their luggage on board without the authorities discovering them? Their host, Mr. Rolt, came to their aid. About midnight, when all was dark and still, the Judsons and Rice, along with a band of coolies to handle the luggage, slipped through the dark streets of Calcutta. With a little judicious oiling of palms, dockyard gates mysteriously opened, and the passengers quietly went aboard. Promptly at dawn they sailed, and three young Americans breathed a collective sigh of relief.

Too soon. Within two days, a dispatch boat from the government pulled alongside with an order forbidding the *Creole* to proceed with its three unauthorized passengers. Somebody had betrayed them. At the little town of Budge Budge, the considerate captain docked so that Rice could hurry back to Calcutta and try again for a pass. It didn't help. The captain finally told them they must disembark because his ship would most certainly be searched. At first Ann stayed on board and Adoniram went ashore, but that night a worried Ann joined him in the small town. In the meantime, Judson had learned of a friendly tavern sixteen miles downriver at Fultah. Maybe they could safely wait there while searching for another ship. Ann returned to the ship to get their luggage because it was too risky for Adoniram to be seen. Next the captain suggested that Ann remain on board until Fultah, as the British likely would not arrest a woman, so Ann returned to shore with the newest arrangement.

Yet even as the Judsons were ashore making plans, the captain felt compelled to take advantage of a favorable wind, and off *La Belle Creole* sailed—*with* the Judsons' luggage but without Ann or Adoniram. Again the question: Now what? Ann left a worried Adoniram ashore while she chased after the luggage. After a nightmare of a journey, Ann and her little skiff caught up with the *Creole* and recovered their baggage. Next she made her way back to Fultah to wait for Judson. Rice had once again gone to try for a government pass.

Ann landed in Fultah, alone and with very few rupees in her pocket. She entered the tavern and waited by herself, perilously close to tears and wondering where her husband might be. Here she was, hunted like a criminal, knowing very few words of Bengali, and alone in a little tavern on a desolate coast in India.[2] Judson arrived some anxious hours later, and so did Rice, but with no pass. Scarcely had the men been seated, however, than a young Indian man approached their table and handed a letter to Judson. Hurriedly he tore it open— a pass. Who could believe it? As Ann wrote in her journal, "We knew not who wrote it, but our hearts were rejoiced, we thanked God, and took courage."[3]

But they were still in dangerous straits. The *Creole* was three days on its way. Again they hired a skiff and chased after the ship. Ann was unable to sleep aboard the tiny boat, but Adoniram managed to sleep through the night. Dawn came, but no sign of the ship. A favorable wind blew, and they sailed throughout the day. Near sunset, they drew near to Saugur at the mouth of the river and sighted some vessels. And there it was, the *Creole*. Three exhausted exiles wearily climbed aboard and again gave thanks; at least they could sail for somewhere.

Now they had time to contemplate that same nagging question: Where on earth to settle? They examined each option, even when it seemed impossible. Ever recurring was the thought of Burma, the first country to capture Adoniram's heart. In spite of all the frightening accounts they had heard, Ann wrote in her journal: "We had almost concluded to go to the Burman Empire when we heard there were fresh difficulties existing between the English and Burman governments. If these difficulties are settled, I think it probable we shall go there. It presents a very extensive field for usefulness…and the Scriptures have never been translated into their language. This is a very strong inducement to Mr. Judson to go there as there is no other place where he could be equally useful in translating. But the privations and dangers would be great."[4] Would it eventually be Burma? At the moment, they were drawing close to the Isle of France.[5] Ann was most anxious to see her friend Harriet. The Newells had sailed in August, and soon it would be January; just five months had passed, but to Ann it seemed more like years. She was eager to see Harriet's baby and to share the news with her friend that she too would be having a baby come summer.

On January 17, 1813, the coast of the island appeared through the mists. The Judsons were exhilarated at the thought of seeing their friends. As the captain dropped anchor, they impatiently waited for the Newells to come out to the *Creole*. Samuel Newell's little skiff finally came alongside, but with a Samuel they scarcely recognized. The Newells' voyage had been a stormy and difficult one, and three weeks out of port, Harriet had gone into premature labor. The tiny baby girl survived the early birth, but two days later, the ship was buffeted by a violent storm. Harriet and the baby were exposed to the elements, and the little girl had died five days later. Harriet's exhaustion and grief combined with the exposure to the weather had been too much for her frail body, and within days she had recognized the signs of tuberculosis. In a matter of weeks, Harriet had died. Samuel was still in shock, and the grief-stricken Judsons tried valiantly to comfort him. Ann wrote in her journal of her own personal sense of loss: "She is gone and I am left behind, still to endure the trials of a missionary life."[6]

Even in the midst of their grief, the Judsons continued to face the issue: Where do we go? They quickly realized that, although they could minister to English soldiers on this island, they would not be allowed to evangelize the slave population. So, where? The two Judsons, Rice, and Newell spent many hours weighing every possibility. Newell was the only Congregationalist left in the group, so he decided to join Gordon Hall in India. Rice faced another problem as well. While in India, he had developed a serious liver ailment that nearly took his life. It had flared up again, and it appeared that his only chance of recovery was to return to America. Nonetheless, all found hope even in that adversity, for Baptists in America needed to be rallied to the cause of missions. There was no central organization, so who better than the dynamic Luther Rice to travel from north to south and raise mission support. On March 12, 1813, Ann wrote: "Brother Rice has just left us, and taken passage for America. Mr. Judson and I are now entirely alone—not one remaining friend in this part of the world. The scenes through which we pass are calculated to remind us that the world is not our home."[7] The one option neither considered was returning to America. They decided to try Penang. That would mean going first to Madras, India, which meant the specter of the East India Company again. Deciding to take the risk, they found a ship and sailed for Madras.

The coast of India came into view on June 4, and Ann and Adoniram were warmly welcomed by the Lovelesses, English missionaries in Madras. Their arrival was duly reported to the authorities; an order of deportation could come any day. Ann's baby was due in just weeks, and this simply added urgency to Adoniram's daily search for a ship headed in the direction of Penang. There were none. Next Adoniram began looking for a ship going *somewhere*, anywhere, as long as it was to sail soon. One and only one vessel was found, the *Georgiana*, that "crazy old vessel" as Adoniram dubbed it. And its destination was the one place that filled them with both dread and anticipation: Burma. The choice was simple. They could go to Burma and try to start their mission there, or they could be deported to England by the Company. The Lovelesses and other friends in Madras all expressed the same emphatic opinion: "Not Burma!"

Judson later wrote a friend: "A mission to Rangoon," he said, "we had been accustomed to regard with feelings of horror,"[8] but Burma was their ultimate choice. Ann recounted: "We now saw the hand of Providence pointing to that region, as the scene of our future labors....My heart often sinks within me, when I think of living among a people whose tender mercies are cruel. But, when I reflect upon their miserable state, as destitute of the gospel,...I feel willing to go and live and die among them."[9] The die was cast. As Ann wrote, "dissuaded by all our friends at Madras, we commended ourselves to God and embarked the 22nd of June."[10]

The voyage on the *Georgiana* was one they forever recalled with mingled horror and sadness. Ann's baby was due. There was not even a cabin, so they contrived a lean-to on deck, making an awning with canvas. To further complicate matters, no one on board other than the captain could speak English. Ann constantly thought about what had happened to Harriet and her baby. All sorts of frightening possibilities raced through her mind. Never had her loving and capable mother seemed so far away. Adoniram tried to ease Ann's fears by hiring a large and apparently healthy European woman to assist when it came time for the birth. Just the thought of capable help comforted the Judsons. To their utter dismay, just as the ship was about to sail, the woman fell on the deck, apparently in a fit. "We made every possible effort to recover her," Ann wrote her family, "but she gasped a few times and died."[11]

There was no time to find someone else; the ship was sailing. Not many days out to sea, Ann became gravely ill and started early labor. Her only assistant was Adoniram, frantic with anxiety as he struggled to help in a situation completely outside of his skills. Ann was deathly ill, and their son was stillborn. Their firstborn, who never drew a breath, was buried in the Bay of Bengal, and the grief-stricken young couple had only each other for comfort.

Ann was so ill that Adoniram agonized over losing his wife as well. To add to their distress, the old vessel would not stay on course, and they were threatened with wrecking on a cannibal shore as they perilously drifted between the Little and Greater Andaman Islands. This stroke of seeming misfortune may have saved both ship and Ann. They were becalmed in a spot where the waters were still as a millpond, and Ann was finally able to rest. Then the ship caught favorable winds, and their goal, Burma, grew close.

Ann and Adoniram were filled with conflicting emotions. They had been striving toward this goal for years. Now they wondered if their dream was actually a nightmare. It was Tuesday, July 13, 1813, when the shores of Rangoon, Burma, appeared on the horizon. What could possibly have been further from the beautiful "golden shore" of the Judsons' early dreams, than the straggling, squalid shoreline assailing their eyes? It was more like a cruel parody of a dream for two soul-weary wanderers who gazed with both dread and anticipation at what lay before them. Their first views of Calcutta had been exciting, colorful. By stark contrast, Rangoon was a wretched-looking place. The city had been flooded by heavy rains, and as Adoniram stood by the rail and strained for his first view of shore, the coastline was shrouded in fog. Ann was still too weak to stand, and Adoniram could only describe for her the depressing sights that slowly emerged through the drifting mist. But they had arrived with the determination that this was literally a "mission for life." As Ann said: "It was in our hearts to live and die with the Burmans, [and we] in this place induced to pitch our tent."12

From the ship's deck, Rangoon seemed scarcely better than a neglected swamp. Occasional tumbled-down shacks with bamboo walls and thatched roofs stood on stilts. Slightly back of the harbor's edge appeared the outline of a timber stockade, some eighteen feet high and stretching a scant mile along the water's edge. Two or three slightly taller structures could be seen peeking over the walls beyond the stockade. Everywhere were scattered the tips of pagodas, some a dull gold, others whitewashed and the air was heavy with the smell of swamp land and decay. Then a break in the clouds occurred, and in the first wavering rays of sunshine, one massive spire glinted in the sun, a spire reaching up over four hundred feet. It was Shwe Dagon Pagoda, laden with gold and one of the wonders of the world. Adoniram's heart leaped. This was the challenge they had accepted, that God's golden scepter of salvation would be lifted high above all else, even the towering Shwe Dagon.

Clustered all around the base of the glittering spire huddled a miserable jumble of streets, huts, dirt, and filth. Adoniram took a skiff to the dock for a brief look. It was most discouraging. He could only contrast this unappealing sight with the image in his heart of their own cool, ordered New England, a world away. He later wrote that all seemed "so dark and cheerless, and unpromising—that the evening of that day…we have marked as the most gloomy and distressing that we ever passed. Instead of rejoicing as we ought to have done, in having found a heathen land from which we were not immediately driven away, such were our weaknesses that we felt we had no portion left here below and found consolation only in looking beyond our pilgrimage.…But if ever we commended ourselves sincerely and without reserve, to the disposal of our heavenly father, it was on that evening."13

Ann, exhausted from the trauma of childbirth and losing their baby, mirrored Adoniram's depression. She too called it the unhappiest day of their lives. But practical and irrepressible Ann, recovering most of her strength and all of her courage, just two weeks later wrote, "We felt very gloomy and dejected the first night we arrived… but we were enabled to lean on God, and to feel that he was able to support us under the most discouraging circumstances."14

They took heart; tomorrow was surely another day, and the next morning, America's pioneer missionaries set foot in Burma. At least Adoniram did; Ann was too weak to walk, so they devised a way to get around. She sat in a contrived palanquin, a chair placed on two poles and carried by four Burmese runners. The Judsons got their first close look at what was to be home, impossible as that seemed in those first hours of confusing smells and sights and sounds.

Where were the beautiful scenes described by Symes in his book? Reality was a noisy, scraggly, arguing mass of humanity, jostling for position in muddy lanes strewn with every imaginable kind of garbage, some of which Ann and Adoniram could identify neither by its fearsome odor nor its rotting appearance. The streets were a jumble of contrasts on every side of Ann's makeshift conveyance. All around were naked children, discounting numerous necklaces and bangles, and many of the little ones were smoking cigars, certainly a shocking sight to the young New Englanders. On every corner were lepers begging for food, some holding out stumps of hands where the disease had eaten away fingers and joints. Monks in saffron robes were everywhere with their begging bowls. And in front, behind, and all around the bewildered young Americans were the crowds, men in their patsos—colorful waistcloths drawn and knotted at the waist—and women with a rainbow of colors making up their silk petticoats and bright scarves. Some had gold earplugs, but others had long cigars stuck through massive holes in their earlobes.

Ann, weak though she was, peered from under her bonnet in astonishment at the strange sights around them and discovered that the curiosity of the women was immense. This was something never before seen—a European woman. The women jostled around the palanquin as the runners set it down in order to have a rest and a cigar. One after another curious face bent down and tried to peer under the odd-looking headgear on the foreigner. A few bold ones reached out tentative fingers and stroked shining curls, at which Ann lifted her head and showed her captivating smile. The delighted audience broke into joyous laughter at the sight of the pale lady with the amber eyes, so like yet unlike their own.[15] The tale of Ann's radiant smile was surely told in many a Rangoon house that night.

The Judson's first stop was the customs house and inspection. Adoniram was searched from the skin out, and the women inspectors were scarcely less thorough with Ann in their search for hidden valuables. They were disappointed at finding none, but never mind. An automatic tithe of all goods that entered the country was the emperor's.

Ann and Adoniram gazed about with inquisitive eyes at the reeking, damp little city where they would live. Just beyond the customs house and inside the stockade was Sule Pagoda—many centuries old already, its shining cleanliness in stark contrast with the squalid refuse scattered around its base. The Judsons stared up in amazement at the white structure, so gleaming and immaculate, and then looked down with dismay at the filth at their feet.

Their little procession made its way through muddy lanes and past a motley collection of dilapidated teak and bamboo buildings. Next they passed the place of execution with its nearby enclosure where dead bodies were burned. Thankful to leave those sights behind, they went out the stockade gate and soon came to the mission house Felix Carey had built a few years earlier. All around the house appeared to be a jungle, with thick groves of trees and bushes, primitive and somehow menacing. The mission house, however, was pleasantly situated with a two-acre garden filled with shade trees and all manner of mango and other fruit trees. What a relief after the sights along the path through the stockade. The Judsons were indeed grateful for a place to stay. The house was not finished and had very little furniture, but it was large and comfortable. Felix was in the capital, Ava, on the emperor's orders, but his Burmese-European wife made them very welcome, using smiles and sign language, for she spoke no English.[16]

The Judson's first order of business was for Ann to regain some strength after her close brush with death, before then engaging a language teacher. Less than two weeks after their arrival, Ann wrote her parents and assured them, "I have entirely recovered my health."[17] Now to their most pressing wish: to learn the language. Here was a new challenge. Where to begin? No one spoke English. Within a matter of days, however, Adoniram had located their first teacher, an elderly Hindu scholar who was willing to ignore caste enough to sit with them, eat with them, and even go so far as to teach a woman. This latter he did with great reluctance and then was amazed at the speed and acuity of Ann's language acquisition.

The Judsons found themselves starting with no books, no grammars, not even a dictionary. There were no such volumes in Burmese. Ann and Adoniram became experts at pointing. They would point and the teacher would name the object in Burmese. It quickly became more difficult as they confronted the complications of adverbs, adjectives, and prepositions, only to discover that Burmese grammar and syntax were completely different from any language they knew. Punctuation and paragraphing were also not used. It was no accident that God had called two brilliant linguists to the task.

Ann's spoken Burmese became exceptionally fluent and she excelled in her verbal command of the language. Ann indeed had more daily practice in the vernacular as she managed the household and could use only Burmese with all those around her from morning until night. Her written skills were also outstanding, and she wrote and translated the first Burmese catechism with surprising speed.

Adoniram had more difficulty with the sounds and intricacies that the tongue required, but his understanding, vocabulary, and written skills in the language are legendary. He had ever been challenged by a puzzle, and Burmese certainly qualified as such. Attacking this challenge as he had done all others in his life, Judson put himself to the task of mastering the tongue with the same exacting thoroughness he approached every undertaking.

The Judsons began by studying twelve hours a day. It was exhausting, fatiguing to mind and body. Adoniram immersed himself in Burman literature, Buddhist teachings, legends, and poetry, so that he could understand the way the people reasoned. Even the thought patterns were different, and how could he reach the hearts of the people if he could not see inside their minds?

One of the first jobs to which Adoniram set himself was the daunting task of preparing a Burmese grammar. This he did with exacting thoroughness. The Judsons' skills in the language were so singular that many years later it was written of them in the prestigious *Calcutta Review*: "Mrs. Judson learned to speak Burman with fluency sooner than he did. But for feeling his way into the heart of a language...till the whole structure stood in characteristic form before his eye, in this he has had few equals and probably no superiors."[18]

Ann recorded Adoniram's routine: "Could you look into a large open room, which we call a verandah, you would see Mr. Judson bent over his table, covered with Burman books, with his teacher at his side, a venerable looking man...with a cloth wrapped round his middle and a handkerchief round his head. They talk and chatter all day long, with hardly any cessation."[19]

Thus it was that the mammoth task of learning the language consumed the greater part of their time and energy, but they were also adjusting to a completely foreign culture. They had only each other for companionship, and a spiritual and emotional bond was forged that they doubtless never would have achieved in a more normal lifestyle, in familiar surroundings, and near family and friends. Such a closeness of heart and spirit resulted that each instinctively knew what the other was thinking and feeling. In the sickness, separation, and suffering to come, this bond became an inner steel that under-girded their emotional stability.

Life was not merely filth and superstition and hardship. Ann and Adoniram quickly learned a love and appreciation for the Burmese people, with their keen minds and inquiring attitudes. This culture was so different that the Judsons were forced to look into Burmese history to understand them. Conservative New Englanders would have been horrified by the philosophies by which the people lived. In their culture, to live was to lie. "How can you not lie?" the Burmans asked in genuine sincerity. "It is essential." Bribery was another fact of life; bribery was the way to oil your path through life. And here was a culture where, on one hand, women were allowed much greater freedoms than in most Asian countries yet were at the same time repressed and regarded as chattel in other areas of daily life. The Judsons sought to understand why the people thought and acted as they did. The fact that they learned so well was the foundation of their success in ministry there.

Ann enjoyed her forays into the markets of Rangoon and quickly became a familiar sight to the shopkeepers. She wrote, "Today I have been into the town and I was surprised at the multitude of people with which the streets and bazaars are filled."[20] She fell in love with the women's dress, which by Western standards would be thought somewhat immodest. The colors were vibrant, the material silky and beautiful, and in time Ann began wearing it, although she could never bring herself to give up her practical New England half-boots, hot though they were in that tropical climate.

Day by day annoyances became routine. Bedbugs, cockroaches, spiders, mosquitoes, long black centipedes, bats, and beetles thrived in the Rangoon humidity, along with legions of rats. On at least one occasion, Ann had to deal with an unwanted visitor to the mission compound when a cobra slithered in.[21] She quickly learned that managing a household in Rangoon required equal portions of ingenuity, patience, and creativity. There was, she wrote, "no bread, butter, cheese, potatoes, nor scarcely anything that we have been in the habit of eating."[22] Finding a variety of meats in the open marketplace was impossible. Buddhism forbade the killing of beef, mutton, or pork. Ann learned how to do interesting things with fruit, fowls, and cucumbers, and occasionally she could procure meat from an animal that had "accidentally" died.

The Judsons reached out in friendship to the Burmans around them. The viceroy was the emperor's chief official in Rangoon and literally held the power of life or death for his subjects in his hands. After living in Rangoon several months, Adoniram felt sufficiently comfortable with the language to pay a visit to the viceroy. Considering the man's power, Judson felt it important to meet him, but his "audience" was not successful. As Ann reported, the viceroy "scarcely deigned to look at him, as English MEN are no uncommon sight in his country."[23]

On the other hand, an English woman was rare indeed, so Ann tried her luck, with much more success. She happily described her first foray into minor diplomacy: "Dec. 11: Today, for the first time, I have visited the wife of the viceroy. I was introduced to her by a French lady....She received me very politely, took me by the hand, seated me upon a mat, and herself by me....One of the women brought her a bunch of flowers, of which she took several and ornamented my cap. She was very inquisitive whether I had a husband and children; whether I was my husband's first wife—meaning by this, whether I was the highest among them, supposing that Mr. Judson, like the Burmans, had many wives; and whether I intended tarrying long in the country."

"When the viceroy came in," Ann related, "I really trembled; for I never before beheld such a savage looking creature. His long robe, and enormous spear, not a little increased my dread. He spoke to me, however, very condescendingly, and asked if I would drink some rum or wine. When I arose to go, her highness again took my hand, told me she was happy to see me, that I must come to see her every day. My only object in visiting her was, that if we should get into any difficulty with the Burmans, I could have access to her, when perhaps it would not be possible for Mr. Judson to have an audience with the viceroy."[24]

But loneliness was always there. Ann wrote to family: "O how I long to visit Bradford! And spend a few evenings by your firesides, in telling you what I have seen and heard. Alas! We have no firesides, no social circle; we are still alone in this miserable country, surrounded by thousands who are ignorant of the true God and the only way of salvation by Jesus Christ."[25]

Her journal also reveals that she was privately examining her own relationship with God and at the same time fighting a battle with severe homesickness. Ann recorded: "Have been writing letters this week to my dear friends....Found that a recollection of former enjoyments, in my own native country, made my situation here appear less tolerable. The thought that I had parents, sisters and beloved friends, still in existence, and at such a distance, that it was impossible to obtain a look, or exchange a word, was truly painful....I am an exile from my country and my father's house, deprived of all society, and every friend, but one, and with scarcely the necessaries of life, [yet]. We would not resign our work, but live contented with our lot, and live to thee."[26]

Homesick as they were, the Judsons had no regrets about investing their lives in Burma. Ann wrote in her journal: "I do feel thankful that God has brought me to this land,"[27] and Adoniram wrote to relatives: "If the world was all before us where to choose our place of rest, we should not desire to leave Burma."[28] To Thomas Baldwin in Boston, he wrote, "I know not that I shall live to see a single convert; but notwithstanding I feel that I would not leave my present situation to be made a king."[29] For the Judsons, the specter of a city shadowed by superstition and cowed by despotism and corruption, had to be dealt with each day. Furthermore, disease was an ever-present possibility. It was soon to become a grim reality.

The First Letters from Home 1815–1818

As cold waters to a thirsty soul, so is good news from a far country.
—Proverbs 25:25

THE JUDSONS WERE BUSY from dawn until late at night, immersed in the all-consuming task of learning one of the world's most difficult languages. An aching feeling of isolation was never far beneath the surface. The two of them would observe the Lord's Supper together, and at such moments, the sense of loneliness was deep within their spirits. They were in a country four times the size of New England, and there was not one other American with whom to converse. Furthermore, they had received no mail from home in two years. They yearned to know how their families fared; so much could happen in just a short time.

Ann wrote to Samuel Newell: "As respects our temporal privations,...they are of short duration and, when brought in competition with the worth of immortal souls, sink into nothing. We have no

A two-thousand-year-old Sule Pagoda in downtown Rangoon greeted Ann and Adoniram Judson as they stepped ashore in Burma in July of 1813.

society, no dear Christian friends, and with the exception of two or three sea captains,…we never see a European face. When we feel a disposition to sigh for the enjoyment of our native country, we turn our eyes to the miserable objects around. We behold some of them laboring hard for a scanty subsistence.…while they vainly imagine to purchase promotion in another state of existence by strictly worshiping their idols,…[and] we forget our native country and former enjoyments,…[and have] but one wish remaining, that of being instrumental in leading these Burmans to partake of the same source of happiness with ourselves."[1]

Meanwhile, Felix Carey had briefly appeared in Rangoon and was astounded at the Judsons' language acquisition. He wrote to his father in Calcutta, "They are just cut out for this mission."[2] Felix was relieved to find such capable missionaries carrying on the work he was about to leave forever. He had been offered an enticing government post in King Bodawpaya's court but felt duty bound first to visit his father in Calcutta to explain his reasons for such a step. Felix had scarcely left Rangoon when the Judsons decided to move to a house inside the stockade walls. Thieves abounded, and the city sounded safer than their isolated mission house. Sure enough, right after they moved, robbers pillaged a house near the mission, confirming their impression that they were safer behind the stockade.

Within two months that changed. One Sunday afternoon, Ann and Adoniram visited Mrs. Carey, who had recently had a baby to join their three-year-old son. Just after they arrived, however, a frightened helper burst into the room with the electrifying news that fire had broken out in the town. The Judsons ran to the stockade and saw flames spreading through the city. Upon reaching the gates, they were astounded to find them locked. The people thought that by barring the gates, the fire could be kept out. Ann and Adoniram frantically pleaded for the gate to be opened, and on gaining access, rushed to their little house to rescue their possessions. The house was a total loss. Mrs. Carey graciously received them back at the mission house, and there they remained for the rest of their years in Rangoon.

In April, Felix Carey returned from Calcutta with mail, and while Ann and Adoniram were thrilled to receive letters from friends in India, it only increased their yearning to hear from family in New England. It seemed like a lifetime since they had left. Felix was soon ordered to Ava, and his whole family went with him. They had not gone far up the Irrawady River when tragedy struck. The boat overturned and all were drowned except Felix himself. Ann wrote: "Heard the dreadful intelligence of the loss of Mr. Carey's vessel, wife and children....He barely escaped with his life. How soon are all his hopes blasted."[3] This shocking news only further exacerbated the sense of isolation the Judsons felt, seemingly cut off from the rest of the world.

Determination and discipline were two traits, however, possessed in full measure by both Judsons, and they doggedly continued intensive language study, further delving into the beliefs of Buddhism that so inexorably colored the Burmans' thinking. Ann recorded what they were confronting: "They [the Buddhists] believe that existence involves in itself the principles of misery and destruction. Consequently there is no eternal God."[4] She explained to her sisters: "They know of no other atonement for sin than offering to their priests and their pagodas. You cannot imagine how very difficult it is to give them any idea of the true God and the way of salvation by Christ since their present ideas of deity are so very low."[5] The Judsons' task was to convey the truth of a loving God who provided for all eternal life to a people who had heard all their lives that life is nothing but sorrow. Small wonder that Ann and Adoniram felt utterly dependent on God's power to break down such daunting barriers.

Eighteen months after their arrival, Ann began to lose weight. Rangoon had no doctors, and the Judsons' medical books offered no clues. The feeling of being literally without earthly help was frightening, and Adoniram insisted Ann leave as soon as possible for India and good doctors. As Ann weakened, Adoniram's sense of urgency increased. Furthermore, Ann was pregnant again. She left for Madras early in January, where she stayed with the Lovelesses. As always,

Ann's personality made a tremendous impact. An early biographer commented that "perhaps few things contributed more to Adoniram Judson's success than this friend-making ability of Ann's."[6] And most certainly her people skills proved to be one of the main means of preserving Judson's life in subsequent years.

The Lovelesses and others overwhelmed her with all sorts of supplies and gifts to take back to Rangoon. She returned to Burma in April in good health and anticipating with mounting joy the baby's arrival. She and Adoniram spent the summer rapidly honing their language skills and began making their first attempts to communicate the gospel. To a people so steeped in Buddhism, the message of a God of love was a foreign concept. The Son of God atoned for their sin? The Burmans would just shake their heads in disbelief and politely say, "My mind is stiff."[7]

September was memorable. After two and a half years without word, mail from home arrived. Pounding hearts and trembling hands made it difficult to break the seal of each letter. The Judsons thrilled to news of loved ones and family happenings, giving fervent thanks for the glorious news of the formation of a Baptist Board of Foreign Missions.[8] Just how elated the two were is reflected in an entry in Adoniram's journal: "These accounts from my dear native land were so interesting, as to banish from my mind all thoughts of study. This general movement among the Baptist churches in America, is particularly encouraging…in furnishing abundant reason to hope, that the dreadful darkness…is about to flee away before the rising Sun.…None but one who has had the experience, can tell what feelings comfort the heart of a solitary missionary, when…[he] has proofs that there are spots on their wide earth, where Christian brethren feel that his cause is their own, and pray… for his welfare and success. Thanks be to God, not only for 'rivers of endless joys above,' but for 'rills of comfort here below.'"[9]

Years later, Judson's son Edward wrote of the cataclysmic effect of the Judsons' decision to become Baptists: "In 1812 the Baptists of America were a scattered and feeble folk.…There was little or no denominational spirit. His summons to the foreign field shook them together. A glass of water may be slowly reduced in temperature even to a point one or two degrees below freezing and remain uncongealed, provided it be kept perfectly motionless. If then, it is slightly jarred it will suddenly turn into ice. The Baptist denomination of America was in just such a state of suspense. It needed to be jarred and shaken into solid and enduring form. Mr. Judson's words: 'Should there be formed a Baptist society for the support of a mission in these parts, I should be ready to consider myself their missionary,' proved to be the crystallizing touch."[10]

Surely one of the most powerful forces in bringing Baptists together was Luther Rice. Rice's leadership role in America was unquestionable. To no other man in the United States was more credit due for the fact that Baptists organized into a denomination. They had been scattered far and wide, from Massachusetts in the North to Georgia in the South. Rice became the man of the hour as he traveled from New England to the Deep South, proposing a national organization and giving thrilling accounts of foreign lands and what Baptists could do there. Commanding in presence, impressive and powerful in speech, he was welcomed everywhere.

Salem's Lucius Bolles, along with Thomas Baldwin of Boston and William Staughton of Philadelphia, were prime forces in organizing a mission-sending agency—and subsequently in May 1814, the first "Triennial Convention" of Baptists was instituted.[11] All of this was happening while the Judsons labored on alone, unaware of what was happening. Such news gave them new heart in their language study.

A completely different source of encouragement also arrived. On September 11, less than a week after receiving the glad news from America, Ann, with Adoniram her only doctor and nurse, gave birth to a healthy, blue-eyed baby boy. The doting parents gave him the eminent name of Roger Williams, convinced there had never been a more beautiful child. He flourished, ate with gusto, and only cried when he was hurting. Two weeks after he was born, Ann wrote: "I know, my dear Mother, you long very much to see my little boy. I wish you were here to see him. He is a little sprightly boy, and already begins to be very playful. We hope his life may be preserved, and his heart sanctified, that he may become a missionary among the Burmans."[12]

Little Roger delighted not only his parents but all who saw him. Even the viceroy was excited at the sight of a chubby little white baby with startling blue eyes—no other such child had ever been seen in Burma. Ann and Adoniram continued their many hours of study but kept Roger right with them. He appeared to have an unusual desire to be with his parents. When they went by his cradle without picking him up, Ann reported in her journal, "he would follow us with his eyes to the door, where they would fill with tears, and his countenance so expressive of grief, though perfectly silent, that it would force us back to him, which would cause his little heart to be as joyful as it had been before sorrowful....He would be for hours on a mat by his Papa's study table or by the side of his chair on the floor, if only he could see his face. When we had finished study...it was our exercise and amusement to carry him around the house and garden, and though we were alone, we felt not our solitude when he was with us."[13] All the loneliness and isolation became much more bearable with the arrival of little Roger.

For seven joyful months little Roger thrived. Then early in May 1816, they began to notice that he had periods of fever and heavy perspiring in the night. They were alarmed, but each time, when morning came, the baby would seem fine. He steadily gained weight. Then the fever became a pattern, always higher at night. One morning Roger began coughing, and this time the fever did not abate. There was absolutely no medical help, so Ann and Adoniram were frantic with worry. For two days they stayed by his side, their hearts torn with anguish and helplessness. The second night, exhaustion overcame Ann, and Adoniram took over Roger's care. Ann wrote: "The little creature drank his milk with much eagerness (he was weaned) and Mr. Judson thought he was refreshed and would go to sleep. He laid him in his cradle—he slept with ease for half an hour when his breathing stopped without a struggle and he was gone!"[14]

Little Roger Judson, aged seven months and twenty-three days, was no more. The grieving parents hardly knew how to cope with such a devastating loss. The joy of their lives was suddenly gone, leaving anguished parents with no comfort but each other and God's grace. On May 7, Adoniram wrote: "Our little comfort, our dear little Roger, has become insensible to our parental attentions and fond caresses....His sweet face has become cold to our lips and his little mind, which to a parent's discernment at least, discovered peculiar sensibility and peculiar sweetness of disposition, has deserted its infantile tenement and fled.

"Had I lost a wife," Judson continued, "I might not thus lament for a little child eight months old....Nothing but experience can teach us what feelings agonize the soul of a parent when he puts his face to that of his dear, his only, child, to ascertain whether there may not be one breath more....Our little Roger died last Saturday morning. We looked at him through the day, and on the approach of night we laid him in the grave."[15]

Ann wrote: "My dear Parents, little did I think when I wrote you last, that my next letter would be filled with the melancholy subject on which I must now write. Death, regardless of our lonely situation, has entered our dwelling....Our little Roger Williams, our only little darling boy, was three days ago laid in the silent grave. Eight months we enjoyed the precious little gift, in which time he had so completely entwined himself around his parents' hearts, that his existence seemed necessary to their own....Thus died our little Roger....We buried him in the afternoon of the same day, in a little enclosure the other side of the garden." Days later Ann finished the letter, saying, "It is just a fortnight to-day, since our little boy died. We feel the anguish a little abated, and have returned to our study and employment; but when for a moment we realize what we once possessed, and our now bereaved state, the wound opens and bleeds afresh."[16]

Their sorrow was further exacerbated by Adoniram's health. It had been deteriorating for some months. He feared he would have to take a sea voyage to Bengal to recover, and that bothered him. He was reluctant to suspend even for a short time his language study. Shortly after Roger's death, however, the pains in his head and eyes were so intense that he could not even bear the sound of Ann reading aloud to him. About this time, one of their friends, a Captain Kidd, came to stay with them for a few days. He suggested a voyage to Calcutta, but news came that George Hough, a missionary printer, and his family were already in Calcutta and preparing to come to Rangoon. Also, the Serampore friends were sending a printing press and type. Adoniram could not bear to leave at such an important time. Captain Kidd was a great believer in exercise and suggested horseback riding. At first, it was jarring and painful, but as Adoniram persisted, his health improved. He decided to get a horse of his own and began the habit of riding each morning before sunrise.

October 15, 1816, was an exciting day for Ann and Adoniram, for the first recruits arrived. They were overjoyed that Hough was a printer, and welcomed him and his wife, Phoebe, with open arms. Things were pulling together to the point that Judson was eager to preach in the language, but he felt the need of a Burman Christian assistant. Possibly there would be one who spoke Burmese on the west coast in Chittagong, where English Baptists had once had a brief mission. He and Ann decided he should go see, since his health was still precarious, and a sea voyage could strengthen him. They found a ship that was to sail to Chittagong on business, turn around and come right back. This seldom happened, and it seemed the perfect solution. On Christmas Day, 1816, Judson set sail with high hopes.

Who could have imagined the events that followed. The winds were contrary and unpredictable, and the ship became unmanageable. For a month it drifted. Furthermore, as soon as they had set to sea, Adoniram suffered the return of an old eye and head pain and had to stay in his bunk. The ship was unable to reach Chittagong, so the captain headed instead for Madras.[17] Even that proved impossible for the crippled ship. Adoniram came down with fever and was in dire straits, filthy, starving, lying half dead in his hard bunk. Twelve weeks later the ship limped into a port in India. Adoniram garnered enough strength to pencil a note to "any English resident" asking for "a place to die on land." Later that day, Adoniram managed to crawl, to the porthole and saw a small boat on its way toward their ship. In it were the red coats of British soldiers and the white coats of

Englishmen. He collapsed on the floor with tears streaming down his cheeks. They appeared to him as angels, those shocked Englishmen who entered the cabin and found a filthy, unshaven scarecrow of a man, so weak that they had to carry him ashore.[18]

Adoniram recovered strength rapidly though his eyes remained weak. The crippled ship could not sail for months, so Judson's only hope was to go by land to Madras, three hundred miles away, and then catch a ship home. He made the trip by sedan chair. In Madras, the Lovelesses welcomed him warmly, but he was dismayed to learn there would be no ship for Rangoon for three months; he must wait, surely the hardest thing in the world for Judson to do. To make matters worse, there was no way to get word to Ann, and he knew how anxious she must be.

He had no way of knowing the dangerous situation in which Ann and the Houghs found themselves. Ann had expected Adoniram back in three months, but those months came and went with no word. Then an ominous message came from Chittagong. Judson's boat had never arrived. Four more months passed with no news. Ann's concern mounted with each passing day and finally reached proportions of near-panic as she wondered if he was even alive.

As if this was not enough, new trouble was brewing. The Houghs, novices in the language of Burma, were heavily dependent on Ann's experience and guidance. One dark morning, George Hough was ordered to the courthouse, and an official tried to extort money from the mission, hinting that if Hough didn't "tell them everything about what he was doing in Burma, they would write with his heart's blood."[19] A thoroughly frightened Hough was in a panic. For two nerve-wracking days, he was continually questioned. Ann puzzled over this new development. Surely this was extortion and not commands from the emperor. Rangoon officials knew that Judson was gone and that Hough was unskilled in the intricacies of Burmese bribery. Never one to lack courage, Ann approached the great viceroy himself, an unheard-of act for a woman. She took a petition outlining the situation and requesting the viceroy's intervention. In the midst of the viceroy's morning court, he looked up and caught sight of Ann. She held up the petition and looked straight at him. The viceroy asked that the paper be read. And that was the end of that; he gave a command that there be no more harassment for "Mrs. Yoodthan" and her group. Immediately Hough was released. Relief engulfed the beleaguered three.

Then more trouble appeared. Cholera broke out, and the death drums never stopped. To further aggrevate conditions, rumors ran rampant that war with England would soon start. Hough became panic-stricken and found a ship headed for India. He insisted that Ann leave also, declaring that a lone woman could not remain. Ann's quandary was dreadful. Was Adoniram alive? Ill? Dead? If he was in India, maybe she could find him there. On the other hand, he might return and find her gone, and then what?

The Houghs begged her to leave. With utmost reluctance, she packed some bags and they were put on the ship. The sailing was delayed, however, and Ann reached the conclusion that she must not go. She ordered her bags ashore and returned to the desolate mission house, writing: "I know I am surrounded by dangers on every hand and expect to see much…distress; but at present I am tranquil…and intend to…leave the event with God."[20] Adoniram had left on Christmas Day. It had been seven months. Ann's determination in the face of peril was more vital than she could possibly know. It is likely that this decision on her part saved the mission and made possible the future of Judson's work for years to come.

Just a few days later, the vessel Adoniram had originally taken to Chittagong showed up in port, and Ann learned the story. He was alive. Soon the Houghs returned to the house as well; their ship had been delayed for several more weeks. Then a messenger arrived at the front door; Adoniram's ship was even now at the mouth of the river. An elated Ann dressed in her brightest garb and headed for the wharf. He was home once more.[21] Against all odds and in spite of the agonizing months of travel, Adoniram had regained the greater part of his strength. The Judsons were together again and looking to the prospect of a possible breakthrough in the task upon which they had embarked.

CHAPTER 7

Maung Nau— The Beginning of Harvest 1818–1819

And as we rise with you to live,
  O let the Holy Spirit give
The sealing unction from above,
  The joy of life, the fire of love.
—Adoniram Judson, "Come Holy Spirit, Heavenly Dove"

The first Burmese convert, U Naw, was baptized in June 1819–six years after the Judsons arrived.

WITH ADONIRAM'S RETURN AND THE HOUGHS' DECISION TO REMAIN IN Rangoon, a buoyant sense of optimism energized the little group. George Hough set up the precious printing press and got to work on Ann's catechism and on Adoniram's first tract: "A View of the Christian Religion." Within six months, Burma had its first look at the message of salvation in its own language.

Adoniram worked on translating Matthew the first part of the day, then met with Burmese men in the evening. He reported to Thomas Baldwin in Boston: "We are just entering on a small edition of Matthew....But we are in great need of men and money. Our hands are full from morning till night. I can not for my life, translate as fast as Brother Hough will print."[1] Ann continued translating as well, working on the book of Jonah and spending satisfying hours in her school for girls. She was plowing new ground, for teaching girls was a novel concept in Burma. Soon another letter to Baldwin contained their momentous news: "I have this day been visited by the First inquirer after religion that I have seen in Burmah."[2] He was well dressed and a man of high standing. After polite greetings, he quickly came to the point: "How long will it take me to learn the religion of Jesus?" In great surprise, Adoniram asked, "How came you to know anything of Jesus? Have you been here before?" "No," the gentleman replied, "but I have seen two little books about Jesus." "Who is God?" Judson asked the man. "He is a Being without beginning or end, who is not subject to old age or death but always is," the gentleman replied.[3] Adoniram immediately recognized his own words from the tract. He could not describe his feeling of exultation. Nearly speechless, Adoniram handed the man a copy of his tract and Ann's catechism. The man wanted "more of this sort of writing." Adoniram explained that he was translating as fast as he could, and gave him the first five chapters of Matthew. Adoniram did not see the gentleman himself for some time but heard from an acquaintance that the man read "those books all the day" and showed them to others.

The Judsons were keenly aware of their dependence on prayer. Adoniram wrote, "We desire, humbly, to repeat to the Board, what the first missionaries from the Baptist society in England said to their friends.…[W]e are like men going down into a well; you stand at the top and hold the ropes. Do not let us fall."[4]

Ann frequently wrote in her journal and to America. Glimpses of her courage emerge on each page as she wrote of difficulties on every hand but repeatedly affirmed the knowledge that the actual "converting" was not theirs. "That is the work He reserves for Himself," Ann wrote. In a letter to a Mrs. Carleton in Boston she said: "Pray much for me, my dear Mrs. C. O pray that I may…be faithful unto death. I have many trials of a spiritual nature. O could you see my heart, my little devotedness to that dear Redeemer,…you would feel that I was very unworthy of the high privilege of living among the heathen."[5] Yet time proved that her confidence in the power of God was never shaken, even in the face of death.

Meanwhile, in the midst of her heavy load of studying and teaching, Ann was also learning Siamese, and somehow she eked out time to translate her catechism, Adoniram's tract, and the Gospel of Matthew into that intricate Oriental language. Those were the first portions of God's Word ever translated into the language of the millions of people of Siam.[6]

The Houghs left for Calcutta where they would continue to print Burmese materials, but other reinforcements were coming. The Judsons joyfully greeted Edward and Eliza Wheelock and James and Elizabeth Colman. Adoniram was now thirty, Ann twenty-eight. The new couples, all in their twenties, seemed incredibly young to the veterans of six years of wanderings, illnesses, tribulation, and painstaking study. They seemed a gift from heaven: "Their arrival has given a new spring to our feelings and exertions," Ann said. "To be again refreshed with Christian society and congenial souls, restores us in a manner to our native land and former enjoyments."[7]

The mission house was scarcely large enough for all three families, but the Judsons quickly made arrangements for each couple to have its own room and a measure of privacy. A major problem was evident. Zeal and courage the two new men appeared to have in abundance, but not good health. They had scarcely settled when they began to cough up blood. The fearful symptoms of tuberculosis were all too clear. Ann and Adoniram helped in making them as comfortable as possible, but there was no doctor to give them medical attention.

Another problem became only too apparent. Eliza Wheelock, only twenty years old, had come with ideals and dreams of the glory of being a missionary. Reality was terribly different, and she was not equipped to handle it. To make matters worse, Edward Wheelock was dying before their eyes. All the others tried to help and to comfort, but Eliza refused their help and could not bear to face the inevitable. She became obsessed with taking him to Calcutta, although Edward had developed a morbid fear of traveling on a ship, as their voyage over had been a nightmare. Eliza insisted that they leave, and sadly the Judsons made the necessary arrangements.

Four heartsick missionaries saw the Wheelocks off, knowing Edward was going to his death. This happened with striking quickness.

Thirteen days out to sea, Edward Wheelock fell overboard, and in the midst of high winds, a rescue could not even be attempted.[8] Meanwhile, back in Burma, James Colman was improving, and the Colmans eagerly began language study. The couple was a genuine encouragement to the Judsons, their loving attitude and willing spirits a welcome balm after the sad experience with the Wheelocks.

Adoniram had always felt that Burma could never be won to Christianity without the Bible in Burmese, but preeminent in his heart was the longing to preach. Years later his son Edward wrote of his father's preaching gifts. "To Adoniram Judson," said Edward, "the most important work was the oral preaching of the gospel—this was his first love. For this, Mr. Judson had rare aptitude and in it he won his most signal triumphs."[9] Judson's voice in those early years was powerful and compelling, but even when illness and disease had reduced his voice to a mere whisper, the power of his message was great in its impact—so gifted was he in speaking to the hearts of his listeners.

"He did not deal in vague abstractions,...His conversation abounded in images," Edward continued. "Behind his words, when he preached, lay the magnet of a great character....There was no mistaking his motives. He had come a long distance and endured great hardships because he loved the Burmans....His figures...were drawn from immediately surrounding objects. Of these, in accordance with Eastern taste, he made great use."[10]

Having invested years in intense language study, Ann and Adoniram were now able to directly share the gospel. They decided to build a *zayat* (zee-yaht'), a small structure raised up on stilts, where they could teach passersby. They bought property adjoining the mission garden, just about two hundred yards away from and fronting on the famed Pagoda Road that led to Shwe Dagon Pagoda. The road was lined with pagodas, and thousands of people passed by each day. What better place to have maximum exposure to the masses? Their Christian *zayat* was constructed on four-foot stilts and was thirty feet long and twenty feet wide. Across the front was the porch where Adoniram would sit and speak. Behind the porch they designed an enclosed room where public worship could be held. In back of this was an area opening into the mission garden, and Ann would teach women there.[11]

A momentous day came in April 1819. Judson wrote, "Today the building of the zayat being sufficiently advanced for the purpose, I called together a few people that live around us and commenced publick worship in the Burman language."[12] There were fifteen adults, many children, and a lot of disorder and inattention. But then, this gathering was something entirely new to Burmans. Ann wrote joyfully of this new milestone and closed her letter: "We trust our American friends will pray, that from the house which we devote to the service of God, streams of salvation may flow to all the surrounding country."[13] Indeed, the audience grew, interest increased, and the Judsons took heart afresh. Every day Adoniram would sit on the porch of the *zayat* and in that deep and compelling voice call out, "Ho! Everyone that thirsteth for knowledge!" It was not a week until someone came seeking, someone who aroused the Judsons' greatest hopes.

One Friday, the last day of April, a quiet thirty-five-year-old man came to ask questions. There did not seem to be anything particularly remarkable about Maung Nau. ("Maung" was a title given to all young men, "U" being used for older men.) There *was* something special about him, though. He was actively seeking hope. Most Burmans by nature were not reticent, but Maung Nau seemed very reserved. That first day he only listened, sitting very still and with keen focus. The next day he was back. Now he asked a few tentative questions. There was nothing in his manner of looking for some philosophical argument, only a genuine desire to learn. Adoniram applied to him the adjectives "modest" and "quiet." Maung Nau kept coming back, and Judson recognized in him "a teachable and humble spirit."[14]

By Wednesday Adoniram was writing in his journal: "I begin to think that the grace of God has reached his heart....The substance of his profession is, that from all the darkness, and uncleanness, and sins, of his whole life, he has found no other Saviour but Jesus Christ,...and therefore he proposed to adhere to Christ, and worship him all his life long." Judson concluded, "It seems almost too much to believe, that God has begun to manifest his grace to the Burmans; but this day I could not resist the delightful conviction, that this is really the case. PRAISE AND GLORY BE TO HIS NAME FOREVERMORE. Amen."[15] The Judsons could scarcely allow themselves to believe what was happening. Six long and arduous years they had been looking toward this very event. The next Sunday Maung Nau openly professed his belief in Christ. The Judsons had difficulty containing their great joy.

Maung Nau was employed by a seller of timber and he had to leave on a trip, but he told Adoniram he hoped he could be baptized as soon as he returned. Surprisingly, he showed up a few days later, having discovered the merchant not to be trusted. There was another job, but it would take him away for as much as a year. He did not want to go, and certainly the missionaries hoped he would not have to leave at such a vital time in his life. They solved the problem by giving him a job copying pamphlets; thus he would become grounded in Scripture even while he worked. Just more than one month after his first appearance at the *zayat*, Maung Nau quietly handed Judson a letter. Adoniram translated it: "I, Maung Nau, the constant recipient of your excellent favor, approach your feet. Whereas my Lord's three have come to the country of Burmah, not for the purposes of trade, but to preach the religion of Jesus Christ, the Son of the eternal God. I having heard and understood, am, with a joyful mind, filled with love."

The letter continued, "I believe that the divine Son, Jesus Christ, suffered death, in the place of men, to atone for their sins. Like a heavy-laden man, I feel my sins are very many. The punishment of my sins I deserve to suffer. Since it is so, do you, sirs, consider that I, taking refuge in the merits of the Lord Jesus Christ, and receiving baptism, in order to become His disciple, shall dwell one with yourselves, a band of brothers, in the happiness of heaven and therefore grant me the ordinance of baptism."[16]

Not a person present had any doubt that Maung Nau had experienced God's grace, but internal troubles in the country prevented his baptism for several weeks. Ominous news had come from Ava. The Golden One was dead, or as the royal proclamation stated: "Listen ye—The immortal king (wearied it would seem with the fatigues of royalty) has gone up to amuse himself in the celestial regions. His grandson, the heir apparent, is seated on the throne. The young monarch enjoins on all to remain quiet, and wait his imperial orders." The edict went on: "It appears that the prince of Toung Oo, one of his uncles, has been executed, with his family and adherents, and the prince of Pyee placed in confinement."[17]

After the countryside had settled down, the long-awaited moment came. On June 27, 1819, Maung Nau stood before the group of worshipers and answered Judson's questions about his "faith, hope and love." Then everyone walked about half a mile to a nearby pond. While a wondering crowd of curious Burmans watched from a hill close by,[18] Adoniram led Maung Nau into the water, and as Ann wrote to the Baptists of America, "We administered the ordinance of Christian baptism to the first Burman convert."[19] Judson's journal of July 4 states: "Lord's day: We have had the pleasure of sitting down, for the first time…with a converted Burman…to administer the Lord's supper in two languages."[20] A gathering-in had begun, and even the Judsons at their most optimistic could not have foreseen the harvest that was to come.

To the Golden Feet 1819–1820

Lord, we would endure, O sift us
clear of weakness, make us strong.
—Amy Wilson Carmichael,
Edges of His Ways

MAUNG NAU INFUSED THE SMALL BAND
of believers with fresh enthusiasm and
zeal. The Burmans visiting the *zayat*
now were not largely curiosity seekers
who came to observe the strange foreigners, but inquirers genuinely interested in finding hope for themselves.
The Burmese custom was to set up a
house wherever one pleased and stay
awhile. Several Burman inquirers built
little bamboo huts in unused parts of
the mission garden and stayed to learn.
One such was Maung Thalah, along
with his sister, Mah Baik, and her hus-
band. Maung Thalah eagerly listened and learned. Ann taught Mah
Baik each day. Mah Baik sought to understand the message of a true
and loving God, but quarreling was her addiction, although she sincerely wanted to learn a better way. Another inquirer was Maung
Byaay, unusual because he could not read as most Burmese men

Ava watchtower, all that remains of the palace of Burma's emperor Bagyidaw, was visible to
Judson from his prison stockade. *Inset:* The ancient monastery ruins at Ava, adjacent to Let Ma
Yoon prison, still stand.

could. He joined a class that Ann and Adoniram were teaching, and they could almost see his mind expand.

About the same time a poor fisherman visited the mission. The Judsons had no way of knowing how the unassuming young Maung Ing would later be used of God to help keep them alive. The newly baptized Maung Nau shared his faith with Maung Ing, who explained that he had "long been looking after the true religion." He read the Gospel of Matthew and asked many questions. Judson recorded, "He says that he wants to know more of Christ, that he may love him more. Lord Jesus, give him the saving knowledge of thine adorable self!"[1]

The great majority who came were average citizens, but one day a man appeared whose soul had the same needs but whose mind appealed immediately to Adoniram's own intellect. Moung Shwa-gnong was "a learned teacher of considerable distinction."[2] Here was a challenge to Adoniram's mental acuity *and* to his missionary heart. Of all the Burmans Judson was to meet and come to love, none did he enjoy as he did the brilliant Shwa-gnong. Adoniram wrote in his journal: "September 11. Moung Shwa-gnong has been with me all day. It appears that he accidentally obtained the idea of an eternal Being about eight years ago; and it has been floating about in his mind, and disturbing his Buddhistic ideas ever since. When he heard of us,...this idea received considerable confirmation; and today he had fully admitted the truth of this first grand principle. The latter part of the day we were chiefly employed in discussing the possibility and necessity of a divine revelation....He is certainly a most interesting case. The way seems to be prepared in his mind for the special operation of divine grace. Come, Holy Spirit, heavenly Dove! His conversion seems peculiarly desirable, on account of his superior talents and extensive acquaintance with Burmese and Pali literature. He is the most powerful reasoner I have yet met with in this country."[3]

Shwa-gnong would come with his followers, and he and Judson would spend entire days discussing philosophy, faith, and the way of life. One night their conversation lasted so long that Shwa-gnong's followers left and Adoniram noticed that his friend's skepticism left as well. He pleaded with Judson to teach him, and when Shwa-gnong finally left, he amazed his foreign friend by prostrating himself. This had never before happened to Adoniram. The Burman *sheeko* was an act of obeisance a Burman rarely made, and then only to a recognized superior.

This one-on-one way of reaching each seeker was what Judson relished, even while continuing the exacting and essential work of translating the Scriptures, which he did directly from the Greek and Hebrew. Coloring every day for the missionaries in Burma, however, was the possibility of persecution and, for the new converts, the danger of death as well. Bagyidaw, the Lord of Life and Death, was not simply a title. Bagyidaw had, with no compunction, ordered the death of his uncle, Prince Toung Oo, and all his family because of their potential threat to his throne. Rumor said the emperor was encouraging the Buddhist priests, certainly disquieting news for adherents of a "foreign" faith. With each new rumor, attendance at the *zayat* dropped off. The Judsons could understand why their friends were apprehensive; as foreigners, they were also in danger, but not as much as a Burman subject.

Maung Ing had become a believer, but his employment required him to leave temporarily. Maung Thahlah and Maung Byaay professed faith but requested baptism in the evening at an inconspicuous time. The Judsons sympathized with the situation confronting the new converts. Judson wrote: "The sun was not allowed to look upon the humble, timid profession. No wondering crowd crowned the overshadowing hill. We felt, on the banks of the water, as a little, feeble, solitary band. But perhaps some hovering angels took note of the event…[and] perhaps Jesus looked down on us, pitied and forgave our weaknesses, and marked us for his own."[4]

The Judsons became increasingly aware of a need for some sort of official sanction. Their situation was precarious, leaving them open to deportation, persecution, or worse. Ann and Adoniram understood the courageous commitment the new Christians had made. A profession of faith made them liable for death itself. Maybe their best recourse would be to go to the Golden Feet in an attempt to receive official approval.

The alternative was worse. Both couples agreed. Judson and Colman would go to Ava, and leave the results in God's hands.

They had to get a pass from the viceroy to go and "lift up their eyes to the Golden One,"[5] and gifts had to be prepared. In Burma, going without gifts was unthinkable. Therefore, gifts were prepared for lesser officials and for the king. They chose an English Bible in six volumes, each enclosed in gold leaf, since gold was so prized in the Golden Land. Shortly before departure, Moung Shwa-gnong reappeared. Danger for Christians was so palpable by this time that he had feared going near the *zayat*, but Adoniram seemed to draw him like a magnet. Shwa-gnong often seemed to deliberately disagree with Judson just to hear Adoniram's explanations, which always appeared to fascinate him.[6] It was encouraging to Adoniram that Shwa-gnong had returned in spite of the danger of persecution.

Early on December 21, Ann, her heart filled with misgivings, quietly told Adoniram goodbye. She watched with great trepidation as the boat pulled away and disappeared into the early morning mists. In spite of anxiety about the unknown that lay ahead of them, Judson was intrigued by the countryside along the great Irrawady River. Travel was slow, averaging about ten miles a day. Judson and Colman encountered thick jungle and all manner of creatures along the banks, from beautiful parrots of brilliant colors to hungry crocodiles and clouds of pesky mosquitoes.

On the way, the two got their first look at Pagan (Bagon), the ancient capital. It was an archaeologist's dream, with thousands of pagodas and temples scattered along the river for more than eight miles. Judson climbed to the top of a high temple to view the ancient ruins. In those moments, he vowed that one day "a voice mightier than mine...will ere long sweep away every vestige of thy dominion. The churches of Jesus will soon supplant these idolatrous monuments, and the chanting of the devotees of Boodh will die away before the Christian hymn of praise."[7]

Five weeks after leaving Rangoon, Judson and Colman reached the capital. The next day they called upon Rangoon's former viceroy, seeking permission to "behold the Golden Face." A sleepless night followed. Judson well knew how tenuous a chance there was at success and recorded: "Tomorrow's dawn will usher in the most eventful day of our lives. Tomorrow's eve will close on the bloom or the blight of our fondest hopes. Yet it is consoling to commit this business into the hands of our heavenly Father—to feel that the work is His, not ours."[8]

Maung Zah, a high-ranking minister, was to introduce them to the king. It was not a propitious day for an audience. They had no way of knowing that the Golden One was preoccupied with viewing a celebration of a recent victory. All foreigners were viewed as potential enemies, and the Westerners' situation was made further precarious by the fact that there was bad blood brewing between Britain and Burma. There was trouble over borders and disputed territories, none of which would incline the Golden Ears to listen with favor to petitions made by foreigners. Maung Zah was in the process of previewing Adoniram's petition when the announcement was heard, "The Golden One is approaching!" It was too late then to wait for a likelier day. Everyone knelt, Judson and Colman as well, and all but the foreigners bowed their heads to the ground. The eyes of the Americans were focused on the king. This immediately drew the Emperor's attention to their white faces and long white surplice-like gowns.

Their first view of the "Lord of Life and Death" was of a man of twenty-eight, about five feet tall and marching with the proud gait of an Eastern monarch. The emperor's forehead was slanted a characteristic inherited from a distant ancestor and his long black hair was enclosed in a turban-like headdress. The most elaborate part of his costume was an ornate sword in a golden sheath.[9]

The Golden Presence stopped his march before the strangers and demanded, "Who are these?"

"The teachers, great king," replied Judson.

Bagidaw was startled. "What! Your speak Burmese? When did you come? Are you teachers of religion?" He peppered them with inquiries.[10]

In flawless Burmese, Judson answered every question thrown at him. Then Maung Zah read his petition for the Golden Ears, requesting permission for them to preach their religion and asking tolerance for Burman converts. Bagyidaw seized the petition in a preemptory manner, read it, and then disdainfully handed it back. Next Judson handed Maung Zah an abridged copy of his tract, "A View of the Christian Religion," and again the king took it and began to read.

Bagyidaw read only the first few lines: "There is one Being who exists eternally—besides this, the true God, there is no other God." The king threw down the tract, even as an assistant opened one of the gold-bound volumes of the Bible and held it up to the royal presence. His majesty paid no attention, and Maung Zah interpreted for them the obvious conclusion: "Why ask for such permission? Have not the Portuguese, English, Moslems, and people of all other nations, liberty to worship according to their own custom? In regard to the objects of your petition, His majesty gives no order. As to your sacred books, His majesty has no use for them. Take them away."[11]

A crushing weight of defeat flooded Adoniram's heart. They had so longed for a positive reception from the emperor and with it, permission to preach the gospel without fear of persecution for the believers. This rejection by Bagyidaw might even mean *increased* danger for the tiny band of believers, and Adoniram experienced a daunting sense of despair. James Colman seemed unable to keep from catching some of the disappointment consuming Judson. Never one to remain in deep despair, however, Judson's spirits rose with the dawn of a new day. The two men reached Rangoon in a matter of days. Judson and Colman were brutally frank with the converts who gathered around for the news. Adoniram had looked at many options. Maybe they should leave Rangoon. As soon as word leaked out, which it assuredly would, open interest in Christianity would be all but dead. The believers would be in grave danger. Maybe the missionaries should go to Arracan where they would be under British protection and could freely preach to Burmans there.

Adoniram had not reckoned with the converts' response. "No. Stay." was their unanimous plea, "At least wait until there are eight or ten believers. Then not even the emperor can stop God's work." The Judsons were overwhelmed. The converts' faith, zeal, and steadfastness amazed and humbled the missionaries. The more the believers heard of possible dangers, the more they appeared determined to hold out. Then Moung Shwa-gnong reappeared, informing his teacher, "I believe in the eternal God, in his son Jesus Christ, for the atonement which Christ had made, and in the teachings of the apostles, as the true and only word of God."[12] This man, more than any of the less educated and well-known, had the most to lose. The Judsons took heart. Long and prayerful hours with the Burmese Christians and the Colmans led to the decision that the Colmans would go to Chittagong and establish a beachhead there. Ann and Adoniram would remain in Rangoon.

So, eight years after beginning a work by themselves, the Judsons were once more alone in the mission—and yet not alone. About them were God's answers to prayer in the face of each believer. Each day they translated and taught, and each day they met with inquirers in the privacy of the mission house in the room vacated by the Colmans, which they dubbed the "new *zayat*."

Ann and Adoniram were often moved to tears by the courageous attitude of the little group. Maung Nau, the first believer, had always seemed submissive and unassuming; now he expressed such zeal and devotion that they began calling him "Peter" among themselves. Maung Thahlah was showing an astounding aptitude for learning Bible passages and talking with inquirers, and his relative Maung Shway-bay became a believer as well.

Shwa-gnong himself appeared to hold back from the open step of baptism, although two of his wealthy, upper-class friends asked to be baptized. Shwa-gnong put forward one objection after another but could never provoke Adoniram to argue with him. "Read what the Word says," was always Judson's response. Judson discerned Moung Shwa-gnong's true reason for hesitation; for someone of his position and public standing, such an open commitment meant sure persecution and possible death. Adoniram admitted to himself, "My heart was wrung with pity....The thought of the iron maul, and a secret suspicion that if I was in his circumstances, I should perhaps have no more courage, restrained my tongue."13

Meanwhile Ann was deep in discussion with Mah Men Lay, an educated, soft-spoken woman of real talent who brought friends with her to learn from "Mrs. Yoodthan." Ann soon realized that Mah Men Lay feared what might happen to her family if she openly believed. Adoniram, watching the growing faith of Mah Men Lay, was genuinely hoping that Ann would soon know the joy of bringing the first Burmese woman to belief. He wished for it in double measure because he increasingly noted the dark circles under Ann's eyes and the sallowness of her beautiful complexion, which was a telltale sign of recurring liver disease. Adoniram's own chronic eye weakness had returned in force. He worked as fast as possible to finish his translation of Ephesians. With deep satisfaction, he was at last able to place it in the hands of the eager little company of believers. Ann's eyes were giving her trouble as well, and then her liver condition worsened and the pain intensified. She must have medical help. She was already too weak to sail without Adoniram, and he privately admitted that he too stood in dire need of medical attention. They were able to procure a berth on a ship planning to sail for Bengal in a few weeks.

Two more applicants petitioned for baptism before the Judsons sailed. Adoniram agreed, and in the small pond near the mission house, they were baptized that night. Then, once again Moung Shwa-gnong came. He had just recovered from a fever and that evening declared, "I desire to receive baptism." Adoniram was astounded. "You say you are desirous of receiving baptism. May I ask when you desire to receive it?" Shaw-gnong's reply was immediate: "At any time you will please to give it. Now—this moment if you please?" Judson asked, "Do you wish to receive baptism in public or in private?" "I will receive it at any time, and in any circumstances, that you please to direct." Adoniram stood in awed silence. Then, to this learned man who so uniquely appealed to his heart, Judson said, "Teacher, I am satisfied that you are a true disciple. I reply, therefore, that I am as desirous of giving you baptism as you are of receiving it."14

The profession of the distinguished Moung Shwa-gnong galvanized believers and inquirers alike. It was no surprise to any that the great scholar was a believer. The astonishing thing was his boldness in making it public and in allowing a foreigner to baptize him, thereby jeopardizing his life. Late that same night Mah Men Lay returned in haste to the mission and insisted on being baptized at once. July 18, 1820, was an unforgettable day for Ann and Adoniram. Moung Shwa-gnong was now an open believer, and Mah Men Lay had become Burma's first woman convert. The dream of ten Burmese believers had become a glorious reality.[15] The Judsons blessed God and took courage.

The Separation
1820–1823

Ann's birthplace in Bradford,
Massachusetts, looks much
as it did when she was
born there in 1789.

When darkness seems to hide his face
I rest on His unchanging grace.
—Edward Mote, "The Solid Rock"

RANGOON'S SUN WAS SCORCHING IN JULY 1820 AS THE JUDSONS STEPPED
into the little boat taking them out to the ship headed for Calcutta.
Ann's skin was yellow from her liver disease. Its debilitating effects
caused her to cling to Adoniram's arm. His step was firm, but the
pain in his eyes was intensified by the sun's glare. Standing on the
dock were all of the new disciples and many inquirers. The women
were crying aloud, not only a Burmese custom but also a reflection
of their genuine grief at seeing the "Yoodthans" sailing away.

As the Burmese waved their last goodbyes, Ann and Adoniram stood at the rail, too moved to speak. Both recalled the July morning precisely seven years earlier when they had first looked on that unknown city that now held so many who were dear to their hearts.

The time at sea was discouraging, for Ann's disease showed no improvement. Upon their arrival in Calcutta, a Dr. Chalmers was happy to treat her and declined any compensation. Her condition would fluctuate, one day improved, the next worse. The atmosphere of Serampore was more conducive to recovery, so they spent two quiet months with their friends the Houghs in that city. The pain in Adoniram's eyes abated, but the doctor felt that returning to Rangoon's climate would be a death sentence for Ann.

On the other hand, a Dr. MacWhirter, equally well-known, studied Ann's case and felt that prescribed medication could allow her to return with Adoniram. They decided to take the latter doctor's advice, so keenly did both wish for her return. As Ann's strength came back, so did her determination to go home to the work she loved. Two months in Serampore and another month in Calcutta did much to shore up the waning strength of both Judsons. Adoniram was only thirty-two and Ann just thirty, but many days they felt twice that age, so difficult had been their circumstances and so debilitating was Rangoon's climate.

Now the Judsons were ready to sail home to Rangoon. On November 23, 1820, they boarded the *Salamanca*, expecting a short and restful voyage. Instead, the little vessel had an unbelievably stormy passage, with ferocious winds, squalls, and the worst thunderstorm either had ever experienced. Out on the open seas, it seemed a miracle that a lone ship could escape the lightning that flashed all around them. The expected two weeks stretched to six until, with overwhelming relief, Ann and Adoniram welcomed the sight of Rangoon's dingy harbor.

How different now their emotions than seven years earlier. On this January morning, Christian friends were waiting on the dock. There was the tall figure of Moung Shwa-gnong, hand raised high in greeting, the other believers clustered around him. The converts rejoiced in having the Judsons home and began telling what had been happening. News of 30,000 troops on the way to war with Siam was troubling. Shwa-gnong had good news, however. All had been anxious about the repercussions of his baptism. In spite of a conspiracy by a leading Buddhist monk to have him persecuted, the viceroy had nipped it in the bud. May-day-men had been the old viceroy who had first befriended the Judsons. He had been returned to authority, and when the Buddhist leader had sent word that "the teacher Shwa-gnong tries to turn the bottom of the priests' rice-bowl upwards," the viceroy had cut him off quickly with: "What consequence? Let the priests turn it back again."[1] And that ended the threat. There was further cause for gladness. Mah Men Lay, radiant in her newfound faith, was opening a school for boys so they would have an alternative to the Buddhist priests' instruction.

Inquirers were coming regularly, and the Judsons experienced great satisfaction in their daily endeavors. Both were meeting with inquirers (as were the converts themselves) whenever they were not hard at work translating Scripture and tracts. Adoniram had Shwa-gnong to help him, and translation took on new satisfaction. Shwa-gnong's knowledge of the language and culture was of great assistance in concise translation, and the scholar flourished with each new truth he learned. Ann wrote: "Moung Shwa-gnong is an invaluable assistant in the translation of the scriptures. He is one of the most indefatigable persons in the world; he sits with Mr. J from 9 in the morning till 5 at night, in which time they get through only 10 or 12 verses, as he will not let a sentence pass, unless the meaning is conspicuous. How great is the mercy of God,…raising up a man of his talents and influence to assist in perfecting the translation of the word of God."[2]

In March 1821, Maung-Ing, the second convert whose baptism had been delayed because of his work, returned and came immediately to request baptism. All the time away he had been gladly sharing his faith, this one who was to become Burma's first home missionary.

In March, it also became apparent that there was no way of hiding the prominent Shwa-gnong's conversion from his home village. The chief accused him before the viceroy of having embraced ideas "subversive" to the Buddhist religion. These accusations were too open for the viceroy to just ignore. He knew the normal response would be to issue a death penalty, but he was deliberately slow to act. Shwa-gnong heard the news, went at once to Adoniram, got a supply of tracts and Scripture portions, and headed upriver. There he settled down and quietly evangelized, utilizing his great teaching skills, and thus the gospel message continued to spread in spite of persecution.

During this time, Ann was at her peak of productivity. Her language skills were remarkable, both in Burmese and Siamese. She was constantly involved in translation, counseling, and teaching at her school for girls. Her liver disease was just barely under control, however, when in late summer both Judsons came down with cholera. For days both lay deathly ill in the same room, neither able to rise. On August 4, 1821, Adoniram was able to write: "Am just recovering from the second fit of sickness which I have had this season. The first was the cholera;...the present has been a fever. The second day after I was taken, Mrs. J. was taken with the same; and, for several days, we were unable to help one another,...[but we] are now in a convalescent state....Mrs. J., however, is suffering severely under the liver complaint which...is making such rapid and alarming advances, as to preclude all hope of her recovery in this part of the world."[3]

Indeed, Ann was failing rapidly. Day by day she grew worse. The couple, so attuned to each other's heart, realized that an agonizing choice confronted them. If Ann were to live, she must go to a colder climate and have the best medical care. Harsh reality told them that they were looking at a minimum of two years for recovery. She would be a severe loss to the mission, but if Adoniram accompanied her, the entire work would stop and all the fruit of the eight-year investment of their lives would be in jeopardy. They made the decision: Ann would go alone.

She and Adoniram stood together with hands locked in anguish the morning of August 21, 1821, not knowing if they would ever stand together again. They were one in a sense far beyond what most couples ever experience. Parting seemed a nearly mortal blow. All the same, although the loss of Ann's vibrant presence and skills would be painful, the thought of temporary separation was more palatable than her death.

Ann's ship was barely out to sea when she became violently ill and actually did not expect to reach Calcutta alive. Against all odds, she managed to regain a measure of strength, arriving in Calcutta with sunken eyes and jaundiced skin, the condition of her disease appallingly evident. Not only was Ann ill, but she was also overwhelmed by homesickness. "Home" was Adoniram and Burma. She wrote a friend: "Nothing but the prospect of a final separation would have induced us to decide on this measure."[4] Ann was bitterly disappointed to learn in Calcutta that the only possible passage to America was prohibitively expensive. Then yet again she recognized the hand of Providence providing a way. A chaplain's wife knew of a ship sailing for England with three children returning to school, and Ann could share their cabin for a minimal charge. Furthermore, even that fare was paid by the grateful father of the children.

Ann Judson arrived in England and was astounded to find herself a heroine. The struggles and exploits of the Judsons were common topics of conversation in Christian circles. Joseph Butterworth, a devout Methodist and a member of Parliament, became her mentor and sponsor. Concerned new friends hastened to make Ann comfortable and help her recover.

Ann's biggest problem was the demands on her time when her body so desperately needed rest. For years she had been corresponding with a friend in Scotland, and in June 1822, she wrote of her recent experiences in London: "My dear Mrs. Deakin,...Striking indeed is the contrast between this splendid city and that wild idolatrous country where all my former letters to you have been dated. Yet I cannot say that the same happy sensations pervade my mind;...though I am in the Christian world...yet I am far away from my world, and feel in a state of constant anxiety relative to my little world which is left far behind."[5]

English friends made every effort to help the traveler in their midst. Ann was shown every kindness and all her expenses paid. Christians were eager to hear firsthand what God was doing in Burma, and friends in Scotland pleaded for Ann to visit them. Her only reluctance was her health and limited physical stamina. Aware of this, her host, Mr. Butterworth, wrote Mrs. Deakin in Scotland: "Repose is absolutely necessary for her....The excitement of friends is too much for her shattered state. I therefore write this as a charge to you...that if you wish to preserve the valuable life of our friend you must keep her quiet."[6]

While in Scotland, Ann heard from the Baptist board in America, suggesting that she return to America on the *Packet*. Scottish friends went a step further, purchasing her passage on the large and comfortable *Amity*. On August 16, 1822, Ann was able to sail for America. Ten years before she had never expected such a moment to arrive, but here she was, soon to see her family again. Joy, however, was tempered by the heartache of knowing that Adoniram was not able to share it. It had been months since she had been able to hear any news from him. The state of her mixed emotions was revealed in a memorandum found years later: "I cannot realize that I shall ever again find myself, in my own dear home at Bradford, amid the scenes of my early youth, where every spot is associated with some tender recollection. But the constant idea, that my dear J. is not a participator of my joys, will mar them all."[7]

Far from Ann or even news of Ann, Adoniram assuaged his own intense loneliness in endless work. The subtle pressure of constantly wondering what the government might do about this foreign religion was draining. Judson learned to go with the flow and daily discover what winds of persecution might be in the air. When there appeared to be no signs of problems, he would focus his energies on teaching. When a hint of danger came, he threw himself into translating. As Judson later reported in February 1822: "About half the New Testament is now finished, and I am desirous of finishing the whole....When that work is disposed of, I expect to feel more free to go forth and encounter the hazards which may attend an open and extensive declaration of the gospel. Difficulties may obstruct...but at the right time, the time marked out from all eternity, the Lord will appear in his glory."[8]

Even under the pressure of impending persecution, Judson's essential optimism asserted itself. A letter Adoniram wrote Ann after she left Rangoon revealed some of the emotions he was experiencing in his lonely work: "Life is short. Happiness consists not in outward circumstances. Millions of Burmans are perishing. I am almost the only person on earth who has attained their language to such a degree as to be able to communicate the way of salvation. How great are my obligations to spend and be spent for Christ! What a privilege to be allowed to serve him…and to suffer for him.…But in myself I am absolute nothingness.…Soon we shall be in heaven. Oh, let us live as we shall then wish we had done!"[9]

A different source of encouragement came in 1821 in the persons of Dr. and Mrs. Jonathan Price and their little daughter, a family sent out by the fledgling Baptist missionary board. Price was a stereotypical New Englander, with one departure: he loved to talk. The word *laconic* was not in his vocabulary. His type of mental prowess was completely different from Judson's; Price was unrefined and with no interest in philosophy or deep thinking. Not only was he absent-minded to a fault but also sloppy in appearance and unconcerned about cleanliness, both of which were anathema to the fastidious Judson. Price was, however, a utilitarian type of doctor who particularly enjoyed removing cataracts. Quickly the news of this rare skill spread through the city, and many came to regard Price as a magician. His language skills grew along with his practice. His Burmese vocabulary was not large and his grammar atrocious, but he possessed a keen ear, and soon he enjoyed talking as much in Burmese as he did in English. It didn't bother him a whit if the Burmese didn't quite understand what he was talking about.[10]

Poor Mrs. Price survived only five months, and the sad little group laid her body to rest in the garden near the grave of baby Roger. Their small daughter was sent to Calcutta to live with the Lawsons. At about the same time, however, the Houghs returned to Rangoon. Hough could still print faster than Adoniram could translate, and he himself had a better command of the language now.

In July 1822, Judson was presented with a dilemma. The Golden Ears had heard about the foreign doctor who could restore eyesight, and he issued an order to Price to report to Ava. Adoniram was deep into translation of the New Testament and hated to interrupt the process. He was constantly aware that he was the only person alive capable of giving the people the Bible in their own language. At the moment, however, a royal order gave him no choice. Price, with his limited language skills and even more limited understanding of the culture of Burma, dared not go before the volatile king without Judson to smooth the way.

But once more, illness ravaged Adoniram's body—first a violent fever, and then cholera again. The deadly effects slowly subsided, but it took his body weeks to recover. The two men finally got away on August 18—although Judson had the immense satisfaction of baptizing the eighteenth Burman convert before their departure.

Price and Judson arrived in Ava late in September. (It was the custom in Burma for a new monarch to rule from a new capital city, and the missionaries arrived while such a move was in progress. King Bagyidaw was rebuilding the ancient capital of Ava, constructing a magnificent palace for himself.) This visit of Judson's to the Golden Feet was vastly different from his first trip. This time the emperor was eager to hear what the magical foreign doctor could do. Initially, he only acknowledged Adoniram as an interpreter. On their second day, Bagyidaw seemed to notice Judson and barked out: "And you, in black—are you a medical person too?" Adoniram indicated to his majesty that he was a teacher of religion. The emperor asked one or two general questions about this foreign faith and then asked the question Adoniram had been dreading, "Have any embraced your religion?"

Judson did not answer directly but quietly replied, "Not here in Ava."

Bagyidaw persisted: "Are there in Rangoon those who have embraced it?"

Here it is, thought Adoniram. Slowly he lifted his eyes to the emperor and began, "There are some foreigners," upon which he paused, then added, "and some Burmans." The moment was weighted with foreboding.[11]

The emperor was silent for long moments and then just as suddenly shifted direction and began asking innocuous questions about religion, astronomy, geography. For some inexplicable reason, the Golden One did not want to pursue the issue. Adoniram had not realized that he was holding his breath until he heard his own sigh of relief. For the moment at least, their little flock of believers in Rangoon was safe.

The weeks and months in Ava were a strange mixture of encouragement and tension. Adonriam often felt he was walking a tightrope. Everybody knew how capricious the Golden One could be, all good humor and affability one moment, the next in a rage. Price was enjoying his popularity as many Burmese with cataracts came for help, wanting the "magic knife" to give them sight again. Meanwhile, Adoniram looked for land in Ava, but none seemed available.

In the midst of translating, Adoniram was repeatedly ill. In December, he wrote, "I am just recovering from the fifth attack of fever and ague." [12] So many fevers made Judson uneasy. He wrote, "My only hope now is, that it [fever] will exhaust itself before my constitution is exhausted....I could wish to live to finish the New Testament and I should also be happy to see a little church raised up in Ava....But the ways of God are not the ways of man." [13]

The momentous day when the New Testament translation was completed came more quickly than Judson had anticipated. How he wished that Ann could have been there that morning. It was July 12, 1823, exactly ten years since they had first seen Rangoon. Adoniram had not been able to receive mail from Ann for months. Lack of news was agonizing, not knowing where she was or if she was recovering. But never one to stay depressed, Judson's basic optimism asserted itself, and he fully expected her to soon be back.

Meanwhile, Bagyidaw had decided he wanted the doctor and teacher to remain in Ava. Adoniram explained that he must first return to Rangoon to fetch his wife. The king ordered Judson to bring her as well and return. What the king wanted, the king got, so land became 'available' for Judson. It was a small plot not far outside the city wall surrounding Ava and the palace. Here Adoniram could build a small house on stilts. With high hopes he returned to Rangoon, confident that there was a possibility of royal approval, and that Ann would soon be back.

In fact, much had been going on in Ann's life. In August 1822, she had sailed from England to America. The first sight of Massachusetts on the horizon was doubly soul-stirring because she had never expected to see it again. Ann had gained a measure of strength during the months in England and hoped that a few more months in the bracing climate of New England would return her to health.

A flood of memories rushed through her mind as the coastline of New England became larger on the horizon. Memories of standing on a deck ten years before and saying goodbye caused her eyes to well with tears. Those idealistic young missionaries of a decade earlier had been tempered in the fires of stark experience. Tears spilled over as Ann remembered Harriet Newell, who had stood with her that day. Harriet had been in a lonely grave nearly ten years, and Samuel was now buried in Bombay. Remembering her lost friends, Ann's longing for Adoniram to share this homecoming was even more overwhelming. The riotous beauty of New England at its peak of autumn color filled her eyes; she had not seen such colors in a decade, but Adoniram wasn't there, and this dimmed its grandeur. Ann would gladly give up all the joy of seeing family and friends again if only she could be well and back with Adoniram.

Just a few days later, Ann sat in the carriage taking her to Bradford. The beautiful young Ann who had left her hometown ten years ago had been vibrant with life, her eyes sparkling with anticipation. This Ann was painfully thin and close to emaciation from the ravages of the disease that had invaded her system, a disease she jokingly referred to as her "Indian constitution." Her heart and spirit had grown deeper, drawing on spiritual wellsprings unknown to her a decade earlier. The bright sparkling eyes were yellowed with jaundice, her skin the same unhealthy hue. Shiny black curls now hung limp and lank about her wan face—but she was gripped by such excitement that she was nearly shaking with anticipation. She was almost in the arms of her family again.

At the sight of their daughter back as it were from the dead, Rebecca and John Hasseltine felt their hearts would burst with joy.

The emotions overflowing in Ann's mind as she tearfully embraced them went far beyond words. The intensity of excitement and emotions of the tender reunion were almost more than Ann's weakened system could sustain. She had not imagined that such joy and exhilaration could bring her to the point of sleeplessness, which in turn further undermined her already precarious condition.

Ann wrote to her friend Mrs. Chaplin in Waterville, Maine, describing her overwhelming emotions: "I had never fully counted the cost of a visit to my dear native country and beloved relatives. I did not expect that a scene which I had anticipated as so joyous, was destined to give my health and constitution a shock which would require months to repair....The idea that I was once more on American ground, banished all peace and quiet from my mind, and for the first four days and nights, I never closed my eyes to sleep!...My health began to decline in the most alarming manner, and the pain in my side and cough returned. I was kept in a state of constant excitement, by daily meeting with my old friends and acquaintances; and during the whole six weeks of my residence at my father's, I had not one quiet night's rest. I felt the cold most severely, and found, as that increased, my cough increased."[14]

Such excitement was so intense that Ann sometimes felt she was smothering. She was shocked to discover that joy could indeed leave her literally breathless. Fortunately, Adoniram's brother Elnathan, a surgeon in Baltimore, realized the strain Ann's body was under. He insisted that she come south to Baltimore, where the more temperate climate would be less taxing on her frail body. Furthermore, she would have the added benefit of rest and quiet, away from the press of those who loved her deeply, but who were unaware that her body was using up energy it could ill afford. In addition, Elnathan was able to procure for Ann the help of the best physicians in Baltimore.

Quietness, a gentler climate, time, and space, these were the things Ann desperately needed. She wrote to Mrs. Chaplin that in Baltimore, with a mild climate and attentive doctors, her body and nerves could begin to recover. Ann was doubly thankful to have time to study several hours a day. Friends and family had been clamoring for her to write about the beginning of the Burmese mission. No one else was qualified to do it, and making such material available to the Christian world was vital in challenging believers to the universality of the Great Commission.

The rest was further a godsend because Ann felt spiritually exhausted. The press and rush of reunion had not allowed the time she felt was essential in maintaining her personal relationship with God. She alluded to these feelings in the letter to Mrs. Chaplin: "Your kind hint, relative to my being injured by the lavish attention of our dear friends in this country, has much endeared you to my heart. I am well aware that human applause has a tendency to elate the soul, and render it less anxious about spiritual enjoyments...since my return to this country, I have often been affected to tears, in hearing the undeserved praises of my friends, feeling that I was far, very far, from being what they imagined; that there are thousands of poor, obscure Christians...who are a thousand times more deserving of the tender regard of their fellow Christians than I am."[15]

By sheer determination, Ann was able to complete her book, *An Account of the American Baptist Mission to the Burman Empire.* This book was to have far-reaching influence on the cause of missions and went into many editions. The name "Ann Judson" came close to being a household word, and after the events of the following three years became known to the world, Ann was to become a heroine—the likes of which America had not known. During this period of rest and quiet study in Baltimore, Ann somehow managed to find time to meet with a few select groups and promote the cause of Burmah. Someone also arranged for a sitting with the famed portrait artist Rembrandt Peale, whose studios were in Baltimore.[16]

Little was known in the nineteenth century about how to treat liver disease. The best medical knowledge of the time said that body fluids needed to be "balanced," and bleeding was a common treatment. Doctors used leeches to suck blood and gave calomel purges. Another common treatment was "salivation," where patients took blue pills containing mercury, which in turn made the body produce more saliva. Medical knowledge in 1823 did not realize the deadly effects of mercury on the central nervous system.

That Ann survived her "treatments" was a miracle, and not surprisingly, her condition worsened. She was bled so frequently that she was in almost total exhaustion. Yet somehow her body began to regain strength. The majority of her doctors declared unequivocally that she must not return to Burma. That would be a death warrant. In Ann's mind, however, there was no choice. She would return. Her heart was already there, both with Adoniram and with the people of Burma. Providence again intervened, and by the spring of 1823, Ann began to mend. The tone of her skin improved, her eyes returned to their normal color and sparkle, and even her hair regained its sheen. Ann managed to have one last visit with her family in Bradford and sailed for Calcutta in June 1823.

This Ann was much like the Ann of old, eager to return to Adoniram and to her work. Two new missionaries sailed with her, Deborah and Jonathan Wade, a young couple who became dear friends of the Judsons and greatly strengthened the Burma mission for many years to come. Never one to waste time, Ann began teaching the Wades the Burmese language on the long voyage, giving them a tremendous head start on that complex language and culture. The three reached Calcutta in October, only to be greeted with the news that war between Burma and Britain seemed imminent. All the advice they heard was to stay put. Not Ann and not the Wades. They located the first available ship for Rangoon and saw the glistening spire of the massive Shwe Dagon on December 5, 1823.

And Adoniram saw the joy of his heart after the longest two years and three months of his life. As the ship drew closer to shore, the vision of Ann on the deck grew clearer, and Adoniram's eyes flooded with tears of elation as he saw the "Ann Hasseltine of other days. Two days later he wrote Thomas Baldwin "I had the inexpressible happiness of welcoming Mrs. Judson once more to the shores of Burmah."[17]

In that moment of joyous reunion, the agony of the long months of separation faded. It would have been difficult for them to evaluate the worth of Ann's convalescent period. They could not view it from the vantage point of history. Ann had written in a letter just the year before about the reasons for this separation: "I know not the designs of God toward me and it is well I do not. I trust however, he will prepare me for all."[18]

Neither could have foreseen the sufferings that lay ahead, but neither could they have known how God would use Ann's influence during those months in America to promote the cause of missions. A later biographer stated: "Adoniram Judson cannot be mentioned without Ann. Apart from her his story would have been very different. Her adventurous nature had been a source of worry to her mother in her childhood days, but it was one of the qualities that made possible her joining so gladly with Adoniram in his missionary enterprise. Again and again, it gave her courage when both sorely needed courage. And she never lost her happy, vivacious spirit, in spite of trials and discomforts and sorrows. Her winsomeness and attractiveness often won an opening when the future looked like a solid wall, and she was always the magnet that eagerly drew Adoniram back to his home. She had a radiant joy in her religious life, and a deep and genuine faith."[19] And Ann was finally back to her heart's home. Once again, as had become their motto, the Judsons blessed God and took courage.

wo ancient gates of Ava that have been restored.

Rumors of War: 1824

Lo, the hosts of evil round us scorn thy Christ, assail His ways.
—Harry Emerson Fosdick, "God of Grace and God of Glory"

TWO YEARS APART. BOTH ANN AND ADONIRAM HAD FELT IT WOULD NEVER end, but in the joy of reunion, those torturous months faded. Adoniram was elated to see Ann so radiant. What a change from the fragile woman who had sailed away in 1821. In reality, Ann felt stronger at the moment than did Judson himself. Frequent attacks of cholera and the constant burning that plagued his eyes left him weakened. Only the discipline of daily exercise had kept him going.

The Wades were a boon, for their arrival meant the Houghs would have help. Ann and Adoniram were proceeding to Ava in a matter of days; Ann's trunks and baggage were taken straight to the boat Judson was preparing for the trip. He was anxious for them to go as soon as possible, for with such a capricious monarch, the winds of acceptance might quickly shift toward antagonism. The situation in Rangoon was encouraging because the Judsons were able to wave farewell to an enthusiastic church of eighteen Burmans and four missionaries.

As they traveled, Adoniram filled Ann in on the apparent change of heart by the king, explaining in a way she quickly grasped about the machinations at court. For months, however, no news had come from Price in Ava, so who knew what might have changed. Even had Price gotten a letter through from Ava, he was clueless about the Burman mind-set. Judson did bring Ann up to date on Price himself. He had operated on a Burmese woman's eyes. and rather than it helping, she was now blind. Price had insisted on marrying her, and when Judson tried to dissuade him, he had been informed that Price would make her his common-law wife if he didn't have benefit of clergy. With real reluctance, Judson performed the ceremony, mentally shaking his head over the most ill-suited couple he had ever seen.

Maung Ing accompanied the Judsons to the capital. His loving disposition and remarkable maturity as a new believer made him a constant source of blessing. Ann was wide-eyed on the leisurely trip up the fabled Irrawady, her first trip north. She was anticipating new adventures in Ava, for Bagyidaw had commanded Adoniram to bring her. No foreign woman had ever been seen at court. In a letter to Butterworth in London, Ann speculated on what lay ahead and reported on the best news of all: the translation of the New Testament was finished.[1]

The trip gave the Judsons six weeks in which to catch up on twenty-seven months apart. Ann wrote home describing the fascinating sights along the river. Mother Nature, not usually generous when it came to climate in Burma, smiled on them with cool breezes and pleasant evenings. Not to go overboard, Nature did decide to throw in thousands of evening mosquitoes, but these were a small price to pay for the thrill of reunion and quiet time together.

The Judsons had hours to enjoy the enthralling scenes along the riverbank. The mighty Irrawady sprang from the Himalayas in the north and wound more than 1,300 miles down to the Andaman Sea. Along its banks the countryside looked almost permanently abandoned to nature. Either side of the river was a thick reed and brush jungle, much of it teeming with wild animals. The few scattered huts in the midst of thick foliage were so surrounded by jungle that they seemed entwined with the clinging vines and trees. Tales of tigers, snakes, and alligators were enough to make the Judsons willing to look at leisure but leave to the imagination what might be in those thickets.

Jungle slowly changed to plains and delta, with many villages along the way. Occasionally their boat would pull to shore so they could stroll in a village. Ann told of meeting villagers along the way: "In one instance…we seated ourselves down, when the villagers as usual assembled, and Mr. Judson introduced the subject of religion. Several old men…entered into conversation, while the multitude was all attention. The apparent school-master of the village coming up, Mr. Judson handed him a tract, and requested him to read,…[and] he remarked…that such a writing was worthy of being copied….Mr. Judson informed him he might keep the tract, on condition he read it to all his neighbours. We could not but hope the Spirit of God would bless those few simple truths, to the salvation of some of their souls."[2]

They frequently discussed an ominous topic: the likelihood of war. After years of rumors, war seemed too close to reality. While Ann had been in Calcutta, she had learned that the Burmese had been firing on British outposts at the shared borders. The British could not continue to ignore such incidents. However, the British simply failed to grasp how uninformed the Burmese court was about the strength of the English. They did not understand that the English forces could utterly annihilate them.

The Judsons would soon reach the exotic capital. Bagyidaw was completing his move to Ava with its splendid new palace.[3] Shimmering with gold trim, it towered higher than any palace preceding it and was constructed with long, elegant pillars carved from Burma's tallest teak trees. The palace was lined with gilded walkways, up and down which the Golden Feet could parade. But within the shadow of such magnificence lay Let Ma Yoon, Ava's infamous death prison. Ann and Adoniram could have no idea of the horrors that sinister spot would portend for their lives as they entered the new capital for the first time.

January 1824 was nearly over, and they were in the heart of the nation, still hopeful about the prospects before them. But were prospects hopeful now? Rumors were ominous. Price greeted them with the news that he was out of favor at court. In fact, all foreigners in Ava were suddenly persona non grata. Word of war intensified daily. Nobles who had been in power when Judson had been there the year before were now dismissed. The change had been so rapid that the Judsons were taken aback.

Ann wrote her family that the situation at court had vastly altered and that she and Adoniram did not know what might happen. One of the Rangoon converts had asked the Judsons to take his two daughters and school them, as their mother had become deranged and he wanted them to have Christian training. Ann, eager to get right to work, quickly began teaching them. The Judsons built a small house in true Burmese style, putting it on the little plot of land designated by the Golden One in the days when he had been inclined to smile on foreigners. Everyone stared at the strange and beautiful foreign woman in their midst, but none dared be open and friendly as the Burmese people normally were. The two Americans kept their eyes and ears ever tuned to the intrigues swirling around Ava.

Late in February, Adoniram wrote to Baptists in America: "Various conditions have conspired to render the king somewhat disaffected toward foreigners....I found that a year had made great changes. My old friends and advocates before the king were missing. Very few recognized me. At length his majesty came forward, just spoke to me, and accepted a small present. But I have seen him twice since without obtaining a word or look." He continued that they had "public worship every Lord's Day at Brother Price's."[4]

Judson explained how the clouds of war were growing heavier and darker each week, but concluded: "In all cases, we trust that we have a few dear friends at home who bear us on their hearts at the throne of grace, and a still dearer and greater Friend at the right hand of the Divine Presence in Heaven....Pray for me, that I may be accounted worthy to hold out to the end, and finally meet with you before the throne."[5]

Meanwhile, Adoniram translated and Ann conducted her school. They made a new friend, an enterprising English businessman who attended their Sunday worship and thrived on conversing with the keen young American couple. Only in his early twenties, Henry Gouger had been in Burma two years and had great language skills. In fact, Judson's Burmese grammar had proved invaluable to Gouger. He displayed an incisive understanding of the Burmese psyche and culture, although not with the depth of experience the Judsons possessed.

The three relished exchanging stories of adventures ranging from unusual to ridiculous. Some considered him a rogue, but Ann and Adoniram found in Gouger an innate sense of honesty and common sense that was endearing. Gouger enjoyed talking about his early days at court, when the Golden Eyes had looked kindly on him. The Judsons were fascinated with his accounts of adventures along the Irrawady, shuddering at violent encounters he or friends of his had had with such varied hazards as poison springs, at least one man-eating alligator, and even a voracious tiger.

The three were fond of exchanging stories of foods eaten and what these morsels had been, or might have been, had they dared inquire as to origin. Gouger had both Judsons laughing and shuddering as he described a dish at court. As a guest he had to eat it: "Being already a favourite, I was permitted to gratify my curiosity by tasting one of the most suspicious-looking dishes. It was a kind of sand-cricket fried crisp—nice enough, except in name....Another favourite insect...is one [with] which I would not offend the stomach...by calling it a maggot, if I could find another word equally appropriate. It somewhat resembles a nut-maggot, magnified to three or four inches long....When fried and spread on toast, it is not to be distinguished from marrow, though I never could...overcome my repugnance to its shape and its large black head, with which it was brought to table entire in undisguised hideousness."[6]

In a more serious vein, the three discussed the tense situation to which they awoke each morning, never knowing what might happen next. Gouger shared his insights into the "royal" mind, feeling that the possession of power spelled ruin for the Burmese character.

Gouger had on one occasion met the most famous of the Burmese generals, the mighty Bandoola, whom he described as "beside himself with pride."[7]

In all he observed, Gouger concluded that the worst habit of Burmans was their utter disregard for truth when an object could be gained by lying. Ann and Adoniram could only concur with such a conclusion but encouraged Gouger with the glad tidings that the Burmese converts had found that they had a new source of help in discarding this vicious habit. The little group that gathered each Sunday saw the situation worsening by the day and sadly reached the inevitable conclusion that war was near and that the Burmese were totally ignorant of both their own weakness and England's strength. This ignorance could only be a recipe for disaster.

Many years later, Gouger wrote a penetrating book about the prison months that all of them were soon to endure, a book revealing his deep admiration and respect for the Judsons. He had held a cynical view of missionaries until meeting them. Shared sufferings radically altered his views, and the influence of the Judsons permanently changed his relationship with God.

The handful of foreigners in Ava had no way of knowing what had already happened in Rangoon. Even had the Judsons known, there was no avenue of escape. They were under constant surveillance. The English had attacked Rangoon, and the Houghs and Wades were immediately arrested and marked for execution. Through a harrowing set of events, they miraculously escaped with their lives and were able to sail for Bengal and safety.[8] In May, Hough wrote to missionaries in Calcutta about those terrifying events and concluded his letter by saying, "It is between two and three months since we have received any letter from Mr. Judson or Dr. Price. It is impossible to predict their fate. We tremble whenever we think of them. We can only pray that God, who has delivered us,…may deliver them also."[9]

Back in Ava, Gouger, Price, the Judsons, and the believers who had accompanied them to the capital were gathered as usual for worship on Sunday morning, May 23, 1824. Clearly the tense situation was daily more volatile and potentially explosive. Henry Gouger was the most vulnerable. He was inescapably English and as such was condemned to bear the mark of "enemy." The Judsons felt relatively safe. They were obviously foreign but were Americans, and after all, Adoniram reasoned, America and England had recently been at war. Surely they would not be blamed for England's policies, yet in the back of his mind, as well as Ann's, was a pervasive apprehension. What could they do? They couldn't leave. That required royal permission, and even the meanest intelligence knew there wasn't a chance in the world that such permission would be granted.

In the midst of worship, the door burst open and a breathless messenger blurted out the chilling news. The British fleet had reached Rangoon, bombarded that city, and captured it. There was no news of their colleagues in Rangoon. The worshipers were gripped by fear as they immediately began to pray for wisdom and guidance. Gouger knew that his presence meant danger for all the foreigners, and they agreed not to be seen together again. Being Americans might help protect them, but realistically the Judsons knew that every hour was fraught with danger. Ann and Adoniram stayed close to home with Koo-Chil, their loyal Bengali cook, MoungIng, and the two little girls to whom Ann had given the names "Mary and Abby Hasseltine." But an ominous new rumor began to slip insidiously down the streets of Ava that all foreigners were spies. Danger was at their door.

Both Judsons understood all too well that the king's power was unrestricted and that he led a court that was ignorant, conceited, and arrogant. Bagyidaw was notorious for the speed with which he could change from smiling monarch to vicious executioner. The lives of others were mere toys to him, and foreigners were the most vulnerable. The invidious power of the Golden One was like a snail crossing the road, leaving a trail of evidence in its wake. The trail left by Bagyidaw tainted all who could not avoid its effect. What possible means of escape from the king could there be?

Late on a steamy Tuesday afternoon, June 8, 1824, Ann and Adoniram were just preparing to sit down to their evening meal when the royal summons reached their little door. A noise could be heard above the usual neighborhood sounds of children at play. It was a banging on their door.

Ann and Adoniram stared first at the door and then in appalled fear at each other. There stood the terrifying "Spotted Face," tattoos branded on each cheek marking him as a murderer. "Spotted Face" was chief jailer of Let Ma Yoon, the death prison, and with him was a band of prison guards. Ann's heart beat so loudly she could scarcely hear the words he spoke: "Where is the teacher?" Adoniram stepped forward, declaring, "Here." Then Spotted Face spoke the deadly words: "You are called by the king."[10] He sprang on Adoniram, throwing him to the floor. Kneeling on top of Judson, he took a hard cord and slipped it around his arms above the elbow. The cord was as effective as a tourniquet, not only an instrument of control but also one of torture. Drawn too tightly, blood would spurt from the nose and mouth, and a prisoner could literally choke to death. Ann stood frozen in horror. The hour of terror was upon them. Their only recourse was total dependence on the sovereign God as they faced the dark pit of the unknown.

CHAPTER 11

Let Ma Yoon—The Death Prison: 1824

Grant us wisdom, grant us courage, for the facing of this hour.
—Harry Emerson Fosdick, "God of Grace and God of Glory"

THE HORROR OF SEEING ADONIRAM WRITHING IN AGONY ON THEIR FLOOR as Spotted Face tightened the cord galvanized Ann, releasing her from the frozen terror that had held her in its grip. She clutched the jailer's arm: "I'll give you money. Stop! Stop!" At that Spotted Face turned on her and barked out a new command, "Arrest her as well—she's a foreigner too!"[1]

Adoniram struggled to his feet and begged the official to leave his wife alone. Spotted Face, seeming to forget his malice toward Ann, dragged his victim out of the house, even as the crowd gathered outside the little house looked on in horror. Ignoring her trembling hands and the sinking feeling in the pit of her stomach, Ann grabbed a

Judson's fellow prisoner Henry Gouger, an English businessman, sketched from memory the interior of infamous Let Ma Yoon prison, c 1824–1825. From *Life of Adoniram Judson* by Edward Judson (Philadelphia: American Baptist Publication Society, 1883).

handful of silver and pressed it into Maung Ing's hands, asking him to follow Adoniram and bribe Spotted Face to loosen the cord before it dislocated his shoulders. Little Abby and Mary were screaming in fear and the servants shaking with dread. But even as Ann waited for Maung Ing's return, her keen mind was at work thinking of what she might possibly do in the face of such horrifying circumstances.

It seemed forever before Maung Ing came back, despair written on his face. One look and Ann knew the news was not good. A bleeding Adoniram had been literally dragged through the streets, first to court and then to the most foreboding place imaginable, Let Ma Yoon, the death prison. Translated, the name was only too descriptive: "Hand Shrink Not" from perpetuating any depravity. The governor at court had been shocked to see the treatment accorded Judson and ordered the cord removed, but already Adoniram's arms were swollen and bleeding. Maung Ing had watched helplessly as Judson was pushed into the inner prison and the door thrown shut.

Upon hearing the news, the inner core of Ann Judson quickly asserted itself. She might be confined in her own house, her husband in prison, with two little girls, servants, and friends ashen with fright and dependent on her, but her brain seemed to be released from its paralysis of fear. She had little time for tears. Ann calmed the little girls, but no one had to tell the others just what the death prison meant. Ann slipped away to her room and fell on her knees.

In less than an hour, the city magistrate came to the door, demanding that Ann come outside and submit to interrogation. He kept shouting, while inside Ann rushed from room to room, destroying all letters and journals; because they were accused of being spies, it would be like suicide to let them fall into Burmese hands. Her mouth was dry with the metallic taste of fear, but this was no time to collapse in despair. Ann stepped onto the veranda and submitted to questioning. The magistrate endeavored to entrap her, but he found himself facing a far quicker and cleverer mind than his own. She parried every question with evasiveness but never with an untruth. He went away grinding his teeth in frustration and leaving behind a guard of ten men to prevent Ann from leaving the house.

Ann went inside and barred the door. This was all the guards needed to arouse their suspicions, and they commanded her to come back out or they would "break the house down." In turn, she threatened to report them to higher authorities in the morning. Incensed, they took revenge by placing her two Bengali servants in stocks. Ann could not bear it. She promised to give them a "gift" in the morning, and the trembling servants were released. If the Burmese lived by bribes, Ann Judson knew how to use such bribes to her advantage. In the months ahead, they became a mainstay in her battle to keep Adoniram alive.

Darkness covered the city of Ava. It had invaded Ann's heart hours earlier. The eerie silence was like a scream. She was perilously close to hopelessness. "The dark night of the soul," was a phrase Ann had heard countless times, but never had it been so real. Was Adoniram still alive? She dared not consider the alternative. Ann realized she must garner her resources and seek divine power and wisdom beyond her own if they were to survive. She could only imagine what terrors the night held for him who was dearest to her. Two years later she was able to write about that infamous night, "You may well imagine that sleep was a stranger to my eyes."[2]

Morning dawned and with it a new determination on Ann's part to somehow help Adoniram. Maung Ing was able to slip away and see what news he could learn. Ann sent food with him. Maung Ing soon returned with news both good and bad. Teacher was alive. However, he was in the inner prison and in three pairs of iron fetters. The blood drained from Ann's face, and again she went icy cold with fear. At that moment, the officious magistrate began banging on the door, once again demanding answers to his questions. Ann begged permission to go and plead for help from a high government official. The magistrate was still sulking from her evasions of the evening before and refused. "You might escape" was his only excuse.

Ann wracked her brain for the next move. She thought of the king's sister; this sister was Prince M's wife and they had been most friendly and interested in Adoniram just the year before. Ann asked if she could send a note to the princess and surprisingly was granted permission. A negative answer came back: Prince M's wife stated that she "did not understand." It was painfully apparent that what she "understood" was her fear of approaching her brother the king.

Now what? Ann rejected one scheme after another as either impossible or impractical. Meanwhile her best move was to befriend the guards. She served them tea and the cigars of which they were so fond. Reasoning that no self-respecting Burman could turn down a bribe, she sent a note to the governor asking permission to call on him with a gift. Her tactic worked and with a flare of hope, Ann set off for a visit, the first of hundreds she would make in the months to follow, approaching all sorts of officials, pleading for the life of her husband.

The governor did not turn her away. She entered her plea for Judson and for Price, stating that they were not English and certainly were not enemies of Burma. The governor informed her that it was beyond his power to have Judson released, or to have the fetters struck off. He then referred her to his chief officer for help in seeing what might be done to alleviate Judson's suffering. The scowling face of the chief officer was anathema in Ann's eyes. Predictably, he demanded a bribe and smilingly informed her that the prisoners were at his mercy. He demanded two hundred ticals of silver, about $100, a princely sum in that day. Ann did not have nearly enough money with her, but the official took all she had, and on a palm leaf wrote the governor's order to allow her to visit the prison. Ann immediately headed toward Let Ma Yoon, the first of what would become endless months of such trips.[3]

At the same time that Ann was devising ways to come to his aid, Adoniram was being introduced to the foul spot that would be his home for many months. The ruler of the prison had met him at the gate with a grin that was forever imprinted on Judson's mind, a look so malicious that it chilled his blood. The prison ruler and every guard in Let Ma Yoon was a convicted murderer and branded as such on their foreheads—the "Spotted Faces." The ruler demanded that Judson call him Father, *Aphe*, in a cruel twisting of the meaning of that title. Through a blur of sweat and blood, Adoniram saw before him a block of wood toward which he was pushed and where

Aphe and the guards joked while three fetters were riveted to his ankles with an iron maul. One misstroke of that maul and he would be forever crippled.

Walking was too dignified a term for the only steps Judson could take; the chains linking the fetters on his legs were mere inches apart. On his first attempt to walk, he fell face first into the filth of the prison yard. He was poked and prodded into the building standing at one side of the prison area, forced to the far corner, and ordered to lie down on the filthy floor.

It was hard to see anything, if anyone could *wish* to see such absolute filth. There were no windows. Even on a sunny afternoon, the only light was that which managed to slip in between the chinks in the walls. When Judson's eyes adjusted to the gloom of the inner prison, he could tell that he was in a room some thirty by forty feet. The only bright spot that met his appalled eyes was a small hole in the roof where a rotten plank had been torn off. At least the hole allowed a bit of the fetid prison air to escape. No such thing as furniture graced the foul floor. There was one piece of equipment, a gigantic row of stocks that could hold more than a dozen hapless sufferers at a time and was eerily like an alligator that opened and shut its jaws on its victims. In the weak light of the inner prison, Judson could make out the shapes of some fifty or more fellow captives. All were nearly naked; most looked more like skeletons than living men.

The air itself defied description. The prison had never been washed nor even swept. Consequently there was a strange sense of permanency about its foul odors. Adoniram's first impulse was to gag, then hold his breath, neither of which helped. There were partial remains of long-decayed animals and vegetables. And there were many animal occupants not needing a broom to keep them moving—insects of every description, shape, and size. These, combined with the remains of the eternal betel juice so universally chewed and spit out in Burma, were added to the odors emanating from scores of bodies that never had a chance to see water. To crown it all, daily temperatures exceeding 100 degrees made the spot seem as close to an approximation of hell as one could find on earth. Such were the appalling conditions that assaulted Adoniram Judson's despairing eyes that fateful evening of June 8, 1824.

He soon made out the dim forms of some of his fellow prisoners, several of whom he immediately recognized. There lay Captain Laird, a bluff Scotsman who had fled his past in Scotland many years ago and tried his fortunes in Burma. An Englishman, Rodgers, married to a Burman, had worked in the customs offices forty years. Old and bent with age, Rodgers lay near Laird. Next to him was Henry Gouger, and it was only a matter of minutes until the small door was pushed open yet again and Jonathan Price was shoved inside. Constantine the Greek, poor leprous man, was added to the motley collection of unfortunates. This merely served to add to the problems already confronting the group. Two Armenians and later the Spaniard Lanciego rounded out the number of non-Burmans who were imprisoned together for how long, they knew not. They were strictly forbidden to communicate in English.

To compound the agony, the foreigners were forced to lie side by side, confined to a bamboo pole passed between their legs and hoisted up so that only their shoulders rested on the ground. In this torturous position, they passed that night and wondered if it was indeed endless or just seemed that way. Dawn came, but inside the foul prison shed it was hard to see clearly. But *feel* they could. As soon as one and then another began to yawn and try to stretch with a clanking of chains and moans and groans from all, the movement of their bodies activated the repulsive vermin swarming in their tattered clothing, sending them scurrying to the next body. The grinning "Father" appeared and inquired in mock concern if they had enjoyed their rest. He lowered the painful bamboo until their feet were barely elevated. The blood began again to circulate in their legs which had long since become numb, and this in itself brought excruciating pain. Then they were taken, two at a time, outside to relieve themselves. The "comfort" break was five minutes at most and was the only one allowed each twenty-four hours. What sanitary problems that caused inside the malodorous shed itself are best left to the imagination.

Judson and the other foreigners who could speak Burmese inquired about food and learned that the "government" allowed each prisoner a basket of rice per month, not one grain of which was ever seen by the prisoners. Had it not been for family help, all the prisoners would have starved to death. (Some died of hunger anyway.) This became one of the many ways Ann saved the life of her husband. She was still under house arrest, but at nine that first morning, she sent Maung Ing with food. He was horrified when he saw Judson. In such a short number of hours, his honored Yoodthan had become so filthy and bedraggled that he was scarcely recognizable.

Later that morning, Gouger was ordered outside, not knowing if this meant he was going to his death or to torture. And even as he "waited" for his turn, he was forced to watch the torture of a young Burmese man who finally fainted from the pain being inflicted on his helpless body. Gouger could only wonder if he would be next. No. He was, however, extensively questioned about his money. The avaricious officials wanted to extract all they could, and Gouger was extremely wealthy. After lengthy questioning, he was returned to the inner prison.

As the day progressed, the prisoners looked around and realized they might be living a little longer. Even in such extremity, it was difficult for a man of Judson's spiritual depth to remain without hope. He and Gouger even engaged in a little gallows humor, commiserating with each other. Slowly the hours passed. By three o'clock, the joking and all conversation died down, first to a whisper, and then altogether. Rumors had already run through the shed that 3:00 P.M. was the daily hour of execution. Exactly at 3:00 P.M., the great gong from the palace grounds pealed out the hour, and the single small prison door was thrust open. Spotted Faces entered and walked toward two men lying with the others on the floor. Not a word was uttered as the two prisoners were led outside, the only noise the clanking of ankle fetters. Those remaining inside began to breathe again. At least for one more day, the great gong had not tolled for them.

The next day, it was Adoniram's turn to be questioned. He too was first forced to witness a Burmese prisoner being tortured. All Judson

112

could do was answer every question about his possessions and then shuffle his way back into the dark hole of the prison shed. He and Gouger could only concur that it indeed looked beyond hope, certainly beyond human help. This was the state of affairs when Ann hurried toward Let Ma Yoon for her first visit, anxiety making her nearly breathless. The only foreign woman in Ava hurrying toward the north gate of the city was a sight that drew every eye like a magnet. Under any circumstances, she was a lovely woman. In her bright Burmese silk dress she was magnificent.

The governor of the north gate had, in the few months the two Judsons had spent in Ava, been slightly more conciliating than any other official. His wife had developed a fondness for Ann, and in an effort to help, she had suggested that Ann always wear Burmese dress. It worked, as people seemed to be drawn to her radiance and pleased to note that she approved of their dress. The governor's wife had given her a beautiful silk skirt and jacket such as the noble rank of women typically wore. Ann was taller than Burmese women, and with her fine figure and graceful erect carriage, she was striking. Her dark hair was pulled straight back and adorned with a flower such as the women wore, and she looked like the women of Burma, with the exception of her feet. Under the lovely silk dress were her sturdy New England half-boots.

This day Ann noticed none of the stares as she hastened toward Let Ma Yoon, the precious government order clutched tightly in her hand, her heart racing with apprehension and dread at what she might find upon arrival. Until her dying day, Ann would never forget that ghastly moment when the guards, having read the governor's order, went to bring Adoniram to the gate to see his wife. From the inner prison shed emerged the figure of her husband, crawling in her direction, dragging iron fetters with him. It had only taken two days for the most meticulous and fastidious man she had ever known to become a haggard, filthy shadow of the vigorous husband who had always been perfectly groomed. His unshaven face and torn and vermin-infested rags made him nearly unrecognizable.

There is an account of that awful moment written thirty years later.

113

Henry Gouger was hobbling across the stockade yard to receive food his baker friend had brought him when he saw Ann Judson standing in horrified silence at the prison gate. Gouger recalled: "Poor Judson was fastidiously neat and cleanly in his person and apparel, just the man to depict the metamorphosis he had undergone in these two wretched days in its strongest contrast. When Mrs. Judson had parted from him he was in the enjoyment of these personal comforts, whereas now none but an artist could describe his appearance. Two nights of restless torture of body and anxiety of mind had imparted to his countenance a haggard and death-like expression, while it would be hardly decent to advert in more than general terms to his begrimed and impure exterior. No wonder his wretched wife, shocked at the change, hid her face in her hands, overwhelmed with grief, hardly daring to trust herself to look upon him,…for though more than thirty-five years have since passed away, [the moment] reverts to me with all the freshness of a scene of yesterday."[4]

Ann nearly gave way. She had already faced the possibility that Adoniram might have been tortured, even killed, yet this degradation defied imagination. But her spiritual resources ran deep, as did her devotion to this man. Ann raised her head, and the two whispered snatches of plans and possibilities. Adoniram's heart was most grieved because he felt so helpless. There was not a thing he could do for Ann, and that hurt him far more than any personal pain.

Then just as suddenly as they had permitted Judson to come to the gate, the Spotted Faces commanded Ann to leave. The figure in the bright Burmese dress was drooping as she turned from the tearful good-bye and began the two-mile walk home. But already her inventive mind was at work, plotting her next effort. The line from Proverbs, "The tender mercies of the wicked are cruel," took on an all-new meaning to Ann Judson after what she had experienced that day. Already her valiant efforts were bearing some results. Before the sun went down, Adoniram and the other foreigners were moved out into the open shed of the prison stockade. At least for a short time each day, they were away from the worst of the filth and decay, and the hearts of those men gave thanks for the unfailing courage of Ann Judson.

Her next move was to petition the wife of the queen's brother. She knew the woman slightly. Ann was not shy by nature, and the appalling conditions in which she had found her husband made her bolder still. As always, Ann took a gift and immediately began telling the princess what was happening: she and her husband were missionaries with no connection to England and yet they were being treated like the vilest of criminals.

"What could your highness do to help right this wrong?" was her piercing question. The princess was lounging in usual Burmese style, or as Ann put it later in a letter, "lolling on her carpet." The woman coolly informed Ann that Judson's case was not unusual; all foreigners were treated alike. Ann refused to accept such equivocation. She reiterated their own unique circumstances and confronted the princess with such injustice. The princess would not meet her eyes, but murmured, "I am not the king; what can I do?" "Place yourself in my situation," Ann countered. "Were you in America, your husband, innocent of crime, thrown into prison, in irons, and you a solitary, unprotected female, what would you do?" There was no reply. Ann refused to withdraw the question that hung in the silence as if roasting over a spit and getting blacker by the second. Reluctantly, the princess made a response: "I will present your petition—come again tomorrow."[5] An exhausted Ann returned to their lonely little house, already considering her next move. News awaiting her there was not encouraging. All of Henry Gouger's possessions had been confiscated. She immediately realized that their possessions would be the next target.

Ann knew that she must retain some valuables or she would not be able to purchase food and give the ever-essential bribes that would help protect Adoniram. She feverishly went to work, gathering silver and valuables, wrapping them in bundles covered with cloth and stealthily burying them in the tiny garden behind their house. In the dead of night, she buried the most precious bundle first: Adoniram's manuscript of the New Testament, so recently completed. Ann sadly recalled how optimistic they had been about bringing God's Word to the Burmans. Now that seemed like another lifetime. One week had changed their lives forever.

Sure enough, the burials weren't a moment too soon. Next morning the Royal Treasurer arrived at her door with some fifty men. Most people would be woefully intimidated, which is exactly what the royal mind intended. Not Ann Judson. That marvelous force of personality, those unerring people skills she had so frequently drawn upon, were hers in full force. She greeted them as if they were the parson coming to call, and personally served tea and refreshments. It was the power of Ann's personality that dominated, not the man of powerful rank. His first question concerned her gold, silver, and jewels. Ann looked him straight in the eye and told him she had no gold or jewels, but handed him the key to the box that held silver. The officials began examining, counting, weighing. They had even brought along scales.[6]

Ann did not intend that they feel comfortable as they did their ugly work. She informed them that this money had been given by disciples of the Christian faith in America. It was sacred money. The treasurer equivocated and suggested that they would list it and maybe it would later be restored. And then he asked if that was all the silver she had. Ann could not bring herself to lie. Instead, she simply told him he was free to search the house as he wished. His search yielded no more silver. And thus the buried treasure remained safe. When the greedy officials began fingering the Judsons' clothing, Ann shamed them by remarking that surely it would offend the Golden One to be handed someone's used clothing. The pilfering stopped.

As soon as the small army of inspectors had left, an exhausted Ann collapsed into the nearest chair. Her courageous stand had drained the very strength from her legs. In that moment, she felt she couldn't stand erect if her life depended on it.

Before she left for the long walk to the prison, she checked on her petition to the princess. Her plan had failed. The prisoners would remain as they were. To Ann, this meant nothing but a temporary setback, and as she continued on her way to the prison, her fertile imagination was already planning the next strategy. She and Adoniram must decide what to do about the New Testament manuscript; they had only moments together. Ann wasted no time on the tears stopped up deep within her heart from the sight of Adoniram's haggard face. They devised a plan; Ann would bind the papers tightly together, cover them in a thick binding, paint on a lacquer layer to form a hard pillow, and then bribe the guards to allow Judson this small comfort.

The next morning, Ann arrived with the crude pillow and slipped some silver into the waiting hands of the jailer. He looked at her, looked at the pillow, experimentally poked it with his spear—and decided it was too uncomfortable to purloin for himself. The irony did not escape Ann. The only existing copy of the Scriptures written in Burmese would be protected right under the eyes of the enemy. Adoniram could use it for a headrest. The two of them looked at one another, their thoughts in perfect accord. The holy Presence was in their midst in that most unholy of places. Once again, they silently blessed God and took courage.

CHAPTER 12

The Heart of Darkness: 1824–1825

No light, but rather darkness visible.
—John Milton, *Paradise Lost*

THE THICK DARKNESS OF THE NIGHTS IN PRISON SEEMED TO LAST FOREVER. The blackness was complete, the sounds of misery constant— clanking chains and groaning men in distress. Though surrounded by uncertainty and danger, Judson, at least for the moment, felt relieved about the pillow. There it lay under Adoniram's head, beneath the enemies' eyes and next to their treading feet.

But there was a new development—and the timing could not have been worse. At thirty-four, Ann was pregnant. She felt a chilling blend of joy and fear. How could a tiny baby possibly survive such conditions? How could she tell Adoniram about the baby? He was already

Site of Let Ma Yoon prison. Judson's great-grandson, Dr. Stanley Hanna, and author Rosalie Hunt stand on the remains of the Judson memorial stone.

grieved beyond words that he was helpless to protect her and must rely solely on God's mercy and his wife's ingenuity. She would not tell him just yet; he didn't need further worry.

They established something of a routine, if the chaos confronting them daily in the capital could be dignified by such a term. Each day, Ann took Adoniram's food to him, or if she was at an official's palace pleading for a concession, Maung Ing would take it. Finding food was difficult; at times she did well to even find rice and *ngape*, the fish mixture the Burmans favored.

Each day for Ann had its differences. They stuck out like little jewels against the dark fabric of long hours of walking and hunger. For months, she haunted the palaces and courts, going from one official to another, interceding on Adoniram's behalf. Some would listen, shake their heads, and tell her again that there was nothing they could do. Often Ann took a gift, a sure way to an open door. Some would pity her and send orders that would temporarily relieve some small part of the suffering of Judson and his fellow prisoners.

One malevolent official made her stand for hours waiting for an audience, with only her parasol to protect her from the deadly rays of the sun. When the official finally condescended to "receive" her, he immediately rejected her plea. Ann took a deep breath, turned, and wearily started down the steps, a reservoir of unshed tears in her heart. "Wait!" the official called out, and turning back with a surge of hope, Ann waited to hear what he would do to help. What he did was to seize her parasol and inform her with a laugh that she didn't need it; she was so thin the sun "couldn't find her." Ann never forgot that remark nor the look on the official's face.[1]

Some days the prison guards would let her see Adoniram. Others they would refuse. Gouger had a faithful servant who often brought him food, and Ann frequently came to Gouger's aid and that of Price as well. Gouger cleverly discovered another source of food. He speared nice fat rats that scurried around close to him and traded them to a jailer's daughter for rice.

As often as the Spotted Faces allowed her to, Ann would bring Adoniram some clean articles of clothing, something he appreciated every bit as much as the food, although it would only be hours before the new garment was besmirched by the filth in which he was forced to live. Sometimes when Ann was not permitted to see Judson, she would slip him a message. One of her favorite hiding spots was in the spout of the teapot she prepared for him.[2]

After the war, Ann wrote Judson's brother Elnathan of her feelings during those months and of her efforts to help Adoniram: "During these seven months, the continual extortions and oppressions to which your brother, and the other white prisoners, were subject, are indescribable. Sometimes sums of money were demanded;…at other times, an order would be issued, that the white foreigners should not speak to each other, or have any communication with their friends without….And how many, many times, have I returned from that dreary prison at nine o'clock at night, solitary and worn out with fatigue and anxiety,…and endeavoured to invent some new scheme for the release of the prisoners. Sometimes, for a moment or two, my thoughts would glance toward America, and my beloved friends there, but for nearly a year and a half, so entirely engrossed was every thought, with present scenes and sufferings, that I seldom reflected on a single occurrence of my former life, or recollected that I had a friend in existence out of Ava."[3]

Occasionally Ann was permitted to spend an hour or two with Judson in the open shed. After a number of months and many bribes, she was granted permission to build a little bamboo lean-to where he could have a tiny bit of privacy. Tiny indeed. It was about five by six feet, scarcely enough space in which to lie down. All too seldom, Ann was allowed to bring Adoniram a container of water for washing. What a treasure, like clear and liquid gold, that little pitcher of water. There was no doubt that cleanliness was one of the luxuries Judson most craved. His distaste for anything less than spotless cleanliness harked back to his childhood and was so deeply ingrained that it made his suffering at Let Ma Yoon just that much closer to unendurable.[4] In later years, it was impossible for Judson to put on clean white garments and shiny shoes, or to take a bracing shower, without remembering what a privilege such a simple thing could be.

Ann realized that she could no longer delay telling Adoniram about the baby. One afternoon in the little lean-to, she divulged the news. Judson's eyes widened in mingled horror and hope; he agonized over his own inability to help her in her time of such desperate need. The very thought brought him to tears. It surprised no one who knew the inestimable fortitude of Ann Judson that her advancing pregnancy did not slow her efforts to do all she could for Adoniram and the other prisoners. She continued to wear her Burmese dress and was a familiar sight in the streets as she went from one official to another, secretly respected and admired as she sought relief for the beleaguered captives.

The weary days dragged on, the heat unrelenting, the boredom itself a torture. Surely one of the hardest things to bear in prison was idleness. Judson, with a burning goal to convert the people of Burma, could do nothing but endure and hope to live to translate and preach another day. Simply enduring became a grievous task. Judson exercised his mental faculties constantly during those months of enforced inactivity. He would recall a passage of Scripture and mentally translate it either into Burmese, Greek, or Hebrew. One afternoon his exercise consisted of versifying the Lord's Prayer in fewer words than the original Greek. His prodigious memory retained the exercise until freedom came and he was able to record it.[5] Prior to imprisonment, Adoniram had read the works of Madame Guyon, a seventeenth-century mystic. While disagreeing with much of her philosophy, he admired her concept of "quietism." Possibly because it was foreign to his own nature, he attempted to employ the concept in meditation. Many times during those prison months, he was able to quiet his heart by quoting some of Guyon's thoughts on God.[6]

The resolute Ann spent much of her mental energy devising some new way to bring relief to Adoniram. Her body became a burden, and it bothered her to realize how poor her own nutrition was and how this could not but affect the baby's health. Still she persevered. Ann later wrote: "The situation of the prisoners was now distressing beyond description. It was at the commencement of the hot season. There were above a hundred prisoners shut up in one room, without a breath of air excepting from the cracks in the boards. I sometimes obtained permission to go to the door for five minutes, when my heart sickened at the wretchedness exhibited. The white prisoners, from incessant perspiration and loss of appetite, looked more like the dead than the living. I made daily applications to the governor, offering him money, which he refused."[7]

The prisoners themselves were an ill-suited bunch. Laird and Rodgers whiled away their time in conversation. Probably the two most similar in mental acuity and sense of humor were Judson and Gouger. They hit upon the idea of playing chess and managed to improvise a set out of bits of discarded bamboo. The two whiled away many hours exercising their minds in a way that even the Burmese guards did not find suspect.

Jonathan Price proved to be a matter of anxiety for Adoniram because he never knew what his fellow missionary might do next. Price loved to do surgery and did not find much outlet for his skills in Let Ma Yoon. He caused his fellow prisoners great alarm when he persuaded a fierce Spotted Face to let him operate on a growth on the fellow's eyelid. Such delicate surgery was questionable under the best of conditions, and their present setting was the worst imaginable. Nevertheless Price talked Spotted Face into surgery. Gouger and Judson mentally held their collective breaths, only able to conjecture what havoc might be wreaked on all of them should the surgery fail. Its chance of success in such filth was negligible. To their amazement, the surgery succeeded, at least partially. Price removed the growth with a penknife; it resembled two or three inches of a large dew-worm, a ghastly sight. Miraculously, the guard was not blinded, but there was a drawback. Price had severed a nerve, and Spotted Face could no longer open his eyelid naturally. He had to open and shut it with a finger, but Price convinced him this was good, because when he didn't need to use it, the eye was covered and protected.[8]

Jonathan Price himself, however, was hard to take close up, and that is what the foreign prisoners undoubtedly were—close. At night, fettered and strung together by the bamboo pole, if one fellow moved, his next neighbor felt it. Judson and Price were placed beside each other. Price liked to sleep with his knees drawn up nearly to his nose. Henry Gouger vividly recalled what it was like during the night and described it in his memoirs over thirty years later. He had already noted that along with all his outstanding qualities, Judson had a quick and hasty temper, but Gouger's nighttime reminiscences revealed his wry sense of humor: "The prison was crowded—the time was midnight. Judson in a sound sleep—Brother Price the same, being next to each other on the row. But Jonathan Price, though a good companion when he was awake, was a wretchedly bad one when he was asleep. I have already said that he was a gaunt, angular, raw-boned Yankee, who could never compose himself to sleep, until he had brought his knees to touch his nose, a custom of long standing, acquired in times of yore—when freedom sanctioned his occupying as much space as he pleased. Now…during the night Jonathan was often disturbed by evil dreams, and when such occurred, he had the ugly habit of launching his terrible knees, well weighted with iron, with fearful force at the back of his unoffending neighbour.…Judson bore these concussions with becoming fortitude for some time, until one of these poundings became more severe than human nature could endure. 'Brother Price! You are a public nuisance. I insist on your sleeping as other people do.'"

Gouger continued: "Price assured him it was unintentional, but failed to convince him that it was unavoidable. Some threats of retaliation passed, in which poor Judson would have had no chance. To restore harmony, I offered to sleep between them, and when the battering-ram assaulted my back, I would awaken the sleepy doctor from his nightmare, and challenge him to a pipe of tobacco.…Besides, I could get him to fall asleep sometimes on the other side, and so bestow a fair share of his attentions on the sturdy frame of old Mr. Rodgers, whose ill-luck brought him to occupy the next place on the line."[9]

One weary day followed another. The executions of Burmese prisoners continued to take place at the evil hour of 3:00 each afternoon. Still, each morning the survivors would open their eyes to find another scorching, dreary day; they were shackled, yes, but with their heads still on their shoulders. Judson longed for the relief of a few books. What a treasure a Bible would be, but he never failed to thank God for the countless passages he knew by heart. In truth, in this unspeakable dwelling that was the epitome of the heart of darkness, the precious truths of the Lord God sustained his aching soul and brought a comfort that went beyond mere words.

Confined in the dark of prison and fighting to maintain his mental and spiritual hold on all that was good and pure, Judson also gained strength from Ann. Just to be able to look on her face and see the determination and tenderness written there gave courage to his heart. She was forever devising some small thing to lighten his burden or cheer his spirits. The food Ann was able to buy was so close to unpalatable and so monotonous that she often tried to think of some new and appetizing dish. Most improbably she managed to make something that looked and tasted nearly like the mince pie Judson had loved as a child. Ann was detained by the governor that morning, so she carefully wrapped the pie and sent it by Maung Ing.

Judson's first biographer described Adoniram's reaction: "When his wife had visited him in prison, and borne taunts and insults with and for him,…when she had stood up like an enchantress, winning the hearts of high and low, making savage jailers and scarcely less savage nobles, weep; or moved, protected by her own dignity and sublimity of purpose, like a queen along the streets, his heart had throbbed with proud admiration; and he was almost able to thank God for the trials which had made a character so intrinsically noble shine forth with such peculiar brightness. But in this simple, homelike act, this little unpretending effusion of a loving heart, there was something so touching…that he bowed his head upon his knees, and the tears flowed down to the chains about his ankles."[10] Plymouth, Mother, home—the memories overwhelmed him. Ann's loving gift had touched an unprotected corner of his heart.

The course of the war moved on. Historians recorded that this First Anglo-Burmese War was the most mismanaged in the history of Britain. As went the war, so went the treatment of the foreigners in Let Ma Yoon. They came to know the signal; two blasts of a cannon meant the Burmese had won a battle. One blast signaled defeat. The prisoners quickly learned that their conditions varied according to the signal. A defeat meant they were confined to the inner prison and Adoniram could not see Ann for days or occasionally weeks at a time. Bandula was now the commander of all Burma's armies and everyone's idol, becoming so powerful that he was the ruler of Burma in all but title. At one point, when Bandula's armies had won a victory and the great man himself was in Ava, conditions were slightly eased at Let Ma Yoon and the prisoners were allowed some daylight hours in small sheds in the open part of the prison yard.[11]

About this time, a new prisoner came to Let Ma Yoon and was placed in a newly barred cage. The reason for his incarceration was a mystery to the motley group of human captives he joined. He was a lordly lion, the king's favorite pet, a gift from some faraway potentate. King lion was in disfavor, however, as it was whispered abroad that the lion was the symbol of British power, a harbinger of bad luck. The lion did not receive an "off with his head" sentence. Instead he was slowly starved to death in front of the eyes and ears of the appalled prisoners. The emperor had decreed that no one could feed him. The roar of the dying beast haunted the prisoners for months to come. However, when the animal finally died, the event indirectly aided Judson. Ann was able to bribe Spotted Face, so eminently bribable was he, and Judson was allowed to spend occasional hours in blessed solitude and comparative cleanliness in the deserted cage of a lion.[12]

Meanwhile, the baby was due. All Ann could do was prepare as best she could to give birth alone. She grieved that Adoniram could not share in the birth and that she would have to go for days without seeing him. But once more she thanked God for the blessing of a faithful friend like Maung Ing, who stood in the gap when they most needed him. Maung Ing and Koo-chil, their loyal Bengali cook, were the only assistance Ann had. Neither knew a thing about childbirth. On January 26, 1825, with two unfledged but willing assistants, Ann gave birth to tiny Maria Elizabeth Butterworth Judson, scarcely longer than her beautiful name.

In the last months of his life, Judson was much given to reflecting on the time of Maria's birth. He confided to his family something of the scene that day when Ann first appeared with Maria in her arms. He described Ann clothed in her beautiful Burmese silk, with her shiny black hair combed back and up—a lovely sight. In her arms was a tiny, blue-eyed, fair-skinned little mite wrapped in folds of plaid silk. Ann was not permitted to enter the prison door. Maung Ing stood close behind her, and the diabolical old jailer was positioned on one side, laughing maliciously and ready to order her away. Adoniram described himself and his companions in misery. Fettered as he was, he hobbled to the door and held out his arms for his sleeping babe. Judson frequently referred to that singular moment etched into his memory and called it the best subject he had ever seen for an artist. "And what figure do you suppose you would cut in the picture?" his family asked. "Ah, I don't know," he said, smilingly; "I suppose I should look like some poor convicted wretch bowing before a Madonna, for with all my efforts, I could not get above the knees."13

There at the gates of the death prison, Judson looked with love at his fragile baby girl. Now Ann could get around again, but what did the future hold? Their first babe was under the sea, and little Roger lay beneath the battleground of Rangoon. Did Maria have any better chance than they had of survival? In the solemn quietness after that tender meeting, the sensitive and creative mind of Judson mentally composed a poem of twenty-four stanzas memorializing their beautiful baby. He wrote it down from memory many months later upon his release.

The prisoners' goals had essentially narrowed to a single wish: survival. As the dreary months dragged by, Judson worked hard at fighting depression. No matter how bleak the future looked, he could not by nature stay disheartened. On the afternoons he was allowed in the open shed, he would seek the shade of a huge tamarind tree standing just outside the prison wall and casting a small square of cooler shade in a corner of the prison yard. From there he could look out at the watchtower visible from Bagyidaw's palace. The tower unceasingly reminded him of the watchful eyes of almighty God who was his sustainer. He could also see several golden spires of glittering pagodas dotting the monastery next to the palace but found something positive even in such a sight. Judson, the eternal optimist, continued to believe that one day spires of churches attesting to the power of eternal God would adorn the skies in Burma.[14]

Judson liked to speculate on how the war could result in the advancement of God's kingdom in Burma. For ten years, they had been translating and preaching in the midst of timid listeners, afraid to openly acknowledge their faith. Perhaps after the war, there would be more openness and the gospel could be preached in freedom. Even the thought lifted his spirits, and indeed, he was prophetic. There *would* be vast change.

Henry Gouger often commented that nothing was so bad that it could not get worse. This certainly was true. Early in March 1825, the prisoners were occupying their little rooms in the prison yard and feeling about as comfortable as such awful conditions allowed. They were even able to laugh at some occurrence so ludicrous that they could do nothing else. But with startling suddenness the laughter was stilled and they were cast yet again into despair. With no warning, a Spotted Face led each prisoner to the now-familiar granite block. One after another was thrust to the stone, and two more pairs of fetters were added to the three they already dragged around. Still not a word was uttered as the prisoners looked at one another in apprehension. Silently the guards thrust them back into the inner prison. Left to themselves in the fetid gloom of that filthy place, they could only guess what might have occasioned such a new punishment.[15]

This was one of their darkest nights. Judson could hear some of the Burmese prisoners whispering that the foreigners were to be killed. Three o'clock A.M. was to be the dreaded hour. Adoniram's chief regret was not being able to say goodbye to Ann and little Maria. He knew Ann's valiant heart well, though; he knew she would find a way to get to the British forces. And he thought of Burma. Christ was sure to win Burma. As to the manuscript, maybe Ann would think of a way to rescue it. Even in the face of imminent death, his mind was going over several passages in his manuscript that he felt he might be able to improve. And somehow the hand reaching out to him through the fog of unimaginable despair was a pierced hand; even in the smothering darkness, his soul felt it. The pagoda bells clanged the hour—one—two—three—the prisoners bowed their heads in prayer, and Judson quietly, calmly lifted his voice in prayer for all. An unearthly calm seemed to descend on that miserable place, and without a word, they awaited their fate. And waited. The wonder of it was when morning broke that, they were still alive.

Ann heard the news from a breathless Maung Ing when he returned from taking food. Yoodthan was now in five pairs of irons. All the foreigners were. Rumor said there were to be executions. Ann rushed to the prison. There was a deathly quiet about the place. The guards refused her admission. Her journal tells of her plea to the governor of the north gate that night: "Your lordship has hitherto treated us with the kindness of a father. Our obligations to you are very great. We have looked to you for protection from oppression and cruelty. You have in many instances mitigated the sufferings of those unfortunate, though innocent beings, committed to your care. You have promised me particularly, that you would stand by me to the last, and though you should receive an order from the king, you would not put Mr. J to death. What crime has he committed to deserve such additional punishment? The old man's heart was melted, for he wept like a child. 'I pity you Tsa-yar-ga-dau (a name by which he always called me). I knew you would make me feel; I therefore forbade your application. But you must believe me when I say, I do not wish to increase the sufferings of the prisoners. When I am ordered to execute them, the least that I can do, is to put them out of sight. I will now tell you what I have never told you before, that three times I have received intimations from the queen's brother, to assassinate all the white prisoners privately; but I would not do it....I will never execute your husband. But I cannot release him from his present confinement, and you must not ask it.'"[16]

And then there was a change in the capital. Bandula had won a victory—the guns boomed twice, signaling the victorious news. His name was on every lip, their hero, the mighty Bandula. How short was fame; April came, and Bandula was blown to pieces by a stray shell. Now the Burmese armies were in great disarray. Panic stalked the streets of Ava. The Pakun Wun, Bandula's rival officer, saw his chance to claim command. He approached the Golden Ears to pour out his plans for quick success. Why, in no time the hated British would become the slaves of the Golden One. A frightened King Bagyidaw was ready to believe any hopeful prediction and made the Pakun Wun the new commandant. This could be a death warrant for the foreigners. The Pakun Wun hated white men with a passion and here was a perfect way of settling old scores.

Meanwhile Adoniram had fallen ill with a raging fever, and Ann feared for his life in the inner prison. The pitying governor wrote an order allowing Ann to see him moved to his little shed, and she was able to bathe him a little and give him medicine and cool water. But the very next morning, May 2, while caring for Adoniram, Ann received a note from the governor ordering her to come to his house. Both Judsons were suspicious, for this had never happened. Reluctantly, an apprehensive Ann left Adoniram's side to go to the governor's quarters.

She was even more puzzled by the time she had left the governor's apartments. He really had no urgent need for her and asked a few seemingly unimportant questions as he continued to detain her. Finally, he looked deep into her eyes: "You can do nothing more for your husband. Take care of *yourself*."[17]

Those daunting words filled her with pervasive fear. Ann was almost running back toward the prison when she was met by one of the servants who was coming in her direction. Pale with fear, he informed her that all the white prisoners had been carried away.[18] In terror, Ann returned to the old governor, who confirmed that he had just learned that the prisoners must be taken to Amarapura. Why, he knew not. By this time, Ann was wild with anxiety and deeply afraid. Even looking at the gate of Let Ma Yoon broke her heart. She later wrote: "My thoughts had been almost entirely occupied in contriving means to get into prison. But now I looked toward the gate with a kind of melancholy feeling, but no wish to enter. All was the stillness of death."[19] An anguished Ann could not but think that the end of hope had finally arrived.

CHAPTER 13

Aungbinle
1825–1826

Grant us wisdom, grant
us courage for the living
of these days.
—Harry Emerson Fosdick,
"God of Grace and God
of Glory"

PANIC PROPELLED ANN THROUGH THE STREETS AND LANES OF AVA, ASK-
ing all she saw if they had seen the foreign prisoners. Some shook
their heads pityingly; others turned and scurried away in fear. Beyond
tears, Ann returned to their little house. Out of the depths of despair
she prayed for strength, even as she recalled Isaiah's words about the
bread of affliction. That bread could not have tasted more bitter. But
true to character, she refused to give up. Remembering the kindly
governor's warning to "take care of yourself," Ann later wrote that
never before had she feared walking in the streets of Ava. Now she
did. Nearly paralyzed by anxiety, she packed their remaining valuables in several trunks and filled a chest of medicine. When darkness
fell, she took them to store at the governor's residence.

At daylight, Ann tearfully bid farewell to Maung Ing, who remained to care for the house. Koo-chil determined to go with her.
With the governor's permit in hand, Ann set off for Amarapura
where the prisoners had been taken. In the rickety little cart were
Koo-chil, the two little Burmese girls, and Maria in Ann's arms. A
year later, she recounted: "The day was dreadfully hot....I procured

Ann Judson Memorial Chapel, built in 1905 on the site of Aungbinle prison. From *The Christian Herald*, 1913.

a cart, but the violent motion…[and] the heat and dust made me almost distracted."[1]

Ann had made some difficult trips in her life, but none had been quite this wretched. The baby cried constantly and the violent motion of the cart caused both little girls to vomit repeatedly. Ann's perseverance seemed about to run out when she reached Amarapura, only to be told the captives had been taken further to Aungbinle. Forever afterwards Ann always referred to it as "that never-to-be-forgotten place."[2] For the remainder of the torturous way to Aungbinle, questions plagued her: Why Aungbinle? And what on earth had happened to Adoniram, so deathly ill with fever just a few hours before?

That morning of May 2, while Ann had gone to the governor's residence, Adoniram had been lying in the prison, wracked with fever and too ill even to eat the food Ann had brought. The moment Ann had left, a Spotted Face rushed to Adoniram and stripped off all his clothing except his tattered shirt and trousers. Adoniram had persisted all those eleven months in wearing his shoes. The result was that the soles of his feet were extremely tender. Without a word, Spotted Face struck off the fetters and tied Adoniram with a rope to the Scotsman, Laird. The white prisoners, bound two by two, were then driven through the streets of Ava. It came perilously close to being a death march, so poor was the condition of the captives. No one who knew them from years past could possibly have recognized the groaning, emaciated men who staggered through the dusty roads beyond the city gate.

The feverish Judson suffered agony from his feet, which were soon torn and bleeding from the stones in the road. Every step was agony, the prints of his feet marked in blood. Kindly Laird, a larger man, tried to bear some of Judson's weight, but weakened by a year in prison, Laird was little help. Gouger later recalled their intense suffering and how, when they had passed near the edge of a gorge, Judson had murmured: "Gouger," said he, "the parapet is low; there can be no sin in our availing ourselves of the opportunity."[3] But Adoniram was bound to Laird; he could not do that to his friend.

Now all the prisoners' feet were burned and bleeding, blisters forming and bursting immediately. Gouger fared better than the others; he was younger and possessed a strong constitution. Within a mile, the poor leprous Constantine had collapsed. He was elderly and frail to begin with, and no matter how much the guards beat him, he was unable to get to his feet again. In disgust, the guards finally thrust him into a cart. After another mile, Adoniram was nearly as far gone. The bottoms of his feet were nothing but a mass of raw flesh. Out of nowhere, a touch of relief came. One of Gouger's Bengali servants had heard the news about the prisoners and came running to help. He looked at Judson's feet and without a word, tore off the turban from his own head, something unheard of for a devout Hindu. Tearing the long strip of fabric into four pieces, he gave two to Gouger and took the remaining pieces and bound up Adoniram's bleeding feet. Next he gave Judson his shoulder on which to lean for the remainder of the march. For the rest of Judson's life, he never forgot that golden act of mercy in his hour of extremity.

By the time they reached Amarapura, Judson was near to fainting from the merciless scorching of the sun, the lack of food and water, and the raging fever. He was surely near to death. For Constantine it was too late. Within an hour after arriving in the city, he was dead. Now the prisoners were turned over to new guards, but no amount of beating and prodding could get them to their feet. These guards, rough and calloused to suffering as they were, were not Spotted Faces. The prisoners were allowed to spend the night where they had dropped. The wife of one of the Amarapura judges had followed out of curiosity, but now out of pity, she gave the prisoners fruit.

By morning, not even the comparatively healthy Gouger could take so much as a step. The judge's wife fed them again, this time with rice, and they were loaded on a cart and hauled the remaining four miles to a prison outside of Aungbinle. By late afternoon, the rough cart had squeaked its way to a building on a grassy plain. The place had clearly been deserted for a long time, its thatched roof collapsed and tilting perilously to one side. The only thing marking its sordid past was a row of stocks in an advanced stage of rot.

The prisoners noticed that the space beneath the prison's stilts was full of dry faggots. One weary captive commented on that being an odd place to store firewood, upon which dawning horror could be seen on several of the haggard faces. One dared voice their common thought, "Remember the rumor we heard in Ava? That we were to be taken out and burned?"[4] By the time Ann arrived at dusk, the frightened prisoners were still chained together, waiting for the roof to be repaired. Adoniram, close to death by this point and as close to complete hopelessness as Ann had ever seen him, opened his glazed eyes and looked at her in disbelief. Her heart ached as he said in despair, "Why have you come? I hoped you would not follow, for you cannot live here."[5] Mercifully, he then fainted and remained unconscious for hours.

An ordinary person under such perilous circumstances would surely have sought refuge in some place where she might recoup. Ann Judson was no ordinary person. Cradling the frail Maria in her arms, she appealed to the jailer, Koh-bai, to allow her to put up a little shelter nearby. He refused. It was not customary. But the look in her fine dark eyes, drooping with a fatigue beyond words, moved his hard heart to pity. He had a tiny two-room house near the prison. His family lived in one room and the other was half full of grain. Ann could live there.

There had been no food to eat all day. There was none that night and no way to get any, out in the middle of nowhere, with moonless darkness surrounding them. Ann, the children, and Koo-chil had boiled water for dinner and tried to fall asleep on the sacks of grain in the sweltering room. Adoniram was not quite conscious of their circumstances or his own, which was a blessing, for all of the captives were put in the stocks and the bamboo pole raised. The mosquitoes from the nearby rice paddies feasted on the bleeding soles of their feet. The suffering defied description.

The dawn of a new day signaled the beginning of organization in the desolate spot. And miraculously food came. A friend of Dr. Price's brought rice and curry, and Ann and the children shared it. Adoniram was still in a sad state and unable to stand up, but gloriously, the air in this country spot was not asphyxiating. The prisoners could actually inhale without filling their lungs with the incredible stench of Let Ma Yoon. Ann and Adoniram gave thanks, rejoicing to discover that the wood stacked under the ramshackle prison building had been placed there to keep the sagging, rotting floor from collapsing. There would be no bonfire of prisoners.

But if there was a tiny ray of hope, it was counterbalanced by a new worry. Mary, the little Burmese girl, was covered with spots. She was the oldest child and had been Ann's helper. Now she was very ill. The tiny room had not so much as a chair, yet somehow Ann coped. Gouger's faithful baker came from Ava with biscuits and salty fish, and Ann found a small market not far away where she and Koo-chil could buy food. She was constantly grateful that she had thought to save some silver and valuables. Otherwise they would have been destitute.

Little Mary's spots proved to be a severe case of smallpox. Ann decided to vaccinate the children as she had seen it done two years before in America. She had been vaccinated herself, so her smallpox was slight, but little Maria had a dreadful case; without the vaccination, she would have died. The jailer's wife wanted her own children inoculated, and next came every village mother. Ann realized the risk she took by administering the vaccine; should the village children die, she would be blamed. Miraculously, not one child died, and again the weary Ann thanked God.

The slight improvement in prison conditions eased Ann's burden, but Adoniram, facing the daily anxiety of the unknown, found his ability to concentrate weakening. And there was that ever-abiding sense of insecurity. This especially caused Judson anguish because he was incapable of easing Ann's hardships. He only exacerbated them, being imprisoned as he was. It added to their grief to realize that the priceless New Testament manuscript was gone forever—ten years of labor left behind at Let Ma Yoon. However, there were bright spots. The air was fresh, vermin weren't crawling everywhere, the chains were lighter, there was a little water for bathing, and there were no Spotted Faces. Fortunately, none of the prisoners was bitten by the deadly snakes that slithered in from the fields around the prison, although they were an alarming sight. After a few days, the new jailer, Koh-bai, realized that these foreigners weren't fierce enemies, but only weak, dejected mortals. Slowly Adoniram's feet healed and he could hobble about the stockade, although Ann wrote that the bottoms of his feet were so torn that it was six weeks before he could stand.[6]

As Judson gained strength, Ann grew weak from dysentery. Her mind was blurred by fatigue, but she knew she must get to their medicine chest in Ava. Leaving the children with Koo-chil, Ann hired a cart and began the torturous trip back to Ava. Fainting with weakness, she reached Ava and got the medicine chest. Then she crawled back into the cart and started back, wracked by anxiety for Maria and the others. At intervals, she gave herself two drops of laudanum. The jolting ride nearly tore her weakened body apart. She later wrote: "I had just reached Aungbinle when my strength seemed entirely exhausted....Koo-chil came out to help me into the house, but so altered and emaciated was my appearance, that the poor fellow burst into tears at the first sight."[7] Ann was close to death for two months. Their faithful Bengali cook thrust aside his taboos about caste and did everything for his beloved Mrs. Yoodthan, never complaining, never receiving wages, only caring for all of them.

During those two months when Ann was so ill, Judson bribed the jailer to allow him to hobble to the village several times a day to beg some kind mother to nurse their baby. Ann was so ill that her milk had dried up, but amazingly, Ann lived, Adoniram lived, and little Maria lived. Adoniram had time to think, too much time those long scorching days in that "never to be forgotten place." He frequently pondered the fate of the precious pillow, abandoned in the filth of Let Ma Yoon. Would he possibly live to translate more? Only God knew the answer.

About this time, when it seemed like the war would drag on forever and their bodies finally fail them, a new rumor reached the white captives. They had all been puzzled as to the reason for the transfer to Aungbinle. Rumor whispered that Aungbinle was General Pakan Wun's birthplace and the plan was to bury them there *alive* as a good-luck charm to ward off the approaching British. They would be an offering to the spirits of war. Whether the rumor was true, they never learned, because great news came within a matter of days. It was brought by Gouger's staunch baker, who stumbled into the prison almost exhausted. The Pakan Wun was dead—actually dead! "Are you sure?" asked Gouger.[8] The beaming baker was *very* sure; he had seen it happen. The king had come to suspect the Pakan of plotting to take the throne. Bagyidaw proceeded to have his own guards drag the general by his hair to the place of execution where the wide-eyed crowd watched as Pakan Wun was trodden to death by elephants. Judson and his fellow captives could only rejoice. Now that there was no commander and the British were fast approaching, panic reigned in Ava.

Rumors abounded. Sir Archibald Campbell, the British commander, was said to have offered the Golden One some form of treaty, but the highly suspicious Burmese had not begun negotiating. Maybe the British weren't really going to march on Ava. Maybe this was a ploy. Then someone at court realized that they would have to deal with the hated British with words. And who could do that? They must have help, an interpreter, a translator. One thoughtful official realized that there was really no one qualified but the American teacher, who spoke and wrote flawless Burmese. Suddenly the emperor needed Adoniram Judson.

On November 4, 1825, a message reached Ann from her friend, the governor of the north gate; an order was being written at the palace for Adoniram's release. Ann could scarcely contain the flood of hope that filled her heart. Freedom? That evening official word came, and the following morning Adoniram's fetters were struck off. Then, unbelievably, they were told Ann could not leave. As a safeguard, the jailers would keep Ann. She was horrified, but all the deprivations and sufferings of the past year and a half had not removed the power of Adoniram's presence, and he convinced the jailers to allow Ann to leave with him by promising them all the food and supplies they had there in Aungbinle. Whatever would they have done without bribes?[9]

By noon, a gaunt and emaciated man and woman, a Bengali cook, two little girls, and a tiny baby climbed aboard a creaking cart and with a jailer, started the bumpy ride to Ava. Judson's personal journal marked the event: "1825, Nov. 5—was taken out of irons and reconducted to Ava," and "1825, Nov. 7—was sent under guard to Maloun, the headquarters of the Burmese Army, to act as interpreter."[10] Ann and Adoniram got only as far as Amarapura before they were again forced to separate. He was taken by guards to the house of Amarapura's governor, and Ann hired a boat to go "home" to Ava and the blessed sight of Maung Ing.

Early the next morning, Ann went to her friend the governor, now promoted to *Woongyi* (deputy ruler). He was able to assure her that although Adoniram was still considered a prisoner, it was just until translating work was done. An anxious Ann had to await the next development. Like Adoniram, she was so much a "doer" that simply waiting was painful. Weariness finally overcame her body and she slept.

Morning dawned and Adoniram was allowed to stop briefly by their house. Many of their belongings had been looted in spite of Maung Ing's efforts, but Ann was able to bundle up a mattress, blanket, and pillow for his trip. Adoniram tenderly held little Maria and once again had to say goodbye to Ann. It was a three-day trip for Judson in a boat not long enough to stretch out in, the days scorching and the nights damp and chill. He arrived in Maloun with a fever that made him nearly incoherent. He was put in a bamboo hut on the blinding white sand beach of the river. The guards realized that Judson was terribly ill, but still they came every hour with papers for him to translate until he lost consciousness. There followed days of delirium and wild dreams before he regained his senses.

Although too weak to move, Judson recovered his ability to think and translate. Clearly, the Burmans were in mortal fear of the British. They were naive regarding anything not Burmese, and Judson had much explaining to do, serving as translator and diplomat. The idea of giving up territory or paying reparations by negotiation was completely foreign to Burmese thinking, so Adoniram conducted a "school of negotiations." If they didn't learn the necessity of wise compromise, things could drag on forever. At all hours of night and day, officials would come to Judson seeking advice. Adoniram frequently thought of the irony; thirteen years ago the British had driven the Judsons from the shores of India, not allowing them to remain there even on a temporary basis. Now the British were completely dependent on the good services of the translator Judson to effect a treaty for them with a warring nation bent on noncooperation.

So disbelieving were the Burmese about the good faith of the British that they asked Judson if he was willing to leave his wife and child behind to be put to death should the English take the money and still march on the capital.[11] Unthinkable to him. Adoniram later recounted that although he was free from leg chains those six weeks and was not deliberately persecuted, he was still every bit a prisoner. Deals and counterdeals were relayed back and forth, and on the negotiations dragged. Emissaries from both sides met in a boat in the middle of the river. A tentative treaty was drawn up; Burma would have to give up four territorial areas and pay one crore of rupees (one million pounds of British sterling). Campbell would allow a fifteen-day armistice for the document to be signed by King Bagyidaw.

Fifteen days passed with no word from Ava. Burma was playing games, and the disgusted British commander began a march on Maloun. On December 17, the Burmese decided that negotiations were completed, and Judson was loaded on a boat for Ava. Not far behind this departure came the British, storming the stockade at Maloun and discovering the original treaty, still unsigned. No Burman had been eager enough to have his head separated from his neck to deliver such a treaty to the king, so there it lay, unheeded.

Adoniram was unaware of the abandoned treaty; his one thought was to get to Ann. They reached Ava the night of December 29, but the guards led him right past his house. No matter how he protested, nothing persuaded his escorts. He was yet a prisoner and was put in an outbuilding by the courthouse—warned that he would be returned to Aungbinle. All the next day, Adoniram was under guard in the sweltering little shed. In the evening, the dear face of Maung

Ing appeared in the doorway; one of the men who had accompanied Judson had met him in the street and told him where the teacher was. Maung Ing explained that, on hearing the news, Ann had immediately asked him to go to the governor to see if Judson could be spared from returning to Aungbinle. Maria was fine, Maung Ing assured Judson; he was not to worry.[12] Seeing Maung Ing buoyed Adoniram's spirits; then he reflected on their conversation. Several times he had asked about Ann and Maung Ing had been evasive. That was not like him. The more Judson thought, the more he feared something was amiss.

There was ample reason for worry. Two weeks after Adoniram had left for Maloun, Ann was hit by "spotted fever," a deadly form of typhus. Ann later wrote of this dreadful time to Elnathan: "I was seized with the spotted fever, with all its attendant horrors. I knew the nature of the fever from its commencement; and from the shattered state of my constitution…I concluded it must be fatal. The day I was taken with the fever, a Burmese nurse came and offered her services for Maria. This circumstance filled me with gratitude and confidence in God; for though I had so long and so constantly made efforts to obtain a person of this description, I had never been able; when at the very time I most needed one, and without any exertion, a voluntary offer was made. My fever raged violently.…At this dreadful period, Dr. Price was released from prison; and hearing of my illness, obtained permission to come and see me. He has since told me that my situation was the most distressing he had ever witnessed, and that he did not then think I should survive many hours. My hair was shaved, my head and feet covered with blisters.…One of the first things I recollect was, seeing this faithful servant [Koo-chil] standing by me, trying to induce me to take a little wine and water. I was in fact so far gone, that the Burmese neighbours who had come in to see me expire, said, 'She is dead; and if the king of angels should come in, he could not recover her.'"

Ann continued: "I now began to recover slowly, but it was more than a month after this before I had strength to stand. While in this…state, the servant who had followed your brother to the

139

Burmese camp, came in, and informed me that his master had arrived and was conducted to the courthouse in town and…it was reported…that he was to be sent back to the Oung-pen-la prison. I was too weak to bear ill tidings of any kind; but a shock so dreadful as this, almost annihilated me. For some time, I could hardly breathe; but at last gained sufficient composure to dispatch Maung Ing to our friend, the governor…and begged him to make one more effort for the release of Mr. Judson."13

Promptly upon receipt of the news, the governor of the north gate came to Adoniram's rescue; he petitioned the highest court for Judson's release and even offered himself as security. Judson was released that morning, December 31, 1825, the end of the year and the beginning of blessed freedom. Fifty years later, Adoniram's son Edward wrote: "With a step more fleet than for the last two years he had practiced, and in spite of the maimed ankles which sometimes almost refused their office, he hurried along the street to his beloved home. The door stood invitingly open, and without having been seen by any one, he entered."14

"The first object which met his eye," the story continued, "was a fat, half-naked Burman woman…holding on her knees a wan baby, so begrimed with dirt that it did not occur to the father that it could be his own. He gave but one hasty look, and hurried to the next room. Across the foot of the bed, as though she had fallen there, lay a human object…scarcely more recognizable than his child. The face was of a ghastly paleness, the features sharp, and the whole form shrunken….The glossy black curls had all been shorn from the finely shaped head, which was now covered by a closely-fitting cotton cap, of the coarsest and—unlike anything usually coming in contact with that head—not the cleanest kind….There lay the devoted wife, who had followed him so unweariedly from prison to prison, ever alleviating his distresses….The wearied sleeper was awakened by a breath that came too near her cheek. Perhaps a falling tear might have been added; for, steady as were those eyes in difficulties, dauntless in dangers, and stern when conscience frowned, they were well used to tender tears."15

Ann slowly opened her eyes and saw the broad forehead, the strict, clean lines of Adoniram's face, and it was a glimpse of heaven. In his turn, Adoniram looked into eyes glazed by the ravages of fever and pain. As he saw the dawning joy as she recognized who he was, it was as if he were seeing into the very corner of her soul. In that moment of pure joy, both could do nothing but weep. Ann looked near death in those frightening moments, but she was actually recovering. In those days of extremity, God had provided. Koo-chil and Maung Ing had been the tools of her survival. At last Adoniram was able to do something for Ann, to lavish his care on her as she recuperated. For so many months, Ann had poured her heart and energies into keeping him alive. Now Adoniram found great satisfaction in giving her his full attention.

And Maung Ing became the unwitting bearer of astounding news. One morning a few days after Judson had returned, Maung Ing came quietly into the room where Adoniram was caring for Ann and carefully placed in Judson's hands a tattered object. Ann and Adoniram gazed down in wonder at the hard inner core of the pillow Ann had made and taken to Adoniram in prison at Let Ma Yoon. Here in his hands was the New Testament manuscript, ten years worth of labor. How on earth could it have survived? Maung Ing became radiant with joy as he realized what the old pillow actually was. The Judsons listened in amazement to his story.

Shortly after Adoniram had been dragged from Let Ma Yoon, Maung Ing had gone to the deserted prison and poked around in the rubble, looking for some remembrance of his honored Yoodthan. And there, in the filth, he saw the remains of the pillow Mrs. Yoodthan had made and taken to the prison. A guard had ripped off the outer cover, thinking it might be of some use, and had thrown aside the hard inner roll. Gently, Maung Ing picked up the core of the pillow and took it home, little knowing the treasure held in his hands that dark day. The Judsons and Maung Ing rejoiced together over the miracle that had occurred. Years later some friend asked about the story of the saved manuscript and wondered how Judson could have borne such a hard pillow upon which to sleep, to which he wryly replied, "When people are loaded with chains and sleep half the time on a bare board, their senses become so obtuse that they do not know the difference between a hard pillow and a soft one."[16]

In the final six weeks of waiting, while all the threats of continued war and bumbling attempts at peace continued, Ann and Adoniram were the guests of the governor, now *Woongyi* and wielding considerable influence. While Ann regained some strength, Adoniram's scars from the long months of wearing shackles healed as well, but the ridges produced by the fetters were forever on his ankles, a daily reminder of human cruelty and the protection of God.

Efforts to conclude the stalled peace talks were speeded up. The Burmese court decided that Judson and Price could be tools to get better terms. Adoniram dreaded the thought. If there was any question at all of his good faith, not only he, but his wife and child, could lose their heads. Judson used all his powers of persuasion to convince the royal court that Price could do the negotiating. Thus it developed that Judson was held as security for Price. Meanwhile, the court was scrambling to get together the necessary silver and gold to pay the required reparations.

Price came back with a message from Campbell: the British would make no changes in their agreed proposals. The indemnity could be paid in four installments, the first within twelve days, and all prisoners held by the Burmese must be given up at once. Campbell actually specified by name the three Judsons. Bagyidaw's response was: "They are not English, they are my people. They shall not go." The British, upon hearing this declaration, angrily refused to consider peace unless the release of the Judsons was part of the agreement.[17]

About this time, an upstart general by the name of Layar-thoo-yah persuaded the Golden One to allow him to attack the British before they reached the ancient city of Pagan. He would fortify the city and drive the foreigners away. Bagyidaw and his queen were so reluctant to see their silver and gold go to the hated British that they agreed to the wild scheme. The general's army named themselves "The Retainers of the King's Glory" and fortified Pagan to the south. With just nine hundred men, the English attacked, upon which the Burmese army broke and ran. For his troubles, the general was summarily executed. Now everyone at court was terrified, and gold and silver from every corner were hurriedly gathered. Within one day the first installment of the indemnity was ready to go downriver.

However, just the sight of those boats loaded with silver and gold from the royal treasury changed the Golden Mind yet again. He would send just one-fourth of the first installment and *promise* the rest. One clever official thought of Adoniram and knew the power of his reputation and word among the British. At the official's suggestion, Judson was forced to go aboard the laden boat with the high Burmese officials to make peace, but he was gratified to discover that Gouger had been released and would go as well.

Sir Archibald Campbell's response to the Burmese proposal of one-fourth of the first installment of the indemnity came as no surprise. Campbell flatly rejected such a feeble portion. He would not stop the British army's march on Ava, but he would move slowly and halt if the remainder of the indemnity reached him before he reached Ava. In addition, he requested that Judson round up all foreigners, and in the presence of both sides, each would be asked if he wished to stay in Ava or to leave. Without their complete release, Campbell threatened, there would be no peace.

Yet again the officials pleaded with the Judsons to stay. "You will not leave us; you will become a great man if you will remain."[18] The Judsons knew better than to agree to any such prevarication. Jonathan Price, on the other hand, the New Englander who had early on become enamored with the royal court, decided he would stay.[19] Judson did not fail to be diplomatic in the tense moment with two opposing sides both asking for him. He quietly stated that his wife wished to go with the British and, of course, he would go with her.[20]

Adoniram's entry in his journal read: "1826, Feb. 21st, left Ava with Mrs. J and Maria, for the British Camp at Yandabo."[21] That evening when the boats loaded with gold and silver started down the river, the Judsons took an affectionate leave of their friend the new

143

Woongyi. Ann, Adoniram, Maria, the two little girls Mary and Abby, along with Maung Ing and Koo-chil, boarded their boat and pulled away from shore. The Judsons gazed back at the spires dotting the city of Ava one last time, their hearts flooded with a multitude of emotions, and outweighing them all was gratitude to God. The boat moved gently downstream, and the Judsons felt overwhelming relief. Twenty-one months of imprisonment made Adoniram appear an old man. Ann, painfully thin and pale, reclined on a cushion, her short dark curls just now feathering her head. She appeared more wraith than reality, as did the fragile Maria, weighing barely as much as a three-month-old infant although she had just passed her first birthday. They all were ragged, weak, and emaciated, but Ann and Adoniram could only thank God for freedom and take courage.

The Letter: 1826

In action, how like a angel. —William Shakespeare, *Hamlet*

THE NEXT MORNING, FEBRUARY 22, 1826, THE WEARY LITTLE FAMILY SAW
before them on the river the masts of the English steamboat *Diana*
gleaming in the bright sun. This imposing vessel had appeared quite
impregnable to Burmese eyes, which had never before seen its like. The
Judsons were taken aboard, and then Adoniram was conveyed just a
short distance further to meet with Sir Archibald Campbell.

To the British officers, Ann Judson was awe-inspiring. All had heard
chilling, nearly unbelievable stories of the heroic American woman
who had managed to keep her husband alive and at the same time gain
the unwilling respect of the Burman court. Even accounting for the fact
that heroic stories tend to become embellished, the English were in awe
to meet someone who had persevered in such circumstances. Here she
stood before them, fragile and painfully thin, a cap of short black curls
framing her fine features. Ann's pale skin was almost translucent, but

The first site of Ann's grave is on a lonely cliff overlooking the Gulf of Martaban.

her dark eyes were warm, looking about at the fine British ship and sailors, and then gazing down at the delicate baby in her arms. The men would never forget the power of those beautiful eyes and could only imagine what suffering and horrors they had seen. She appeared to them that day like a genuine angel. They treated her accordingly. Nothing was too good for Mrs. Judson. For Ann, who had endured insults, taunts, and denigration for nearly two years, the experience was especially gratifying and a balm to her weary heart.

Sir Archibald invited the Judsons to be honored guests in his camp. Ann wrote: "We feel that our obligations to General Campbell can never be cancelled. Our final release from Ava, and our recovering all the property that had there been taken, was owing entirely to his efforts. This subsequent hospitality, and kind attention…have left an indelible impression on our minds.…We daily received the congratulations of the British officers, whose conduct towards us formed a striking contrast to that of the Burmans. I presume to say, that no persons on earth were ever happier than we were during the fortnight we passed at the English camp. For several days, this single idea wholly occupied my mind, that we were out of the power of the Burmese government.…Our feelings continually dictated expressions like these, *What shall we render unto the Lord, for all his benefits toward us.*"[1]

Campbell had the largest tent in the camp, complete with a veranda, pitched for the Judsons next to his own. They were his guests at every meal. Adoniram drew up the final draft of what became the Treaty of Yandabo; by this time Gouger had arrived and was basking in freedom with them—infinitely more precious now and ever after, having been deprived of it for so long. That sublime sense of joy was described by Judson twenty years later in his reminiscences of this singular moment. A family member recorded those memories: "One evening several persons at our house were repeating anecdotes of what different men in different ages had regarded as the highest type…[of] enjoyment derived from outward circumstances. 'Pooh!' said Mr. Judson; 'these men were not qualified to judge. I know of a much higher pleasure than that. What do you think of floating down the Irrawady, on a cool, moonlight evening, with your wife by your side, and your baby in your arms, free—all free? But you cannot understand it, either; it needs a twenty-one months' qualification; and I can never regret my twenty-one months' of misery, when I recall that one delicious thrill. I think I have had a better appreciation of what heaven may be ever since."[2]

Biographer Courtney Anderson related a crowning incident at the state dinner General Campbell gave for Burmese officials at the end of negotiations. No doubt Campbell wished to impress the "Golden" court with British pomp, and he succeeded. The Burmese were not the victors, after all, and they were clearly ill at ease in the British camp. Flags and banners were flying, the regimental band trumpeting the dinner hour. Walking alone at the head of the procession, Campbell, in full regalia, stopped at the Judsons' tent. The band stopped. No one moved as the general entered the tent and emerged with Ann Judson on his arm. Ann was beautifully dressed, thin but erect, and with a twinkle in those fine eyes that reminded Adoniram of her eyes when they had been courting. The dark eyes were dancing with life and a touch of mischief.

She was led to the seat of highest honor next to Campbell, and surely each Burman heart was beating more rapidly than usual. This honored guest was the same person who had appeared countless times at their doors, pleading for mercy for her husband. They could not maintain eye contact with Mrs. Yoodthan. Each trembling heart knew that had the situation been reversed, he would have extracted satisfying revenge of the most ominous type. Ann knew them well— all too well. It was as if she could look straight into their souls. One plump official was so perturbed that it was obvious to everyone present. At this table loaded with all sorts of interesting dishes, he could scarcely lift a bite to his mouth without a portion of it dropping off his trembling fork.

This attracted Campbell's attention: "What is the matter with the owner of the pointed beard over there? He seems to be seized with a fit of ague."

Ann looked at him carefully. "I do not know," she said, "unless his memory may be too busy. He is an old acquaintance of mine.

Probably he considers himself in danger now that he sees me under your protection." She described Adoniram in fetters in the inner prison, half dead from fever, and how it was to this man's house she had walked early one day to plead for help. This man had kept her waiting in the hot sun until noon, had heard her request indifferently and refused it contemptuously. It was he who had noticed her silk umbrella and snatched it out of her hand, he who had laughed and said, "The sun can't find a woman as thin as you."

The English officers found it difficult to keep a courteous silence as she told the story. But their looks at the shrinking official spoke even louder than their few indignant words, and he seemed to know what Ann had said. His face paled with fear. His hand shaking uncontrollably, he tried to wipe the perspiration that trickled down his stricken face. Ann took pity on him. In Burmese she reassured him softly, "You have nothing to fear."[3] Ann explained to Campbell what she had said to Pointed Beard, and she and Adoniram had to enjoy a rare moment of laughter later that night as they recalled the events of that immensely satisfying state dinner.

The accolades heaped on Ann during those two weeks were neither sought nor even desired by her, but they were a special blessing to Adoniram. He had been keenly aware those many months that he could never repay Ann for her devotion to him. It gave him immense gratification to see her so highly esteemed. And the British paid her great tribute years later in the *Calcutta Review*, quoting the incisive words of Henry Gouger: "Mrs. Judson was the author of those eloquent and forcible appeals to the Government, which prepared them by degrees for submission to terms of peace, never expected by any, who knew the hauteur and inflexible pride of the Burman court."

"And while on this subject," Gouger continued, "the overflowings of grateful feelings...compel me to add a tribute of public thanks to that amiable and humane female, who, though living at a distance of two miles from our prison, without any means of conveyance, and very feeble in health, forgot her own comfort and infirmity, and almost every day visited us, sought out and administered to our wants....While we were all left by the Government destitute of food, she, with unwearied perseverance, by some means or other, obtained us a constant supply." Gouger concluded: "When the unfeeling avarice of our keepers confined us inside, or made our feet fast in the stocks, she, like a ministering Angel, never ceased her applications to the Government...(for) a respite from our galling oppressions."[4]

Adoniram as well was held in the highest regard by the entire British army. Their admiration for his linguistic genius *and* his stature as a man of great integrity only increased as they observed him in action.[5] John Crawford, the leader who represented Britain in the Court of Ava, wrote his estimate of Judson's contribution: "The service of Dr. Judson from his local knowledge, his intimate acquaintance with the Burman language written and colloquial and his general good sense and discretion I consider highly beneficial to the interests of the government. He understood the Burman language, his subject,...and was besides a power in every respect of distinguished good sense and intelligence."[6] Judson's contributions during that difficult and delicate period of time were even more remarkable when considering the conditions in which he had lived.

With hearts lighter and prospects brighter than they had been in almost two years, Ann and Adoniram boarded the gunboat *Irawaddy* on March 6, 1826. Ann wrote of their speculations on the past dreadful months, and what good, if any, might accrue from them. Second-guessing their move to Ava was difficult. Ann stated: "All we can say is 'It is not in man that walketh, to direct his step,'...but two years of precious time have been lost to the mission, unless some future advantage may be gained....We are sometimes induced to think, that the lesson we found so very hard to learn, will have a beneficial effect through our lives; and that the mission may, in the end, be advanced rather than retarded."[7]

They reached Rangoon in March.[8] They had been gone more than two years. Their house was a ruin but still standing. Both the Wades and Houghs had been in Calcutta since the beginning of the war, and now, thirteen years after first arriving, the Judsons were again alone in the mission. Their first concern was the band of believers. Maung Shway-bay had stayed in the mission house. Dear Mah Men Lay, the first woman convert, had just returned to Rangoon. Moung Shwa-gnong was in the interior. They did not yet know the fate of the others.

Ann and Adoniram faced a choice. Rangoon remained under Bagyidaw, but the British controlled Arracan and Tenasserim in the south. There they could have liberty to preach and teach. Thousands of Burmans were streaming south to escape the repressions of the Golden One. Finally, the Judsons decided to move, for the possibilities for future work in the south were encouraging.

John Crawford was appointed as the civil commissioner under Lord Amherst. It was Crawford's task to select a new capital, and he immediately asked Judson to go along and help make vital decisions. Adoniram had not lost his early love of adventure, and this was a perfect opportunity to scout out where they could settle and begin work again. After ten days in Rangoon, Adoniram told Ann goodbye again, but this time they both knew it was a brief separation, and high hopes buoyed their spirits. A spot in South Burma with a good harbor was selected and named for Lord Amherst. Judson himself concluded the ceremony for the opening of the new city with a prayer of dedication.

Just ten days after leaving, he was back in Rangoon. Judson took down their dear old Rangoon *zayat* and sent it by river to Amherst. Most of the converts decided to move as well. Four of the Burman families went ahead, including Maung Ing and Maung Shway-bay. Crawford made another proposal to Adoniram. The Treaty of Yandabo called for a follow-up commercial treaty, and Crawford desired Judson's help. Judson refused. Crawford continued to plead, and then dangled the carrot of the possibility of inserting a clause that would guarantee religious freedom for all Burmese people. Ann realized what this would mean for future work and added her persuasions. It took a lot of convincing. Adoniram agreed with great reluctance but insisted that first he go and help Ann and little Maria get settled in Amherst.

On July 2, 1826, the Judsons landed at the mouth of the Salwen River in Amherst. Captain Fenwick, the civil superintendent, insisted on vacating his little home for Ann's use while she supervised the building of a house. Adoniram left for Ava in just a matter of days, but this time he and Ann parted with light hearts, excited about the future. Adoniram could leave even little Maria without worries. She was much improved. As Ann described her to a friend in England: "Our little Maria is now fifteen months old, a lovely child with blue eyes and light hair."9

Amherst seemed ideal to Ann. The air was clear and fresh, the view of the ocean beautiful, and the sense of freedom exhilarating. There were only about fifty houses in the raw little town, and everything had a heady pioneer feel about it. Ann delighted in the progress of the school where she already had ten students. She put Maung Ing in charge of the class, and he was doing an excellent job. Ann conducted the Sunday services with the group of believers who had moved to the new territory, and they all rejoiced in being able to worship together again.10

Occasionally Judson received a letter from Ann, reporting on the new school, worship services, and the progress of their new house. Then he received another letter from her written September 14, which made him ache to get home to be with his family. Ann wrote of how she and Maria would be completely happy if he could be there with them. Adoniram worried about Maria, for Ann said: "Poor little Maria is still feeble. Sometimes I hope she is getting better; then again she declines to her former weakness. When I ask her where Papa is, she always starts up and points toward the sea....May God preserve and bless you, and restore you in safety to your new and old home, is the prayer of your affectionate Ann."11

And then he received no more letters from her. In the middle of November, he received a communication from Captain Fenwick who reported that Ann was extremely well. This was soon followed by another letter from Fenwick saying that Mrs. Judson had been stricken with fever but already seemed to be improving. Still Adoniram did not hear from Ann herself. The slowness of communication in Burma created a situation in which Adoniram could only wonder what might be happening to his family those many miles away. Unknown to him, ominous news was already on its way; it took a full month in arriving.

Maria had been dreadfully ill. Ann had lost much sleep caring for her but was elated when Maria's condition improved dramatically. Then in October, Ann was taken with a fever. At first she seemed to rally, but then the seriousness of this attack became apparent to her beloved Burman friends and all-too-discernible to the English doctor attending her. The diagnosis was cerebral spinal meningitis. Had Ann been her usual strong self, she could likely have fought it off. Her constitution, however, had been severely weakened by nearly two years of malnutrition, stress, smallpox, and repeated bouts with cholera and typhus fever. Ann's debilitated frame could not fight off this violent new attack.

Captain Fenwick found the wife of a British officer to care for Maria, and this seemed to relieve Ann's distraught mind. The intensity of the fever would occasionally abate and give her friends renewed hope. Then once again it would worsen, and she would lie for days barely moving and nearly insensible. Occasionally she would start and rouse, inquire about Maria, and then subside in ease when assured that her baby was happy and well cared for. Ann spoke very little. The last day or two she lay on one side, for the most part unmoving, reclining her head on one arm. Once, she opened her eyes, glazed with the deadly fever, and said: "The teacher is long in coming, and the new missionaries are long in coming; I must die alone and leave my little one; but as it is the will of God, I acquiesce in his will. I am not afraid of death, but I am afraid I shall not be able to bear these pains. Tell the teacher that the disease was most violent, and I could not write; tell him how I suffered and died; tell him all that you see; and take care of the house and things until he returns."[12] Her last request was that they take good care of Maria until her father should return. The small band of Burmese Christians gathered around their beloved friend, weeping in helpless anguish as they saw her life slipping away. At 8:00 on the evening of October 24, 1826, Ann Judson murmured one last phrase in Burmese, and died.[13]

Edward Judson described the scene: "The hands so full of holy endeavors were destined to be suddenly folded for rest. She died apart from him to whom she had given her heart in her girlhood, whose footsteps she had faithfully followed for fourteen years, over land and sea,…sharing his studies and his privations, illumining his hours of gloom with her beaming presence, and with a heroism and fidelity unparalleled in the annals of missions, soothing the sufferings of his imprisonment. He whom she had thus loved…was far away in Ava.…The Burman converts…gathered helplessly and broken-heartedly about their white mama."[14]

One month later, Judson received a black-sealed letter. Realizing that the black portended death, he immediately thought that little Maria had died. Adoniram could scarcely bring himself to open the letter from the assistant superintendent of Amherst. Strange. With trembling hands, he carefully broke the seal and read: "My dear Sir, to one who has suffered so much and with such exemplary fortitude, there needs but little preface to tell a tale of distress. It were cruel indeed to torture you with doubt and suspense. To sum up the unhappy tidings in a few words—Mrs. Judson is *no more.*"[15] In that moment, Adoniram Judson's world crumbled about him. Ann, beautiful, heroic, loving Ann—gone. Anguish bowed him sobbing to his knees. It was precisely as if the world had stopped. For Judson, in the utter desolation of his grief, it had.

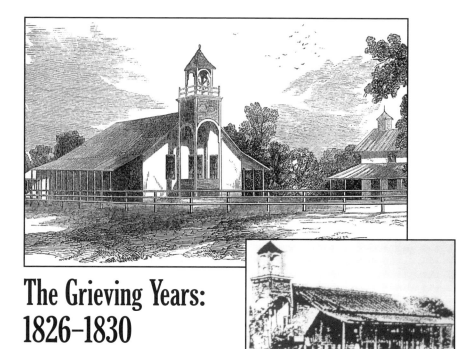

The Grieving Years: 1826–1830

What restraint or limit should there be
to grief for one so dear?
—Horace

HOW COULD ADONIRAM BEAR SUCH A BLOW? HE HAD GONE THROUGH
two years of torture, prison, fevers, and malnutrition, but this was far
worse. Ann was his heart, the one who had sustained him. Ever afterward he could not recall how he survived those first weeks. With a
sense of disbelief, he went through the mechanics of rising each morning and going through the motions of completing the treaty that he
now felt was meaningless. Ann had encouraged him to work on it

Early sketch of Moulmein church. Courtesy Dr. Stanley Hanna. *Inset:* Only known photograph of
that building. Courtesy the American Baptist Historical Society.

because of her hope that it might address religious freedom. That hope was dead, and it seemed to Judson that all hope was now extinguished for him as well. There was a numbing sense of unreality about everything. In his mind he still saw a smiling Ann standing at the door of the house, Maria cradled in her arms, an aura of new beginnings about them.

Waking up—that was the most daunting time of all; it hit him fresh each morning. Ann was gone forever. Adoniram wrote to Ann's mother and told her of the dreadful blow: "I will not trouble you, my dear mother, with an account of my own private feelings—the bitter, heart-rending anguish,...[W]hile I am writing and you perusing these lines, her spirit is resting and rejoicing in the heavenly paradise."[1]

By mid-December the treaty was finalized and Judson was once again on the *Diana*, the same steamboat where just months before he had been with Ann and Maria, basking in the thrill of freedom. Now he was bent with grief. They stopped in Rangoon; rebels were attacking on every front. There was no way to go beyond Rangoon's defended stockade. While finishing up treaty details on board the *Diana*, Judson received the news that his scholar-teacher Moung Shwa-gnong had died of cholera. In the sorrow of loss, however, Adoniram gave profound thanks that his friend had spent his final years sharing his faith.

Their old mission house was outside the stockade surrounding Rangoon. Adoniram could not go there because of the rebel guns, but by climbing onto a high roof, he could see the spot. Only the post and a forlorn little part of the roof remained. A desolate Judson could only think of the years he and Ann had studied and preached there, and of the grave of little Roger somewhere under all the rubble. With mingled relief and dread, Judson wrote the final lines of the treaty and sailed for Amherst. Now he must face reality—no Ann at the door to welcome him home, and only God knew what Maria's condition might be.

A new year began, but Adoniram's dark cloud of sorrow did not lift. On January 21, 1827, the *Diana* reached Amherst. Jonathan Wade was waiting for Judson at the dock; the Wades had arrived in

Amherst shortly after Ann's death. They had moved into the house Ann had built and assumed the care of Maria. She was alive, Wade assured Judson, but exceedingly frail. Wade and Judson began the walk to the house, and as they grew closer, Maung Ing and the faithful believers saw their approach. They came on the run to meet Judson, all of them weeping for their honored Yoodthan. Deborah Wade came to the door holding Maria in her arms. The little girl did not recognize her weeping father. She would not go to his outstretched arms. Adoniram's sorrow came in great waves, and he swallowed repeatedly in an attempt to speak.

Judson needed to see the place where Ann lay. It was near, close to the little garden by the house. At the head of her grave was a little hope-tree (*hopia*). Friends had built a small fence to protect the area. Judson's eyes were so blinded by tears that he could scarcely see. Long minutes went by. He finally turned and walked to Captain Fenwick's house nearby, the house where Ann had been living when he kissed her goodbye last summer. He looked once more at the place where they had knelt for their last prayer together and exchanged a parting kiss. Returning to the house Ann had built, Judson climbed the stairs to see the room where she had died. By looking from the window, he could see her grave. He was overwhelmed by memories, memories of fourteen years of life with Ann.

On February 7, Judson was able to talk with the physician who had cared for Ann those final weeks, and that gave him a small measure of comfort. The doctor assured Adoniram that even had he been there, he could have done nothing to save her life. The doctor was fully convinced that all the suffering, disease, and malnutrition of the past two years had rendered her body too weak to fight off the final deadly fever. Again Adoniram wrote Rebecca Hasseltine, telling her about Maria and describing the comfort the child was to him. He valiantly endeavored to help her gain strength, but her frail little frame held few powers of recuperation.

In the middle of April, George Dana Boardman and his wife, Sarah, arrived with their six-month-old little girl. The contrast between the healthy babe and fragile Maria was daunting to observe. Barely had

156

the Boardmans arrived before, on the afternoon of April 24, exactly six months to the day that her mother had died, Maria Elizabeth Butterworth Judson breathed her last. Gentle George Boardman made a little coffin for Maria. Boardman spoke of Adoniram's condition in those days of suffering, wrote, "He looks as if worn out by sorrow."[2]

Judson had to write yet another black-sealed letter to Maria's grandmother: "My little Maria lies by the side of her fond mother….She ceased to breathe on the 24th instant, at 3 o'clock P.M., aged two years and three months. We then closed her faded eyes, and bound up her discolored lips, where the dark touch of death first appeared, and folded her little hands on her cold breast. The next morning we made her last bed in the small enclosure that surrounds her mother's lonely grave…And I am left alone in the wide world. My own dear family I have buried; one in Rangoon, and two in Amherst. What remains for me but to hold myself in readiness to follow the dear departed to that blessed world."[3]

Months later Adoniram wrote to Ann's sisters in response to a letter in which they sought details about Ann and the prison experiences. His reply revealed why Judson was always so reluctant to talk about the prison months: "You ask many questions about our sufferings at Ava, but how can I answer them now? There would be some pleasure in reviewing those scenes, if she were alive; but now I cannot. The only pleasant reflection—the only one that assuages the anguish of retrospection, is, that she now rests far away, where no spotted faced executioner can fill her heart with terror; where no unfeeling magistrate can extort the scanty pittance which she had preserved through every risk, to sustain her fettered husband and famishing babe; no more exposed to lie on a bed of languishment, and stung with the uncertainty, what would become of her poor husband and child, when she was gone. No, she has her little ones around her, I trust, and has taught them to praise the source whence their deliverance flowed."[4]

Yet Judson persevered and resumed his work, that work he had dreamed of being able to do once again, during endless months in prison. Just two days after reaching Amherst, he had conducted his first worship service in Burmese, after three years of being unable to do so. Meanwhile, Amherst was *not* going to be the capital of the new British territory. General Campbell had decided on Moulmein, twenty-five miles upstream, for the British headquarters.

Then Adoniram witnessed the death of little "Abby Hasseltine," who along with her surviving sister, "Mary," had lived with them through the horrors of Ava. And in July, Judson received a letter telling of his father's death in November 1826. Adoniram Sr. had become a Baptist the last ten years of his life. The death of his father flooded the son with memories, even as far back as to the gratified sire who had beamed at the little reader in his lap and proudly said, "My son, some day you will be a great man." Adoniram could only wonder what his father would think now. Here was his son, thirty-nine, widowed, childless, and with permanent scars on his body. Judson wondered if the scars might be etched on his heart as well.

A few weeks later, the small band of Christians, working hard at regrouping, lost elderly Mah Men Lay, the first woman convert, that educated woman who had begun a school and ministered to others. Mah Men Lay had been sinking quite rapidly yet still expressing her joy and faith. She talked of entering heaven itself and meeting her dear Mama Judson there. On one of her last days she declared: "But first of all, I shall hasten to where my Savior sits and fall down and worship him, for his great love in sending the teachers to show me the way to heaven."[5]

Adoniram did not slow in his work of preaching and translating. Sometimes he felt as if moving by rote, but move he did, and labored hard not to be borne under by grief. He could not seem to keep from returning repeatedly to the graves under the hopia tree—kneeling, praying, weeping. The Wades were concerned about the condition of his mind but could do nothing except be there for him.

Judson and the Wades paid a visit to Moulmein where the Boardmans had begun work, and in October they decided to move there to center work in that fast-growing capital. There Judson established the first permanent church in the country, a church that survives to this day and will celebrate its bicentennial in 2027. Judson spent the bulk of his time revising the New Testament, that precious manuscript that so miraculously survived the death prison. He also began work on the Old Testament and prepared catechisms for use in the Burman schools the small mission group established. Sundays were spent in leading worship services. Most days of the week, services were also held from the *zayat* Adoniram had built in front of his home.

Maung Ing was set apart by the mission and believers to be the first Burman missionary, and that act was a moment of intense satisfaction for Judson, who thought back to the time when Maung Ing had become a believer and had followed them to Ava and devotedly helped them. Could he ever forget that Maung Ing had found and saved the New Testament manuscript?

Only through iron self-discipline was Adoniram able to continue his work. Many days and every night, grief threatened to overcome him. He translated, preached, and wrote, and then repeated the process by sheer force of will. During those dark nights, Judson often recalled the letter he had written his fiancée, Ann, on a snowy New England New Year's Day. He had spoken of the change to come in their lives and speculated on what might confront them overseas, concluding: "We shall probably experience seasons when we shall be 'exceeding sorrowful, even unto death.' One of us may be unable to sustain the heat of the climate and the change of habits; and the other may say, with literal truth, over the grave—'By foreign hands thy dying eyes were closed; By foreign hands thy decent limbs composed; By foreign hands thy humble grave adorned;' But whether we shall be honored and mourned by strangers, God only knows. At least, either of us will be certain of one mourner."[6]

The words haunted him now. Writing of a distant speculation was far easier than being the one left alone. Still he refused to give up. The idea of throwing up his hands and quitting may have crossed Judson's mind, but it never lingered. To him it was in every sense a mission for life. But sometimes, most unexpectedly, there would strike his heart "the echo of a distant pain" and he would experience afresh the agony of loss.

Early in 1828, the Boardmans moved to Tavoy, more than one hundred miles south of Amherst. George Boardman had a great depth of dedication, real personal charm, and special language ability. Sarah Boardman matched George in gentleness and dedication and surpassed him in linguistic brilliance. They had studied Burmese while waiting out the war in Calcutta. The Boardmans now took with them to Tavoy a new believer named Ko Tha Byu.

Ko Tha Byu was from a wild jungle people called the Karens, many thousands of whom lived in the jungles near Tavoy. The Karens shied away from others in Burma and were seldom seen in a town. Ko Tha Byu had been as wild as his people, and while still a teenager, he had become a robber and a multiple murderer. He had been put on sale as a slave to pay his debts. One of Adoniram's assistants, Maung Shway-bay, had pitied him and bought him. Ko's temper was so vile, though, that Shway-bay had gladly turned him over to Judson. Over time, Adoniram got through to him. Ko learned to read the New Testament and came to faith, and his entire life changed. In Tavoy, Ko flourished under the tutelage of the Boardmans and influenced thousands of lives, coming to be known as "The Apostle of the Karens."

Back in Moulmein, Adoniram still attempted to submerge his grief in work, but inevitably the pain had to catch up with him. Post-traumatic stress disorder had not been identified in the nineteenth century, but that did not prevent Judson from suffering with it. He struggled every day with his loss. Meanwhile, several new missionaries had come and the work was strengthened. Adoniram was unquestionably their leader, the driving force propelling the whole group, yet something within him seemed to have died along with Ann.

The years immediately after her death were a strange period in Judson's life. He attempted to subdue both his flesh and his spirit in ways entirely unlike his usual, positive response to life. As the prison years had been for Ann, the years after losing Ann were for Judson "the dark night of his soul."[7] Again, Adoniram remembered Madame Guyon and her theories of "quietism." He had always found merit in some of those theories, but now it seemed he tried to implement them by isolating himself from nearly all that gave him pleasure or stimulated his mind. Adoniram found it close to impossible to forgive himself for not being there for Ann when she needed him most. She had always been there for him. How could he have failed her so miserably?

Judson decided he should keep none of the compensation given him by the British government for his services in negotiating peace. He sent these funds, along with his inheritance, to the missionary board. The total was about $10,000, an impressive sum in the early 1800s. The Wades joined him in giving up a twentieth of their salaries, already quite small, to serve as a challenge to ministers in America. Still later Adoniram reduced his own salary by one quarter, determined that love of money would be no motivation in his life.

Judson's self-abasement cut deep at what he felt was one of his besetting sins—pride. Had not he long ago thought how magnificent it would be to be America's very first foreign missionary? Now he cringed at ever having felt pride in such a vain ambition. Next he wrote the *American Baptist Magazine* to inform them that he "resigned" his honorary doctor's degree; he wished to be addressed without that title. Judson even wrote his sister and mother and asked that they destroy all his letters. In addition, he destroyed all his papers, some of which were irreplaceable. This brilliant man who loved people now avoided all that had pleased him about society. His biographer and friend Francis Wayland said, "No one enjoyed intelligent and cultivated society more keenly than he; and he surrendered it only in obedience to those principles by which he designed to govern his life."[8]

Judson then went one step further. He built a retreat, a little place in the woods a short distance from where he had lived, calling it his "mourning place." He worked and lived there for well over a year. Sometimes he would go to the Wades for the evening meal. Other times he would simply eat alone. The Wades grieved over his anguish but felt helpless to relieve it. For one disturbing forty-day period, Judson went even further into the jungle, to a deserted and dangerous area that was home not to people but to tigers. Without Judson's knowledge, one of the faithful disciples built him a little bamboo shelter. For six weeks Adoniram remained, praying and reading his Bible and eating only a little rice. More disturbing, he had a grave dug, and for days at a time, he would sit beside the open pit and consider how he would look lying there.[9]

Judson slowly came to the point of joining life again, delving into his translation work and preaching, his sense of call again sounding in his heart. By the third anniversary of Ann's death, the sense of paralysis started lifting. News came that his brother Elnathan had died, but that at the very end, he had believed. His last words were, "Peace. Peace."[10] This gave Judson a measure of peace that his wounded heart sorely needed.

The new decade of 1830 seemed to be a turning point for Adoniram as he poured himself into translating the Old Testament and preaching at every opportunity, even as he was training Burmese disciples. All who knew him sensed a new attitude of looking to the positive and finding the encouraging. This in turn invigorated the work of the other missionaries and disciples. The Burmese believers caught his sense of optimism and were inspired to work even harder. Adoniram could finally think of Ann's favorite statement and make it his own again: I will bless God and take courage. That was what he fervently desired. There was a world of need out there, a need for hope.

ဗျာ၊မြ့·ဗျာလဿဘာသာမျ့ုတို့မှဆရာယုဒ္ဒသာန်
ဘာသာပြန်သောဓမ္မဟောင်း:ဓမ္မသစ်သမ္မာကျွမ်း
စာဧစာင်ကိုကျ့ုပုံနှိပ်တိုက်ခန်း:၌ ၁၈၄၀
ခုနှစ်·တွင်ပဌမအကြိမ်ပုံနှိပ်သည်။

THE COMPLETE BURMESE BIBLE TRANSLATED
BY THE Rev. A. JUDSON FROM THE ORIGINAL
HEBREW AND GREEK WAS FIRST PRINTED
IN THIS ROOM IN 1840

Judson's great-grandson, Dr. Stanley Hanna, stands by the tablet commemorating the first printing of the Bible. *Inset:* Only the press building remains on the old Moulmein Mission compound.

C H A P T E R   1 6

"Teacher, give us a writing": 1830–1834

For the word of God is quick and powerful and sharper than any two-edged sword. —Hebrews 4:12

THE YEAR 1830 MARKED A TIME OF OPTIMISM IN THE MISSION GROUP and among the believers. More missionaries were arriving, and increasing numbers of Burmans were being converted. Cephas and Stella Bennett arrived in Moulmein. Here was an experienced printer; tracts could be printed in bulk, and the masses would be able to read the Good News. Judson appeared as a venerated figure to the other missionaries. The Burmese believers were rather in awe of what they considered a miracle; "Yoodthan" had lived forty days alone in a jungle teeming with tigers and then returned to Moulmein unscathed. Even unbelievers marveled at this man of God who survived such an experience. All looked to their senior missionary for guidance.

Judson decided to go to Rangoon, arriving in May 1830. Most of the early believers there had either moved to Moulmein or other provinces; some had died. Tha E was preaching in Rangoon on his own initiative and was pastor of the small church. Judson had heard of Tha E's work and liked what he heard: "He is as solicitous and busy as a hen pressing about her chickens. It is quite refreshing to hear him…and see what a nice careful old shepherd he makes."[1]

But Adoniram felt Burma's interior tugging on his heart. It was with trepidation but determination that he hired a little boat and headed up the Irrawady toward Prome, about half the distance to Ava. Maung Ing and several of the disciples went with him. Everywhere they stopped, people wanted tracts. The first afternoon that Judson went ashore in a village and began conversing, a dozen people asked for one. On returning to the boat at sunset, he could see people on boats and others on shore reading the tracts, friends clustered about them asking questions.

Every day he heard it: "Teacher, give us a writing, give us a writing." Everyone wanted to hear about the "new gospel."[2] As Judson reached Prome, however, the atmosphere shifted. Prome had been badly terrorized during the war, and those memories were vivid in minds there. But by the end of June, Judson had been able to obtain an old *zayat* near a pagoda and to begin teaching. In less than a week, however, he was under suspicion as a "spy." Even hearing that word automatically brought a chill of dismay and too-vivid memories of persecution not too many miles distant. For some, the sight of a white face seemed frightening. Many appeared eager to hear his message anyway, while others turned away, fearing to be associated with a "foreigner."

Judson talked with all showing an interest, giving them tracts. More and more frequently, someone would approach him and say, "Are you Jesus Christ's man? Could you give me a writing?" Each time he heard it, it brought him up short. They literally looked to him as Christ's man; it was sobering.

Then word got to Ava that Judson was in Prome. This was a potential problem, for King Bagyidaw had never forgiven Judson for "deserting" him and leaving Ava. However, Judson continued to teach and give out portions of Scripture, only returning in September to Rangoon where he could better combine preaching and translation. All difficulties aside, he felt a quiet sense of satisfaction as their little boat started back down the Irrawady. He had been able to distribute five hundred tracts and knew of at least one convert. And just as he was leaving Prome, Maung Kwet Ni, secretary to the deputy governor, who had come many times to talk and listen, came to say goodbye: "Mark me down as your disciple," he called out. "I pray to God every day. Pray for me also." This warmed Judson's heart and rekindled his hope.

Enroute to Rangoon, he gave out five hundred more tracts. Whenever they would stop, people came to plead: "Teacher! Are you asleep? We want a writing to get by heart." Judson wrote to friends: "There is no period in my missionary life that I review with more satisfaction...than my sojourn in Prome."[3] Unfortunately, by the time he reached Rangoon, the Wades had left the city and the believers were under surveillance. Many people who were interested in hearing were intimidated by the threats of government reprisal, and few were bold enough to come as inquirers. Judson taught all who did come and immersed himself the rest of the time in translating.

Never far from his mind was the burning need to finish the Bible, and not just to finish it but to make it as accurate and perfect as possible. He admitted that he had a "lust to finish," a drive to make the entire Bible available to Burma. The disciples occupied the lower floor of the old house, while Judson translated in the "garret," a small room with little furniture but with hordes of bats flitting around every evening. On January 19, 1831, he recorded that he had completed Genesis, twenty chapters of Exodus, Psalms, Song of Solomon, Isaiah, and Daniel.[4] His inspiration in the midst of the slow and sometimes painful process of translating was the fact that inquirers still came. The government's menacing presence always lingered nearby, but still the people came to get "a writing" from the teacher, and to learn from him the Good News.[5]

In 1831 the great annual festival at Shwe Dagon pagoda was in February. The next week Judson wrote that he had distributed "nearly ten thousand tracts, giving to none but those who ask. I presume there have been six thousand applications at the house. Some come two or three months' journey, from the borders of Siam and China—'Sir, we hear that there is an eternal hell. We are afraid of it. Do give us a writing that will tell us how to escape it.' Others come from the frontiers of Kathay.…'Sir, we have seen a writing that tells about an eternal God. Are you the man that gives away such writings? If so, pray give us one, for we want to know the truth before we die.' Others come from the interior of the country, where the name of Jesus Christ is little known—'Are you Jesus Christ's man? Give us a writing.'" And to Baptists in America, Judson constantly stressed the need for more workers and support: "And thanks be to God, our labors are not in vain. We have three lovely churches, and about two hundred baptized converts.…O, if we had about twenty more versed in the language, and means to spread schools and tracts, and Bibles, to any extent, how happy I should be!"[6]

Word came that Deborah Wade's health had failed and they must take a sea voyage. Judson packed his translation materials and soon sailed for Moulmein. On July 31, his boat docked and joyful Burman Christians and the mission group celebrated his return. It was 1831, and Adoniram Judson had been in Burma seventeen years. A total of twenty-four missionaries had been sent during that time, including Ann, himself, and Luther Rice. Only twelve remained; the others had died or left. The Wades, Bennetts, and Kincaids were in Moulmein. Bennett was fully occupied with printing; the Wades had to leave because of Deborah's health, and Kincaid was pastor of the English-speaking church. There was only Judson to preach in Burmese.[7]

Then tragic news came from Tavoy, where the Masons had joined the Boardmans. George Dana Boardman had just died of tuberculosis. In spite of rapidly failing health, he had gone with Sarah, little George, and Francis Mason on a three-day journey into the jungle.

The Karens carried Boardman on a cot for he was too weak to walk. From a bamboo chapel beside a stream, Boardman watched as Mason baptized thirty-eight Karens. A huge thunderstorm hit and Boardman was soaked; the next morning, still wet and cold, he was placed on a boat, but it was too late. Sarah, little George, and hundreds of grieving Karens were with him as he died.[8]

Adoniram wrote to Sarah: "My dear sister, You are now drinking the bitter cup whose dregs I am somewhat acquainted with. And though, for some time, you have been aware of its approach, I venture to say that it is far bitterer than you expected....I can assure you that months and months of heart-rending anguish are before you, whether you will or not,...yet take the bitter cup with both hands, and sit down to your repast. You will soon learn a secret, that there is sweetness at the bottom."[9] Judson encouraged Sarah to stay. The Karens loved and respected her, looking to her for leadership. Sarah decided to remain. Little George had been the only one of their three children to survive, and he went everywhere with his mother as she traveled and taught. Among the Karens, Sarah became something of a legend herself.

Progress in all areas of the work was encouraging to Judson. His health was amazingly good; he was forty-three but looked younger. In light of what Judson had endured, that was astounding. He regularly walked and exercised. The years in fetters had changed his gait, making his steps rise higher, as if to compensate for the weights which so long had dragged on his feet. What time he could spare, Judson spent preaching in the jungles; the pioneering spirit had never left him, never mind that he was senior missionary and looked to from every side for advice. Adoniram knew the language and the people better than anyone outside their culture; everything the Burmese knew about God had come from him, either directly or through his writings and translations. Ann's catechism also continued to be widely used and highly effective.

In September, Judson spent two weeks on a preaching trip to the jungle, reveling in the direct contact with eager listeners. Then fever struck, and he reluctantly returned to Moulmein but took with him three Karens to attend an adult school he had opened. They trained there and then returned to their people to share the message.[10] Wade had studied the Karen language and was able to translate Ann Judson's catechism and Adoniram's "A View of Religion" into Karen. This put tools in the hands of the believers.

The new year of 1832 arrived. Judson was well and returned to the jungle with several disciples. The rivers were their roadways, and the farther they went, the more difficult became the journey. Disciples got on-the-job training. Many people along the trails believed and were baptized. People gravitated to this magnetic man who had a special gift for making them feel loved.

In the village of "Newville," Adoniram heard the story of an elderly couple. A couple who resided in the jungle and had never seen a foreigner, had obtained the blessed "writing" and died in the faith. The husband, just before his death, requested his friends to lay the tract "View of the Christian Religion" on his quieted breast and bury it with him.[11]

The six weeks Judson spent in the jungle was as strenuous as any trip he had ever made and sorely tested his stamina, but he was exhilarated upon his return to Moulmein. The response of the "wild Karens" had been inspiring, and he had baptized twenty-five new believers.

Much of what Judson believed about the importance of the church and of evangelism is clear from reading his journals. He sent sections of the journal to the Baptist missionary magazine, and running like a golden thread through his records was his theory of missions: learn by doing and being. Experience became his great teacher. In a letter to Hamilton Theological Institution, he addressed those considering mission service, warning potential candidates about the reality of "culture shock," although that term was unknown in the 1800s. Judson explained how candidates needed to be prepared for fatigue and disappointment, to beware of pride, to maintain physical exercise, and to choose a spouse carefully. Above all, Judson stressed that a true missionary spirit was for life, making the point: "Do not fancy that you have a true missionary spirit, while you are intending all along to leave the heathen soon after acquiring their language. Leave them!—for WHAT? To spend the rest of your days in enjoying the ease and plenty of your native land?"[12]

Judson had learned by *living* the missions experience. One of his many adaptations was his style of preaching. He had adopted the Burmese custom of speaking in a *zayat*, where interested passersby could drop in, sit, listen, and discuss issues. Judson sat when he preached and knelt for prayer. His work was real oratory but done in a way appealing to the Burmans. He usually sat in an armchair beside a plain table placed upon a low platform.

Adoniram's sermons abounded in word pictures, a method particularly appealing to the Eastern mind. One who frequently heard him reported that when he preached, "Every hearer sat motionless, with every eye fixed immovably upon the preacher....Every countenance seemed to change with every varied expression of sentiment; now beaming forth joy as though some joyous news from the other world had just reached them, which before had never gladdened their hearts; now depicting a feeling of anxiety, as though their immortal all...was at stake....'Though I did not know the meaning of a single sentence he uttered,' said one visitor [a new missionary], 'still my attention was never more closely riveted on any sermon I ever heard. It was impossible to escape the conviction that his whole soul was in his work.'"[13]

One day Judson recorded a very special journal entry—the baptism of Mah-ree (Mary Hasseltine) when she was twelve years old. Mary was the only child from Ann's school in Ava who had survived.[14] Adoniram's journal revealed how seriously the believers took baptism: "Several applications for baptism have lately been refused, the applicants being relatives of professors of religion, and influenced, we fear, by the example and persuasion of others, rather than by the impulse of grace. To-day, however, a clear case occurred—an old lady eighty years of age, mother-in-law of a petty chief, who is one of our bitterest opposers. She commenced her inquiries several months ago with a great deal of timidity. And though she has acquired a little courage, and is a person of considerable presence, she almost trembles under a sense of the great

169

responsibility of changing her religion. Such being her character, the promptness with which she answered our questions, before the church, affected us even to tears. 'How old are you, mother?' 'Eighty years.' 'Can you, at such an age, renounce the religion that you have followed all your life long?' 'I see that it is false and I renounce it all.' 'Why do you wish to be baptized into the religion of Jesus Christ?' 'I have very, very many sins; and I love the Lord, who saves from sin.'...Her name is Mai Hlah."[15] Adoniram joyfully baptized her.

Cephas Bennett was giving full time to printing. Along with tracts, he had already begun printing Judson's newest version of the New Testament. Judson became convinced that he must concentrate on completing the Bible. About one-third of the Old Testament was finished, and Adoniram felt that if he could give himself exclusively to this task, he could finish the whole in two years. Otherwise it could drag on interminably.[16] The Wades were back and agreed to take charge of the Moulmein church. Adoniram prepared a room "at the end of the native chapel" and set to work. It was as if for two years he shut himself into this spot and poured out his intellectual might into a finely tuned, intensely accurate translation from Hebrew to Burmese. The entire community of believers keenly felt the importance of his task and did their part in making it possible for him to accomplish this immense undertaking.

An unusual story came to light half a century later, told by Daw Lone Ma of Moulmein. Young Lone and her parents had lived near the mission compound, and they, like all the Burmese believers, knew of the *Sayagyi's* vital work of translating. She related: "From his house to the chapel there was a covered path about fifteen feet long, and at one end of the latter, there was a little room in which he spent his time in literary work. In going to his study one day, he stopped to drink water from a stand put for public use....My mother, hearing of this incident, entrusted me with the duty of filling a small chatty of water with which I would daily creep into his study and leave it there, covered with a clean napkin. It was a joy to me to do this service for one I revered very much."[17]

Throughout 1832 and 1833, Adoniram applied himself to painstaking translation. The Wades' health was shattered yet again, and they had to leave for America for a period of time. Bennett was printing the new revision of the New Testament even as Adoniram labored to complete the Old. He set himself a goal of twenty-five to thirty verses a day. The assignment Judson had set himself was massive, but that early trait was still very evident; he never did anything by halves. His intellect and energies were dedicated to this consuming goal: the whole Bible in Burmese. The dark days of sorrow had evolved into a sense of loss and loneliness, but Judson's focus was clear and his heart committed. He was determined to complete the translation.

CHAPTER 17

The Family
1834-1845

Only extant photograph of the original Judson house
in Moulmein. Courtesy of Dr. Harold Haswell.

A lovely lady garmented in light from her own beauty.
—Percy Bysshe Shelley, *The Witch of Atlas*

AS THE MONUMENTAL TASK OF TRANSLATION NEARED COMPLETION,
Adoniram's emotions, so long immobile, began to respond again.
The old Judson had been optimistic and sociable, and his former sensitivity to emotions, to beauty and great thoughts, began to reappear.
He developed deep friendships with missionaries who had quietly
encouraged him during his years of grieving. Adoniram often called
the Bennetts and Wades his dearest and best of friends.

Judson's perspective on life broadened as he drew near to the fulfillment of his goal of completing the Burmese Bible. There was a special satisfaction about this project, for it was one he and Ann had
embarked upon together, one fundamental to their aim of making the
gospel accessible to Burma. Ann would have been elated that the task
was complete.

His journal had the usual short entry denoting milestones: "1834, Jan 31st, finished the translation of the Old Testament."[1] Later that day he wrote: "Thanks be to God,...I have knelt down before him, with the last leaf in my hand...[and] I have dedicated it to his glory."[2] The work had been twenty-one years in the making. In a real sense, Adoniram began a new life. Just weeks after the completion of the Bible he received a letter from Sarah Boardman: "February 17, 1834. My Dear Brother, The translation of the Bible into Burmese is an event, to which thousands have looked forward with joyful anticipation...and through which, thousands yet unborn will praise him for ever and ever....I have, for the last four years, been in the daily practice of reading attentively the New Testament in Burmese; and the more I study it, the better I am pleased and satisfied with the translation...and think many of the doctrinal passages are expressed with a force and perspicuity entirely wanting in our version. How much of this is due to your vivid manner of expression, and how much to the nature of the language, I do not know." Sarah concluded, "Last Lord's-day, while reading a portion of Scripture, I was affected to tears, and could scarcely proceed, as is often the case, in reading striking passages; and the effect was also observable on the old Tavoyan, for he managed to bring a great part of it into his prayer, which immediately followed. Yours affectionately, Sarah H. Boardman."[3]

Judson had long admired the Boardmans and had grieved when George died. His respect for Sarah only grew as he saw her continuing commitment even when she was alone and with the responsibility of a child. Maybe the idea had been growing in Judson's mind that when he completed his great task, he could consider his personal life again. No one knows. No records remain of other correspondence between Judson and Sarah in the months before April 1834.

However, on April 1, Adoniram left Moulein for Tavoy. Arriving on April 6, he made an entry in his journal four days later. Most entries were one or two lines; this one took four: "1834, April 10, was married to Mrs. Sarah H. Boardman, who was born at Alstead NH Nov. 3, 1803, the oldest daughter of Ralph and Abiah O. Hall, married to George D. Boardman July 4, 1825, left a widow Feb. 11, 1831, with one surviving child, George D. Boardman, born Aug. 18, 1828."[4] Adoniram was usually impulsive in decision-making and Sarah more deliberate. Apparently, they found swift agreement together in the matter of their marriage.

Fifty years later, their son Edward wrote of "that beautiful and intrepid woman," saying that in her Judson had found a "kindred spirit."[5] She validated the truth of that commendation many times over, and the following years further illuminated the purity of her soul and ministry. Edward was unable to write about Sarah from his own memory because he was just eight months old when she died. Instead, Edward described his mother through the eyes of those who had known her. He wrote about her "faultless features, moulded on the Grecian model, beautiful transparent skin, warm, meek blue eyes, and soft hair, brown in the shadow and gold in the sun."[6]

Adoniram grieved in years to come that there was no known portrait of her: "I exceedingly regret that there is no portrait of the second as of the first Mrs. Judson. Her soft blue eyes, her mild aspect, her lovely face and elegant form, have never been delineated on canvass. They must soon pass away from the memory even of her children, but they will remain forever enshrined in her husband's heart."[7]

Shortly after Sarah's birth, her parents, Ralph and Abiah Hall, moved first to Danvers and then Salem, Massachusetts, where Sarah grew up, the oldest of thirteen children. The Halls never prospered financially, and Sarah's formal schooling was sporadic at best. Her mother depended heavily on Sarah in caring for the little ones. Even as a child, Sarah was characterized by both a gentle spirit and a strong determination to learn. She was largely self-educated. Gifted intellectually, the more she learned, the more she longed to study. She was converted as a teenager and baptized by her pastor, Lucius Bolles, the same Bolles to whom Adoniram had written in 1812, appealing for Baptists to organize a mission board.

Sarah showed an early talent for poetry. The idea of missions and a world in need captured her heart. When news came that the Judsons' little Roger had died, thirteen-year-old Sarah composed a poem of tribute. The plight of American Indians also caught Sarah's imagination, and as a teenager, she heard the story of heroic young Catherine Brown, an early Cherokee convert. Catherine had become the first Indian teacher at Creek Path Mission in Guntersville, Alabama. Catherine died of tuberculosis when only twenty-three and was buried near the mission school. On hearing of her death, Sarah wrote a beautiful poem of tribute titled "Catherine's Grave."[8]

Sarah also learned of the death of young James Colman who had gone to Burma and died so prematurely, and she wrote an elegy to him that greatly impressed the Christian community in Salem. When Ann Judson made one of her rare public appearances in 1823, Sarah was there. She was thrilled to see the famous missionary in person, but was mortified when several of the leaders insisted that she read before Mrs. Judson her elegy to James Colman. Sarah remembered years later how embarrassed she was to read publicly before the esteemed Ann Judson. Never in her wildest imagination could she have foreseen how their lives would one day be linked.

The mission zeal and poetic skills of young Sarah naturally reached the ears of George Dana Boardman, a missions volunteer. Having read of the death of Colman as well, Boardman determined to go to Burma himself. He was eager to meet Sarah Hall and was as amazed by her beauty as he had been impressed by her missions interest. The inevitable happened, and two years later they were married by Lucius Bolles. So loved was Sarah by her congregation that when the members learned that she was marrying Boardman, one lady exclaimed, "Oh dear, why couldn't they have taken someone to be a missionary that everybody didn't love!"[9]

Shortly after the wedding, the Boardmans sailed for Burma. The war there was in full spate, so they made their way first to India, using their time in Calcutta to study Burmese. Both were linguistically gifted and learned Burmese with formidable speed. Sarah made an impression on Indians and Europeans alike, her beauty and grace widely acknowledged.

The Boardmans had arrived in Moulmein early in 1827, just days before the death of little Maria Judson. They began work in Moulmein, and it was purely a pioneer experience, from tigers and cobras from the jungle just beyond the cleared area, to encounters with robbers. As the mission began to grow, the Boardmans moved to Tavoy and began work among the Karens. It was also in Tavoy that Sarah buried her young husband. There too were the graves of two-and-a-half-year-old Sarah Ann and the baby Judson Wade, dead at eight months old.

Friends described Sarah as "singularly modest and retiring."[10] The easy route for the young widow would have been to return to America with her surviving son, six-year-old George. Most expected her to do so, although in Judson's letter of sympathy, he had encouraged her to remain in her vital work. Sarah clearly knew that she had been called to missions many years earlier. When the Bolles wrote from Salem, inviting her to return to America and live with them, Sarah read the letter and wept—and remained in Tavoy.

The Karens' "White Mamma" assumed the full load of the work when Boardman died, devoting to the task all her skills and talent. Boardman had preached in remote Karen areas deep in the jungle, and Sarah did the same. One biographer pictured her making her way through wild mountain passes, following obscure jungle paths and fording streams.[11] Little George traveled on the shoulders of one of the Karen disciples and went right along with his mother into the depths of the jungle. Several biographers tell the story of an English hunter alone in the wilds, who one morning looked up and saw a beautiful white woman walking toward him through the mists, and he thought for a moment it was "an angel visitant from a better sphere."[12]

Sarah wore many hats, personally instructing Karen women and continuing her translation work. Not only did she care for little George and make frequent jungle trips, she also directed the seven Karen schools that she had begun. They became part of the Bengali school system, and Sarah would only agree to operate them if Christian instruction was allowed. So successful were her methods that the British agreed to her condition, learning from her great success how to administer and conduct schools over a vast area of British territory.

With her marriage to Adoniram in 1834, Sarah assumed a new role: still a missionary and wife of Burma's pioneer missionary. Years later when asked about Sarah, Adoniram proclaimed that he had been "much blessed with two of the best of wives," that he could say in truth that Sarah was in every point of natural and moral excellence, the worthy successor of Ann Hasseltine Judson.[13] On April 16, the Judsons arrived in Moulmein, which was much changed since Sarah had last lived there. Their house was right in the middle of the mission compound, a clear indication that Adoniram was no longer a recluse. The printing press was only about a hundred steps from their door.[14] Clearly, a new chapter in life had begun for the Judsons.

No chapter in the life of an early missionary family, however, was ever uneventful. Six days after they were married, Adoniram and Sarah's boat docked in Moulmein. But no sooner had they arrived than the dysentery that had affected Sarah so often in Burma struck with renewed force. She was extremely pale and lost what little appetite she had, becoming so weak she could not get out of bed. At one point, doctors despaired of her life. On good days, Adoniram would carry her to a couch for a change of scenery. During her recuperation, however, Sarah had time with George, giving him her undivided attention, something she had seldom been able to do.

As Sarah began to gain strength, Adoniram got her a small horse, and after several months of steady exercise, Sarah was greatly improved. The horse died a few months later and was mourned by all of them, but by that time Sarah could begin walking with Adoniram early each morning in the hills above Moulmein. The little family group was enjoying life together, but a painful separation was to come.

Sarah had decided years before that in order to ensure that her son would have a chance to live to adulthood, he must go to America. Too many children had died in the Orient of the early 1800s. It was the hardest decision Sarah ever faced. Though scarcely able to bear the thought, she felt there was no other choice. In December, the *Cashmere* arrived with new missionaries. Two of them, J. T. Jones and William Dean, were going on to Singapore and could care for little George; later, from Singapore to Boston, the crew would assume his care. Judson's journal read: "1834, Dec. 13, George D. Boardman embarked on the *Cashmere* for America."[15]

The description of his parting from his mother is wrenching. George was six years and four months old. Sarah wrote her sisters about the parting moment: "My eyes are rolling down with tears and I can scarcely hold my pen. Oh! I shall never forget his looks, as he stood by the door and gazed at me for the last time. His eyes were filling with tears and his little face red with suppressed emotion. But he subdued his feelings and it was not till he had turned away and was going down the steps that he burst into a flood of tears."[16] Adoniram had to leave Sarah on her knees, weeping. He carried George in his arms to the boat that would take them out to the *Cashmere*, anchored some miles away. Adoniram comforted the sobbing child as best he could, and after getting him settled into his little cabin and introducing him to the friends who would care for him, he too had to leave and told little George that he would go "comfort Mama."[17] All the missionaries on board fell in love with the winsome six-year-old. After a brief stay in Singapore, the ship was ready to head for Boston. Missionaries Jones and Dean took George with them on a small boat out to where the *Cashmere* was anchored some fifteen miles offshore.

It was a blessing that Sarah Judson did not know what happened next or how close to death her son came. The experience would have terrified anyone, to say nothing of a sheltered little boy. George and the missionaries were rowing to the *Cashmere* when there appeared out of nowhere another boat with three fierce-looking Malays rowing in their direction. The Malays came alongside and innocently asked for some fruit; J. T. Jones stood up to hand it to them, whereupon the Malays violently pushed him overboard. George hid as best he could under a bench and saw everything. Another of the pirates stabbed William Dean with a fishing spear, and the little boy watched in horror as his friend's blood dripped to the floor of the boat. The pirates spied a metal box of mission letters, and thinking it treasure, they grabbed it and took off. Jones, not quite drowned, was hauled back on board, and a petrified little boy and two wounded missionaries were finally rescued by a fishing boat. George D. Boardman never forgot his first experience on the high seas—the images haunted him the rest of his life.

When a version of the terrifying adventure reached Sarah over a year later, she could only tremble and give fervent thanks for protection. Sarah never saw her eldest son again, but how her heart would have rejoiced to see the grown George D. Boardman Jr. as pastor of First Baptist Church, Philadelphia, and the author of many books.

The year 1835 was really the beginning of married life for Sarah and Adoniram. Her loving and gentle spirit was balm to his lonely heart. Both Judsons were so endowed with skills essential to effective evangelization, that the problem became how to best use all their gifts. In spite of other demands, the language abilities of both required that they spend much of their time in translation. The majority of Moulmein's people were Peguans (also called Talings or Mons.) Already fluent in Burmese and Karen, Sarah turned her talents to yet another sphere, learning Peguan and translating tracts and catechisms into the language of those people.

Adoniram was already busy with *revising* the Bible. Always a perfectionist, he felt every word must be perfectly accurate and perfectly Burmese. One of the secrets of his stellar translation was that it was absolutely unambiguous to any Burmese who read it. Judson was both chagrined and amused when, shortly after his marriage to Sarah, an elderly Christian came to him much disturbed and confessed that he was fearful that "Yoodthan" would be among the lost. "You know," the old man explained, "the Bible says that God will deliver his children from the snare of the 'widow.' But he has not delivered you; you have been snared by the widow." Puzzled, Adoniram turned to the passage, Psalm 91:3. The feminine form of the word *hunter* had been used, which in Burmese meant "widow." Judson revised the passage with great haste.[18]

Sarah had another ability that mirrored Adoniram's: doing a multitude of tasks and excelling at all of them. She organized prayer meetings and mothers' classes in addition to writing hymns that became the foundation of the Burmese hymnbook. Meanwhile, Adoniram had more tasks than time, including preaching seven sermons a week. Early every morning, he and Sarah would take a brisk walk and then meet with the assistants who did daily preaching.

Judson listened to them, prayed with them, and trained them in evangelism. He possessed a remarkable ability for discerning and developing the individual talents of each assistant.[19] Judson was also pastor of the Moulmein church. He knew every one of the one hundred members personally and spent time nurturing them.

A favorite task of Judson's was performing baptisms. One was memorable; it was Koo-chil, the Bengali cook who had so faithfully served Adoniram and Ann during the years of separation and imprisonment. Several times as Ann's sole caregiver, Koo-chil had saved her life. Ann's death had devastated him, but he remained with the mission the rest of his life. Koo-chil had maintained an allegiance all those years to Mohammed, whom he feared. He married a Burmese Christian and then came with great deliberation to that commitment himself. Judson wrote: "The process was slow, the struggle strong...and when he made his formal request for baptism, he trembled all over. Poor old man! He is above sixty; his cheeks are quite fallen in; his long beard is quite gray; he has probably but a short time to live....He affectionately remembers his old mistress, and frequently sheds tears when speaking of the scenes of Ava and Amherst, where he saw her suffer and die."[20]

Judson reported each year on baptisms in each station. One hundred twenty were baptized in 1835, bringing the total number to 786. By 1838, he wrote his sister in Plymouth that there were more than a thousand converts in the various churches. At the end of 1835, when Judson sent the final sheet of the Old Testament revision to press, he wrote his mother, recalling an earlier time: "I used to think when first contemplating a missionary life, that, if I should live to see the Bible translated and printed in some new language, and a church of one hundred members raised up on heathen ground, I should anticipate death with the peaceful feelings of Old Simeon."[21]

Naturally, he was not satisfied, even though all those goals had been surpassed. Judson's nature was such that he possessed a "divine unrest," always wanting to achieve more.[22] And, typical for Judson, who was never typical, he was at forty-seven becoming a new father again. On the last day of October 1835, little Abigail Ann Judson was born, named for Adoniram's sister and in memory of Ann Judson. By the time visitors arrived from America in February 1836, little Abby was becoming, as Adoniram described her, "a sweet, fat baby."[23]

Missionaries arrived on the *Louvre* to strengthen the mission. Howard Malcom was also on board, the first-ever member of the Baptist missionary board to visit mission fields. Malcom was eager to meet Judson, who had become almost a legend in America, having been in Asia longer than any missionary alive. Meeting the man himself did not dim the fascination. Malcom called him "the most interesting man alive."[24] Adoniram himself did not realize how Burman he had become, attuned to Burmese thinking in a way no foreigner had ever been. Until Malcom arrived, Judson had not heard a sermon in English for fourteen years.

As the *Louvre* docked, Malcom saw a middle-sized man quick-stepping toward the landing, calling out joyfully, "Mr. Malcom, you have brought me treasures!"[25] Malcom was amazed at his first sight of Judson. This was the man who had endured prison for almost two years? He was forty-seven? Judson's thick auburn hair showed no gray. Bright and vigorous, his look and his step belied his years.

During those quiet years in Moulmein, Adoniram related that he wished he could write more interesting communications, "but what can be expected from a man who spends his days at a study table?"[26] Compared to Adoniram and Ann's early adventures and trials, this quiet family life seemed a world away. And for Sarah, this domestic tranquility was a whole new life.

After the birth of "sweet, fat baby" Abby Ann, came Adoniram Brown Judson, born April 7, 1837. (Adoniram's mother's surname was Brown.) Judson's letters to his mother and sister were full of the sayings and doings of the little Judsons. In spite of massive schedules, he and Sarah were loving and involved parents. When the smallest Judson, called Pwen (meaning "flower") by the doting Burmans, was about a year old, Adoniram wrote his family about their "highly intelligent little ones." "Little Adoniram," wrote his proud father, "is one of the prettiest, brightest children you ever saw....Abby is growing fast. She runs about, and talks Burman quite fluently, but no English.

I am not troubled about her not getting English at present, for we shall have to send her home in a few years, and then she will get it of course. She attends family and public worship with us, and has learned to sit still and behave herself. But…Pwen, as the natives call him, when he is brought into the chapel, and sees me in my place, has the impudence to roar out Bah (as the Burmans call father), with such a stentorian voice, that his nurse is obliged to carry him out again."[27]

Son Elnathan was born July 15, 1838, and a little over a year later, on December 31, 1839, another son, Henry, arrived. Adoniram commented: "Master Henry came into notice the last day of the year but there was no earthquake or anything."[28] Sarah was now the mother of four children under the age of four and was obliged to ask James Haswell to assume most of the Peguan translation.

Adoniram, now fifty, realized he had severe throat and lung problems. He had a constant cough and began to lose his voice, that preaching tool he used with such consummate skill. The tuberculosis that would eventually take his life had already begun. He could no longer preach; even conversation was a strain. The usual prescription of the British doctors was given again—a sea voyage. Consequently, shortly after Henry's birth, Judson left on the *Snipe*. He had never been away from his young family for more than a few days, and it was a painful goodbye. Judson's throat was improved by the time he reached Calcutta, and he visited friends there and at Serampore. His last time in that city had been in 1812. The "Serampore Three" (Carey, Ward, and Marshman) were no more. Judson lamented that "the glory had departed from Serampore."[29]

The Judsons' letters to each other during this separation vividly mirror the depth of their love. Sarah's letter written just after Adoniram sailed was a poignant tribute to the tender feelings they shared. Sarah wrote: "As soon as you left the house, I ran to your dressing-room, and watched you from the window. But you did not look up—oh, how I wished you would! Then I hastened to the back veranda, and caught one last glimpse of you through the trees…and I gave vent to my feelings in a flood of tears….I have often wondered that I should have been so singularly blessed as to possess that heart,

182

which is far more precious than all the world beside."[30]

Judson was ever a master letter writer, and his to Sarah were no exception. He wrote: "I should have been so happy to have had you with me. If such exquisite delights as we have enjoyed with those now in paradise, and with one another, are allowed to sinful creatures on earth, what must the joys of heaven be? Surely there is not a single lawful pleasure, the loss of which we shall have to regret there. What high and transporting intercommunion of souls we may, therefore, anticipate, and that to all eternity!"[31] When he wrote Sarah that he was returning, he concluded the letter, "And how joyfully do I hope to see your dear face, and take you in my loving arms, and find again 'that home is home.'"[32] Adoniram's lungs and throat seemed almost totally healed, but Moulmein's rainy season soon brought the trouble back. He was able to carry on conversations, however, so the rest of his work continued unabated.

With four small children and a host of responsibilities, Sarah still managed to complete a remarkably accurate Burmese translation of *Pilgrim's Progress*; it is still in use. Years later Adoniram told her parents in America: "It was marvelous to me how she could accomplish so much and in so many ways. She would sit with one child in her arms, another by her side, and translate and write at the same time."[33] He praised her language, saying that none surpassed her in either speaking or writing Burmese. High praise indeed, considering Judson's own linguistic ability.

Adoniram loved to play with the children. He would romp with the boys and often ended up on the floor on his hands and knees playing horse. One biographer recounted what it was like during the family years in Moulmein: "Bluebeard and Jack the Giant Killer...were familiar figures around the mission compound, for Judson's boys were real boys and Abby was a boy with them. And Judson had not forgotten his own boyhood love for good stories. The stone baptistery when drained was a fine place to play. One day it was a den of lions, with Elnathan...as Daniel and Abby Judson...[and friends] as the roaring lions....Occasionally they even had a 'baptismal' service, with young Adoniram taking the place of his revered father and one

of the smaller children serving as the candidate—summarily interrupted one day when they heard a voice up on the bank and recognized it as that of Papa Judson."[34]

"Papa" was always aware, no matter what he was doing, that
completing a dictionary was high priority. The grammar had been
difficult to prepare but was quite concise. A Burmese-English,
English-Burmese dictionary, however, was essential for use by all missionaries and was a massive undertaking. There was no other person
capable of the endeavor. Judson himself much preferred "the real
work" of a missionary, but knew that a dictionary was a priority.
Reluctantly he set himself to the task but continued his "real" work
as often as possible. He wrote a friend that the dictionary was "such
a chaotic affair and seems to me so unmissionary, that I am constantly hoping that something will turn up to relieve me from the work."[35]
Something did, but not something he would ever have chosen.

Sarah: 1845

This photocopy of Sarah Judson's portrait is the only possible likeness of her thought to exist. Used by permission of the American Baptist Historical Society.

Give sorrow words: the grief that
　does not speak
Whispers the o'er-fraught heart,
　and bids it break.
—William Shakespeare, *Macbeth*

TROUBLES SELDOM SEEMED TO COME singly. All the children became ill with whooping cough and three of them were also hit with dysentery. Then on March 8, 1841, Sarah gave birth to a stillborn son, Luther, and was struck herself with dysentery. Adoniram nearly lost her and two of the children. Doctors insisted they go to sea, and in June, the suffering family embarked for Calcutta.[1] To compound their woes, the voyage was terrible. The ship was blown off course, hit a shoal, and then limped into port in Calcutta. Serampore seemed to be the best place to rest and recover, but the weather there was scorchingly hot. Doctors prescribed yet another sea voyage, this one to a more temperate climate. Then an old friend came calling—Captain Hamlin of the *Ramsey*, whom Adoniram had met years ago in Rangoon. He volunteered to take them to sea, so Sarah and the older two, improved now, went to Calcutta to buy needed supplies.

Meanwhile, eighteen-month-old Henry was growing worse. On July 28, his condition became critical, and Judson sent word to Sarah to return at once. She arrived in the middle of the night. Adoniram wrote to his mother and sister of the marks of death on Henry's little countenance: "We spent the day hanging over our dying babe, and giving him some liquid, for which he was always calling, to relieve his burning thirst. When I said, 'Henry, my son,' he would raise his sinking eyelids, and try to stretch out his little arms for me to take him; but he could not bear to be held more than a moment....In the afternoon he became convulsed for a few moments, and our hearts were rent to witness the distortion of his dear little mouth and face....In the evening he had another turn of convulsion. His mother lay down by his side, and, worn out with fatigue, fell fast asleep. About nine o'clock I had gone into another room, and was lying down, when a servant called me. He began to breathe loud, indicative of the closing scene. I let the mother sleep—sat down by his side, and presently called, as usual, 'Henry, my son,' upon which he opened his eyes, and looked at me more intelligently and affectionately than he had been able to do for some time; but the effort was too great, and he ceased to breathe. I instantly awoke his mother; he then gave two or three expiring gasps, and it was all over."[2]

Once again, Adoniram and Sarah endured crushing loss. They would forever remember the sorrow of Rangoon, Amherst, Tavoy, and now Serampore. Eventually the desolate family set to sea, and in spite of violent squalls, reached the Isle of France, spent a month there recuperating, and arrived back in Moulmein six months after leaving, just before Christmas.

The following February, they moved into a more convenient house. Adoniram had a little guest house built, hoping to persuade his sister, if she were left alone, to come and stay a long while. Judson did not yet know that his mother had just died. Abigail Brown Judson had lived to be eighty-three. She had not seen Adoniram in thirty years. (His sister Abby never made it to Moulmein.) Adoniram realized that Sarah's health was indeed frail, and he gave an increasing amount of time to caring for the little ones. And their number increased yet again. Henry Hall, named for his little brother buried there in Serampore, was born July 8, 1842, and then in December 1843, Charles was born. There were now five living children.

On December 27, 1844, Edward was born, and Sarah was further weakened by all the childbearing. Dysentery hit again. As usual, a sea voyage was prescribed, and nine-year-old Abby went sailing with her mother. For those six weeks away, Adoniram wrote fond letters to his only daughter and kept her abreast of all that was happening with her little brothers. In one letter, he described the youngest family member: "Edward has become a fat little fellow; I am sure you would not know him again. He begins to look pleased when he is played with. But he has not yet made any inquiries about his absent mother and sister. Indeed, I doubt much whether he is aware that he has any such relatives...and does not know what a fair, beautiful, fond mother he has at Mergui, who thinks of him every day. However, when he gets larger, we will tell him all about these matters."[3]

But Sarah did not improve. Adoniram was shocked by her appearance when she returned; something had to be done. Sarah's doctor informed him that her only real hope was the cooler, more bracing climate of America. There seemed no other choice. Adoniram had never planned to return to America. His was a mission for life. But Sarah was a vital part of that life. They would go. A painful decision had to be made; they must leave Henry, Charlie, and Edward with missionary friends. The family's plight was devastating, for Henry was only two and a half, Charlie sixteen months, and Edward not quite four months old.

On April 26, the ship *Paragon* sailed with Sarah, Adoniram, and the three older children. Those children were leaving the only world they knew for the alien world of America. They must remain there for an education, far away from home. Parents and children alike dreaded the thought of parting. Sarah was so weak that she had to be carried aboard ship. There was some comfort in knowing that the little ones were in loving hands. Mrs. Haswell in Amherst would keep Henry; Mrs. Osgood would care for Charlie. Mrs. Stevens made the baby Edward like her own. But there was no good remedy for the aching heart of the frail mother who must leave them.

Adoniram devoted the days and nights to Sarah, making her as comfortable as possible.[4] Rough seas plagued them. Judson was a seasoned sailor, but on this trip, all of them were seasick. The Judsons had seldom known a smooth voyage. About the time they were passing near the Isle of France (Mauritius), the *Paragon* sprung a leak, and the captain decided he must put in at Port Louis for repairs. As they made for port, the weather was beautiful and the Indian Ocean under a canopy of stars, a sight the three children would never forget. One such night on deck, Sarah sang for all of them "The Star of Bethlehem." Forever imprinted on the minds of the Judson children was their mother singing so movingly that tribute to the Christ Child.[5]

Judson had written the mission board of the absolute necessity of the trip to save Sarah. He admitted his own reluctance to leave the work but keenly felt the urgency of caring for her. Adoniram explained that what he desired was a "quiet corner, where I can pursue my work…undisturbed and unknown." For thirty-three years, he had given himself to the mastery of Burmese, not just the language, but the very thought patterns and culture: "In order to become as acceptable and eloquent preacher in a foreign language," he wrote, "I deliberately abjured my own. When I crossed the river, I burned my ships. For thirty-two years I have scarcely entered an English pulpit or made a speech in that language…[and] the burned ships cannot now be reconstructed.…I can scarcely put three sentences together in the English language."[6]

It wasn't just lack of practice in English that was a problem for Adoniram; it was also lack of voice—literally. Judson's once-powerful voice had been greatly affected by his lung infection. He explained that his voice was very weak, and if he tried to preach, it would break down yet again. "I hope," he wrote, "that since there are thousands of preachers in English and only five or six Burmese preachers in the whole world, I may be allowed to hoard up the remnant of my breath and lungs for the country where they are most needed."[7]

In the long night reaches, Adoniram would think about those he would see in America. His sister had only been twenty-two when he left. She must be greatly changed. Judson felt that he himself had changed almost past recognition. He was wrong. He looked remarkably like the Adoniram of 1812, astounding in light of the sufferings of Ava. His face was slightly fuller and he had a few wrinkles around the eyes, but he did not look close to fifty-seven.[8]

Much of the essential Adoniram had altered, however. Twenty-four-year-old Judson had been self-confident to the point he could appear arrogant. Then prison and Ann's death had thrown him into a period of guilt and self-abasement, but the deeper, the real Adoniram had emerged and come to grips with life. Marriage to Sarah had mellowed and honed him. He exuded a genuine humility and compassion that blessed all those around him.[9]

This was the Judson who thought he could find a quiet corner to continue his work while helping Sarah recuperate. Neither happened. Upon reaching Port Louis, both Judsons were full of optimism. Sarah was stronger. The two reached yet another painful conclusion. Sarah was so much improved that she insisted she could go on alone and take the three children. Adoniram should return to Burma to care for the three little ones and continue his translations. On a piece of scrap paper, Sarah pondered the parting soon to come and wrote a poem about it, probably the most beautiful of all the excellent work she had produced. It began: "We part on this green islet, Love, Thou for the Eastern main, I for the setting sun, Love, O when to meet again?"[10]

As soon as they docked in Port Louis, Judson found an American ship due to leave in a few weeks. The seaworthy *Sophia Walker* was sailing directly for Boston, and so they could reach America a month faster. But as they waited for the ship to sail, Sarah had a massive relapse. There was no way Adoniram could leave her now. All five Judsons sailed on July 25. As they reached the Cape of Good Hope, the weather was colder and more bracing; Sarah rallied, but it didn't last long. She was one day improved, the next failing. Within weeks, they were nearing St. Helena, and it was painfully obvious that Sarah did not have long to live.

On August 26, the ship anchored. Sarah realized that she was dying; Adoniram knew it all too well. The children could not quite grasp such a reality. No such massive loss had entered their sheltered world as did this calamity. Life waned, and with Adoniram by her side during the night-watch, assuring her of his love, Sarah quietly ceased to breathe. The desolated Judson lovingly closed her eyes and dressed her for the final time. Then in sheer exhaustion, he threw himself down to sleep. Adoniram woke to the sounds of three weeping children, gathered around their mother, begging her to answer their cries.[11] The finality of death struck them—the mother who had been their joy and anchor all their short lives was gone.

The Christian community of St. Helena rallied round and took the grieving little family to its heart. Rev. James Bertram, a local missionary, had long heard of the Apostle of Burma. He came to the ship and had prayer with Adoniram and the children. The community pitched in to help, preparing a coffin for Sarah's body and mourning clothes for the children. Bertram accompanied them in a boat to shore. It was a sad and strange little funeral procession that left the ship. Judson and the children rode in a small boat, and in front of them was the boat bearing Sarah's body. St. Helena's shops closed in respect as the small procession went through the town.

People had chosen a beautiful shady spot beneath a spreading banyan tree for Sarah's resting place. Adoniram himself led in prayer to end the service. As he later wrote in his beautiful tribute to Sarah: "In the language of prayer, which we had often presented together at the throne of grace, I blessed God that her body had attained the repose of the grave and her spirit the repose of paradise."[12] In the flyleaf of a volume of Burmese hymns written by Sarah is an inscription written by Adoniram in which he says: "The wings of the Moulmein songstress are folded in St. Helena."[13]

The service had been at six in the evening. After a short rest in one of the homes, the exhausted and grieving father and children made their way back to the *Sophia Walker*. She sailed immediately. Adoniram wrote the next day to a friend that by "this morning, the rock of the ocean, where reposes all that is mortal of my dear, dear wife, was out of sight. And O, how desolate my cabin appears and how dreary the way before me!"[14]

To another, Judson said: "For a few days, in the solitude of my cabin, with my poor children crying around me, I could not help abandoning myself to heart-breaking sorrow. But the promise of the Gospel came to my aid, and faith stretched her view to the bright world of eternal life, and anticipated a happy meeting with those beloved beings whose bodies are mouldering at Amherst and St. Helena."[15] Adoniram doubly dreaded what lay ahead. He must part with his three oldest children and then go on alone. The task felt beyond him.

The *Sophia Walker* took six weeks to sail from St. Helena to Boston, six of the longest weeks of Judson's life as he and his three older children grieved. Adoniram reflected not just on his loss, but on all the ways Sarah had blessed him and all those around her. Time and time again he recalled her gentle touch, her loveliness that went soul-deep. Sarah was the one who had helped him turn the fluctuating beginnings in the Moulmein mission into phenomenal growth, and she had given him her absolute love and devotion. Now Judson's world was bereft of the blessing that had been Sarah. His indomitable spirit, however, rose above the crushing sorrow of loss and contemplated what lay ahead. Adoniram's personal wish would be to return at once to Burma and his work. This was impossible; his oldest children must first be settled in America. Judson's own emotions were an uneasy mixture of joy and dread. He would soon set foot once more on American soil. After nearly thirty-four years in an entirely different culture, he was facing change yet again. How much, he could not fully imagine.

The *Sophia Walker* reached Boston on October 15, 1845. Abby Ann, Adoniram, and Elnathan, those children of Burma, saw before their rapt eyes a noisy, bustling, and strange new world, completely foreign in sight and sound. Their weary father found it nearly as foreign. When Ann and Adoniram Judson had left in 1812, the struggling young nation was facing a second war with the British. Now the frontier stretched all the way west to the Pacific Ocean. James Polk was the eleventh president, and news of his election had traveled across the country by the new electric telegraph. Industrial cities were springing up, roads were fast multiplying, and railroads linked all of America's major cities. Small wonder it was difficult for Adoniram to find anything familiar before his eyes.

Tears clouded those penetrating eyes as he recalled the great anticipation and excitement of a handful of young, foolhardy missionaries who had sailed off from Salem and Philadelphia to conquer the world with the gospel. As far as Judson knew, he was the sole survivor. Ann lay under the hopia tree in Amherst. Luther Rice had died of ill health while still quite young. Samuel Mills had died at sea returning from Africa, and Samuel and Harriet Newell had been dead many years. Gordon Hall had died in India in 1826. Samuel and Roxanna Nott's fate he did not know, but he feared that they too were no longer living.

Rip Van Winkle had nothing on Adoniram Judson. Van Winkle had slept for only twenty years. Judson saw before him his "old" world all changed and new, but he had certainly not slept away the intervening years. He had instead become America's mission pioneer.

Immediately upon docking, Adoniram's hopes of a quiet spot to recoup and regain strength were dashed. He had been wondering where he and the children might find lodging that first night. Yet here before them, filling the quay of Boston Harbor, were throngs of people. Unbelievably, they were there to greet the famous Adoniram Judson, America's missionary hero. It was a stunning and difficult experience for a weary man who sought to avoid any spotlight.

That proved to be impossible. For over thirty years, religious publications as well as the secular press had recounted the exploits of Ann and Adoniram Judson. A nation had vicariously followed their struggles and their triumphs and had waited anxiously for "the next chapter" during the two interminable years of prison in Ava when no news came. Now everyone wanted to see this larger-than-life man. Ironically, of the thousands of Americans eager to greet the missionary hero, probably not even fifty had ever met him before. A new generation had grown up, but the press had made Judson seem very personal to Americans. As a youth, Judson had fought pride. Adulation had been a dream to the young Judson. Now with his maturity and depth of character, he literally shrank from publicity and the limelight.

Immediately Judson was thrust on platforms from city to city, and he recoiled from being on exhibition. To compound the problem, that deep and compelling voice had been nearly silenced by disease, and he could only manage to converse in a low voice. What could he do? He frequently commented on how he felt like he was being put on display, finding it distasteful to be so publicly eulogized. As Judson expressed it, he knew his own heart, shortcomings, and sins all too well, and he knew he was not all those grand things people were proclaiming.

Once while Judson was listening to words of eloquent praise heaped on him in the presence of a great crowd of people, "his head sank lower and lower until his chin seemed to touch his breast."[16]

What escape was there? The meetings began almost immediately. The ship had docked on Wednesday. By Friday a public meeting was planned in Boston to welcome the hero home. News spread, and the large Bowdoin Square Church was packed, both pews and aisles. The air was electric that night. To the hundreds crowded into the sanctuary, the wiry, medium-sized man standing on the podium was an almost mythic figure. After the introduction, Judson arose, and with a voice too frail to be heard in that vast auditorium, spoke softly to William Hague, pastor of Federal Street Church, who repeated Judson's words for all to hear. Judson said: "Through the mercy of God I am permitted to stand before you this evening a pensioner of your bounty. It is one of the severest trials of my life not being able to lift up my voice and give free utterance to my feelings."[17] He begged their continuing prayers for his brethren in Burma. Judson was unable to speak further, and Hague continued by telling of current circumstances in Burma.

Meanwhile, an elderly man was making his way slowly down the aisles, crowded as they were with listeners. The man did not hesitate but made his way up to the platform where Judson was sitting. Judson looked up at him, looked again, then leaped to his feet, clasped the man's hand, and embraced him. It was Samuel Nott. Adoniram had thought him long dead, but here he stood. He and Roxanne had been forced by ill health to return from India thirty years earlier. The two rejoiced in a reunion they had never dared hope would occur. As the congregation raptly watched, the message spread of just who this was. The eyes of an entire congregation welled with tears at the drama of that reunion.[18]

That first public meeting was the precursor of many to come. It was not that Judson was antisocial. He loved people and by nature was a sparkling conversationalist. But here was a man in frail health, weak of voice, and thrust into a new world. He longed for a short respite, some privacy and time with his children who were overwhelmed by their puzzling new world as well.

Judson felt rather like a freak in a sideshow, constantly on display yet practically mute. He would be so keyed up after a meeting that he could not sleep, which took a further toll on him. The Monday after his return, the mission board held a special meeting, and again Judson felt smothered. It was like the sensation of "everybody knows me—but I don't know anybody."

Within a week, however, he was able to get away and deal with the question of just what was best for his children's care. Adoniram first visited the Hasseltines in Bradford. When Adoniram had last seen Ann's mother, she had been younger than he was now. Rebecca Hasseltine was now eighty-four, and Ann's father had died. Next he visited the Halls, Sarah's parents and the in-laws he had never met, and he recounted to them in person the beauty of the life and ministry of their oldest child.

Adoniram had a severe cold, and winter was fast approaching, but there was much to do. He decided to place Adoniram and Elnathan with Dr. and Mrs. Newton, his friends in Worcester, where Sarah's seventeen-year-old son, George Boardman Jr., was also living. It was a poignant moment when the half-brothers met for the first time. In the meantime, Judson sent Abby Ann to his sister in Plymouth, and he followed a few days later. Plymouth was the home of his youth, the place where he had last seen his parents. Only Abigail remained, living alone in the house on Pleasant Street. Abigail had a great welcome for the brother she adored. She was nearly his sole remaining kin. Of all that Adoniram saw in America, one of the few scenes that looked like the memories of his youth was the view from his favorite window there in the Judson home. As he looked down at the familiar sight of Plymouth Harbor, he exclaimed, "This is the most natural scene I have looked upon in America!"[19]

The following months were a kind of "triumphal march" of the Apostle of Burmah, as some called it, with Judson speaking in the nation's largest cities and to small, select groups. A young mission volunteer who heard Judson speak at Hamilton Seminary wrote to his fiancée about Judson's address: "I feel I can hardly pass this Sabbath evening more profitably than in recalling to my own mind and seeking to convey to yours the hallowed scenes of the past day. It is a day I shall never forget—one of those days that make an indelible imprint on the memory....Judson has been here. Though he could speak but few words with his lips, the man spoke volumes. What a world of associations cluster around him."[20]

Judson's appearance—indeed, just his presence—was an energizer to the cause of missions and recruitment. His poignant plea at the special meeting of the Triennial Convention, where delegates had met to discuss retrenchment due to a $40,000 debt, led to the debt being completely erased and the work abroad expanded. Judson's influence was not limited to religious groups; he received secular honors as well. Soap magnate William Colgate wrote to his daughter concerning Judson in Washington: "Senator Marcy introduced him to...President [Polk] as the greatest ecclesiastical character now living....Mr. [Daniel] Webster offered to introduce him to the Senate but by some oversight it was not done."[21]

Everywhere Judson went, people wanted to hear of the thrilling exploits, adventures, and trials of his many years in Burma. They were usually doomed to disappointment. Judson brought messages through an "interpreter" and preached the story of salvation. Once a friend told him that people were disappointed.

"Why, what did they want?" Judson asked. "I presented the most interesting subject in the world to the best of my ability."

His friend explained, "But they wanted a story."

"Well, I am sure I gave them a story," replied Judson, "the most thrilling one that can be conceived of."

"But they wanted something new of a man who has just come from the antipodes," the friend insisted.

Judson was emphatic: "I am glad to have it to say that a man coming from the antipodes had nothing better to tell than the wondrous story of Jesus' dying love....When I looked upon those people today, and remembered where I should next meet them, how could I stand up and furnish food to vain curiosity—tickle their fancy with amusing stories, however decently strung together on a thread of religion?"[22]

This wasn't always the case. When Judson spoke in Plymouth, a young boy was in the congregation, Daniel Faunce, who later became a leading pastor. He never forgot the impact of the missionary's presence: "The old church was crowded, and I was able to find a seat only in a corner of the gallery. Shall I confess my disappointment, at first, when a slim, worn man, with a weary voice, rose in the pulpit…and gave out his text, 'These are they that follow the Lamb.'"

"Trained in a religious household," continued Faunce, "where missionary names, and especially those of Judson and Rice, were familiar words, somehow, in my boyish fancy I had thought of him as a great orator, with a loud voice and commanding tones, who would sweep down all before him with a resistless eloquence. Hence my disappointment. But as he went on, in simple language, to unfold his thought, and repeated over and over again his one theme, pleasing Jesus, somehow I forgot all about eloquence. There stole over me, a boy convert of only a few months' standing, a great tenderness. Was this venerated man influenced in all he had done by the simple thought of pleasing Jesus? Well, then, might not I, boy as I was, strive to please Jesus also? My eyes began to fill, and my heart was in my throat. Was there anything I could do to please Jesus? A hundred times since, the single simple thought of that sermon has come to me…[that] if that is eloquence which gets its thought written imperishably upon the heart of an auditor, then the simple, almost childlike words of that hour were truly eloquent."[23]

Judson tended to reveal only part of himself in these public appearances, and was perceived as solemn and serious. On one hand, he was those things. But, when free of the limelight and among friends, he was youthful and cultured, altogether a fascinating person. He never failed to charm. Those who knew something of what he had endured for those many years could only be amazed at his youthful vitality. At one small gathering, a friend asked to see the marks on his wrists left by the fetters over twenty years before. Matter-of-factly, Judson pulled back the fabric from his wrists, revealed the deeply imbedded scars, and then immediately changed the subject and engaged the group in conversation.[24]

Biographer A. C. Kendrick, who knew Judson personally, characterized him as having "an inextinguishable warmth of heart, a delicacy of taste, a breadth of culture and an exuberant joyful spirit."[25] When speaking to small groups, Judson became more personal and direct, especially when talking to young people committing their lives to missions. Speaking before the Boardman Society at Waterville College, he declared: "You will expect me to speak of missions and missionary life. I have seen so much of the trials and responsibility of missionary labors, that I am unwilling to urge any one to assume them. The urging must come from a higher source. One important thought just occurs to me. You have but one life to live in which to prepare for eternity. If you had four or five lives, two or three of them might be spent in carelessness. But you have one, only....Now, my dear brethren, if the Lord wants you for missionaries, he will set that command home to your hearts. If he does so, you neglect it to your peril."[26]

At the conclusion, he prayed what Francis Wayland, president of Brown University, described as one of "Judson's prayers." Wayland sensed in him a man very aware of his total dependence on heavenly guidance, of his own sinfulness and need of mercy. Wayland concluded, "Such, I believe, was the habitual temper of his mind, that the more his brethren were disposed to exalt him, the more deeply did he seem to feel his own deficiencies."[27]

There were very few areas of Christian life in which Adoniram Judson did not make an impact those months in America. Yet all this time he was longing for peace and quiet, for time with his children, and above all, to go home to Burma. News came belatedly from Moulmein that little Charlie's frail grip on life had slipped in August. Charlie had already been in heaven to greet his mother when she arrived in September. Adoniram yearned to be back with little Henry and the baby Edward again, to go home to the work that still remained his mission for life.

Yet in just a few weeks, his life made a new and totally unexpected turn. Providence had in store for him something, or rather, someone, who was to give him a new lease on life and renewed hope for how God would continue to use him. There was much more to come.

CHAPTER 19

Emily: 1845

Her every tone is music's own, like those of morning birds,
And something more than melody dwells ever in her words.
—A. C. Kendrick, *The Life and Letters of Emily Judson*

IT IS RARE THAT ONE MAN, NO MATTER HOW GIFTED, HEROIC, OR HIGHLY favored, should in the course of his lifetime be blessed with three exceptionable wives. Ann Hasseltine Judson was noted as "remarkable in any era, unexcelled in her own."[1] Sarah Boardman Judson was a genius of linguistics and possessed prodigious abilities as mother, poet, and translator. That there should be yet another woman of such exceptional abilities who would fall in love with the widowed Judson is like a scarcely credible conclusion to a work of fiction, but indeed it happened in real life.

Emily Chubbuck and Adoniram Judson met through a series of improbable events, coming face to face for the first time on a snowy

On Judson's one trip back, he revisited where he and four others were ordained as overseas missionaries on February 6, 1812 and sat on this deacon's bench in the Tabernacle Church.

Christmas morning. Their meeting was totally unlooked for and altogether unexpected. Their falling in love was breathtakingly swift. Judson, lionized by the Christian community of America and greatly admired by the general public, was fifty-seven. The average life expectancy of a missionary on the field during the first half of that century was a painfully short five years. Adoniram had already lived through thirty-three years in tropical Burma, including two years of torture and suffering in a death prison.

Here was a man keenly aware of his own mortality, knowing that not only was his voice all but gone, but that the privations of those arduous early years were taking a toll on his entire constitution. Judson desperately wanted to get back to Burma and his little boys and to a chance to complete his work there. At the same time, he was deeply concerned about what would happen to his older children when he left America. Sociologist Joan Brumberg called Judson's unexpected third marriage the "dramatic representation...of the point where religious and popular culture converged,...this 1846 marriage of the venerated missionary Dr. Judson to the popular fiction writer Fanny Forester [Emily Chubbuck]."[2]

Charles and Lavinia Chubbuck had moved from New Hampshire to Eaton, New York, in 1816, hoping for a better life. Charles tried many jobs but never earned enough money to adequately support his family. He was looking for the proverbial pot of gold in the Valley of the Alderbrook near Eaton. It never materialized.[3] Emily was born August 22, 1817, so fragile that her mother was told she would "have her but a short time."[4] But live Emily did, though the day-by-day effort to stay clothed and fed was ever a struggle and affected the way she viewed life.

The year Emily turned ten, the Chubbucks were so poor they did not have enough food. Before she was eleven, they felt compelled to put the frail girl to work in a nearby factory. Emily worked from dawn until dark and earned one dollar and twenty-five cents a week. She recalled, "My principal recollections during this summer are of noise and filth, bleeding hands and aching feet, and a very sad heart."[5] Ice was a blessing that winter, for it stopped the water wheel and the factory was forced to close, allowing Emily to go to school for three months.

Many of Emily's early memories centered around her older sisters, Lavinia and Harriet, both much older than she. Her first examples of deep and genuine faith centered around these sisters. As long as she lived, Emily recalled how they loved God with unwavering trust. Lavinia died of tuberculosis when Emily was eleven. Shortly after Lavinia's death, Emily first read of America's heroine, Ann Hasseltine Judson, and her little Maria, both of whom had recently died in far-away Burma. Upon reading the news, the young Emily first had the thought cross her mind: "I will be a missionary."[6] She never forgot that early tug at her heart.

Conditions did not improve. Emily said of her thirteenth winter: "We suffered a great deal from cold this winter, though we had plenty of plain food. Indeed, we never were reduced to hunger. But the house was large and unfinished and the snow sometimes drifted into it in heaps....Father was absent nearly all the time, distributing newspapers....Mother, Harriet and I were frequently compelled to go out into the fields, and dig broken wood out of the snow, to keep ourselves from freezing. Catherine [Emily's other older sister] and I went to the district school as much as we could."[7] In November 1830, Emily wrote: "Father's attempt at farming proved, as might have been expected, an entire failure, and...he determined to remove to the village. He took a little old house on the outskirts, the poorest shelter we ever had....I got constant employment of a little Scotch weaver and thread-maker at twisting thread."[8] Then tragedy struck again. In 1831, older sister Harriet died of tuberculosis. Two sisters were gone.

Emily never really knew a childhood, but those years refined and defined her. Life was a constant round of work, snatches of studies and more work, often not getting to bed until one or two, then rising a few hours later to do washing before school. Her mother, anxious for Emily to have steady employment, wanted her to apprentice with the local milliner. Emily could not bear the thought and on her own initiative, got a teaching job. She was slender and small. One of the men who interviewed her shook his head in amazement at the thought of this slight young girl teaching hulking farm boys double her size. But teach she did, and most effectively. Her parents were amazed at the assertiveness of their shy Emily. Sheer determination also kept her studying diligently on her own.

Emily came to personal faith and was baptized by William Dean at age seventeen.[9] She was mature beyond her years, unselfish in nature and thoughtful of those around her. A biographer remembered her as having an "almost prodigal generosity,...a self-reliant will, and an almost masculine energy of action."[10] During the time Emily taught in Hamilton, she wrote the elderly pastor of Eaton church, Nathaniel Kendrick, of her desire to commit herself to a missionary life. This was quite remarkable, for in the 1830s, single women did not go as missionaries. Kendrick did not discourage her but advised her to "wait the opening of Providence."[11] Somehow this longing never left her heart, even during times when she did not think it could be possible. Emily told a friend, "I have felt ever since I read the memoir of Ann H. Judson when I was a small child that I must become a missionary. I fear it is but a childish fancy, and am making every effort to banish it from my mind; yet the more I seek to divert my thoughts from it, the more unhappy I am."[12]

While teaching, Emily was also writing poetry and short stories and being published in a local newspaper. She seldom wrote of *imagined* suffering, for she had tasted too much of the bitter cup of reality to spend time soaring in a fantasy world. Her writing, always realistic, was incredibly picturesque and evocative, her imaginary people and their struggles and triumphs coming to glowing life for the reader. Emily painted a wonderful word picture. By age nineteen, Emily the writer and teacher was the sole support of her parents and surviving older sister, Catherine (who was called Kate).

Emily was pretty enough to be noticed anywhere. Childhood illnesses had left her with a slim figure and milky-white skin. Her hair was dark and her features were almost classical.[13] During these years, she had at least two proposals of marriage, although early biographers make no mention of them. She wrote her brother Walker in Wisconsin about a young doctor, stating that, at age twenty-three, she was "thinking some of getting married…but I don't care a fig for him…[so] what shall I do? I don't love him and I don't hate him and I don't believe I ever should do either."[14] She spoke of her determination to write and teach: "I am not very healthy but I can work and I will. I shall have neither Hough [an earlier suitor], nor Dr. Redfield, for I don't like them and can live alone. Besides, I calculate to take care of Pa and Ma."[15]

In 1840, Emily entered Utica Seminary, first as pupil and then as teacher. Anna Maria Anable, who became her closest friend, wrote of meeting Emily: "I remember well her first appearance in Utica as a pupil. She was a frail, slender creature, shrinking with nervous timidity from observation; yet her quiet demeanor, noiseless step, low voice, earnest and observant glance of the eye…began to exert a quiet but powerful influence in the school.…Miss Chubbuck had a heart full of sympathy and no grief was too causeless…for her not to endeavor to remove them. She…became a favorite with the younger, as with the older and more appreciative scholars. Her advice was asked, her opinions sought, and her taste consulted."[16] Observing Emily, the seminary administrators were able to "detect the rare gem concealed in the shrinking exterior."[17]

Emily was pushing her frail constitution by day and by night, teaching, counseling, and writing. She loved writing but did not write solely for the joy of it. Emily continued to write poems, articles, children's stories, and moral tales for the Baptist Sunday School publishers. Her first children's book, *Charles Linn*, earned about fifty dollars. In truth, the record of her rise to eminence as a literary figure "had all the trappings of a female success story."[18] It wasn't exactly "rags to riches." There certainly were privations in the cold, early years, yet the Emily who gained renown as "Fanny Forester," did not remain "Forester" long enough to become rich.

It forever bothered Emily, the product of nineteenth century Victorian America, to *sell* the products of her imagination. She wrote: "I have always shrunk from doing any thing in a public capacity, and that had added a great deal to my school-teaching troubles. But O, necessity! Necessity! Did you ever think of such a thing as selling brains for money? And then, such brains as mine! Do you think I could prepare…a small volume of poems that would produce the desired—I must speak it—cash?"[19] Yet Emily was unable to make enough to get out of debt for the house she had purchased for her parents. For three years, she was published in various magazines, but all her efforts never produced enough earnings to allow her to erase the debts.

Edward Judson recounts Emily's frustrations: "As Miss Sheldon [director of Utica Seminary] was at one time passing near midnight through the halls, a light streaming from Emily's apartment attracted her attention, and, softly opening the door, she stole in upon her vigils. Emily sat in her night-dress, her papers lying outspread before her, grasping with both hands her throbbing temples, and pale as a marble statue. Miss S. went to her, whispered words of sympathy, and gently chided her for robbing her system of its needed repose. Emily's heart…overflowed in uncontrollable weeping: 'Oh, Miss Sheldon,' she exclaimed, 'I must write, I must write; I must do what I can to aid my poor parents.'"[20]

Like many creative writers, Emily was never quite satisfied with her writing. She was now being published frequently in *Mother's Journal*, *Godey's Lady's Book*, and *The Baptist Register*. Two of her children's stories were published by the American Baptist Sunday School Union, *Effie Maurice* becoming exceptionally popular with youth.

Emily made her first trip to New York City in 1844 and wrote a clever letter about "the big city" to New York's leading literary critic, signing the letter "Fanny Forester." N. P. Willis, who edited the flourishing *Evening Mirror*, recognized exceptional talent. He gave Emily a chance, and "Fanny Forester" was catapulted into prominence. She became a quick success—almost dizzying to one who by nature was an introvert. However, there was nothing introverted about her writing. Willis went so far as to say, "You are more readable than any female writer in this country."[21] Upon examining the quality of her work, Willis wrote: "Nobody could ever read a line of yours and see anything but merit over modest, for," he continued, "there is no writing well without coloring from one's own heart....There are two worlds, my dear,...one imaginative and the other real life—and people of genius have separate existences in both."[22]

One aspect of "fame" that Emily had never considered was one she abhorred. She was fast losing her anonymity, and for a person with her wish for privacy, this presented a problem. Emily shrank from overly bold criticism and comments, particularly from those who did not know her. Yet little though she knew it at the time, the public limelight, both in literary and religious circles, was soon to be focused squarely on her. That proved extremely painful.

"Fanny Forester's" personality was an interesting study in contrasts. Personally introspective, she nevertheless had a natural exuberance of spirit that spilled over in her writings. Emily revealed a many-faceted character. Her poetry exuded idealism, yet she was blessed with great common sense. Historian Winfred Hervey noted some of her unique characteristics: "Her union of qualities seemingly contradictory, poetic ideality joined to plain and efficient common sense,...at once a child of genius and a child of want, who, while starving alone in a cottage, can build castles far away, and people them with her own noble and royal guests,...the rare compound of...fancy and reason."[23] Emily was a self-taught writer and poet. The well-springs were within her own mind and thoughts, a God-given gift, and she recognized it as such. Her writing was a juxtaposition of strength and elegance.[24]

That fateful year of 1845, little did Emily, or anyone else for that matter, know what God had in store in the blending of two such divergent personalities as Emily Chubbuck and Adoniram Judson, the two so different and yet so amazingly complementary. Although far apart in age, they were uncannily similar in perspective. One of the amazing facets of Judson's personality was an ever-present youthfulness, readily apparent in relaxed times with friends and associates. It was especially remarkable, considering the agony of the hardest years in Burma. He once commented in those later years in a letter to a friend about love being that which "we will cherish in the young corner of our hearts, an oasis in the desert."[25]

These two were soon to meet. In the winter of 1845, Emily's doctors urgently advised her to go to a warmer city for the sake of her health, so she spent about six weeks in Philadelphia during the coldest part of the year, staying in the home of A. D. Gillette, pastor of Philadelphia's Eleventh Street Baptist Church. On Christmas morning, 1845, while Emily was receiving a vaccination for smallpox, a visitor arrived at Gillette's door. The vaccination that morning was not proof against the arrows of what Judson later called "that scamp Cupid."[26] The rest is history.

The Engagement 1846

We feel that God has directed us in this affair, and we may hope that he will grant his rich blessing. And if he bless us, we shall be blessed indeed.
—Letter from Adoniram Judson to Emily Chubbuck
April 2, 1846

An 1846 engraving of author Emily Chubbuck, a k a Fanny Forester, who became the third wife of Adoniram Judson. Courtesy of Dr. George Tooze.

IT WAS CHRISTMAS EVE, 1845, AND Adoniram Judson was weary. His children were scattered—the little ones in Moulmein, Abby in Plymouth, the boys in Worcester, and he was headed to meetings in Philadelphia. Such gatherings seemed endless for they had not stopped since his arrival in America just over two months earlier. Judson would never become accustomed to being idolized. He understood human nature all too well—most people preferred the idealized image to the reality of the man.

He had endless invitations to speak, or rather to "appear." Judson had to turn down far more than he accepted. Arthur Gillette had come to New York specifically to insist that Judson come to his city; now the two men hoped to reach Philadelphia and a bit of rest soon. Then an accident along the tracks caused a three-hour delay. Judson was not accustomed to wasting time. Noticing Judson's restlessness, Gillette found in the hands of a nearby acquaintance a book well-known to himself. He borrowed it, hoping it would help pass the time for Adoniram.

Trippings in Authorland—not Judson's usual reading. His own life's "trippings" had been anything but light and relaxed. Undeniably bored, he accepted the book and began flipping through the pages. An occasional phrase caught his eye, then another, and before he knew it, Judson had read the entire book. Much to his own surprise, he had just been highly entertained for two hours by stories light but engaging, cleverly written and highly evocative in imagery. This was a welcome relief from adulation on the one hand and his own grief on the other. "This book is written with great beauty and power," he commented. "Who is Fanny Forester?"

"Actually," Gillette smiled, "I know her personally." Immediately Judson asked, "Is she a Christian?" "Yes," Gillette confirmed, "and a Baptist." Judson suggested that he would like an opportunity to meet her and talk with her about her talent and writing, expressing the opinion in his usual forthright manner that such creative abilities needed to be more worthily utilized. Beaming broadly, Gillette informed Judson that Forester was in fact Miss Emily Chubbuck, who currently was a guest in his own home. They certainly *could* meet.[1] Gillette suggested that Judson come visit the next morning. He readily agreed, for reading stories of characters who rose above misery to triumph had encouraged him, and he looked forward to meeting such a writer. It promised to be an interesting Christmas Day.

Indeed, Providence came knocking that Christmas morning, and Emily Chubbuck opened the door. At that moment, the last thing on Judson's mind was romance, but this turned out to be the beginning of the rest of his life. People who knew one or the other of them only casually must surely have thought this the most unlikely couple imaginable, but theirs was actually an amazing "meeting of the minds."

Neither Judson nor Emily had any inkling of how their lives were about to change. Adoniram arrived at Gillette's home to find Miss Chubbuck getting a smallpox vaccination. Taking a nearby seat, those perceptive eyes missed nothing as he observed Miss Chubbuck. Here was a young woman involved in a medical procedure but not cast into confusion by the arrival of one of the most well-known men in America. Emily had no chocolate-box prettiness, but her inner emotions seemed to illuminate her face. The moment the procedure was complete, Judson walked with her to a nearby sofa and began discussing with her the book that he had just read. Emily felt honored that her writing had captured the attention of a man she had revered all her life, yet she talked to him very naturally, without either coyness or affected manners.

Adoniram went straight to the point, suggesting that she was wasting great ability on frothy stories. Emily might appear to be reserved, but there was no counterfeit meekness about her. With someone else, she might have answered sharply. Not with Judson. In spite of his quick criticism, there was about him a genuine warmth and sincerity that disarmed her, and she perceived that he honestly admired her talent. She gave her reasons frankly, sketching her life's circumstances and explaining how her parents depended on her support. Emily admitted that she personally did not prefer this light type of story, but face it, it sold. Emily in turn asked Judson if he faulted her for that.[2] Adoniram assured her that he did not. Her reasons were noble. And then quickly, as he did most things, Adoniram made up his mind about a matter he had been considering. He wanted a memoir written about Sarah. Much was written of Ann, but nothing about Sarah. Emily's gift with words had impressed him. Would she consider helping him with such a book? She would. Thus, Christmas morning 1845 began a new chapter in two lives.

There is no record of Emily's initial impressions of Adoniram Judson. She must have been amazed at how at home she felt in conversing with such a famous man nearly twice her age, one who had traveled the world and experienced several lifetimes of adventure. Not long after their first meeting, however, Emily wrote a wise friend in the literary world explaining what had most impacted her about Judson: "I am a great admirer of greatness—real, genuine greatness; and goodness has an influence which I have not the power to resist."[3]

One of the many traits the two held in common was an uncanny perceptiveness. Each was gifted in discernment. Emily had heard all her life of Adoniram Judson. Now she could see *why* he affected others as he did. The missionary in a large gathering had an aura about him that could not be simulated. Just being around him caused people in city after city to fill with emotion at his presence.[4] In private conversation, Judson was smiling, humorous, friendly. Emily was not proof against his charm. Among other unique qualities was the speed with which he had always made decisions, and seldom did his impetuous resolve prove wrong.

Some events and developments of the couple's courtship are not recorded, but a look at the beautifully written love letters between the two makes fascinating reading. Their first meeting was December 25, 1845. Eleven days later, Adoniram wrote in his journal: "1846, January 5th, Commenced an acquaintance with Emily Chubbuck."[5] For Judson this was tantamount to "I am going to propose." In recently discovered letters, the morning of January 6, Emily wrote her friend Anna Maria that "It [the romance] has grown into a serious matter." Judson had not yet proposed, she explained; it "had not come to that. It will, though, if I don't prevent it." She pleads: "What shall I do?"[6] Later that same day, she wrote her sister that Adoniram *had* just proposed to her.

Each day during Judson's time in Philadelphia, the two were together discussing the memoir of Sarah. The more they conversed, the more each recognized a kindred spirit. Always with Emily, even as he had with Sarah, Judson spoke of his love for Ann and their life together. He opened his heart to Emily about the blessings of those two unique women. Only a month later, in the most tender of love letters, he first expressed his heartfelt love for Emily, and then talked of Ann and Sarah, writing, "How thankful and joyful do I ever feel, that your kind, sweet love allows me this precious privilege of saying that I am thine. Heaven will be brighter to me for thy presence. Those will be with Ann and Sarah—we shall join in the same song of love and praise. And how happy we shall be in beholding one another's faces glow with heavenly rapture."[7] Certainly an unusual love letter, but clearly, it worked.

As the relationship grew, their private letters reveal that Emily had many doubts as to how news of their marriage would be received. She feared the criticism that would be aimed at Adoniram for marrying a "lightweight," a frivolous author of fiction. Conversely, Adoniram was unconcerned about what others thought. He always had been. His perspective was—I feel this is God's guidance and therefore this is what I will do. Long years before, when all had advised against trying to start a mission in Burma, he and Ann nevertheless had set their faces toward that forbidding land and proceeded to follow what they had felt was God's will. Judson felt the same about marriage, even telling Emily in one of his letters that experience had hardened him considerably to the opinions of others, especially others not of like heart.

Adoniram's first love letter to Emily was typical of his skill. Those two shared a magical way with words. One historian called Judson "one of the finest epistolary writers in our language—simple, elegant, passing spontaneously from delicate playfulness into those regions of sacred thought in which he habitually dwelt."[8] Truly amazing, for English was now Judson's second language, after thirty-three years totally immersed in the intricacies of literary Burmese.

The tacit implication of Adoniram's first letter to Emily is that they had already discussed the possibility of marriage. It is apparent from its tone that the two had already revealed their love to each other. Their original love letters, some sixty of them, make for marvelous reading. The hearts of two unusual people are beautifully framed in these glimpses into their courtship. Reading them is rather like peering into the window of a private parlor. Adoniram Judson might have been fifty-seven, but he was a master of beautifully crafted declarations of love.

On January 20, he sent Emily a watch he had first given to Ann many years before and wrote: "I hand you, dearest one, a charmed watch. It always comes back home and brings its wearer with it. I gave it to Ann, when a hemisphere divided us, and it brought her safely and surely to my arms—I gave it to Sarah, during her husband's life-time, not then aware of the secret, and the charm, though slow in its operation, was true at last. Were it not for the sweet indulgences you have kindly allowed me, and the blessed understanding that 'love has taught us to guess at,' I should not venture to pray you accept my present, with such a note. Should you cease to 'guess' and toss back the article, saying—'Your watch has lost its charm. It comes back to you, but brings not its wearer with it!' O first smash it to pieces, that it may be an emblem of what will then remain of the heart of Your devoted—A. Judson"9

Four days later Emily wrote her friend Miss Sheldon: "My good doctor has now gone away, and I have just said to him the irrevocable 'yes,' though I must acknowledge that I have acted it slightly before."10 The cities from which Judson wrote his letters to Emily serve as a guide to his itinerary for the next several months. He left Philadelphia for Washington and Richmond. Wherever he traveled, Judson always wrote of God's presence in their relationship. And in one of her early letters, Emily declared: "I thank God for sending you to Philadelphia, and for giving me your priceless affection. I can not become worthy of it, but dear, dear doctor, you shall teach and guide me and I will do the best I can; I can love you at least, and will. Heaven guard you! So prays your Emily."11

Adoniram wrote Emily from Washington and told of an interesting day in the Senate and House. He bemoaned a meeting at which "the most appalling praises were poured out on me, so that I felt obliged to get up and disclaim the praise and confess my sins and beg the people to join me in praying for pardon."12 Judson tended to fill his letters equally with beautiful literary allusions and references to God's goodness. In the same letter he closed: "Christ went about doing good—May it be our glory to imitate his example!…My spirit clings to thine, love."13

Judson's next stop was Richmond, Virginia, although he had neither strength nor time to go south. He concluded, however, that it was vital to attend a meeting of the newly formed Southern Convention, which had just the previous year broken from the Triennial Convention over the issue of slavery. Judson was interested in promoting mission zeal among Southern Baptists. There was no hint of dissension in the meeting; Southern Baptists received him with open arms, and Judson did nothing but stimulate their interest in the cause of missions. Southern Baptists viewed Judson as their own father of missions, part of their foundation and heritage.

Judson was asked to speak in many southern states but simply did not have the luxury of time to honor these requests. One such invitation was from Judson College in Marion, Alabama, a burgeoning new college for women founded in 1838 and named for the heroic Ann. In answer to their request, Judson wrote, "I regret exceedingly that my health will not permit me to visit the Institute bearing the name of 'that incomparable woman' Ann Hasseltine Judson."[14]

Adoniram's letters made frequent reference to a longing for privacy. The teenage boy who had daydreamed of being a "hero" now longed for the opposite. He spoke of the joy of being able one Sunday to "sit in a pew like other people, and...join in worship unmolested."[15] Nearly every letter to Emily included news about his children, his love and concern for them, and how he rejoiced that they would have a new mother. Emily frequently wrote about her need for more depth in her relationship with God. Occasionally Adoniram would comment on his or her "low state of religion," referring to those moments when they did not feel they were living to their spiritual utmost. He encouraged Emily to look to God for every need, assuring her: "You will find the throne of grace accessible; he will help you come out of this trouble with a grateful, joyful heart and you shall shine brighter for it, for all eternity."[16] And from Maine on April 11, 1846, he wrote, "May he bring us together 'in love and happiness' is my ardent prayer."[17] In the remarkable collection of letters that Adoniram wrote Emily, the very flow of his soul can be felt. Emily found him irresistible, whether on paper or in person.

While Judson made trips to meetings he felt were absolutely essential, Emily settled temporarily in Utica to prepare for their wedding and sailing to Burma. Adoniram made no attempt to paint a rosy picture for her about what life as a missionary to Burma would be like. His frankness did not frighten Emily. "Dear Doctor," she responded to his honesty, "only love me, do not see too many faults, censure gently, lead me 'to the enjoyment of higher religion, and to more extensive usefulness,' *trust* me, and no place on earth is half so pleasant as 'grim Burmah'....The *place* is not what constitutes my home— it is your presence."[18]

In March, Adoniram met Emily's friends in Utica and her family in

Hamilton. On that Sunday in Hamilton, Adoniram was honored to sit on the platform with Leonard Woods, his old Andover professor who had been a great influence on him. Judson, that young Andover student who called himself a "poor blind skeptic," had received encouragement and enlightenment from this professor. Here they were once more together after half a lifetime.[19]

The engaged couple met and then parted yet again, both preparing for the months ahead. Among other business, Adoniram paid off the debt on Emily's parents' home, bringing her immense relief. When news of the impending marriage came out, reaction was immediate and quite what they had expected. The literary world mourned the loss of the brilliant Fanny Forester, throwing herself away on an "old man" and burying herself a world away. Surely the missionary had seduced her mind and influenced her with his aura! One article called Judson a "wizzled old widower," and another, a "bluebeard."[20]

The religious community was just as extreme, those who knew not the man but the name. How could the great Apostle of Burma do such a thing, and so *quickly*, as to marry a spinner of "novels"! For such people, the legend of Judson was shattered.[21] To much of the religious public, Judson was a mythic figure, not a real man.

Emily was frequently devastated by what she read, more for Adoniram's sake than her own, but the public bothered him not. Judson commented that so many grievous events had been part of his life that he was quite inured. In truth, the bedrock Adoniram Judson had never been affected by what people said, and his attitude was a tremendous shelter in the time of storm for the sensitive Emily. Sometimes "the public" downright amused Judson. He wrote Emily in May about a large meeting in one of the great cities. "After the affair," he wrote, "the pulpit was thronged and among the rest one grave gentleman wanted to know, looking earnestly at my apex, whether I wore my own hair! I meekly assured him of the fact, and he seemed to go away edified."[22]

The busy couple still managed to find time to write one another. Adoniram could change from a serious tone to playfulness in an instant. He had numerous pet names for Emily, which delighted and amused her—from "Miss Nemmie Petty" to "Miss Blidgims" and "Miss Peakedchin"—and she called him her "Darling Nome." Fanny Forester was the well-known writer, but her "Darling Nome" constantly amazed her with his quick and clever turn of phrase. In one letter he asked, "What are meetings here but partings? Any novice can answer that. For meetings, with those we love, when continued at least for a while, are the balm of existence. Religion is indeed the philosophy, but love is the delicious poetry of life. Religion may be the roast beef, most nutritious, but love claims to be the cake and the pie."[23]

When the time came to return to Burma, the goodbyes to his children were painful for Judson. He wrote of the tears they shed, the hugs they could scarcely bear to end, of his own great weeping. Yet he felt a sense of urgency about returning to Burma, his work, and the younger boys, Henry and Edward. Adoniram realized he would likely never again see his older children, and he died a small death with each goodbye.

Both Emily and Adoniram were more than ready for the partings to end and the wedding to take place. Nathaniel Kendrick, Emily's elderly pastor in Hamilton, New York, performed the quiet ceremony. This was one of Kendrick's last public appearances. Adoniram arrived in Hamilton on June 1, 1846, and they were married the next day. A whole new life and world opened to Emily and a new beginning for Adoniram Judson as well. He felt alive and hopeful once again; Emily had given him a new lease on life. They were soon to sail, and those who knew them both and loved them well rejoiced for their unexpected happiness.

The Final Years 1846–1849

A sketched map of Burma (Myanmar) gives both the ancient and modern names for important locations in missions history.

Oh, if we are so happy here amid our toils and pains,
With thronging cares and dangers near, and marr'd by earthly stains,
How great must be the compass given our souls to 'bear' the bliss of heaven!
—Emily Chubbuck Judson to Adoniram Judson, 1847

IN JULY 1846, JUDSON STOOD ON THE DECK OF THE *FANUEIL HALL*, LOOK-ing at the crowd waving farewell to their missionaries. He remembered another morning in 1812. That had been no summer day with crowds of well-wishers. There had been wintry winds laden with sleet, a tiny vessel with four foolhardy young people embarking on a "wild romantic adventure," and a handful of hardy souls waving goodbye. Of those original four, only Adoniram survived; the others were all in scattered graves. For Emily, however, everything was new. Her extraordinary talent with a pen captured impressions of those months on the Pacific, her depictions a form of praise: "Up curls the mist...curl on curl, it winds in silvery beauty and meeting the sun, falls back in gorgeous showers of million-colored rainbows...gloriously beautiful! The sea, even as 'the earth, is full of thy riches.'"[1]

There was another first-time sailor aboard. Emily wrote about their fellow passenger the day they sailed: "We have everything for our comfort and convenience, even to a cow which the doctor bought yesterday."[2] In a later letter from Moulmein, she reported that the cow had made the voyage in fine style: "She's a very popular madam. Everybody flocks to see the American cow."[3] It was a pleasant voyage, unusual for Adoniram—a sea journey with no gales, seasickness, or pirates. They passed close enough to St. Helena to see the promontory of rock where Sarah had been buried. Judson had earlier shipped a gravestone to St. Helena. It was in place by this time, marking Sarah's grave. Even on the voyage, Adoniram was working on the dictionary, but he still managed to find time to begin teaching Emily Burmese. Just as he had predicted, she proved a facile learner. Her keen mind was aware of the magnitude of the task ahead of her: new wife, new mother of two little boys, new country, and new language. But Emily had never ducked a challenge. Her body was frail, but that was completely eclipsed by the strength of her determination.

Four months later, the Judsons stood on deck watching Burma's coastline emerging slowly out of the mists. Emily was getting her first look at the land that was to be home. There was a special landmark to note as they neared Amherst. On a "green bank sloping to the water" was Ann's grave.[4] That night Judson wrote: "The members of my own family are scattered far and wide; for the mounds that mark their graves stud the burial-places of Rangoon, Amherst, Moulmein, Serampore and St. Helena. What other place shall be added next to the list?"[5]

Adoniram was returning home to his adopted land and people, but all the scenes before Emily's eyes were new and exotic. The ship anchored off Amherst that night before proceeding to Moulmein. Emily recorded her first impressions: "Here we are at last in queer, ridiculous, half-beautiful, half-frightful, exceedingly picturesque Burmah....As they drew sufficiently near to be distinguishable by their features, one of our number [Adoniram]...leaned far over for a moment gazing at them intently, and then sent forth a glad wild hail. In a moment the glancing of oars ceased, a half dozen men sprang to their feet to the imminent peril of the odd nut-shell in which they floated, and a wilder, longer and if possible more joyous cry, showed that the voice of the salutation was recognized. Christian [Adoniram] beckoned me to his side. 'They are our Amherst friends,' he said; 'the dear, faithful fellows!' And these were some of the Christians of Burmah!...Men born in idolatry...redeemed and marked for His crown in glory! What a sublime thing to be a missionary! In a few moments the men had brought the boat along side, and were scrambling up the sides of the vessel....Then came a quick grasping of hands, and half-choked words of salutation...which he only to whom they were addressed could understand; while I, like the full-grown baby that I am, retreated to the nearest shadow, actually sobbing."[6]

Dawn broke on November 30, and Moulmein came into view. Adoniram once more held his little boys in his arms. A whole new existence lay in front of Emily; the two children she took to her heart. Shortly after arrival, she wrote: "I do love the dear children that a saint in heaven has left me. I love them for their own sakes; for sweeter, more lovely little creatures never breathed....I love them; I pray to God to help me train them up in His fear and love."[7]

Adoniram wrote his older children about their little brothers in Moulmein, painting in words for them the scene in the house that they remembered so fondly: "I can hardly realize that I am sitting in the old house, where we all lived together so long; and now your mamma, yourselves...and little Charlie are gone...your new mamma has just put your little brothers, Henry and Edward, to bed. They lie in the room where you used to sleep....Henry is singing and talking aloud to himself,...'My own mamma went away, away in a boat. And then she got wings and went up. And Charlie too, went up, and they are flying above the moon and the stars.'"[8] Judson wrote his sister: "Emily makes one of the best of wives and kindest of mothers to the children that ever man was blessed with. I wish you were here to make one of the family."[9]

217

Judson was gratified by the progress he found in the mission, reporting that the "native church" was not much enlarged but much improved. The schools were stronger, the Karen department "never more promising," and the printing office was producing a lot of material.[10] All of these things made Judson look with great longing to Burma proper. A big portion of his heart was in that first spot, Rangoon. It seemed obvious to him; here was Moulmein with nearly thirty missionaries, but there was Rangoon with a forbidding government and *no* missionaries. And in the back of his mind, always close to his heart, was Ava, with no witness at all.

Adoniram made the decision to scout out Rangoon and see if they might be able to reestablish a work there. Emily was amazed at how the temporary separation affected her: "I did not think that I should feel so sad to be left alone only these few weeks; but the prospect actually makes my heart faint. We have been daily and hourly together ever since our marriage, and his presence is my very life. I hear his step now, as he goes from room to room, making all the arrangements in his power for my comfort. So thoughtful! So tender! So delicate! O, there are few on earth so blest as I...I will venture to assert that it required a far greater effort in Ann H. Judson to leave her husband (such a husband!) in Rangoon, and go to America alone, than to play the heroic part in his presence, and for his sake, that she did at Ava."[11]

Judson knew only too well the perils that doubtless lay ahead in Rangoon. Nevertheless, he determined to give it his all and wrote that he was "quite willing to leave the event in the hands of God. 'Trust in God and keep your powder dry' was Cromwell's word to his soldiers; trust in God and love one another is, I think, a better watchword."[12] He reached Rangoon the last week of January and remained for about ten days. Fortuitously the city's governor was an old acquaintance, one who knew the peace treaty services Judson had rendered for Burma.

Adoniram's priority on this scouting mission was to find a place suitable for him and his family to live. The old mission house was long gone, destroyed many years earlier. He located a huge brick house on the "street of the Musselmans [Moslems]." It came to be known by two rather dubious names: "Bat Castle" and "Green Turban's Den." It was to this enticing location that the four Judsons moved in February 1847. Emily depicted "Bat Castle" so graphically that the bugs seemed to come to life. She described huge, echoing rooms, windows (holes) covered not with glass but by plank shutters, and thick walls: "The partitions are...very thick, and the door sills are built up so that I go over them at three or four steps, Henry mounts and falls off, and Edward gets on all-fours and accomplishes the pass with more safety."[13]

Adoniram wrote about the "creatures" in the castle and his war of extermination: "We have had a grand bat hunt yesterday and today—bagged two hundred and fifty, and calculate to make up a round thousand before we have done. We find that in hiring the upper story of this den, we secured the lower moiety [half] only, the upper moiety thereof being preoccupied by a thriving colony of vagabonds...and the sound of their wings is as the sound of many waters."[14]

Emily described other residents: "Besides the bats, we are blessed with our full share of cockroaches, beetles, spiders, lizards, rats, ants, mosquitoes, and bed-bugs,...and the ants troop over the house in great droves, though there are scattering ones besides. Perhaps twenty have crossed my paper since I have been writing. Only one cockroach has paid me a visit, but the neglect of these gentlemen has been fully made up by a company of black bugs about the size of the end of your little finger—nameless adventurers."[15]

The food predicament was still worse. Even staples were difficult to obtain. The Judsons were not being picky; common vegetables and fruits were scarce, and in this Buddhist city, meat was rare. The children weren't getting adequate food, and Adoniram worried about Emily. She was often ill, and Judson pictured her "as thin as the shad that went up Niagara."[16]

Emily wrote her sister, Kate: "As for living, I must own that I am within an inch of starvation, and poor little Henry says...'I don't want any dinner—I wish we could go back to Moulmein'....Our milk is a mixture of buffaloes' milk, water, and something else which we cannot make out....The butter we make from it is like lard....I must tell you, however, of the grand dinner we had one day. 'You must contrive and get something that mamma can eat,' the doctor said to our Burmese purveyor; 'she will starve to death.' 'What shall I get?' 'Anything.' 'Anything?' 'Anything.' Well, we did have a capital dinner, though we tried in vain to find out by the bones what it was. Henry said it was touk-tahs, a species of lizard, and I should have thought so too, if the little animal had been of a fleshy consistence. Cook said he *didn't know*, but he grinned a horrible grin which made my stomach heave a little, notwithstanding the deliciousness of the meal. In the evening we called Mr. Bazaar-man. 'What did we have for dinner today?' 'Were they good?' 'Excellent.' A tremendous explosion of laughter, in which the cook from his dish room joined as loud as he dared. 'What were they?' '*Rats!*'"17

The infested house, scarce food, and threat of illness were constant specters for the Judsons. There was an epidemic in Rangoon and many were dying. At one point, all four Judsons were ill. Adoniram's diarrhea came close to being critical. Then Henry came down with "Rangoon fever" and scared all of them. Meanwhile Emily was wracked with a variety of ills, and for more than a month, she was unable to sit up for an hour at a time. Adoniram feared he would lose her. To compound an already serious situation, Emily began to suspect that she was pregnant.

Then Edward became deathly ill. It was erysipelas (St. Anthony's fire), a violent skin disease. Emily wrote of trying to save him: "Edward awoke this morning, his face so swollen that his eyes are nearly closed, shining and spotted purplish;...[then] the spots on his face became red, instead of purple. I think my dose of calomel saved his life....The sweet little fellow is still a great sufferer....I went to bed late at night with one of my very worst nervous headaches. I was awakened from troubled sleep by Edward's screams; but as soon as I raised my head I...fell back helpless. As soon as possible I made another attempt, and this time reached the middle of the room, where I fell headlong. I did not venture on my feet again, but crept to the bed on my hands and feet, and finally succeeded in soothing him. All this time the Doctor was groaning terribly, and he managed between his groans to tell me that he was in even greater agony than when he was first seized. I was unable to do anything for him, however, and so crawled over to Henry's cot. Oh, the predicament that he was in!...[and] I expected that both Edward and the Doctor would die....Henry is left a pale, puny child, without appetite; and poor Edward, really the greatest sufferer, is still in an alarming situation. There is an abscess in his forehead and the acrid matter has eaten back into the bone, we can not tell how far; there is another immense one on the back of the head in a shocking state....He is the loveliest child that I ever saw; there is something which seems to me angelic in his patience and calmness. He could not help crying when his papa lanced his head; but the moment the sharpest pain was over, he nestled down in my bosom, and though quivering all over, he kept lifting his eyes to my face, and trying to smile, oh, so sweetly! He watched his papa while he sharpened the lancet to open another, and when it was ready, turned and laid his little head on his knee of his own accord."[18]

Somehow, all four of them survived. They were able to remain in Rangoon for only seven months, but in spite of the mausoleum of a house, the hordes of unwelcome creatures, the lack of basic food, and several serious illnesses, they looked back upon that period as one of the happiest of their lives. In many respects, those months in Rangoon seemed to them like a period out of time, as if a spell had been cast over all of them. Emily described it in a letter: "'I have seen all this before!' was a feeling that flashed upon me,...producing a momentary confusion of intellect, that almost made me doubt if 'I was I'; and then came the reflections; when?—how?—where? And finally it would creep into my mind; why I learned about it in Sabbath school when I was a little child."[19]

Those months in Rangoon, Adoniram worked on the dictionary, met with seekers, and encouraged the little band of believers. Emily studied Burmese, began work on Sarah's memoir, and cared for two growing little boys who felt she was indeed their "mamma." It was a poignant time for Adoniram. He wrote the mission board in

Boston: "I have just returned from baptizing a Burman convert, in the same tank of water where I baptized the first Burman convert, Maung Nau, twenty-eight years ago. It is now twenty-five years since I administered baptism in Rangoon."[20] Maung Nau still came to Judson's mind frequently. That gentle first believer had died during the horrors of the war; no one knew the exact circumstances.

They also walked in memories when Adoniram took Emily to the overgrown English graveyard that had once been the gardens of the mission house. Emily wrote: "The first child of European parents born in Burmah had been buried there; and there was a strong tie between that mouldering little one and ourselves. Over the grave of little Roger stood, but slightly broken, the rude brick monument which was built thirty-three years ago; and a tall azalea…had grown out from the base almost overshadowing it. It was strange to stand and muse beside that little grave, with one parent by my side, and the other so irrecoverably a being of the past. Oh, how she had wept there!—and how human she grew—she whom I had formerly only wondered at—while my own tears started in sympathy."[21]

While in Rangoon, the Judsons received bad news from Moulmein. Thinking to protect their most valuable possessions and records, they had left them stored at the home of the Stevenses. A fire had swept that house, and both families lost virtually everything they owned. Yet in the face of such a blow, Adoniram rejoiced that the New Testament and other manuscripts were not totally lost. He wrote Edward Stevens, who had also suffered so many losses in the fire: "The Lord gave and the Lord hath taken away; *blessed be the name of the Lord.*…'Blessed be God for all, For all things here below; For every loss and every cross, To my advantage grow.'"[22]

All this while Judson had been working very quietly so as not to attract the attention of the authorities. One Sunday he baptized a young man, and next morning word came—the young man's father had been arrested. The noose of surveillance continued to tighten. The presence of the Judsons now endangered the believers. Then word came that the mission board had retrenched and there were no funds to keep them in Rangoon. It was an added blow; they must return to Moulmein. Adoniram found it wrenching. His ties to Rangoon went back thirty-four years.

Unusual experiences with creatures, governments, and illness notwithstanding, the Judsons emerged from those months in Rangoon with positive spirits and goals in place. Judson wrote: "My sojourn in Rangoon, though…trying in some respects [he was ever a master of understatement], I regard as one of…the brightest oases, in the diversified wilderness of my life. If this world is so happy, what must heaven be?"[23] Emily, who by this time knew she was pregnant, added her coda: "God counts the scattered hours, God gave the wasted powers—our judge is he!"[24] As they left Rangoon, Judson looked for the last time on the city to which he had given a major portion of his life.

By September 5, they were back in Moulmein. Judson continued to hope to get back to Ava.[25] He even had permission for such a trip from the old governor of Rangoon. Then bitter news came; the board had decided on further cuts and there were no funds for a trip to Ava. It was like a blow. All over America Adoniram had heard calls for more missionaries, for greater giving. Now this? He told Emily, "I thought they loved me, and they would scarcely have known it if I had died."[26] Judson's comments to a missionary friend were pointed: "It is my growing conviction that the Baptist churches in America are behind the age in missionary spirit. They now and then make a spasmodic effort to throw off a nightmare debt…and then sink back into unconscious repose. Then came paralyzing orders to retrench,…and applicants for missionary employ are advised to wait.…The Baptist missions will probably pass into the hands of other denominations, or be temporarily suspended; and those who have occupied the van will fall back into the rear."[27]

However, with his usual bedrock resilience, Judson recovered from the disappointment and determined to continue his tasks as best he could. Conditions in Moulmein were so much easier to deal with that the Judsons could concentrate on their work and the children. They enjoyed the society of the Christians and missionaries in Moulmein, and the boys loved the many playmates they had acquired.

On December 24, 1847, life changed again with the birth of Emily Frances, who was healthy from the start. Emily wrote a beautiful tribute to her, "My Bird." The first stanza read: "Ere last year's moon had left the sky, A birdling sought my Indian nest, And folded, O, so lovingly! Her tiny wings upon my breast."[28] When "My Bird" was two months old, the family moved back into their old home near the chapel. Emily gained strength quickly, and the year 1848 was one of the healthiest, happiest, and most productive of Judson's entire life. Adoniram and Emily rose every morning before sunrise and took a fast walk, as much as two or three miles. They would go up and around the hilltop overlooking the city and glory in the sunrise. Many of the missionaries marveled at their method of getting down the hill—a regular race. It was hard to believe, watching them, that Adoniram Judson was sixty years old.

Henry and little Edward thrived on having Bah (Daddy) at hand and as their companion in play. In his biography of Judson, Edward wrote: "One of them [Edward himself] well remembers how his father used to come into his room in the morning and greet him upon his first awakening with a delicious piece of Burmese cake, or with the joyful tidings that a rat had been caught in the trap the night before." Judson wrote a friend: "I have to hold a meeting with the rising generation every evening and that takes time. Henry can say 'Twinkle twinkle' all by himself and Edward can repeat it after his father! Giants of genius! Paragons of erudition!"[29]

Always close in thought and prayer were the older children. In one letter to Abby Ann, Judson said: "We are a deliciously happy family; but we think much of the three dear absent ones, and my tears frequently fall for your dear, dear mother in her lone bed at St. Helena. And any time I enter the burial-place here, I see the white gravestone of poor little black-eyed Charlie. If you should die, would you go to them too? O that I could hear of your and your brothers' conversion!" "You can never know," he continued, "how much I want to see you, how much I think of you, how much I pray for you, always when I pray for myself."[30] In every letter, Judson expressed his great hope that they would each have a personal relationship with Christ.

Adoniram loved to write about family news. To friends in Philadelphia: "Have I written you since the birth of little Emily Frances?…The little thing will be one year old on the 24th instant. She is a great pet of her brothers…and her mother has taken to the two boys as if they were her own, so that we are a very happy family, not a happier, I am sure, on the broad earth."[31]

Emily wrote a former Moulmein missionary about Edward: "When you left, I believe the little fellow could not talk, but now he has become the veriest chatterbox in the mission. While we resided in Rangoon the children became great cowards (I suppose they caught the infection from us) and…I was obliged to take great pains to break it up. One night Edward, who slept in a little room by himself, called out that he was 'afraid,' and would not be comforted. I have never taught them a prayer to repeat, because I do not like the formality, but I assist them in discovering what they need, and then have them repeat the words after me. So I prayed with little E., kissed him good night and left him apparently satisfied;…soon…I heard him call out, as though in great distress, 'O Dod!' The poor little fellow had not sufficient acquaintance with language to know what to say next; but this up-lifting of the heart evidently relieved him, for in a few minutes…he again called out, 'O, Dod!' but in a tone much softened.

"I stepped to the door but hesitated about entering. In a few minutes he again repeated, 'O, Dod!' but in a tone so confiding that I thought I had better go back to my room, and leave him with his Great Protector. I heard no more of him for some time, when I at last went in and found him on his knees fast asleep. He never fails now to remind me of asking 'Dod to tate tare of him,' if I neglect it, and I have never heard him say a word since of being afraid."[32]

Both parents had more to do than hours in a day, and they liked it that way. Emily described a "normal" mid-morning: "Factotum gone to buy dinner; little Master Henry at his lesson, which I must hear very soon; Edward rolling on the carpet, with his heels in the air, and spelling 'b-a bas,' with all his might; husband, as usual, digging at his dictionary, with his two assistants; and I by just such a confused, littered up table as you used to see at home, with baby asleep on my knees,…my portfolio in a chair on one side, and a half dozen Burman books on the other."[33]

Adoniram was responsible for overseeing the work of the mission, and he was again pastor of the church. A listener described a typical sermon: "All give close attention as he preaches, for he is as forceful and eloquent as ever, often dramatic, sometimes humorous, always direct and impressive. As he closes the sermon the congregation rise to sing, perhaps one of his own hymns, like…'Shwe Pyi kaungin san logyin le' [I long to reach my golden shore]."[34] And more and more, the theme of Judson's preaching was "love." Sometimes he would be so personally overcome by the magnitude of God's love that he would weep as he repeated again and again, "Oh, the love, the love of Christ."[35]

Judson spent endless hours on the dictionary. As he bent over his desk at the tedious work, the lines on his face mapped the intensity of the spirit within. He was convinced that the dictionary's completion would serve as an indispensable tool for missionaries yet to come, proving vital in bringing in the kingdom of God. Emily described his boundless industry: "The good man works like a galley slave; and really it quite distresses me sometimes, but he seems to get fat on it, so I try not to worry. He walks—or rather runs like a boy over the hills, a mile or two every morning; then down to his books, scratch-scratch, puzzle-puzzle, and when he gets deep in the mire, out on the veranda with your humble servant by his side, walking and talking (kan ing we call it in the Burman) till the point is elucidated, and then down again—and so on till ten o'clock in the evening. It is this walking that is keeping him out of the grave."[36]

Son Edward wrote of his father's outlook: "Though he had come to the ripe age of sixty, he had within him the fresh heart of a boy. It has been truly said of him that his spirit was intensely, unconquerably youthful,…[for] in a life of self-sacrifice, he had discovered the perennial fountain of joy.…To his fellow missionaries his wide experience and affectionate disposition made him an invaluable advisor and friend." Edward personalized it when he confided, "The pressures of his public cares and other labors did not make him moody or absent-minded at home. His love for his children was deep and tender."[37]

Once a month on a regular basis, Adoniram would take his turn in leading a meeting for the children in the missionary families—some twenty of them. He delighted in the little ones and sprinkled his talks with humor. Sixty-year-old Judson never lost the love of puzzles the boy Adoniram had reveled in, and he loved confounding the children with a favorite conundrum.

Judson looked back on the completion of the Burmese Bible with a genuine sense of satisfaction. Now he was as equally determined to finish the dictionary. The more advanced he became in translating, the more he wished he could make that longed-for visit to Ava, to meet with the most learned Burmans and consult literary works not accessible in Moulmein. Just at this juncture, however, a Burmese scholar came to Moulmein, and Judson was able to get his assistance. By the end of 1848, the English-Burmese section of the dictionary was completed and came off the press several months later. The first section alone had been six hundred pages, and Judson was already busy on the second; it would likely be as long.[38]

Emily's work as well was constant and varied. Within six weeks she completed the main work of Sarah's memoir, plus mothering three little ones, mastering an intricate language, and leading Burmese women in Bible classes. Emily made exceptional progress in the language and completed the "Scripture Questions" that Sarah had begun several years earlier.

Emily had more limited time for correspondence than she had the first years. In mid-1848 she wrote friend and mentor Cynthia Sheldon: "Since my first letters (all written running), I have been censured more than I deserve for being a negligent correspondent. Now, there are two special reasons why I write so little. The first is want of time. When I first landed I was a spectator; now I am a worker—in the smallest of all ways, to be sure, but still I am busy. Every moment seems inexpressibly precious, and how few the days before we shall be in the grave."[39]

She ended the same letter with a pointed commentary on the depth of "true mission zeal" among Baptists in America: "If I were sitting by you,...I would tell you of a time when we were hungry for want of palatable food; when we were ill, and had neither comforts nor physician; when we were surrounded by the spies of a jealous and unscrupulous government, without any earthly friend to assist us, or any way of escape,...[but] my first *real* missionary trial...was when, amidst sufferings,...a letter came telling of retrenchments,...[and] how could we carry out our plan of going to Ava, while we lacked even the means of remaining where we were? There was nothing left us but to retrace our steps; so we came back to good, comfortable, pleasant Moulmein, making a decided gain in the Egyptian 'leek and onion' line,...[so] do please, tell me your own opinion. Is not the great interest in missions, which makes so much noise at the present day, very much a matter of moonshine—more on the tongue than in the heart?...I think if some of our rich American Baptists could occupy our point of vision for a little while, it would plant a most salutary thorn in their consciences."[40]

It was ironic that in the summer of 1848 Adoniram and Emily finally received news from America: they could go to Ava. At long last the money had been appropriated. But now it was too late—by this time the political climate in Ava was extremely antagonistic to foreigners and religious tolerance. Such a trip to the Golden Feet would no longer help.[41]

Meanwhile, Judson seemed to find a new dimension of satisfaction as shepherd of the Moulmein flock. One of his main themes became the need for disciples to "love one another." Amazed at the progress of Christian missions just in his lifetime, he would frequently exclaim: "What wonders God has wrought." His fellow missionaries often remarked that even his preaching had become increasingly spiritual in tone. His attitude was contagious in the mission, as he inspired his fellow workers, both Burman and American.[42]

Then came a change in the Judsons' health. Late in 1848, Emily, with her weak lungs, was attacked by a worsening cough. In January, she began to improve, but about that time the baby, "Emmy Fan," became so seriously ill they feared losing her. The toddler recovered, but *Emily* grew weak again—so weak that in March, Adoniram wrote her friend Anna Maria, "A dark cloud is gathering around me.

A crushing weight is upon me. I cannot resist the dreadful conviction that dear Emily is in a settled and rapid decline. I sent her to Tavoy in a steamer, on a visit to the missionaries there. She was gone ten days and returned thinner in flesh and weaker than ever. I now take her out every morning in a chaise, and this is all the exercise she can bear. She is under the care of a very skillful doctor, who appears to be making every possible effort to save her, but the symptoms are such that I have scarcely any hope left. She is thinner than she has ever been; strength almost gone; no appetite; various pains in the region of the lungs; a dry cough, which has hung on pertinaciously for two or three months."[43]

Then, just a week later, Emily rallied and they all took heart. Emily wrote her sister that she was stronger and hoped that her life would be spared, for the sake of the little ones, for Adoniram, and for the work she felt she had left to do. She wrote: "I want the privilege of doing a little for Christ before I die, and I leave it to Him to determine where the work is to be performed."[44] How long could they continue? Most would have faltered long before this. But the Judsons, with their usual unequivocal faith, together thanked God and took courage.

CHAPTER 22

His Golden Shore: 1849–1854

I long to reach my golden shore.
—Adoniram Judson

ADONIRAM JUDSON HAD ENDURED MORE SUFFERING IN HIS LIFETIME THAN most people could even imagine. Now Emily was to experience some extremely painful lessons, to bear a new crucible, one even exceeding the varied adversities that had already marked her thirty-two years. Spring of 1849 turned into early summer, and the Judsons were in improved health. Both had been ill so many times that they knew how to appreciate a measure of health. In June, Emily wrote Anna Maria: "We are all getting well again.…Mr. J. is looking, I think,

In 1851, Emily and the three youngest children returned to America accompanied by Nancy, a Burman convert. From *The Life of Adoniram Judson* by E. Judson.

much younger than he did in America and is so well as to be a proverb among the Europeans. For myself, I feel as though I had received the same blessing that Hezekiah did....There was at one time little hope for my recovery....But I feel so very grateful for that illness—My Heavenly Father revealed Himself to me as He never did in health."[1]

She wrote her sister the next month: "I am very well indeed, though not so strong as before my late attack. We sometimes think that I have received a blow from which I shall never fully recover."[2] Her lingering chest weakness and sore throat bothered her. "The doctor assures me that I am in no more danger from consumption than any other person of equal delicacy of constitution; but physicians are not in general over endowed with frankness."[3]

Emily noticed her own ambivalence as her health fluctuated: "The cloud is a little lifted—I am still growing stronger and stronger. Strange that my heart bounds back to earth so joyfully, when I have been accustoming myself to the thought of being with Christ,...but I can not but feel that my work is unfinished...[and] until He call, I pray for length of days and a wide field of usefulness."[4] For both Adoniram and Emily, light had again appeared to pierce the clouds.

During the late summer, Emily realized that her suspicions were true; she was pregnant. They would have another child sometime in April 1850. This added yet another dimension to her already-fragile health. It was a fact, however, and facts must be accepted. Those months of 1849 were a "golden evening" in Judson's life.[5] All who knew him felt that his spirit had never been more vital. "We have both tasted of these bitter cups once and again; and we have found them bitter and we have found them sweet too,"[6] Judson wrote to Sewall Osgood, whose wife had just died: "Every cup stirred by the finger of God becomes sweet to the humble believer."[7]

Emily later wrote a remarkable letter to Adoniram's sister, describing Judson's thoughts and demeanor those final months of his life. "There was something exceedingly beautiful in the decline of your brother's life," she wrote, "more beautiful than I can describe....He was of a singularly happy temperament, although not of that even cast which never rises above a certain level, and is never depressed. Possessing acute sensibilities,...he was variable in his moods; but...his trust in Providence was so implicit and habitual, that he was never gloomy, and seldom more than momentarily disheartened."[8]

As the months went by, Emily wrote, love was the ever-constant theme of his conversations: "'As I have loved you, so ought ye also to love one another,' was a precept continually in his mind, and he would often murmur, as though unconsciously, 'As I have loved you—as I have loved you'—then burst out with the exclamation, 'O, the love of Christ! The love of Christ!'"[9]

"Toward the close of September last year," Emily wrote, "he said to me one evening, 'What deep cause have we for gratitude to God! Do you believe there are any other two persons in the wide world so happy as we are?'"[10] That same night, one of the little ones became ill. Judson got up to help Emily cope, and the damp air and chill led to a dangerous cold. Adoniram developed a high fever and could not get rid of it. By November, more than a month later, Adoniram's condition was so serious that he could not even hold a pen. The disease settled in his lungs, and he never recovered from this blow.[11] In January 1850, the doctors felt a sea voyage might help, so Adoniram and Emily took a steamboat together to Mergui. It seemed to help slightly, but not long after returning, Judson's health failed again. Then they went to Amherst and stayed a month by the seaside, very close to the hopia tree and Ann's grave.

Emily became truly alarmed there, for Adoniram continued to weaken and there were no doctors. When Judson thought no one was looking, he would hold on to furniture for support. He would frequently reminisce and recall all God had done. He especially enjoyed recounting early adventures: his boyhood, the years at Brown, his call. And always, Emily noted, he returned to his favorite thought, "O, the love of Christ! The love of Christ!"[12]

The Judsons discussed their situation, and the looming possibility of Adoniram's death at length. Emily recalled their conversation one evening: "'It is the opinion of most of the mission,' I remarked, 'that you will not recover.' 'I know it is,' he replied; 'and I suppose they think me an old man, and imagine it is nothing for one like me to resign a life so full of trials. But I am not old—at least not in that sense; you know I am not. O, no man ever left this world, with more inviting prospects, with brighter hopes or warmer feelings—warmer feelings,' he repeated and burst into tears."[13] Adoniram also related to Emily his vision of the wonders awaiting them in glory, speaking of the millennial glory, which he felt would begin after the year 2000.[14] As his condition deteriorated, they returned to Moulmein and medical care—and to a new house at the back of the compound. Doctors had long declared the old one unhealthy, and Judson's condition *did* improve. However, it was only temporary, and doctors concluded that the only hope was a sea voyage.

Judson had never approached life as a pessimist. He honestly believed he would recover, weak though he was. He wrote one more letter, this to Solomon Peck at the American board: "I cannot manage a pen; so please to excuse pencil. I have been prostrated with fever ever since the latter part of last November,...I think I am convalescent for the last ten days; but the doctor and all my friends are very urgent that I should take a sea voyage of a month or two....My hand is failing; so I will beg to remain yours affectionately, A. Judson"[15]

That March, Emily was just weeks away from giving birth. While waiting for a ship to take Adoniram to sea, Emily used her masterful pen to compose a poem picturing her "Watching" at his bedside. She described the sounds of the pagoda bells "as if a choir of golden-nested birds in heaven were singing,...and drop like a balm into the drowsy ear."[16] The outpouring of Emily's heart ended on how the thoughts of a future alone would affect her personally. Those tinkling pagoda bells, moved by the air, "Turn to a dirge-like, solitary moan; Night deepens, and I sit, in cheerless doubt, alone."[17]

Adoniram never gave up hope, this extraordinary man who had survived Ava and Aungbinle. "I am not tired of my work," he said, "neither am I tired of the world; yet when Christ calls me home I shall go with the gladness of a boy bounding away from his school." Death held no fear for him. He asserted, "Death will never take me by surprise—I feel so strong in Christ."[18]

One evening, Judson's back gave way as he tried to get into bed; after that he would never again stand. Ten day later, on Wednesday, April 3, he was carried aboard the *Aristide Marie*. Repeatedly Judson said, "If it should be the will of God to let me die here, what a mercy!"[19] The Burmese Christians agreed; they had been loud in their pleas for Judson not to set sail. If he must die, they wanted him to die there in Burma, where he had planted his heart and life. Yet they must try to save his life, and a voyage held the only hope. After all, Adoniram observed, there was something pleasing in the thought of being buried at sea. He loved the sea, its wideness and its freedom. If he had a choice, he actually preferred burial at sea.[20]

Because of Emily's advanced pregnancy, there was no question of her accompanying Adoniram. The mission had appointed Thomas Ranney, who now headed the printing press, to go with Judson. Panapah, a faithful Bengalese helper, would go to aid in any way possible. Sailing was delayed five days, but the one advantage of such a delay was that Emily was able to board the ship and be with Adoniram several times. She wrote: "I was on board the greater part of four days, and had the privilege of arranging everything for his comfort in the way that I knew he liked."[21]

On Monday, April 8, the ship set sail across the Bay of Bengal. For Emily, with a baby due any moment, the terrible wait began. It was the most harrowing period of her life, those four months when she was unable to receive any news of Adoniram. Had he survived? Was he gone already? She lived in agony.

Meanwhile, several of the Burmese Christians remained on board until the ship reached open waters. Adoniram had rallied slightly, and Ranney sent a letter to Emily saying Judson was slightly improved and had even been able to have a little tea and toast. Judson had told Ranney to let Emily know that he had a strong belief it was the will of God to restore him to health.[22] The pain fluctuated, sometimes agonizing and then subsiding. By Tuesday, however, the swelling began, especially in his right side, and Adoniram began to vomit, no longer able to retain any food or liquids. Wednesday, even the air at sea was hot and humid, making it difficult for him to breathe. The pain grew so intense that Ranney gave him laudanum and even ether. Each time he vomited. The pain was so agonizing that he prayed to die and know the joy of heaven, but even in the misery of those final days, his faith never faltered. He assured Ranney that he had no fear that Christ was not near.

By Thursday, Adoniram was close to comatose, his eyes quite glazed over. The pain was torturous all day, and late that night when Ranney felt his feet, they were cold. Friday morning dawned and still he lingered. Mid-afternoon, Judson spoke in Burmese to the faithful Panapah who stood weeping at his side: "It is done; I am going."[23] His last words were a request for them to care for Emily. The pain left. Judson lay quietly with Ranney holding his hand. Ranney wrote: "His death was like falling asleep. Not the movement of a muscle was perceptible, and the moment of the going out of life was indicated only by his ceasing to breathe. A gentle pressure of the hand, growing more and more feeble as life waned, showed the peacefulness of the spirit about to take its homeward flight."[24] The time was a quarter past four on Friday, April 12, 1850. Judson's golden evening had changed to the infinitely greater illumination of heaven. His golden shore was now a glorious reality.

The entire crew of the *Aristide Marie* had watched and waited, showing deep concern for the remarkable stranger who had boarded their ship. They carefully prepared a strong coffin weighted with sand so that it would sink. Judson's mortal remains were gently placed in it and the lid sealed. That same evening, those remains were committed to the open sea, latitude 13 degrees north and longitude 93 degrees east, just northwest of the Andaman Islands.[25] Adoniram Judson had always loved the open sea—the freshness and freedom of its wide expanse; there would be no enclosed, dark, earthen resting spot for him. Months later, Emily's description of that moment formed a tribute to her husband: "Neither could he have a more fitting monument than the blue waves which visit every coast; for his warm sympathies went forth to the ends of the earth, and included the whole family of man."[26]

But that mid-April, Emily had no idea what had happened. A baby was due any moment, three little children were completely dependent on her, and Emily's heart was nearly paralyzed with anxiety. She realized she had no way of getting news for months. Even after the *Aristide Marie* reached a port, a letter would take months to reach her. The odds were staggering that never again would Emily see her beloved, yet she refused to relinquish hope. Emily poured out her grief in poetry. Several lines captured her anguish of soul: "While here from out my dreary prison, I look as from a tomb—alas! My heart another tomb."[27]

Next she wrote the children in America about their father, trying to prepare them, "My very dear children: I have painful news to tell you—news that I am sure will make your hearts ache....Your dear papa is very, very ill indeed, so much so that the best judges fear he will never be any better."[28] She wrote them of the events of the past weeks, explaining that it would be three or four months before there could be any news. That sorrowful task completed, she waited for the baby to arrive, this child who would be another link with Adoniram. That hope changed to anguish when on April 23, only fifteen days after his father had sailed, the tiny baby boy was stillborn. He never drew a breath, and Emily was crushed under the weight of yet another sorrow, this one totally unexpected. Baby Charlie had come, but was already gone.

Some of the circumstances of those dark days were only discovered a century later. Emily wrote two letters to Adoniram in April and May, when she did not know his fate, keeping her own hopes kindled by writing to him as if he were still able to respond.[29] The letters were preserved by Judson descendants and recently came to light. Emily had begun hemorrhaging, and on April 23, right before midnight, the baby was born dead. She wrote Adoniram: "He was a beautiful boy—my dear little Charley, you know—perfect in his formation, and so like you that everyone spoke of it, but very thin—indeed wasted to a skeleton even before he was born."[30]

Emily's letters underscored how keenly she missed Adoniram: "Dr. M thought the child had been dead about twenty-four hours, and hastened the burial on that account. Oh, darling, how I have longed to have you here, for me, to take me in your arms, and make me feel there is somebody that loves me exclusively."[31] Emily concluded the letter with news of the little ones: "The boys pray for 'dear papa' every night, and even baby has learned to say 'God-take-care-papa.'"[32] The recently found letters shed new understanding on the situation in Moulmein while Emily waited to learn Judson's fate. As she so frequently did, Emily poured out the overflow of her heart in poetry. Her "Angel Charlie" is poignant. The first stanza sets the tone of her tribute to the child she held so briefly: "He came—a beauteous vision—Then vanished from my sight, His wing one moment cleaving The blackness of my night."[33]

The long-awaited, long-dreaded news of her husband reached Emily in August, more than four months after he had sailed. Rev. Dr. Mackay, a Scotch Presbyterian minister in Calcutta, sent her the bleak news. In the following days, Emily unleashed her grief in letters to family and friends in America. In all she wrote, one stark sentence summed up her pain: "Oh, it is a terrible thing to lose a friend and guide like him."[34]

As Emily's shattered health gradually improved, her greatest wish was to stay with the mission. Her heart and work were there. She was needed. She longed to use her Burmese language skills and put her writing experience and gifts to the greatest use. Then came the rainy season, and Emily had a relapse. It was painfully obvious that she must come to some decision. Her lungs were so vulnerable that a severe illness could spell sudden death. Then where would three little children be? Her responsibility was a heavy weight, and she reached the inescapable conclusion that her supreme task must be to care and provide for the future of the little ones.

She wrote Anna Maria in October: "You will not think that I do not love you when I say that it is more painful for me to return to America—to leave all—than it was to come away from you originally."[35] Leaving America five years earlier seemed a distant dream now. She told Anna Maria: "My heart is here—I love the missionaries, love the work, and love the precious Christians that have been accustomed to gather round me for prayer and instruction. They sobbed like so many children when I announced my purpose of returning. My knowledge of the language is too important to be thrown away, and my knowledge of the habits and character of the people is probably (from peculiar circumstances) greater than that of many who have been longer in the field. But the state of my health and the good of the children require a sacrifice of feeling which, from your distance, you will be unable to appreciate."[36]

Emily's plan was to gather all the Judson children together under her roof, wherever that would be, and make a home for them. She finished her duties in Moulmein and sadly prepared for the voyage home.[37] A weeping Emily and three bewildered little children sailed from Moulmein on January 22, 1851. Burma was the only home the three had ever known, and it had become Emily's heart home.

By the time the ship landed in Calcutta, Emily's health was slightly improved, and the welcome given her by India's Christian community was balm to her weary soul. Emily summed up her feelings about the time there: "I feel like setting up an Ebenezer in this place before I go, for surely the Lord has thus far helped me."[38] After stops in several ports along the way, their steamer, the *Canada*, reached Boston in October. More than five years had passed since Emily had seen that harbor, and she received a wonderful welcome on her return. Emily had proved herself beyond all expectation. As one biographer put it: "She had gone through the ordeal and come out, like gold from the furnace, approved and refined."[39]

Emily's great task was helping prepare, inspect, and arrange Adoniram's letters and papers. She often grieved because many irreplaceable documents were gone forever, whether destroyed of necessity at Ava, burned by fire, or purposely destroyed by Judson during his period of deep grief following Ann's death. Emily was delighted that Francis Wayland, president of Brown University, a highly respected leader, and Judson's personal friend, was to be Adoniram's official biographer.

The three little ones remained with her until her frail body failed. Emily never regained health. Each new illness left her weaker than the one before. So, although she tried to gather all the children in one place so she could watch over their growth, their education, and spiritual welfare, her failing strength simply did not allow it. She got them together as often as she could, caring for and nurturing each one. She lived in Hamilton, her old hometown, and cared for the three little ones. Whenever possible, the older children came to stay so they could be together as a family. Emily tried writing in order to support all those dependent on her, but her health was so tenuous that she was able to do little more than edit previous work and gather selections from it to be republished. She worked on Judson's biographical material and wrote a few short stories. Her greatest joy those final years was seeing Adoniram, Elnathan, and Abby Ann baptized.

Emily had ominous bleeding from her lungs, and the winters were painfully difficult. Familiar with the signs, she knew her days were numbered. Emily found homes for each of the children, her "bird" Emmy Fan going to her friend Ann Maria Anable. As Emily's biographer described it: "She set about her arrangements with the calmness of one going to visit a friend."[40] Her last weeks brought great suffering, but she never gave up, even when the effort just to speak brought pain that was torture. Somehow Emily lingered until June— her favorite month and the month of her marriage to Adoniram. Her sister, Kate, cared for her those final weeks.

On the morning of June 1, Emily opened her eyes as Kate said: "Emily, do you know that it is June?" "Yes," she replied, "my month to die."[41] Kitty dressed her, and Emily was carried downstairs. Terrible attacks of agonizing suffocation came and went. Late that evening, the pain finally subsided. Tranquilly, without even a sigh—Emily died in the arms of her sister. In just two hours it would have been the eighth anniversary of her wedding. Thus it was, on June 1, 1854, that Emily Judson, that inimitable woman, entered heaven.

Emily had always expressed her deepest soul in poetry. Her last poem, a tribute to Judson, she titled "My Angel Guide." It defined Adoniram's profound influence on her life and described her expectation of what it would be like to reach heaven at last. "My Angel Guide" ended:

> Yet firm my foot, for well I know
> The goal can not be far,
> And ever, through the rifted clouds,
> Shines out one steady star—
> For when my guide went up, he left
> The pearly gates ajar.[42]

The race was over, the victory won. The matchless legacy lives on, and even with the passing of two hundred years, its influence is remarkable.

Finding the Footprints

May the footprints that we leave lead them to believe.
—Jon Mohr, "Find Us Faithful"

EVEN A SINGLE VISIT TO PRESENT-day Burma (Myanmar) provides proof positive that the Judson legacy is alive and thriving. More than a century and a half have passed since the death of Adoniram Judson, but the impact of his legacy continues to expand. The first sight in Burma that caught his eye on that historic 1813 morning was the fabled golden Shwe Dagon pagoda. In this new millennium, that gleaming spire is still the magnet that inevitably captures the eye as it pierces the smog of a bustling, crowded city, but the city of Rangoon (Yangon) over which it towers is no longer completely pagan, because on that long-ago day, Ann and Adoniram Judson planted their lives in Burma.

The size of that giant monument of gold must have stunned the Judsons, for it reaches nearly as high as the great pyramids of Egypt. Legend takes its founding back 2,500 years. This incredible mass contains over sixty tons of gold, more than is housed in the Bank of England. The spire is covered with more than 13,000 gold plates, the

Immanuel Baptist Church in downtown Rangoon, founded in 1855, is one of Burma's oldest and largest churches, conducting services in five languages.

vane at the top studded with 1,400 precious rubies and sapphires and crowned by 5,000 diamonds weighing 2,000 carats. One enormous 76-carat diamond is positioned to catch the first light of the morning sun.[1] There is nothing of poverty about Shwe Dagon, Buddhism's most sacred shrine, yet it looms over a city and country so impoverished by a military regime that, in spite of rich natural resources of teak and precious gems, Burma ranks among the world's ten poorest nations.

In one sense, since the young mission pioneers stood in this same place, little has changed. The Judsons were appalled at the opulence of the Shwe Dagon in the midst of poverty. Poverty still blankets the nation, and the hearts of a repressed people still long for help. However, something is strikingly different. Along with pagodas, now mingle the spires of churches, a compelling tribute to that 1813 beginning. In fact, at the 1913 Judson Centennial in Rangoon, one seminary student summed it up: "July 13, 1813, was Burma's Christmas Day!"[2]

Rangoon abounds with efforts at modernization in spite of a government that has basically stripped its 50 million people of fundamental rights. The streets throng with people who are by nature friendly and welcoming but have been molded by leadership that chooses to shun the outside world.

It is a small wonder that unanimity is difficult to come by in this nation of three thousand years of history, more than sixty racial groups, and two hundred languages. Beginning in the eleventh century, a series of mighty kings ruled the land—the "golden period." King Anawrahta consolidated a kingdom in A.D. 1044, and various subsequent kingdoms rose and fell. King Bagyidaw, a despotic ruler, came to the throne in 1819. Sixty years later, in 1885, Britain's decisive victory in the third Anglo-Burmese war ended the era of Burmese kings, and Burma became a colony, part of Britain's vast Indian Empire. Burma was granted a portion of self-government in 1923 and twelve years later became a separate colony from India. The people of Burma suffered greatly under Japanese occupation during World War II. Britain granted them full independence in 1948.

When military rule began in Burma in 1962, things changed. There was an even greater crackdown in 1988, and very few personal freedoms remained. Repression of student protests led to the closing of universities. The military did allow an election in 1990, and Daw Aung San Sui Kyi, daughter of Burma's national hero, was overwhelmingly elected as leader. Although awarded the Nobel Peace Prize in 1991, she was not allowed to lead her country, and she was under house arrest most of the next years.[3] A military regime continues today.

Sprawling Rangoon, with its nearly 5 million people, is crowded with decaying buildings aged beyond their years. These relics of colonialism are scattered along the streets and alleys, reminding everyone of the Burma that once was. The streets are alive with honking buses, cars, taxis, bikes, and trishaws, and people of many tribes and nations brush shoulders as they hurry through the day. The favorite dress is still the ubiquitous *lungyi*, some six feet of material wrapped around and knotted at the waist. This has been the "national dress" for centuries. Men wear them, women wear them, and bright tribal patterns are popular—just as they were in the Judsons' day.

Another persistent tradition remains popular. Men and women, and sometimes even young boys and girls, may be seen smoking cigars. "Smoking a stogy" seems to be something of a national pastime. Amazing—to think that this same sight greeted the Judsons on these identical streets. The substance staining modern Rangoon sidewalks also decorated these paths long ago: betel juice. The areca nut, a mild stimulant, is a favorite chew throughout the land, and it produces bright red juice that is spat along the street, against the side of buildings, and on the floors of many houses—the same red juice that marked the prison floors at Ava and Aungbinle when Judson was there.

Where in this fascinating old city—in the sprawl of buildings, industries, people, and vehicles—had a young couple found a place to live and begin their work? Ann and Adoniram had arrived in Rangoon of 1813 to find only a small town standing in swamp land, the jungle held at bay only by a wooden stockade. How isolated and marooned they surely felt. It is easy to stand on a street corner in modern Rangoon and imagine the Judsons passing that very spot, on foot or maybe riding in a cart. Street names have changed, but the city's layout is essentially unaltered.

Curiosity about the early mission evolved into a quest to find the Judson trail in this huge city. A tiny bookstore in downtown Rangoon was reported to specialize in hard-to-find books. Pagan (pronounced Bay GAHN) Book House was itself a colonial relic. When asked if he knew of Adoniram Judson, the proprietor, U Ba Kyi, who looked ageless, creased his wrinkled face into a delighted smile. He responded in beautiful English, "Yoodthan! Of course I know of Judson! Just a moment," and holding up an admonitory finger, shuffled his way into a back room. In moments he was back, holding a first edition of Courtney Anderson's biography of Judson. It showed its fifty years in the tropics but was remarkably intact. On a nearby table was a brightly covered volume titled *Burmese-English Dictionary*, by Adoniram Judson—still in print.

All along the lanes and alleyways in the city were tiny bookstalls. Old rubbishy volumes and dusty copies of elderly *National Geographics* rubbed shoulders with modern Burmese paperbacks. At stall after stall, clerks would nod and say, "Oh yes! I know who Yoodthan was!" Here were people to whom the name *Judson* was a household word. Those pioneer footprints were beginning to emerge.

Finding actual Judson historical sites, however, was not simple. There were no maps with the old colonial street names. Then a hotel shop revealed a treasure, a book by British historian B. R. Pearn, with a foldout map of Rangoon, circa 1810. There were no street names; there were scarcely any streets. However, the map marked the outline of the old stockade, the harbor, the dreaded execution ground, Sule Pagoda, and yes—the mission house. Now to figure out how this ancient map juxtaposed with a more modern one and locate where this first mission house had been. Somewhere in this city there must be a map using the street names of colonial Rangoon.

This marked the beginning of an absorbing journey of exploration, beginning with a visit to the offices of the Myanmar Baptist

Convention near downtown Rangoon. It is housed in Cushing Hall, the main building of Burma's Judson College in the first decades of the twentieth century. Several convention officers recommended a trip north to Mandalay, where the prison sites were located, and to Moulmein in the south, which had become the center of Baptist work. One leader mentioned a Judson memorial stone that had stood on the site of the Ava prison but was now gone. Rumor said it had been "thrown into the sea." "No," another leader disagreed, "it was buried." Such ambiguous information made a visit to Ava seem doubly intriguing.

One convention officer suggested talking to Paul Johns, pastor of Immanuel Church and known to be knowledgeable about Judson history. Johns, whose English was impeccable, was a classic blend of Burmese and Indian cultures. His family was Indian-English-Burmese back five generations and Baptist nearly that long. For many years his mother had been a deacon at Immanuel Church, where her son was now pastor. It is Burma's largest church and among the oldest in the nation. With his rich heritage, Johns was keen on history and eager to share his knowledge of Baptist roots.

Immanuel Church stands very near the spot where the old execution gate once stood, just yards from where Ann and Adoniram first entered the city. Johns suggested a "Baptist tour" of Rangoon, seeing where Baptist hospitals, schools, press, and college had once been. Baptists from America had been a profound influence in this city. Just beyond the present-day Bogyoke Aung San market in downtown Rangoon is the central railway station. In the yard of that station the original mission house had stood. Paul Johns reminisced, "When I was a small lad, my great-grandfather brought me here and showed me where the Judsons had lived." How amazed Ann and Adoniram would be to see the spot today. That old teak house had stood high on its stilts, marked by a two-acre garden on one side and jungle on the other. Now the site is a noisy, busy thoroughfare, with masses passing each day, unknowingly walking upon history.

The gardens of that first 1800 house had given welcome shade to the young couple who walked there, and in these gardens little Roger

Judson had been buried in 1816. Historian Pearn wrote that "to this mission house was attached a burial ground which became the English cemetery of Rangoon."[4] A memorial plaque once hung on a lamppost on the street. The plaque is gone, but the memories linger.

It proved much more difficult to pinpoint the spot where the first baptism had taken place. No Baptist leader seemed clear about the location. There were few references to the exact spot in the Judson papers. Many biographies spoke vaguely of a pond or tank in the direction of the Great Pagoda Road, the main thoroughfare leading to Shwe Dagon. Tanks were very common in early-nineteenth-century Rangoon. All have disappeared, buried beneath the load of modernization. The Judsons had written that they built their *zayat* (worship place) on property they had purchased next to their own land—toward Pagoda Road where many passersby trod each day. On the 1819 Sunday that saw the baptism of U Naw, the little congregation first gathered for worship and then walked from the *zayat* to a nearby pond. Several secular Burman accounts tell of a wondering crowd standing on a hill watching a white foreigner doing an exceedingly strange thing—putting his hands upon a Burmese man and dipping him under the water. *Burma Baptist Chronicles* records that this baptism took place just to the east of "Scot's Kirk,"[5] but there is now no such Presbyterian church.

After several promising leads led nowhere, a young pastor came with the answer. Scot's Kirk is now a Methodist church, and yes, it stands on a hill, near the railroad yards. Sure enough, there was the church on a hill and below its gentle slope ran the road in the direction of Shwe Dagon. Under this road are the remains of the old tank used for the first baptism. Would not U Naw be astounded that he, as humble as a man could be, held a revered place in the hearts of a denomination?

Back in the United States, the search for an authentic old map began. It took months, but one turned up in a Pennsylvania basement. Russell Brown, retired missionary and former pastor of Immanuel Church, proved to be the source. The map was large and clear—old Rangoon, all streets clearly marked. On a subsequent trip to Burma, this colonial map verified both the location of the 1813 mission house and the site of the first baptism.

Each July, Baptist churches throughout Burma/Myanmar celebrate "Judson Day," commemorating the arrival of Ann and Adoniram Judson in 1813. At the 1999 memorial service at Immanuel Church, the speaker gave thanks for the nearly 4 million believers in Burma, concluding: "Let Judson's life be a challenge to us. He has passed on the torch. We must take it up." In January 2001, Immanuel commemorated the 185th anniversary of the established church in Burma.[6]

Meanwhile, several hundred miles north of Rangoon were more spots that were vital links in the Judson legacy. Mandalay had two ancient prison sites close by, one of which offered the mystery of the memorial stone. The puzzle regarding its whereabouts begged to be solved. Surely the footprints at Ava and Aungbinle must be visible somewhere along those ancient paths.

CHAPTER 24

"On the Road to Mandalay"

On the road to Mandalay / Where the flying fishes play
And the dawn comes up like thunder / Out of China 'cross the bay.
—Rudyard Kipling, "On the Road to Mandalay"

MANDALAY. THE NAME CONJURES UP THE EXOTIC EAST: PALACES, PRINCES, temples, and jungles. A modern-day flight from bustling Rangoon to the other Burma—of priests and pagodas—takes just over an hour. In 1823, Ann and Adoniram's trip up the mighty Irrawady took *six weeks*. Burma, now known as Myanmar, is Asia's third largest country and the size of France and England combined. The Irrawady rises high in the Himalayas in the north and flows down to the Gulf of

Present-day Judson Baptist Church, built in 1905 and later expanded, stands on the site of the Aungbinle prison.

248

Martaban in the south, over one thousand miles. On the Irrawady of the 1820s, the Judsons could easily have heard the faint paddling sound made by forty royal oarsmen rowing the emperor's magnificent gilded barge, blindingly bright in the tropical sun. Such decadent splendor is now just a memory, but small trading vessels still ply the mighty river.

Marco Polo visited this spot in the thirteenth century and described the teak jungles "teeming with elephants, unicorns and other wild beasts." Myanmar is still producer of 75 percent of the world's teak. And the mythical unicorn aside, the Judsons saw more wild animals than they could have dreamed of at home in New England: elephants, leopards, tigers, and even a few of Burma's astounding fifty-two varieties of poisonous snakes. There are some 2,000 tigers left, four times as many as in neighboring Thailand, and one-third of all the Asian elephants in the world, numbering 10,000, are found there.[1]

The Judsons saw small villages along the riverbanks, and vast jungle areas alive with animals. Ann had described life along the river: "Our boat was small,...[but we] arrived in safety in six weeks.... We often walked through the villages; and though we never received the least insult, always attracted universal attention. A foreign female was a sight never before beheld, and all were anxious that their friends and relatives should have a view. Crowds followed us through the villages, and some who were less civilized than others, would run some way before us, in order to have a *long* look as we approached them."[2]

Some things are little altered since 1800. There would be much in modern Myanmar that Ann and Adoniram would readily recognize, like ancient Bagan (Pagan). The Rangoon to Mandalay flight touches down briefly in this deserted city, which was abandoned even when the Judsons walked its streets. Bagan dates back 2,000 years, and at its height was covered with a staggering 13,000 pagodas, more than any other city in the world. Bagan is truly a ghost city now, holding the remains of thirty square miles of pagodas. As a living city, it was abandoned in 1287 when Kublai Khan's hordes descended, but at last count, there were still more than 2,200 pagodas. Whether viewed from the air or by walking on its echoing streets, it is an amazing sight.[3] Ann described it to her sister Mary: "The Burman system of religion is like an alabaster image, perfect and beautiful in all its parts, but destitute of life…[and] it provides no atonement for sin. Here, also, the gospel triumphs.…This is the grand difference—this makes the gospel 'good news' indeed, to the heavy laden and sin-sick soul."[4]

The Judsons reached Ava in February 1824, and their lives were never the same. In this new millennium, anyone interested in missions history and its legacy must be affected by a visit to this spot. Less than ten miles from the ruins of Ava is Mandalay, the last royal city and the most Buddhist in all Burma. Sixty percent of the tens of thousands of monks and nuns who walk the villages and cities of the land, barefoot and begging bowls in hand, live in Mandalay.[5] It was just a straggling village in the heyday of those exotic ancient capitals that surround her—Sagaing, Ava, Amarapura. Even the names ring like the thousands of temple bells that echo constantly in the wind. The royal kingdom met its doom here in Mandalay, and the main thing now found walking its sprawling, dusty streets is nostalgia for long-gone days.

Mandalay watches the meandering Irrawady flow by on its way to the sea. The city is young for Burma, but only Rangoon is more populated. Mandalay, hot and nearly treeless, is sprawled out over twenty-five square miles. The royal palace, King Mindon's "Golden City," is now in ruins. Mindon moved the capital here the same year America began its agony of civil war. The last king, Mindon's son Thibaw, was exiled by the British in 1885, but not before he managed to kill eighty of his relatives. His choice of methods—having them sewn up in red velvet sacks and clubbed to death or trampled on by the royal elephants. The elephant method, he had learned as a child, was one of the favorite tactics used by his ancestors.[6] The palace must have been a spectacular sight at its zenith, a perfect square, more than a mile in each direction, and its immense walls rise more than twenty-six feet high. All but the walls were consumed by flames in 1945 when British and Indian troops advanced on the Japanese who controlled it.[7]

Far more intriguing, however, is the Judson impact on this area.

Baptist influence is very visible. The steeple of Judson Centennial Church pierces Mandalay's blazing blue sky. It was built in 1888 on the one-hundredth anniversary of Judson's birth; hanging near the entranceway is the Roger Williams memorial bell, a gift from the women of First Baptist Church, Providence, Rhode Island. Two blocks away is the former American Baptist school that educated thousands before the present regime "nationalized" it. A Baptist congregation still meets in one of the buildings.

The cities of Ava, Sagaing, and Amarapura, all surrounding Mandalay, actually provide the real fascination. Sagaing, west and south of Mandalay and just across the Irrawady from Ava, was the capital in the 1300s, but when it fell to the Shans, Ava became the new center of the kingdom for some four hundred years—longer than any other capital in Burma's history.

It is about eight miles from Mandalay to the ferry crossing to Ava, but the condition of the roads makes the distance seem farther. Dust and bumps carry travelers into another world—a deserted kingdom. "Ferry" is a dignified euphemism for the ancient little boat powered by a decrepit putt-putt motor that offers transport for five "chat" (about two cents) into this ancient world. Ava means "city of gems," and it is genuinely a jewel in the crown of missions history. A canal was cut to join the Irrawady with the Mytinge River, so ancient Ava has become an island. Dedicated archaeologists would enjoy being marooned with such a treasure trove. Ava was abandoned as Burma's capital in 1841, but the ghosts of a thousand years still walk about.

There are three historical "Avas." The first Ava of 1824 witnessed the suffering of the Judsons; then there was the 1915 Ava, when that prison spot actually belonged to the Baptists of Burma, who placed a monument here. The third Ava is that of the twenty-first century, where believers can approach the place where it all happened and see little but the evidence of their hearts to commemorate the courage of the Judsons. When approaching the deserted area called Let Ma Yoon, the recollection of the suffering of those two young missionaries is sobering. The events of 1824–1826 made stunning news in America; surely the echo of the Judsons' sacrifice and perseverance still reverberates in this lonely, timeless spot.

Stepping off the ferry onto the island is stepping back in time. A queue of horse-drawn carts waits to transport pilgrims to an earlier era. One of the drivers is U Thaw, tall and thin, probably fifty years old. He was born less than a mile from Let Ma Yoon. His sunburned face brightened. "Yood-da-than?" Of course he knew who Judson was! And Let Ma Yoon? "Certainly. I have lived right here since I was a little boy." U Thaw takes travelers directly to Let Ma Yoon. Obliging horses amble along the dusty, uneven paths that serve as a road, each new bump causing the bells on their harnesses to jingle merrily in the breeze. The ruts themselves must be ancient. They are certainly deep and plentiful. The experience of Ava is rather like being caught in a time warp; it is easy to imagine the same scene two centuries ago.

The outline of the palace walls is still visible in places, as is the moat that surrounded it. There are two gates guarding the deserted city—both have been restored.[8] The spires of the aging pagodas of Maha Aungmye Bonzan, the old monastery that was adjacent to Let Ma Yoon, still remain. Nanmyin, the emperor's ninety-foot watchtower, was the highest point on the horizon. It is the one intact remnant of the ancient palace.[9] The prison once stood next to that royal residence, and it is still bordered on one side by centuries-old trees. The place where Judson lay fettered is now a deserted field of overgrown scrub. The towering trees call to mind Ann Judson's journal, recording the rare occasions when she could bribe the guards to allow Adoniram to sit in the prison yard, in a corner where he could catch the shade of a tree standing just outside the stockade. These ancient trees had given blessed shade to Judson nearly two centuries ago.

Reflecting on the suffering that occurred here and on the enduring strength of a spirit sustained by grace makes it a poignant moment. Ann wrote of Adoniram looking at these nearby pagodas at Maha Aungmye Bonzan and envisioning the day when *church* spires would be found throughout Burma. He often gazed at the crumbling old watchtower, just about a thousand feet away, and recalled, "O Lord, thou art my buckler, the horn of my salvation, and my high tower,"

The cart driver, U Thaw, knew the location of two marble slabs—all that remained above ground of the Judson memorial stone. There are some fragments of the bricks from the palace wall scattered over the immediate area. U Thaw spoke with certainty: "Here is where the stone is buried." The story he related matched that of an elderly Baptist leader living in Mandalay.

The vast stone was placed on its marble base in 1915, its variegated marble seven feet long, and six feet wide at one end, four feet at the other. It read in Burmese and English: "In memory of Adoniram Judson, D.D., and Ann Hasseltine Judson, his wife, missionaries of the American Baptist Missionary Union. This memorial is erected on the site of Ava 'Let Ma Yoon' prison, in which Dr. Judson, sustained by his faith in the Lord Jesus Christ, and by the devoted ministrations of his noble wife, suffered imprisonment from June, 1824, to May, 1825 A.D."[10]

In 1988, Buddhist leaders persuaded authorities that such a stone honoring a foreigner was "politically incorrect" for a sacred Buddhist site. Authorities first demanded that the villagers take the stone and throw it into the Irrawady. That was easier said than done. The stone was massive, and try as they might, the village people could not lever it up. The authorities next brought in a bulldozer, and *that* also failed. Suddenly, in the midst of the villagers' reluctant efforts, the earth began to tremble and move. It was an earthquake, but such a thing had not occurred at Ava in the lifetime of these peasant farmers. With one voice, the villagers adamantly refused to have another thing to do with moving "the stone." They would not touch it. The government most reluctantly sent in troops, who dug a hole and managed to roll the stone into it. There it remains, an invisible but stirring tribute to exceptional courage.

A deeply rutted dirt road goes around the perimeter of the ancient capital. This is the same dirt road that Ann Judson trudged each day between her home and the death prison to feed her husband and sustain his life. The exact location of Ann and Adoniram's little house, somewhere outside these crumbling city walls, is lost in history, but it had stood some two miles from the palace and the prison.

But the Judsons had suffered much more after Ava, for Adoniram had been in yet another prison. That spot was in the town of Aungbinle, just twelve miles away, but for one who was feverish, dehydrated, and malnourished, walking those few miles on bare, bleeding feet must have seemed a lifetime. Today's road from Ava to Aungbinle is hardly less bumpy, and retracing the route of the prisoners leads to reflection on what must have been going through Adoniram's mind as he suffered with each step. Paramount was surely the thought of what Ann would think when she returned to Let Ma Yoon and found him gone. And then he would weep inwardly over the pillow with its priceless New Testament contents, abandoned there at Let Ma Yoon.[11]

On the site of Aungbinle prison now stands Judson Baptist Church. What superb irony: a church where once the prison stood, named for one of the prisoners. On the right side of Judson Church, running from the roof to the door, is a large, jagged crack.[12] The rift occurred in the earthquake of 1988, the same one that hit Ava. A low brick wall surrounds the property, and at the back of the church is the pastor's home. This house likely sits on the land where Ann had lived in one little room and kept three children as well as her husband alive. Memories of her courage still linger at Aungbinle.

Silas Saw, the pastor at Judson Baptist Church, is a Karen, and his father had been pastor before him. Reverend Saw knows the Aungbinle story well and loves recounting what happened there. The church was founded more than one hundred years ago, and the building was completed in 1905, largely through the fund-raising efforts of Judson's son Edward. Two wealthy donors, one from Ohio, the other from Minnesota, never had the opportunity to visit the place but wanted future generations to remember Aungbinle. The first small building was named the Ann Hasseltine Judson Memorial Chapel, and it has since been enlarged. Inside the church hang pictures of Adoniram and Ann and a photograph of the memorial stone taken many years earlier. This historic little church also holds a special treasure, a large first edition of the Burmese Bible printed in 1840.

Several years ago, a committee of biblical scholars from across

Burma met to consider a new edition of the Bible. After long meetings and much consultation, the committee reached its conclusion: Judson's remarkable translation was so beautiful and so compellingly rendered that the scholars could not improve upon its accuracy and purity. The committee disbanded.

At one time, the Aungbinle church held other unique relics as well. When the foundation was dug for the church around the beginning of the twentieth century, workers uncovered rusted old stocks and fetters left there when the foreign prisoners had finally been released. The church kept the fetters in the sanctuary as a memorial to Judson and his fellow prisoners. During the Japanese occupation in World War II, those artifacts "disappeared" and have never been found.

Another treasure turned up in Mandalay; this one was living. Daw Khin Nu, a pastor's daughter, was for thirty years principal of the Baptist High School. In her late eighties, she lived in a house near Mandalay's Judson Centennial Church. Daw Khin Nu spoke flawless English and loved reminiscing about Judson history in the Ava area. Her father had been pastor of the Sagaing church, working there with A. C. Hanna, Judson's youngest grandson. She recalled playing with the Hanna children and remembered clearly when the youngest son, Stanley, was born in 1920. Daw Khin Nu and her father were the ones who had carefully preserved the rare first edition Bible and presented it to the Aungbinle church on its seventy-fifth anniversary.

Missions history in the Mandalay area is rich, but there was more. Far to the south lay new opportunities to see what was happening on the spiritual foundation laid long ago. The Judsons made the trip to Amherst by water, but present-day pilgrims can brave *modern* highways and look for other treasures of missions history yet to be explored.

The Monuments of Moulmein and Amherst

By the Old Moulmein
 pagoda, / Lookin' lazy at the sea
There's a Burma girl a settin' /
 And I know she thinks o' me.
—Rudyard Kipling, "Mandalay"

THE FIRST PROBLEM WITH VISITING MOULMEIN (MAWLAMYINE) IS FINDING a way to get there. To the question "What is the best way to get to Moulmein?" the response is an incredulous look or a slight shake of the head. Once there were two flights a week; now there are none. That leaves train, public bus, or hired car. If relative convenience is a priority, strike the first two. Travel guides are candid about the challenge of the trip. One guide declares: "The 'Road to Moulmein' as opposed to Kipling's 'Road to Mandalay'—has deteriorated alarmingly and would assuredly have upset the old master. It is little short of diabolical. Travelers these days will sample mouthfuls of dirt and grit, [and] experience a constant stream of straggling lorries throwing up snowstorms of dust....It is possible you will reach the river crossing at Martaban in about eight hours (punctures and errant goats permitting)."[1] This daunting picture proves all too accurate.

Had Rudyard Kipling's famous "On the Road to Mandalay" indeed been "On the Road to Moulmein" instead, he would surely

Dr. Stanley Hanna, great-grandson of Adoniram Judson, and author Rosalie Hall Hunt stand with Harriet Bahn and Juan Myint, great great-granddaughters of the first Burmese printer, Ah Vong, by the grave of Ann Judson.

have been making poetry out of pain. As the guide promised, it is *not* a journey for the faint of heart. The end result, however, is worth ten or more hours of bumps, twists, turns, and whatever the weather throws in the path. No place in Burma is richer in missions history, and what happened there makes the trip worth the effort.

According to the map, the distance from Rangoon to Moulmein is not far, about 185 miles. The roads make reality far different. The cross section of life along the way, however, is both varied and engrossing. Clusters of little villages, houses elevated on stilts, domestic animals roaming freely, and little children happily splashing in the mud could easily have been the same sights the Judsons saw. The ubiquitous monks of Burma are much in evidence in the villages. Each morning, they walk in lines with their begging bowls held out, no matter what the weather. The order is often according to height—the youngest little novices, maybe seven years old, in their saffron robes leading some twenty people, with the older monks bringing up the rear. Occasionally the lines are reversed, with the oldest and tallest first. Less frequently a line of nuns can be seen as well, with their heads shaved and wearing pink robes with saffron scarves.

In some rural areas, the one-lane roads mean that approaching vehicles must decide who pulls off the road. All sizes and shapes of cars, rickety buses, and rundown trucks share the roads with ox-drawn carts, bicycles, and pedestrians. The 185-mile trip should require about four or five hours, but each of three trips to Moulmein took longer than the last—from ten to fourteen hours. Even taking a rest stop is a problem; there are no service stations, and cars must haul their own gas containers.

Finding information about Baptist landmarks in Moulmein was *another* challenge. Old biographies and documents in archives finally yielded some basic information. A hand-drawn map of the old mission compound found in the American Baptist Historical Society archives is the only known map of that historic spot. "Living links," however, revealed details about Baptist beginnings.

The best source of "live" information was the sole living great-grandson of Adoniram Judson (and wife Emily). Dr. Stanley Hanna, in his eighties, is a retired professor of physics at Stanford University and a man who clearly inherited the tremendous intellect of his great-grandparents. Hanna is steeped in family history and has vast stores of family anecdotes and materials in both his memory and in the family keepsake trunk. To make his testimony even more compelling, he himself was born in Burma and grew up there.

More living links to the Judson heritage are Burmese Baptists whose spiritual foundations go back to Judson in the early years in Moulmein. Harriet Bain, born in Burma, is now a U.S. citizen. She is a piece of Baptist biography, part of distinguished Burmese Baptist history on both parents' sides. The account of her family is a saga in itself. Harriet's great-great-grandfather was Ah Vong, the first Chinese-Burmese printer in the 1830s. He married Daw Lone Ma, who was baptized by Judson at the age of twelve.[2] That unique couple had twelve sons, many of whom became Baptist leaders. Four of the granddaughters of Ah Vong and Daw Lone Ma are still living. They were born and raised in Moulmein and now live together in Rangoon. At the beginning of the new millennium, these venerable ladies ranged in age from ninety-two to one hundred. Daw Ngwe, the oldest, clearly remembered her grandmother, who had lived with them and had often spoken of the early years and Dr. Judson. Daw Lone Ma had lived to a ripe old age. The keen minds of the four Nyein sisters belied their many years. They studied the one-hundred-year-old map of the old Judson compound and added firsthand information, for they had grown up in a house just one block away.

Moulmein, with its quarter million people, was the capital of British Burma from 1827 until 1852 and retains an ambience of post-colonial decay. The scenery approaching Moulmein is still as beautiful as it was two centuries ago. Driving in the direction of the Gulf of Martaban, the pagodas the Judsons saw every day are still visible to the east, nestled among the trees on the hills near the city. They glimmer through the morning mists, lending a touch of the exotic to the landscape. The arrival of the new century also marked the opening of a welcome addition to the old city: a comfortable hotel. It is on the Strand by the Andaman Sea and looks out on one of the world's most beautiful sunsets. As an unexpected bonus, the Nge Mwo Hotel is less than two blocks from where the Judsons once lived. These are the same sunsets that had warmed their hearts.

Adoniram Judson could never have predicted beginning the second phase of his ministry here. However, after the horrors of war, land in the south was ceded to the British, and the Judsons had felt the most effective work could be done here in an atmosphere where they had freedom to tell the message. The British had first chosen Amherst, about twenty-eight miles south of Moulmein, to be their capital. That is where Ann began work, building a house and starting a school and church while Adoniram went back north to translate the commercial treaty. Then the British moved the capital to the fine port town of Moulmein. The grieving Judson had moved here in 1827, determined to continue the work they had begun together and for which Ann had died.

Three blocks from the Nge Mwo Hotel is Judson Baptist Church with its towering steeple. Every few years it is whitewashed, but that color soon becomes weathered in the tropical climate. A large sign at the right side states: First Baptist Church, Founded by Adoniram Judson, 1827. The present building was erected in 1937. Inside the sanctuary is a massive white marble tablet paying tribute in both English and Burmese to the foreign missionaries and Burmese leaders who poured their lives into ministry here: "Dedicated to the Glory of God and in Grateful Memory of all who have by life and work helped to build Christ's kingdom in Moulmein. 1827–1977." The list begins: Adoniram Judson, Ann Judson, Sarah Boardman Judson, Emily Judson—an honor roll of heroes.

In front of the church are several graves. The Baptist (European) cemetery, only two blocks away, was nationalized in the mid-1990s, so church members moved several graves to the church. One is that of Emily Margaret Hanna, granddaughter of Adoniram and Emily, who died in missionary service in 1911 at age forty-one. The other Judson marker etches in words the pain of Sarah and Adoniram Judson: "The grave of CHARLES JUDSON, son of Adoniram and Sarah B. Judson who died August 5, 1845, aged 1 year and 7 months."

Scattered around Moulmein are many Baptist churches and schools. Those schools, built and run by missionaries for more than a hundred years, are now nationalized. The government has taken over Ellen Mitchell Hospital, named for the first missionary doctor, but in large red letters over the portico the words remain: "The Son of Man came not to be ministered unto but to minister."

A singular spot of Baptist history, the Christian Leprosy Hospital, continues to minister as it has for more than a century. Much-loved missionary teacher Susan Haswell, herself the daughter of pioneer missionaries, founded the ministry. Chief reconstructive surgeon, Saw Wah Htoo, has been operating here for more than a quarter of a century, and his wife, Freedom, is the physical therapist. There remain thousands of lepers in Burma, but health education by the hospital staff is reducing that number each year.

The heart of Baptist beginnings in Burma is less than two blocks from the present Judson church. The old, hand-sketched map pinpoints this compound, rich in Baptist history. Most of the area is now the sports field of the high school located here. Classes are conducted in the one remaining building, which held the first printing press of Burmese Baptists, the place where the first edition of the Bible was produced. A memorial tablet is embedded in the wall of the school commemorating the event. On what is now the soccer field stood the church Judson founded in 1827. A covered walkway led from the church to the Judsons' house. In front of where the house once stood are the stumps of two massive trees Judson planted in the 1830s, but the focal point is the northern corner of the old compound. A little creek, long dried up, flowed through this spot, and it was here those pioneers built a tank for Burma's first constructed baptistry. At the eastern end of the large compound is Ebenezer Baptist Church. Judson had organized it primarily as a ministry to the many English soldiers garrisoned in Moulmein. The building was badly damaged by bombings during World War II. Inside the reconstructed sanctuary, members placed the cornerstone: "English Baptist Church Moulmein. Founded by Dr. A. Judson March 1829. Centenary 1929." And on the wall in large letters in both Burmese and English is the text from 1 Samuel 7:12: "Call its name 'Ebenezer' for he said Hitherto the Lord Has Helped Us."

The rest of the missions story of Moulmein is actually a recounting of what occurred so long ago in Amherst, two hours to the south. Ann and Adoniram had first landed there in 1826. Ann never made it as far as Moulmein. Her memory did, however, and lives on as an encouragement to an entire body of believers. Amherst waited to be explored.

Very few have made the trek to the remote little town. Small wonder. The spot is now painfully isolated. Kyaikkami, the present name for the old Amherst, sounds exotic enough, but the route to reach the town is bumpy, winding, and intensely uncomfortable. Until recently, the government itself would not permit tourists to travel these roads, calling them "brown zones." The authorities attributed the danger to Mon and Karen insurgents lurking in the nearby jungle areas.

There is plenty of history on the road to Amherst, along with motorcycles, ox carts, and ancient trucks. The route leads through the little town of Thanbyuzayat, which was the western end of the notorious railway featured in the movie *The Bridge on the River Kwai*. In World War II, the Japanese, wanting an alternate route to infiltrate Burma and nearby countries, calculated it would take five years to link Burma and Thailand by rail by normal means. The Japanese army forced prisoners of war to complete the line in just sixteen months. Literally thousands of Allied POWs were compelled to labor under unbelievable conditions, and 16,000 died. Japan used the line for twenty months before the Allies bombed it in 1945. Of all those thousands of POWs, only one, aided by Karen guerrillas, escaped. Even more shocking than the deaths of so many Allied soldiers was the number of forced laborers from Burma and surrounding countries who perished. Between 90,000 and 100,000 of them died in the construction process.[3] Here in the little town of Thanbyuzayat is Htaukkyant War Cemetery, which testifies to the tragic history. The road into town actually crosses the tracks laid down by those doomed prisoners. Some 3,771 Allied prisoners are buried here, each marked by a single white cross standing on the quiet and beautiful grounds, somber reminders of a painful past.

Only a few miles south is Amherst, but the roads are such that it takes close to an hour to drive it. A significant spot in missions history lies at the end of the rough road. Entering Amherst, the western shores of the Gulf of Martaban lie to the right. A windswept cliff rises some fifty feet above the waves. Ann's first grave once lay beyond the edge of the current cliff. Because the sea was eroding the cliff, her grave was moved many years ago to a nearby spot. Then *that* ground, also perilously close to the water's edge, began sinking. In the 1960s, Ann's grave was moved to its present location, some four acres of land less than 300 yards from where Ann and Adoniram had first landed in Amherst. It is actually the site where Ann built the first little house and began worship services.

Walking up to the grave and memorial at the top of a gentle rise is a poignant experience. The original marker stands at the foot of Ann's grave. The small stone reads: "A. H. Judson 1826." Around 1914 the beautiful marble tribute was added: "Erected to the memory of ANN H. JUDSON, wife of ADONIRAM JUDSON, missionary of the Baptist General Convention in the United States, to the BURMAN EMPIRE. She was Born at Bradford, in the State of Massachusetts, North America, Dec. 22, 1789. She arrived with her husband At Rangoon, in July 1813; And there Commenced those MISSIONARY TOILS which she sustained with such Christian Fortitude, Decision and Perseverance, amid scenes of Civil Commotion and Personal Affliction, as won for her Universal Respect and Affection. She Died at Amherst, Oct. 24, 1826." This is also inscribed in elegant Burmese script. Little Maria is buried next to her mother, that blue-eyed babe who never had a chance to grow up. Near the close of the last century, Burmese Baptists added to the memorial a tall gleaming white cross, visible in every direction.

The grave and monument are adjacent to the spot where Ann started worship services in 1826. The early church building was destroyed in World War II, although the bell survived. Now the little Amherst congregation is once again active and has a new pastor.

Work on a new building has begun just yards from where Ann built her little house in 1826. Burmese Baptists decided to rebuild this "oldest" church of all. On October 24, 2001, exactly 175 years to the day that Ann died here, a groundbreaking service for the new Ann Judson Memorial Church was held right next to Ann's grave. There could be no more perfect tribute to that remarkable woman. And to bring history full circle, in December 2002, a dedication service was held for the church then under construction, and the first plinth stone[4] was laid by Judson's great-grandson, Stanley Hanna.

The fruits of Ann Judson's ministry are still visible throughout Burma, as the legacy of her devotion is passed on. Through the years, accounts of lives that Ann touched have surfaced in many places. One hundred years ago, a long-time Baptist missionary recounted what had happened to an elderly colleague in southern Burma in the generation after Ann. Murilla Ingalls and her husband went to Burma in 1851. When Ingalls died, Murilla continued her work alone for more than forty years, often making jungle trips to nearly inaccessible areas. On this particular day, Mrs. Ingalls was telling of Creator God and his love for all. In the crowd was an elderly man who begged her to come to his remote village and tell his neighbors this wonderful story too. Mrs. Ingalls inquired, "Where do you live?" He told her the location of his village, and she explained that her present itinerary was headed in the other direction, but she promised, "I will surely come and visit you."

And she did. The villages welcomed her gladly that day, and she was given a seat on a veranda from which to tell the gospel story. The crowd grew and grew, and as she was telling of Christ's coming and of his sacrifice, she suddenly heard a voice coming from the far end of the veranda, "That's the rest of it! That's the rest of it!" "Mother, what do you mean?" Mrs. Ingalls asked an old lady, who had stood up and spoken so eagerly. The elderly woman pushed her way through the crowd and drew near to Mrs. Ingalls.

"Long, long ago," she explained in excitement, "when I was young, I lived in Ava; my husband was one of the king's courtiers. During a part of the time, there was a white foreigner, a lady who was destitute and in great anxiety about her husband. He was lying in chains in the death prison," the venerable old lady recalled. "I pitied her and used to carry her rice and eggs, and she would talk to me about her God, and how he had provided a way of salvation from our sins...But later," she continued, "my husband fell under the king's displeasure and we fled to the river, and taking a little boat, we hastened down the Irrawady. After many days, we dared to land and hide away in this jungle. But," she fervently declared, "I never forgot the white lady and what she said about the one true God who created all things: but I could not remember just how we could get rid of our sins. Now you have told the part that I had forgotten—and that is the 'rest' of it!" Mrs. Ingalls heard the story in amazement. The elderly man who had invited her to this village was the son of this woman. The Lord had remembered this lady's kindness to "Ann of Ava" and had permitted her to hear the rest of the story. She believed, as did her son, and they were joyfully baptized. Not many years later, she joined Ann in glory.[5]

First hearing of the living legacy and then seeing the actual places where the missions pioneers had invested their lives prompted the next step in the search for a powerful heritage. The Judson legacy in Burma is both alive and evident. How has it fared in America? That became the next compelling search.

CHAPTER 26

The New England Trail

Faith of our fathers, we will love.
—Frederick Faber, "Faith of Our Fathers"

FIRST EXPLORING THE FOOTPRINTS OF ANN AND ADONIRAM JUDSON IN Burma, and *then* going back to search for their roots in New England is a bit like reading the conclusion of a book before discovering how it begins. There are no difficulties with travel or governmental red tape in America, but a subtle difference is apparent. The Judson name and influence are strong throughout Burma. Yet in America, the land of the Judsons' birth, their legacy has not always been carefully passed on, and many in the community of faith have little knowledge of their unique heritage. This made locating information a challenge.

The birthplace of Adoniram Judson, which was built in 1651 and restored in 1724, is also the oldest standing house in Malden, Massachusetts.

Nonetheless, libraries and archives across the nation yielded invaluable material, much of which had never before been researched.

Vital locations in the Judson legacy are concentrated in Massachusetts. Ann's birthplace was a logical starting point. Bradford, dating back to 1639 when Ann's great-great-great-grandfather Robert Hasseltine settled there, is a beautiful little town packed with history on every street.[1] And Ann followed in his footsteps as a pioneer—America's first woman missionary and a heroine to her generation. Her mother, Rebecca, used to shake her head in loving dismay at this adventurous young daughter, fearing she would never be satisfied with her rambling. Ann never was. In time, Rebecca was astounded to see the distance to which that daughter would ramble.

The Bradford Commons is beautiful, just a block from Bradford Academy, which Ann's father, John, helped found in 1803. To one side of the Commons stands 1692 Kimball Tavern where the town fathers voted the academy into being, and on the other, the gleaming white Congregational church. The Commons was set aside in 1751, when the third church building was constructed here. In this sanctuary, Ann worshiped as a young woman. A monument marks the spot: "The American Board of Commissioners of Foreign Missions was organized June 29, 1810, in the church that stood here. It has carried the gospel into many lands and ministered to millions through churches, schools and hospitals." Just west is Bradford Academy. One of two buildings fronting the street is Hasseltine Hall with its memorial tablet to Abigail, the academy's principal, and Ann. Sadly, after two centuries, Bradford Academy closed its doors in 2000.

Crossing Kingsbury Avenue, a house now stands on the spot where the first academy building was placed in 1803, right next door to the Hasseltine House. In the 1890s, the house was moved less than two blocks away to Greenleaf Street. The beautiful old place bears its years with dignity, but the deep wrinkles of old age are obvious. The building needs a facelift. The two-story house is large and deep, with weathered shingles of a fading apricot patina. In the rear is the addition where John Hasseltine had provided Bradford youth with the "Hasseltine Dance Hall." Today the house is apartments. Near the entrance is a weather-beaten plaque now barely legible: "Birthplace of Ann Hasseltine Judson, 1789."

A knowledgeable source of Hasseltine lore emerged at Haverhill library. In 1896, little Bradford was swallowed up by Haverhill, the town just across the Merrimac River. Gregory Laing, Haverhill Library's archivist, actually has Bradford Hasseltines in his own family tree. As a result, Laing has a special interest in the venerable Hasseltine House and personally knows the owner and tenants. He arranged a visit to view the interior of the house. Walking up the front steps and entering the original front door is stepping back in time. Immediately facing the door is the staircase that the child Ann climbed thousands of times. The lovely, old, original banister is still in use. To the right is the west parlor. In this room Ann and Adoniram first met, and in front of the solid old fireplace they stood to exchange their wedding vows. The rooms in the house are fairly small, but there are many of them. There have been no structural changes in the home's more than two centuries of existence. Of the three houses so important in Judson history, this one is the most unchanged *and* the most in need of attention.

Haverhill Library contains files and pictures preserving Hasseltine history and a clue or so as to possible collateral descendants of Ann. Most of the search for descendants from her immediate family ends with names on tombstones and no progeny to carry on the Hasseltine line. Finding some surviving ties to Ann's family became an ongoing challenge.

Bradford's oldest cemetery, circa 1600s, is less than a mile from Ann's house. The graves of John and Rebecca Hasseltine are there among the thickets and brambles. Next to their marker is the grave of Bille, Ann's baby brother who did not survive his first year. The marker simply says: "William." Ann must have visited this spot many times as a child. Her own grave is half a world away, but the imprint of her life is a continuing memory in the town of her birth.

An hour's drive south is Malden, a town more than 350 years old. Just as Mount Vernon is remembered as the birthplace of Washington, the father of his country, to those of the community of faith, Malden is the birthplace of Judson, the father of American foreign missions. When Judson was born on August 9, 1788, Malden was already old. The Judson home, a large, white, two-story house at 145 Main Street, is the oldest extant building in Malden, first built in 1651. It burned in 1724 and was rebuilt the same year by Joseph Emerson, the great-grandfather of Ralph Waldo Emerson. The original low stone wall surrounds 145 Main Street, and one stately old tree still stands in the parsonage yard.[2]

The Judson house has had some internal changes, but the north upstairs bedroom remains as it was in 1788 when Adoniram was born there. The original stairs the little boy climbed so many times remain, and the foundation stones in the basement look much as they did three centuries ago. Another intriguing bit of history is tied to the house, for in the nineteenth century, it became a stop on the Underground Railroad, and crawlspace in the basement provided refuge for weary people seeking freedom. Malden's First Baptist Church, constructed of pink Quincy granite, is also on Main Street and displays on one wall the well-known tribute to Judson written by Samuel F. Smith and concluding with the words: "His Record Is On High."[3]

The Judson family had moved from Malden in 1792, first to Wenham and then to Braintree. In 1802, when Adoniram was thirteen, his father became pastor of the newly formed Third Congregational Church in Plymouth. No place could be more historical in America than Plymouth, but it became associated with missions history as well because of the Judsons' residence there. Present-day Church of the Pilgrimage was founded in 1801 as Third Congregational Church. This was to be Adoniram Judson Sr.'s longest pastorate, because he did not resign until 1817, when he became a Baptist. Church staff and historians in the congregation provided some information about the early years. The present building stands in the center of Old Plymouth, near the foot of Burial Hill, site of the original 1621 fort. A tablet in front of the classic white building is dedicated to the Pilgrims and their successors, who "at the time of the Unitarian controversy in 1801 adhered to the belief of the Fathers" and were the heirs of those 1620 Pilgrims. The original church structure is about two blocks away, on Pleasant Street and directly facing Training Green. It is now a private residence and still in excellent condition.

Records made no mention of a parsonage, which seems to indicate that Adoniram Judson Sr. had provided his own housing. The Judson house is identified as 17 Pleasant Street, but the present owner (herself a descendant of three *Mayflower* passengers) had been told the house was built between 1810 and 1825. A 1903 article in *Baptist Missionary Magazine* stated that Pleasant Street had at one time been called the "Road to Jordan" and then "Judson Street."[4] William Davis, Plymouth's most famous historian, wrote that Pleasant Street was an old road across private land until 1802 and did not lose its old name of "Judson Street" until 1823.[5]

But when was the house built? The most accurate source of information proved to be Plymouth's Registry of Deeds. After many months, the Registry located the original deeds that solved the questions of date and location. Reverend Judson Sr. had been installed as pastor in May 1802, and the first deed was dated July 1, 1802, indicating that Judson's purchase was on the "southwesterly side of Pleasant Street, so called," and south of the grist mill by Jenny Pond. The Judsons' home was built just west of Burial Hill, the center of old Plymouth. Subsequent deeds reveal that Judson Sr. bought more property between 1804 and 1810, including much of Watson's Hill, where Chief Massasoit, Squanto, and Samoset had camped in 1621.[6]

Among the deeds was one poignant document alluding to great pain in Adoniram Judson Jr.'s past. His sister, Abigail, had requested his signature on papers related to their mutually inherited land. Judson would only agree to sign a quitclaim if Abigail would promise to destroy all his letters and papers she had saved through the years. At long last and with great reluctance, she did so. In the Registry of Deeds is the document Adoniram signed in 1834, relinquishing all his claims to any Judson land to his sister, Abigail—for one dollar.

The house at 17 Pleasant Street stands just five houses up the street from the original Congregational church. Its present owner has lived in the place for over half a century. This house, like the Bradford and

Malden structures, has survived long enough to become an apartment house. The inside configuration has been altered, but the original house remains intact, two centuries old and solid as the rocks that form its foundation. The basement has sixteen brick pillars supporting the three floors. An original two by four from 1802 reveals the sturdy handmade wooden pegs and square-headed nails with which the house was constructed. In this house, as with the previous two, the centerpiece is the original staircase and beautiful oak banister. Adoniram had stood at this front living room window in 1846 and looked down at Plymouth Harbor, the only truly familiar sight he had seen in America after thirty-four years away.[7]

These unique Massachusetts houses have become missions Ebenezers, true stones of remembrance, a stirring heritage for all in the community of faith. It begs the question—how long will they remain? Two hundred years is a long life for a house, and Adoniram's birthplace is closer to three hundred years old. None of the three is a registered National Historic Landmark, and all need preserving.

More Judson footprints are not far away. Some fifty miles from Plymouth is Providence, Rhode Island, where Adoniram entered Brown University in 1804. One building comprised the entire campus that year and is still affectionately known as "Old Brick." Old Brick now serves as an administrative center. Just across the street is John Hay Library, its special collections featuring a Judson display. A first-edition Burmese Bible and other memorabilia of Brown's famous son Judson are included in the collection. Nearby is the beautiful First Baptist Church in America, founded in 1638 by Roger Williams. The graceful white edifice, with its towering steeple, seats close to fourteen hundred people on its eighteenth-century pews. In 1807, Adoniram Judson gave his valedictory address in this sanctuary, where Brown still holds its commencements.

The last period of Judson's formal education was at Andover Seminary. Just nine miles south of Bradford, Phillips Academy was founded in 1788, and Andover Seminary began on the same campus in 1808 with Judson as one of its first students. In the fall of 1808, very few buildings dotted the rural landscape. Only two remain from that original campus; one of these, Phillips Hall, now called Foxcraft, has mellowed gracefully.[8] Adoniram attended classes in this building. One more historic spot remains at Andover, the picturesque pond and wooded area where Adoniram frequently walked and meditated. It later earned the name "missionary woods." A large boulder marks the spot where Judson dedicated himself to missions. The memorial boulder commemorates the brave young men known as "The Brethren" who talked and prayed the beginning of a mission-sending society into existence.

Another city in Massachusetts is equally significant in missions annals. Salem is famous as the second oldest of all New England settlements, circa 1626, and known for its infamous witch trials of that century as well. Salem's part in the beginnings of America's foreign mission enterprise, however, exceeds in eternal significance those other claims to fame. Salem's missions legacy seems almost "prearranged" as a walking tour. Just as Boston has its Freedom Trail, so Salem has a "Missions Trail." There is Tabernacle Church where Roger Williams was pastor shortly after its founding. Tabernacle was the place where America's first foreign missionaries were commissioned on a freezing day in February 1812. The slender "deacon's bench" where those five young men knelt for the ordination prayer is still in the church. Later biographies record that in 1846 Judson paid a brief visit to Tabernacle Church, sat again on the bench, and wept as memories engulfed him.

Just a stone's throw from Tabernacle Church is historic First Baptist Church. It celebrated its two hundredth year in 2003. Its first pastor was a founding father of American Baptist foreign missions, Lucius Bolles. One of the early members of the church was beautiful young Sarah Hall. Bolles performed her wedding ceremony to George Boardman in 1825, shortly before they sailed for India. The round stained-glass window behind the pulpit in the sanctuary is priceless, a beautiful depiction of the *Caravan* as it sailed from Salem's harbor with the Judsons on board on February 19, 1812.

A mere two blocks away is Peabody Essex Museum. Among its many treasures are two that are especially cherished by missions historians. Two of the most prized Judson family portraits are in its collection: Rembrandt Peale's 1823 oil of Ann, and Henry Cheever Pratt's famous 1845 portrait of Adoniram with quill in hand. Very close to the museum is Salem Harbor. From this spot the young Judsons sailed in 1812, fully expecting never again to see these shores.

Beyond Bradford and Malden, past Plymouth and Providence, the Judson name still adorns numerous churches and institutions. More than thirty churches scattered across America are named for Judson. Probably the most famous is Judson Memorial on Washington Square in New York City, founded by son Edward Judson in 1890. There is even a town named for Judson; after the Civil War, a colony of Northern Baptists founded Judsonia, Arkansas. The names of some of the streets read like a missions text: Judson, Hasseltine, Carey, Boardman.[9] The American Baptist publishing house, Judson Press, in Valley Forge, Pennsylvania, continues to produce fine books and materials. Dynamic Judson College in Elgin, Illinois, named for Adoniram Judson, was founded in 1963, and beautiful Judson College in Marion, Alabama, was named for Ann Hasseltine Judson upon its founding in 1838. There was also a Judson College founded in 1841 in Tonica, Illinois, that flourished until 1858, and a Judson College founded by Conservative Baptists in Oregon that closed sometime in the 1980s.

The American search for Judson roots proved just as fascinating as had the hunt in Burma. What would prove even more enthralling was the search for the stories of the Judson sons and daughters. What had happened to Judson's children? And *their* children? Who was left in this new millennium? These were stories waiting to be discovered.

The New Generation: George and Abigail Ann

Footfalls echo in the memory. —T. S. Eliot

IN 1899 *HARPER'S* MAGAZINE NAMED ADONIRAM JUDSON AS THE SECOND most recognized name of the century in America. He and his wives have been the subject of significant writings, however, extraordinarily little has been written about the offspring of this nineteenth-century hero, making it difficult to uncover information about their lives.

One 1980 volume does touch on the lives of three of the Judson children, however. In *Mission for Life*, Joan Brumberg looks at Judson's stepson, George Dana Boardman Jr., daughter Abigail Ann,

George Dana Boardman Jr., Sarah's oldest son, was pastor of First Baptist Church, Philadelphia. Abby Ann Judson, only daughter of Sarah and Adoniram, was founder and head of Judson Female Institute in Minneapolis, Minnesota. Courtesy of Dr. Stanley Hanna.

and youngest son, Edward. She stated of the Judson children that their "decision to pursue secular careers was a response to both the influences of the Gilded Age in which they grew up, as well as to the dislocation and harsh realities they experienced as children of pioneer missionaries."[1] Surely those realities affected all the Judson children. Yet two of the three offspring that Brumberg scrutinized, George and Edward, became outstanding ministers. True, none of the children became "foreign" missionaries, but Edward Judson's ministry in the heart of immigrant New York City was a prime example of "home missions" at its finest, and George Boardman became one of America's strongest advocates of world peace.

From the perspective of two centuries of experience, it is easy to see the effects of early separation on missionary children, as well as the consequences of the profoundly difficult living conditions confronting any child in an alien culture. And as always happens with children, even those raised in the same home and under similar circumstances, responses are highly individual. What seems to crush one child seems to strengthen another. The widely varying courses taken by Judson's surviving offspring (thirteen children were born to Adoniram with seven dying in infancy) illustrates this diversity.

The second generation did have survivors who lived and grew and did honor to their parents. Such was George Dana Boardman Jr., Sarah's son. Sarah Boardman and her first husband, George, had arrived in Burma in time to build a coffin for tiny Maria Judson. Sarah's first child, also named Sarah, was a healthy eight-month-old at the time. The Boardmans soon moved to Tavoy to begin work among the Karens. George Boardman Jr. was born August 18, 1828, a frail little fellow. Before he was a year old, his older sister had suddenly grown ill and died. Judson Wade Boardman was born when Georgie was two but only lived eight months. And George was just two when his father died of tuberculosis while on a jungle trip.

Sarah could not bring herself to leave their post. The Karens needed her desperately, and for the next three years, she carried on the work, taking little Georgie with her wherever she went. If a four- or five-year-old had been able to keep a daily journal, what tales that child could have recorded—jungle adventures, complete with tigers and other lurking dangers, rivers to ford, and forests to penetrate. All that time Sarah was wrestling with what was to become one of the most wrenching decisions of her life. If she expected her child to reach adulthood, he would have to be sent to America. It tore her to think of facing such a moment. When George was five, Sarah married Judson and the new family moved to Moulmein. George gloried in having a father once again. Sarah's resolve did not falter, however, and in December 1834, she and Adoniram arranged for George to go to America on the *Cashmere*, since there would be missionaries on that passage.

A speech given by a Captain John Codman in 1895 sheds new light on that memorable ocean voyage, traumatic enough for anyone, to say nothing of a little six-year-old who had never been away from his mother, even for one night. It was an amazing coincidence that John Codman's father had been a classmate of Judson's at Andover, and his mother a schoolmate of Sarah's in Boston. Sixteen-year-old John was the youngest sailor on the *Cashmere*, so the captain told him to "look out for" little George. Codman went to the Judson's home that day the ship sailed and sixty years later recalled: "Let me tell you,…she [Sarah Judson] was one of the most beautiful women I ever saw."[2] Sarah, grieving silently, gave all sorts of orders to young John about the care George needed and sent the boy's pet goat along so he would have milk to drink.

Sarah would have been horrified had she known what trauma her child would experience. First he witnessed the appalling encounter with the pirates before reboarding the vessel in Singapore harbor,[3] and then the *Cashmere*'s sailors killed his dear goat and had it served for dinner. The sailors threatened to "search him out at midnight" if he ever told anyone. Many years later, Boardman told about arriving in Boston: "I shall never forget my feelings when I realized I was free from the sailors," he said. "I knelt down and took some of the soil in my hands and kissed it in my joy."[4] That voyage gave George nightmares for many years to come.

There are scores of letters written in the ensuing years—from Sarah to George, George to Sarah, and letters concerning George written by

Sarah to her numerous relatives. There are almost certainly many more that did not survive the years. It is doubtful that George himself ever realized the full extent of agony his mother experienced in sending him to America when he was so young and how she suffered from missing him each day for the rest of her life.

Reading Sarah's letters gives a poignant look into her heart. She loved each of her children in a special way, but even having a "quiver full" did not diminish her pain at losing George. In a letter written to a sister just one day before Abby Ann was born, Sarah anguished that she still had no news about her child. It had been eleven months since he had sailed away. Sarah had asked her pastor in Boston, Lucius Bolles, to find a good home for him, setting out meticulous instructions as to his care. She feared his grandparents would be too "indulgent," so she wanted him to live elsewhere.

George first lived with "Mr. and Mrs. Lincoln" and then with a Captain and Mrs. Childs, and he seemed content in both settings. Then Mrs. Childs grew extremely ill and George left to live with Dr. and Mrs. Newton. He was still there when his half brothers joined him late in 1845. By that time, George had been in America ten years. Sarah remained as closely involved in George's upbringing as 10,000 miles and woefully slow mail permitted. In an 1838 letter to her sister Frances Bullen, Sarah fretted that because George had been quite ill with a cold, it might mean he had inherited his father's weak lungs. In reply to a letter from her sister Harriet in 1839 when George was eleven, she couldn't believe that he was nearly as tall as his father had been, reflecting that she could not picture him nearly grown. In her mind's eyes, "He is still a little 'chubbed' [chubby] boy in frocks and riding the hearth broom."[5]

George enrolled at Judson's alma mater in 1846, and Judson's correspondence indicates that, prior to sailing back to Burma, he had personally arranged for all of George's college expenses. Brown's president, Francis Wayland, personal friend and great admirer of Judson, became a profound influence on George. Boardman's journal recounts his social and religious life, indicating he often attended Quaker meetings. A world free of war became an ardent wish of his heart. Then, for some reason, he left Brown in January 1848, later stating in a letter that he left because of "spiritual shipwreck" and a wish to study law.[6] George went West, trying first one job and then another, from working in a variety store to making political speeches. He did study some law, and then switched to medicine. In the midst of this apparent wanderlust came an attack of cholera, and this time his life permanently changed directions. He felt a genuine sense of call to Christian ministry, and a newly focused George Boardman returned to Brown in 1849, graduating with honors in 1852.[7]

A special memory concerning Dr. Wayland stuck in Boardman's mind, and years later he related it. Friends dared him wear one of Judson's own high collars, which came up to his eyes. Boardman recalled: "The president fastened that majestic gaze upon the ridiculous linen and sternly said, 'What fashion of collar is that you have on, sir?' 'It is my step-father's Dr. Judson's, sir.' 'I apologize,' Wayland retorted, 'pray wear it every day of your life.'"[8]

After Brown, George attended Newton Theological Institution, graduating in 1854. He met Ella Covell while attending Newton, and they married in 1855. There is no record of their having any children. George always referred to Ella as his source of inspiration, and Ella's favorite name for him was "seraph."[9]

George's first pastorate was in Barnwell, South Carolina. He was ordained there but remained only seven months. Slavery was a big issue in the 1850s, and George was deeply antislavery. His next call was to the Second Baptist Church of Rochester, New York, and it was a happy and fruitful eight-year ministry. In 1864, he was called to the prominent First Baptist Church of Philadelphia. It was a thirty-year love affair, George for the people and they for him. His influence was far-reaching, not only from the pulpit, but in personal contacts and through his writing as well.

Boardman had evidently inherited much of his mother's literary talent; he wrote hymns and poems and became a well-known author of numerous books. However, he maintained that biblical exposition was his principal arm in the ministry. He wrote in retirement: "I am one of those old-fashioned students who believes that…the Bible is still true."[10] George Dana Boardman Jr. was one of Philadelphia's most loved and influential citizens in the last decades of the nineteenth century. Those who knew him well observed that, around him, "You should never forget that you were in the presence of a refined cultured Christian gentleman."[11] Well-known pastor and contemporary Walter Rauschenbusch said in a tribute to Boardman that "His soul lived in a many-windowed turret."[12] Possibly his foreign mission background influenced this character trait. George took an outspoken stand for peace among all people and nations.

Boardman lived to be seventy-five years old. One eulogist spoke of his death in 1903 as his "coronation."[13] A memorial tablet hangs in the sanctuary of First Baptist Church, Philadelphia, summing up the impact of this remarkable man: "As a pastor his chief work was the up-building of character. As a Christian his sympathies embraced all who loved the Lord Jesus Christ. As a scholar he made all learning tributary to the exposition of the scripture. As a citizen he was an uplifting force in the community. As a man his saintly character and blameless life made him beloved of all men."[14] Sarah would indeed have been proud of her son.

In fact, Sarah would have been gratified to learn of the sterling character of each of her children, as well as the significant achievements of several of them. It was pure joy for her in 1835—the birth of little Abby Ann, named for her paternal grandmother and aunt and for Ann Judson. Adoniram wrote his family the morning after the baby's arrival, sharing the happy news and seeking to "engage your prayers for our little Abigail."[15] He wrote George, "Your sister Abigail is a sweet fat baby. You would love her very much if you were here."[16] During the years of Judson's grieving following Ann's death, he had written only spasmodically to his family and even less to others. Following his marriage to Sarah, however, and especially after Abby Ann's birth, this changed. Adoniram kept his mother and sister informed about their namesake. When she was a toddler, he wrote: "Abby is growing fast. She runs about and talks Burman quite fluently, but no English."[17] Abby Ann would become the big sister of a regular little ball team of Judson boys. She was the only girl, surviving several bouts with tropical fevers and violent dysentery.

But, by the time Sarah had given birth to the last of the seven sons, her body was worn out with childbearing. Throughout her years as a missionary, Sarah had been intermittently plagued with severe dysentery, and shortly after the birth of Edward, the illness became life threatening. Abby was nine at the time, and she went with her mother on a sea voyage along the coastline of Burma in an unsuccessful attempt to restore Sarah's health. Throughout the voyage, Abby Ann wrote her father frequent reports on Sarah's condition, and Adoniram wrote all the little details of life at home: "My Dear Daughter: Your letters to me and your brothers, together with the shells from Mergui, arrived this afternoon in the Burmese box....They have already written some letters to you and Mamma....It is now between eight and nine o'clock in the evening. I have had a little meeting with Adoniram and Elnathan, and now they are asleep. Edward has become a fat little fellow. [He was two and a half months old.] I am sure you would not know him again. He begins to look pleased when he is played with. But he has not yet made any inquiries about his absent mother and sister. Indeed, I doubt much whether he is aware that he has any such relatives....I am getting the carpenters to make a new cot for you, longer than your old one. That I have given to Adoniram, and his to Elnathan. Both the kittens are dead, and the old yellow cat has been missing for several days....Alas! Poor pussy!"18

Abby Ann relished the reports on her brothers and pets and felt grown-up and appreciated by her father who had entrusted her with Sarah's care. During those weeks at sea, Abby had an unparalleled opportunity for one-on-one time with her mother. This was rare, as Sarah was normally occupied all day with six children, her translation work, and trying to overcome the debilitating effects of chronic dysentery. The disease was sapping the life from her. Years later, Abby recalled the many conversations she had with her mother during those weeks and how Sarah had revealed that she had never felt "good enough." Long afterward, Abby Ann wrote: "My precious mother, so loving, devoted and intuitive, was troubled at times by painful doubts.

I well know this from the conversations I heard as a child. There was in her a constant strife between her determination to cling to what is called orthodoxy and her intuitive perceptions of infinite justice and love. My father, less intuitive, more aware of the logical deductions from certain laid-down premises, held her by his stronger will to conclusions which he never doubted. And yet how faithfully she labored! How earnestly she sought to bring all with whom she came in contact into salvation through the blood of Jesus!"[19]

Sarah and Abigail returned to Moulmein, and the family began the voyage to America, which Sarah did not survive. Abby Ann never forgot her wrenching grief when she entered her parents' cabin that morning and found her father on his knees beside the body of her mother.

Later came more separation, Judson returning to Burma and Abby living first in one place, then another, and her two older brothers in still a different town. The letters Abby wrote her father and stepmother in the ensuing years give a poignant look into the heart of a lonely child. In one such letter, she told her father, "I am now at Worcester and enjoying a visit to my brothers whom I have not seen for more than two years." In a letter written on Judson's birthday, twelve-year-old Abby wrote: "I wish I could see you, if it were not for more than five minutes. I wish you could always be fifty-nine, because sixty seems so much older."[20]

Actually, in the letters Emily and Adoniram exchanged before their wedding, Emily suggested they take Abby back to Burma with them, listing her very good reasons. Adoniram replied that they would talk about it when they next met but that he had several strong reasons why that plan would not be best. Their conversation about Abby when they did meet again is not recorded, but since Abby remained in America, Adoniram's reasons must have prevailed.

Abby Ann appears to have divided her time between "Aunt Judson" in Plymouth and her two "Aunt Hasseltines" in Bradford, where she attended Bradford Academy. Her Aunt Abigail was the academy's director. Most of Abby's expenses seem to have been provided for by Aunt Judson. None of Abby's primary caregivers during those crucial teen years had children of their own. However, whatever emotional needs may have gone unmet, clearly Abby's education was superb and she became an accomplished teacher. In her early adult years, she taught in various cities in Massachusetts and also was a governess in both New York and Massachusetts. She later taught high school in Plymouth, Massachusetts, and lived with Aunt Judson.

Few details and mementos remain of Abby Ann's years of teaching. There *is* a photograph of Abby taken in 1861 when she was twenty-five, elegant in a formal gown of that period. Later in life she wrote: "I did not marry. Circumstances kept me from mingling with liberal, worldly persons, and the devout ministers or laymen who were attracted to the daughter of the missionary soon found that she was not in sympathy with much that they held dear, and we drifted apart."[21]

In 1879, Abby Ann founded the Judson Female Institute in Minneapolis and became its principal. Even then, she was wrestling with great confusion and studying Spiritualism, although she kept silent about it for many years. Her small book *From Night to Morn or: An Appeal to the Baptist Church* reveals her thought processes and how she clung to some biblical principles while rejecting others. She seemed especially annoyed with the apostle Paul and felt he put far too much emphasis on the doctrine of grace and not enough on works. Abby closed her school in 1890 and left the Baptist church. In the next seven years, she traveled extensively, speaking about the "light" that had been revealed to her. Apparently, she relied heavily on her famous father's reputation to gain an audience. She told of her "visitation" from both her mother and father and how this comforted her.

In *From Night to Morn*, Abby said of her parents: "Their other children who still dwell in the earth plane are living for the right. Some of them are actively engaged for human progress. Our parents rejoice in the good they accomplish. But though my brothers may never recognize the fact,...our parents rejoice over me with a yet greater joy, because to me it has been vouchsafed to receive direct evidence of spirit existence and of life, in spite of death and the grave, and to know that they are often with me, directing my work and cheering me with their sympathy and love."[22] Then in her *The Bridge Between Two Worlds*, Abby wrote of "feeling" her father's arms, of speaking to him and he to her. She explained that he didn't actually materialize but held her spirit body in his spiritual arms.[23]

In 1894, Abby spent twenty-four hours with her brothers, Edward, the minister, and Adoniram Brown, the surgeon—the first time they had been together since Abby had left the church. Abby reported that they were "right brothers" and that they didn't love one another any less because of their differences.[24] Edward and Adoniram Brown never discussed the reunion, so how they felt or what they said to Abby will never be known. Abby seemed to gain comfort from the "visitations" by her parents, and no doubt this was the crowning appeal of Spiritualism to many who embraced it—seeking to ease their grief over dear ones who had died.

Several of Abby's statements in *From Night to Morn* expose a startling amount of residual pain from her early years. The hurt locked in her heart is revealed in a disclosure she made: "I never returned to Burmah, for Father was not there, and my work seemed to be to teach in this country,…[yet] I was always interested in the missionary work in Burmah. But…as the development of events showed how much I had suffered from being deprived of my parents' care at the age of ten, and the deleterious effects on some of my brothers, of being orphaned, as it were, at an early age, I came to have serious doubts regarding the propriety of parents' putting their own children into other persons' hands for the sake of teaching the heathen. I idolized the memory of my father and mother, believed them to have been most conscientious and self-sacrificing, but I thought that in this regard they had been guided by a mistaken sense of duty. And it seemed more and more unlikely to me that the heathen would be tortured forever for not accepting a Savior of whom they had never heard."[25]

What a lonely little girl—one who felt deserted and who had been compelled to leave all that was known and loved and familiar. Abby's life might have been very different had she been able to return to Burma in 1846. After 1896, Abby lectured only around her home in Worcester, Massachusetts, and she cared for her brother Elnathan the last year of his life. That had to have been a monumental task. He was fifty-eight and had been mentally ill more than thirty-two years.

Abigail died tragically in December 1902, when she was sixty-seven. She had been reading in bed and a lamp accidentally overturned. Some of the hot oil fell on the bed and soaked her nightgown. The garment caught fire and she ran into the yard, a mass of flames. She died as a result of her massive burns.[26] For those who knew her, there remained the images of the rosy-cheeked toddler who gave such joy to her parents, the bright but lonely young girl and teenager, the gracious young woman, the capable and effective teacher and administrator—yet forever the image of the lost little girl. That girl had struggled for many years to recapture the security of those loving arms that she felt had deserted her far too early in life.

All the Judson children shared many of the same early experiences in Moulmein, but their lives later took widely divergent paths. Some lived to achieve eminence; others seemed to follow a tragic path of unfulfilment and loneliness. Students of human nature always speculate as to how much is "nature" and how much "nurture." The four sons of Adoniram and Sarah who lived to adulthood were much alike, yet vastly different—interesting studies for such a psychological puzzle. Their directions in life were notably different from Abby's. Two were bleak. Two were memorable.

CHAPTER 28

Adoniram, Elnathan, and Henry

Be kindly affectioned one to another with brotherly love.
—Romans 13:10a

PIECING TOGETHER THE LIVES OF THE JUDSON CHILDREN IS LIKE WORKING an antique puzzle with missing pieces. What *is* known is that they were brilliant, orthodox, unorthodox, exceptional, enigmatic, lovable, sad, admirable, and pitiable. Among the seven surviving children, there was certainly diversity, although their early years and influences were similar. Why did one succeed and another drift? Intriguing facts about each child have emerged.

After Abby Ann, Adoniram Brown was born, a strikingly beautiful child nicknamed "Pwen" (flower) by the Burmese who doted on him. As a young child, he was called "Fenelon" at home. Years later Adoniram Brown wrote about his name "change" when he was still small: "One day family prayer was made more serious than usual by a ceremony in which father changed my name from Fenelon (a French

Adoniram Brown Judson, Sarah and Adoniram's oldest son, became an orthopedic surgeon. Elnathan, their second son, had a tragic life. Their third son, Henry, called himself a "widowed wanderer." All photos courtesy of Dr. Stanley Hanna.

mystic and writer) to Adoniram. Probably friends at home had failed to approve of his transient surrender to the meditations of the mystics."[1]

In 1915, an elderly Dr. Judson wrote recollections of his Moulmein childhood. His reminiscences are full of the derring-do of children living on the edge of a jungle, short on toys but long on imagination. He recalled the tiger that came into Moulmein to explore and was killed and mounted on a cart to be paraded through the compound. An enraptured collection of small children had delicious shivers as they watched its stately progress. Pwen was wide-eyed at the hapless animal. He also recalled making "regulation guns" from the stems of banana leaves and firing volleys at his playmate enemies. He particularly relished occupying a *howdah* (seat) on the back of a massive elephant and going for a sky-high ride, and he related tales of little brothers Henry and Edward working at "converting the heathen" at one of the compound gates.[2]

Then it was 1845, and eight-year-old Adoniram Brown Judson was headed to America for the first time. He never saw Burma again. The bright spot of the voyage for him was the night his mother, Sarah, sat on the deck of the *Paragon* and sang "The Star of Bethlehem." The haunting melody never left the memory of her son, and he recounted the moment some sixty-nine years later at the 1914 Judson Centennial.[3] The memories of that voyage grieved him ever after as he recalled waking up one morning near the shores of St. Helena to find his mother dead.

Adoniram and his younger brother Elnathan lived with Dr. and Mrs. Newton in Worcester, Massachusetts, where half-brother George also lived. Later the younger two boys lived with Dr. and Mrs. Bright. Bright became one of the guardians for the Judson children. There are many letters in the Valley Forge archives written by Adoniram Brown to his father and stepmother, and many from them to him, the ties of love very evident. "Addy" and Emily's letters reveal their special bond, although they could seldom be together. His letters always began "Dear Ma" and related little everyday happenings. He wrote of money and gifts that "Aunt Abigail" sent and very carefully itemized his expenses. In another, obviously written in haste, with sloping lines and swirls, the future doctor added a postscript: "I guess this letter will look as if it had rickets!"[4]

Adoniram graduated from Brown in 1859 and studied medicine at Harvard. During the Civil War, he was an assistant surgeon in the U.S. Navy.[5] Later becoming a specialist in orthopedic surgery, he was head of the New York Hospital outpatient department for thirty years. A prolific writer, Adoniram published more than fifty papers. He also helped organize the American Orthopedic Association and became its president in 1891.[6] Adoniram married Ann Haughwont, but the search to find children born to the couple was lengthy and unsuccessful. In his biographical file in Brown's alumni office, Adoniram listed under the category Children: 0.

Scattered records give a picture of his character. The *Dictionary of American Biography* called Adoniram "a friendly, companionable man of unusual modesty."[7] T.A.T. Hanna, who became husband to Judson's daughter, Emily Frances, compared the two most prominent of his brothers-in-law. "Edward," said T.A.T. "was the one in the presence of the public. Was there ever a man in America who had so many Christian friends as he? On the other hand, Adoniram Brown was like 'Isaac, a plain man, dwelling in tents.'" Hanna described Adoniram Brown by using a Civil War analogy: "It was as General Meade was asked, at the beginning of Gettysburg, how many men he had. He answered, 'Enough for the purpose.' Adoniram Brown Judson was equal to the task, whatever it might be."[8]

In 1916, the year he died, Adoniram reflected on what might be the biggest tragedy of missionaries' lives—separation from their children. It was wrenching for both parent and child. Adoniram Brown could have been thinking about several of his siblings when he wrote: "Children of the missionaries in the Far East have to be taken back to the homeland to grow up, far away from their parents....It was early found that such offspring could not survive the climate conditions....A divided and scattered family presents the saddest and most perplexing problem of missionary life."[9]

The lives of his brothers Elnathan and Henry were much harder to explore, for little was written about these two. What can be gleaned is often poignant and sometimes tragic. Elnathan was the second son of Judson and Sarah Boardman, born July 15, 1838. His early experiences were like those of his big brother and sister; he too never forgot his mother's death aboard ship just weeks after his seventh birthday. Six weeks later, the family reached America and separation came again, as "Ennie" (or "Elly" as his siblings called him) and "Addy" went to live with the Newtons. The brightest spot for two grieving boys was that they had each other; at least one person was familiar in their alien world.

In 1846, during Judson's hectic months in America, he had few opportunities to be with his children. In March, he wrote Emily of reaching Worcester to find the three boys at the depot waiting for him: "They have both [the younger two] grown some and appear to be in excellent health. And how glad we all were to meet and what hugging and kissing ensued! I am sure you will love them when you see what dear nice fellows they are. And all testify that they behave well in the house and at school and are better scholars than any of their age."[10] Judson wrote of goodbyes and how he indulged in a good cry "about my poor dear children. I left the boys crying yesterday....Abby Ann I took on to Bradford and left her crying at the Hasseltine's."[11]

Details of the following years are scant, mostly snippets found in letters "Elly" wrote his father and stepmother, and then to Emily alone after Judson died. Emily and Elly corresponded regularly. Elnathan called her "Mother" and signed his letters, "Your very loving son Elly." The longing can be heard in the signature—this child who had lost his own mother when so young.

Elnathan must have been a promising child, which only adds to the tragedy of his life. In an 1852 letter, when he was thirteen, Emily bragged on "Elly and Eddie." "I am as proud as ever I can be of them. I don't think there is a one in the whole lot less promising than Abby," Emily wrote, for she felt Abby very talented. "They all *can* be anything they like, and Elly and Eddie are going to be something. You will fall in love with Elly."[12] The brothers were close, and being able to live together was a comfort to both. Fourteen-year-old Elnathan wrote Emily of going "walnutting" with Addy and described their attic room—where they had "a great deal more room—a beautiful prospect. I hope that you may be able to come here sometime the following year to see our arrangements."[13] But that next year, the valiant Emily lost her grip on life.

Personnel records at Union Seminary indicate that Elnathan graduated from Brown in 1859. On July 4, 1860, however, while rowing in a regatta in Providence, he suffered serious sunstroke. His family felt that this incident caused major damage to his system. He went on to graduate from Union Seminary in 1862, but subsequent problems may have stemmed from that earlier illness.[14] Those problems were summarized obliquely years later in his obituary: "After painful struggle and vicissitudes, he was placed in the Maclean Hospital for the Insane in Somerville, Massachusetts, January 24, 1864."[15] In November 1874, he was transferred to an asylum in Worcester. All those years, his sister and brothers kept in contact concerning his condition as best they could. There are few records of that period. A glimmer of news appears in 1895, when Abby Ann wrote to the *Banner of Light*, a Spiritualist publication, that she was now making her headquarters in Worcester where her "invalid" brother was in the hospital. She referred to his mental problems as "brain fever," writing that she was unable to forsake him and sent birthday and Christmas gifts, and visited him "from time to time." Abby reported that the visits gave her "great pain."[16]

In January 1896, Elnathan suffered a second stroke that paralyzed the left half of his body, and Abby was allowed to take him to her "hired rooms" to live. She took over the sole care of Elnathan, who was both mentally ill and paralyzed. After his death, she revealed that he had been a "less-than-docile" patient, and that sometimes she had to solicit help in subduing him. In a rather harrowing account, she described the extremities of his condition, "alone in the house with him as his screams forbade other[s]."[17] Nevertheless, she characterized his last four months as "calm and sweet."[18] It must have been Abby who wrote Elnathan's obituary, for it is filled with Spiritualist phrases such as "the deserted house of clay" and "his freed spirit has entered the home of the soul." Abby also recalled the character and personality of Elnathan Judson that his family and friends remembered: his integrity and purity, his sweet disposition and polished manners, his bright intellect and tender heart.[19]

Henry is almost as much a mystery as his older brother Elnathan. His was a life whose productivity was also stymied. This third surviving son, born July 8, 1842, was given the name of older brother "Henry" who had died in India. Sources for tracing the life of Henry Hall Judson proved scanty; his great-nephew has what remains of direct information, a thin file containing a picture of the young college student, a letter the teenaged Henry wrote his older brother "El," and his honorable discharge from the U.S. Army. There was also notification of his death from the chaplain of his veterans' home for disabled soldiers, and a copy of his will—scant remnants of a life of seventy-six years.

Henry was closest to his younger brother Edward. Only two years separated them. When their parents had to leave Burma in 1845, Henry remained behind and lived with the Haswells. In letters Jane Haswell wrote Emily, she said that Henry was truly dear to her heart and would always be "her boy." All through Emily's letters those four years she was in Burma are references to her "beautiful boys" Henry and Edward. The bonds were strong, and the boys loved her like the mother they could not remember. Emily often wrote about the antics of the boys: "Henry is seven only and just like a wild colt; people ask me if I ever saw him *walk*—he is so forever on the jump. He is a clever little fellow though, reads beautifully, writes decently and studies geography and history like a little sage. He has a pretty Grecian face—people say like his own Mamma's."[20] Emily carefully supervised the boys' education and saw to it that they didn't depend on servants, as was the tendency for foreign children in that culture. The boys learned to be independent. Who could have foreseen how vital such skills would soon be to them?

Emily and the three youngest Judsons last saw Moulmein in February 1851. Henry was eight and leaving the only world he knew. An ocean voyage was at once exciting and scary, and all that lay before him was strange and a little terrifying. Caring for the three youngest children was almost more than fragile Emily could handle. In America, she tried on every possible occasion to get all the children together, but illness, school schedules, and weather prevented that from happening frequently. Each child cherished the rare occasions when they could be together.

By early 1854, Emily knew she was dying and must make final plans for her children. For a time, Henry and Edward lived with a Mr. Osborne in Hamilton. Henry wrote in one letter that Mr. Osborne had to get onto them for playing around when they should have been studying. In fine handwriting, the child talked about his past three days of transgressions, "I am very sorry for these sins that I have done in so little a time."[21] Henry concluded: "I went to the anxious seat in the meeting the first time I ever went in my life before."[22]

James Granger and Edward Bright became executors of the Judson estate when Emily died, and they helped with Henry's upbringing. In 1860, Henry enrolled at Brown, but in 1861 transferred to Williams College.[23] In January 1864, Henry enlisted in the 15th of New York Heavy Artillery. Before the engagements at Petersburg, Virginia, however, family tradition says he was permanently disabled when a horse kicked him in the head. The sparse records available in the archives of Brown University only add to the mystery. A short paragraph states that from June until August 1864 a wounded Henry was lying sick in a hospital. In December a surgeon's certificate states: "General debility and feebleness of mind (patient states was caused by sunstroke at Cold Harbor, Va. June 3 while in line of duty)."[24] What a strange twist of fate that two brothers should both suffer permanent damage from sunstrokes. Many years later, Henry answered a questionnaire from Williams College, stating that he really had no information to give them, other than that he was a "widowed wanderer."[25]

Henry's honorable discharge from the army was not issued until November 1885, twenty-one years after his hospitalization. That in itself seems unusual. The discharge was signed in Plymouth, Massachusetts, and lists his occupation as "traveling agent."[26] That corroborates the "wandering" description Henry gave of himself. According to Brown University archives, he lived for several years in Illinois and then divided time between Cape Cod and Florida. In 1883, he was living in Plymouth. Evidently Henry spent some time in New York City, as well, where two of his brothers lived, because a tribute to him in the *Watchman-Examiner* stated that "for several years prior to his death Henry Judson had been a member of the Judson Memorial Church."[27]

At the time of his death, however, Henry was residing in the National Home for Disabled Soldiers in Virginia. Could it be that he went there after the deaths of his brothers Edward and Adoniram?

Henry Judson died January 11, 1918, of diabetes. The chaplain who sent the family Henry's death notice wrote, "The end was a genuine example of Christian fortitude."[28] Henry was the last of Judson's children to die. He was seventy-six, and in the final reckoning of his accounts, he still had a portion remaining of his "Adoniram Judson estate," which he bequeathed to his nieces and nephews.

Much of the life of Henry Hall Judson remains shrouded in mystery. Where did he live? Whom did he marry? Were there any children from that union? What did he actually do all those years between 1864 and 1918? A few of the questions found answers in pension records held by the Department of the Army. There was even a mention in the files of his physical appearance; it brings to mind Emily's early description of the beautiful child Henry. Army records describe him as having a fair complexion, with light hair and blue eyes. And there *was* a wife. On a form submitted in the 1890s, in answer to the question, Are you a married man? Henry wrote, "My wife is dead, her name was Mrs. Emily Holland." They had married in Illinois in 1869. To the question, Have you any children living? Henry answered, "I never had any children." It would be easy to become sentimental. Poor Henry. His wife, Emily, had lived only nine years after they married, and he was left alone. However, the next form has a follow-up statement to the question about being married. This time Henry wrote, "I am not married, thank God." And on another army form, he answered the question about marriage by saying, "Married only once and that was enough."[29] So Henry had married an "Emily," as had his father, but clearly not with the same splendid results.

Henry's file was sadly small. In contrast, there are volumes of information about his younger brother, Edward, and descendants of his half-sister, Emily Frances, live on and have more tales to tell.

The Final Two: Edward and Emily Frances

It is so old a story yet somehow always new.
—Heinrich Heine, *Lyriches Intermezzo*

EDWARD JUDSON WAS THE LAST of the children of Sarah and Adoniram, and the one who most resembled his parents. The finest traits of both Sarah and Adoniram seemed to be intertwined in the extraordinary character of this child. Throughout life people commented on his uncanny physical resemblance to his father as well as to their similarities in ability and character. That was especially singular since Edward had so few years with his father before Judson's death. The year that Edward died, he spoke at the 1914 Judson Centennial in Boston and told the thousands there: "My father's example has always been an inspiration to me. I keep on my desk before me a portrait of him as a young man. We need human guides to keep us in the footsteps of the great pathfinder....I have often thought that my father's influence upon my life has been greater than it would have been had he been spared to me through all these years."[1]

Edward was strikingly like his mother in gentleness and loving spirit. A fellow minister declared: "He had a talent for winning love

Edward Judson, the youngest son of Sarah and Adoniram, became a prominent pastor and denominational leader. Emily Frances, only surviving child of Emily and Adoniram, is the only Judson offspring to have descendants living into the twenty-first century. Courtesy of Dr. Stanley Hanna.

292

because he had a talent for loving. He brought out the good in people because he believed in them and made them feel he did."[2] Another termed Edward "a gentleman...[who] gave to everything he undertook a touch of chivalry that was none the less human because it was born of an exquisite sense of beauty and divine love."[3]

This outstanding pastor, linguist, and leader nearly died before his first birthday. Sarah was extremely frail when Edward was born in Moulmein two days after Christmas in 1844. Dysentery and bearing eleven children had drained her health. When she was put on a ship in April in an effort to save her life, Sarah kissed her four-month-old son goodbye, knowing she likely would not live to see that precious face again. She didn't. In a few months, Sarah was dead.

Lizzie Stevens took tiny Edward to her heart. Because of her loving care, he lived. The Stevenses' daughter, another Sarah, became a missionary herself, and sixty-eight years later at a Judson Centennial, she recalled: "I have a very distinct picture imprinted on my memory of Dr. Judson entering the door with the wee, puny little baby in his arms, and handing him to my mother and lovingly did she fulfill her trust. The poor little man had had a hard struggle for life, because of the serious condition of his mother's health....My mother had a baby of her own only a few months older,...healthy and plump. She was convinced that the only way to save the life of baby Edward was to give him the chance which little Emma had enjoyed. She believed that she would be running no risk in weaning her own child...[and] had the joy of returning him to his father, two years later, in perfect health,...the masterful, sturdy little man, my foster-brother."[4]

Edward was just short of two when his father was once more able to hold him in his arms and introduce him to his new mama, Emily Chubbuck Judson. Edward ever after looked on Emily as his mother, and she loved and nurtured him as her own. Several of Edward's fellow MKs became missionaries themselves and recalled those early years. Edward was a vivid memory to them. Sarah Stilson, a few years older than Edward, remembered his recitation when he was two. Dr. Judson was having a session with the MKs and they were repeating verses. "As we repeated our little verses around, I well remember little apple-cheeked Edward standing up to say his: 'Tij religion what can give, thweeteth pleasthuresh while we live.'"5 And his father wrote big sister Abby, describing her little brother during those early years, "Edward is a stout chunky fellow," said Adoniram, "another John Bull."6

In his biography of his father, Edward wrote about that period, calling his father their "ardent companion in play."7 Those joyful memories were all too few, for death again intervened. Judson weakened quite rapidly when Edward was five, and soon died. Adoniram Judson was far too early only a cherished memory in his son's heart— but one that never faded. Emily's own health was precarious, and she reached the difficult conclusion that she must leave Burma with the three little ones, since both they and the three older ones already in America depended on her.

The trip to America was a point in time between two worlds for Edward: "The ocean voyage seems as a dividing line, making the earlier recollections more vivid."8 The voyage helped restore their health. Emily wrote: "The sallow cheeks of my children are aglow with English roses."9 They got to Boston in October 1851, and for the first time Edward, Henry, and little Emily Frances saw their big brothers "Addy" and "Elly" and sister Abby Ann. Emily settled in Hamilton, New York, where her parents lived. By the next winter, however, she was forced to go to Philadelphia for a milder climate, and the boys remained in Hamilton, cared for by Mr. Osborne. Emily kept close tabs on the boys' progress. In a letter to a friend when Edward was nine, Emily wrote: "The boys...are doing nicely, especially Eddy. Mr. Buell says he is the best Latin scholar in the class....Eddy is going to make a fine speaker. He is cheered every time he goes on the floor. Of course this is partly because he is a little fellow, but then he speaks surprisingly well. He is indeed a most promising child, not so much on account of his talents, which are great, but he has a large soul, a generous warm heart and he is industrious, persevering and brave. I don't think I have heard him say 'can't' once since he has been in school."10

Beautiful little gems written by Edward to Emily during 1852 and 1853 reveal a loving, active, sharp little boy. When he was seven, he wrote in clear printing about his daily activities—and loneliness. "My Dear Mama, We are haveing [*sic*] fine times in the snow. Henry and I are very lonely and want Emmy [his younger half-sister] to play with. On Saturday I fell down and bumped my nose and cryed [*sic*] very much,…your effectionate [*sic*] little son Edward Judson."[11] A few months later he wrote, "I love you very much and hope to see you again next summer in Hamilton.…I send a bushel of love and kisses to you and Emmie.… I would have written to you sooner if I had thought of it. Your effectionate [*sic*] little sonny Eddy."[12] In another note, he came up with a creative way to describe a lie: "I am very sorry I disobeyed and told a wrong story about it. I read the Bible every day."[13]

But tragedy lay just ahead, and in June 1854, Eddy and his brothers and sisters became orphans indeed. Edward was fortunate in his new home, going to live with Ebenezer Dodge, professor and then president at Madison University (Colgate University). The Dodges had no children and took Edward to their hearts. A classmate recalls: "Dr. Dodge was proud of him,…[and] Mrs. Dodge was an excellent woman of rare intelligence and kindness.…Edward had a smile in his boyhood days that was very charming. You could see his whole soul behind it."[14]

Biographer Charles Sears commented: "Few lives have been touched by so many men and woman of genius as was his."[15] This, along with his astounding linguistic skills and winning personality, left a trail of goodwill. Edward, like brother Adoniram, graduated from Brown. He delivered the classical oration and won a Phi Beta Kappa key. Edward began teaching at once and became principal of Leland and Gray Seminary in Vermont. He taught there two years, showing remarkable ability as a teacher, but he was torn. He loved teaching but felt that a pastoral ministry was more needed. This became a conviction, and even while teaching, he looked upon his school as a kind of church and congregation, leading prayer meetings several times a week.

The inner conflict about what to do with his life kept him disturbed. In a letter to his sister Abby in 1867, he described this internal struggle:

"I have a growing conviction that the conversion of sinners is the noblest business of life,…[but] one of the bitterest curses of life is the fact that we are called on to make the most important decisions— decisions which involve our whole future happiness, just at that time in life when we have the least experience."[16] In the fall of 1867, Edward began teaching at Madison University, and in 1868, when only twenty-four, was named Professor of Latin and Modern Languages. About this time, he began applying his language skills to a study of the Bible. From then until the week of his death, Edward read portions of the Old and New Testaments each day in two or more languages. He recorded his daily studies, and the record is astounding: Hebrew, Greek, Latin, German, French, and English.

Edward fell in love with Antoinette Barstow, whose father was a Congregational pastor in a nearby town. Their marriage was remarkable for its strength, and Antoinette was a vital part of his ministry. The young couple went to Europe in 1874 to study for a year, and Edward resigned his post at Madison. While abroad, the North Orange Church in New Jersey called him as pastor. Beginning in 1875, Edward was pastor there only six years, but it was really a lifelong relationship. Just prior to Edward's death, the son of a member wrote: "You must derive great comfort, Dr. Judson, from the knowledge that there are so many persons scattered over the country who bless you for the help you have been to them spiritually. And then think of the many who have gone before who were led into the kingdom by you!"[17]

Like his father, Edward Judson wasn't the type to take the easy path. He left a flourishing, loving church in New Jersey and entered the heart of New York City—bustling, crowded, and teeming with immigrants. Here Edward faced the biggest challenge of his life. This Judson was a pioneer of *home* missions work, and there on the lower west side of New York City, he developed the goal of establishing a memorial to his father.

Such a task was not easy. Berean Church was the base from which the vision developed as Edward invested his life in the dream that became Judson Memorial Church. For thirty years he gave himself to a city pulsing with need. It was such a magnificent conception that the dollar costs were every bit as great as the mental and emotional price he paid. John D. Rockefeller became a close friend and benefactor of the project, yet Edward was never out from under financial pressure. Nevertheless, that did not affect the essence of the man nor that indefinable sweetness of spirit that touched everyone who knew him. During his first seven years as pastor, seven hundred people were added to the church.

Judson Memorial Church was a beacon. Edward watched wealthier people moving to the suburbs—leaving the poor behind and need on every hand. He established the first mission of an individual church among New York's non-English-speaking people and began the first church kindergarten, as well as boys and girls clubs. The church also opened a gym, provided training in sewing skills, maintained a dispensary, and established a children's home. No wonder finances were a burden. A century later, the church continues to adjust to community needs and reach out to all ages. The Judson vision became far-reaching and long-lived.

Even in the midst of such overwhelming tasks, Judson the pastor never stopped preaching and teaching. Just as Judson the father had trained young pastors and evangelists, so did Judson the son gather young theological students and train them in preaching and evangelism, even finding time to teach occasionally at the University of Chicago and Union Theological Seminary.

Edward himself never stopped studying. In the midst of such a busy life, he managed to do advanced study at Union Seminary and write two books: *The Institutional Church* and *The Life of Adoniram Judson*. The dedication Edward made in the latter book is a poignant reminder of the little child whose compelling and tragic early years imprinted his life forever:

TO THE CHILDREN OF MISSIONARIES
The involuntary inheritors
Of their parents' sufferings and rewards,
THIS BOOK IS AFFECTIONATELY DEDICATED
BY ONE OF THEIR NUMBER[18]

297

Judson could have named his pulpit or his position. He served as a trustee of Brown and of Vassar and turned down the presidencies of both Brown and Colgate, not because he didn't love teaching but because of his sense of commitment to God's call to him in New York City. Edward's biographer characterized him as completely genuine, not a preacher of "sensationalism" but of matchless skill in using a conversational tone to convey the gospel—like one friend talking to another. He did not preach from notes. The listener was convinced that the sermon was entirely extemporaneous and from the heart. Edward's preaching was not some display of literary or oratorical expertise, but instead the expression of a great soul and personality. He worked to win his audience, not command them. The last weeks of his life, there was an evident depression about Judson, no doubt due to the strain of such responsibility and the loss of Antoinette in 1914.[19] He only outlived her by five weeks.

Edward's expression of his philosophy of life gives an intimate glimpse into the man. He felt that "the important thing is not to undertake some great piece of work, but to live by the day, having the mind that was in Christ Jesus."[20] He maintained that "large undertakings require more than a lifetime for their fulfillment."[21] Edward's message was the highlight of the 1914 Judson Centennial. Edward spoke a profound sentence that reflected both his heritage and his own life: "If we succeed without suffering it is because those who preceded us suffered without succeeding."[22] Five months later, Edward died, active until the week of his death.

Tributes came from near and far. Not least among his attributes was an inextinguishable sense of humor. He never missed a gleam of fun, even in the midst of gloom. Occasionally Edward would show flashes of a quick temper, but his sense of humor was much stronger. His church members loved to hear him pray, "Help us to be decent, and to keep sweet." Those members, fellow pastors, classmates, and a host of others called him a man of genius—in languages, in preaching, in people skills. A leading New York pastor proclaimed Judson the greatest planner he ever knew—in a day he could fashion more plans than any dozen other men could think of in a year. Like his father, Edward Judson was a pioneer—the father in overseas missions.[23] Like father, like son, rare in ability, rare in spirit, and unforgettable.

When he was three, Edward, youngest son of Sarah and Adoniram, gained a little sister, Emily Frances, who is the only surviving child of Emily and Adoniram. "Emmy," became his beloved playmate. Much has been written of Edward, gifted professor, sterling pastor, and talented author, but little is known about Emily Frances. However, the beautiful poem her mother Emily wrote to welcome her to the world stands as a classic of its generation and gave tiny Emily Frances the nickname "My Bird." Her mother actually wrote it the same night her child was born, pretty amazing in itself. One of the later stanzas of "My Bird" captures the awe of a new mother's heart and the sense of wonder she felt:

> The pulse first caught its tiny stroke,
> The blood its crimson hue, from mine—
> This life, which I have dared invoke,
> Henceforth is parallel with thine.[24]

Emily Frances was born Christmas Eve, 1847, and was the delight of big brothers Henry and Edward. A letter written by Emily to her parents when Emily Frances was just three weeks old gives a proud mother's view of her newborn: "I beg leave to introduce to your notice one Miss Frances Judson, usually mentioned in these parts as…little Fanny and who claims to be your grand-daughter and niece. She is a very nice little affair—is my black-eyed baby, and oh so fat & healthy! She beats all the babies in the mission…in size. 'Such a head!' everybody says to us, and 'How handsome she is!' and all that sort of thing; and as she doesn't know enough to be vain, I have to be vain for her.…You will naturally inquire whom Miss Fanny resembles.…The shape of her head, her forehead & eyes are mine. The lower part of her face, nose, & mouth and chin—it takes longer to develop, you know, but we think they are Judsonian.…How I wish you could come & dine with us today;…we would bring birdy Fanny out, & little fat

Edward would clamber over your knees & play with your nose & eyebrows, while he teazed you to…'dive' him 'a ittle dirl dolly';…what a time we would have!"[25]

Adoniram wrote big sister Abby about baby Emily Frances when she was eleven months old: "Your little sister Emily Frances is a fine healthy child. She has got your teeth and can almost stand alone.…It is generally said that she looks like you."[26] In another letter, Emily describes baby "Emmie" as "fat as a ball of butter."[27] There was a period of several months in early 1849 when the whole family thrived. Emily wrote her friend Anna Maria, "We cannot be unhappy," and told of the contented domestic scene that very evening, "Teacher" going off to lead his little flock and merry tones rising from the veranda, with the baby trying the Burmese alphabet and her older brothers shouting with laughter—and baby laughing in glee along with them.[28]

That little girl all too soon became an orphan, but she grew up to be the only Judson child to leave descendants to the next millennium. Emmy was just six when her mother died. She went to live with "Aunty" Anna Maria Anable, her own mother's closest friend and confidant. "Aunty" and her sisters directed a finishing school for young women in Philadelphia, and Emmy became the daughter of "Aunty."

Small glimpses into the heart and life of Emily Frances come mostly from anecdotes passed down in the family. "My Bird" attended the finishing school administered by her Aunty Anable and was a teenager there during the Civil War. Emily Frances's youngest grandson remembered his own father telling him about this grandmother as a teenager. One afternoon during a break from class, Emily Frances was standing at a second-floor window when she was attracted to noise and movement in the street below. Looking down, she saw a company of smartly uniformed young Union soldiers briskly marching by. Young Emily was much taken by the splendor of their attire and by the eagerness and purpose written on their faces and evident in their steps. Turning to a friend standing next to her, Emmy declared, "One of these days I'm going to marry just such a soldier!"

Some daydreams have a way of coming true. Emily ended up marrying a "soldier of the cross." Her brother Eddy introduced her to a

classmate of his, young Thomas A. T. Hanna, a promising ministeri-
al student. He was a childhood immigrant from Ireland, of strong
Baptist background. In 1870, the year of their marriage, Emily was
twenty-two, and T.A.T., at twenty-eight, was pastor of Central
Baptist Church in Williamsburgh, Long Island.[29] Emily became a
pastor's wife in the best sense of the word, a partner with her husband as they ministered and did domestic missions work among
Germans in Connecticut.

Emily did something that no other Judson child had done; she had
children who had children who had children, and the Judson heritage
still lives on through her descendants. In the possession of Emily
Frances's youngest grandson is a small photo album, about the size
and shape of a diary, much used, its hinges rather loose and fitted
with a clasp. It must have been carefully put together and much cherished by one of Emily's children, for labeled in the album are numerous pictures of "Mother"—Emily Frances—from the time she was a
glowing young girl in finishing school, to a wedding portrait, and on
to later pictures. The little album included portraits of Emily's dear
"Aunty" and poses of Emily with several of her half brothers.

Emily Judson Hanna had eight children, three daughters and five
sons. Her oldest and youngest children became missionaries to
Burma, and four of the eight children had children who had children,
and thus "unto the third and fourth generations." Several of those
children would make contributions to the world that would have
delighted the hearts of Adoniram and Emily Judson. Emily Frances
died of cancer at age sixty-four, and she left behind a legacy of love
that touched many lives.

Being a Judson was surely a privilege for those children of
Adoniram and Sarah and the daughter of Adoniram and Emily. At
the same time, it carried an equal burden of difficulty and responsibility to which they responded in vastly different ways. They had so
much in common, and yet those six lives took widely divergent paths.
Some excelled. Some simply coped. Each one at some point in life
gave evidence of their goodly heritage. And so the Judson legacy has
been passed on to the third and fourth generations.

CHAPTER 30

Unto the Third and Fourth Generation...

Tell your children of it, and let your children tell their children, and their children, another generation.
—Joel 1:3

THE THIRD GENERATION OF JUDSON DESCENDANTS WAS ACTUALLY QUITE small, considering the total number of children born to Judson, those sons and daughters of Ann, Sarah, and Emily. High mortality rates in the nineteenth century, especially in Burma, was a factor. Six of the thirteen Judson children lived to adulthood, four of whom married: Adoniram Brown Judson, Henry Hall Judson, Edward Judson, and Emily Judson Hanna. Adoniram and Henry had no offspring, Edward and Antoinette had two daughters, and Emily Frances and T.A.T. Hanna raised a total of eight children.

Edward's oldest child was Sarah Elizabeth, born in 1877. Records are scant. This may have been intentional, for Edward's biographer stated that his two daughters requested that nothing of a personal nature concerning them or the family be included in the story of his life. Consequently, many questions are left unanswered. There are a few entries in the archives of Vassar and Yale, where Sarah Elizabeth obtained degrees. She graduated from Vassar in 1903 and received a

A.C. and Hazel Ames Hanna and their three oldest children in Burma in 1921. A.C. was Judson's youngest grandson and himself a missionary to Burma. The small child in the portrait is Dr. Stanley Hanna, Judson's youngest great-grandson. Courtesy of Dr. Stanley Hanna.

Ph.D. in physiology from Yale in 1916. In 1920, at forty-three, she married Emil Bauman, and they lived in Toronto, where Emil taught. Sarah left no record of having taught subsequent to her marriage. She died in Scarsdale, New York, in 1952 when she was seventy-five.

Margaret, the second daughter of Edward, was born in 1880. She also graduated from Vassar in 1903 and later studied at Yale—three different times, in fact—for a total of six years. Before, during, and after Yale, she was an English teacher at Simmons College, professor and dean of women at Ohio's Denison University, and associate professor at Vassar in New York. After 1919, there is no record of where Margaret lived or what she did. On a 1939 biographical questionnaire at Vassar, she did not indicate having ever been married. Margaret was nearly sixty by this time. She died in New York in 1963 when she was eighty-three.

There was a third generation of Judsons. Emily Frances, that intrepid daughter of Emily and Adoniram, had a quiverful. All five sons and three daughters survived, and six of them lived out their lives in the United States. The oldest Hanna child was another Emily, the third in a line of "Emilys." She lived to be an honor to the name. The third-generation Emily was born in 1871, and she was known into adulthood as "Little Miss Hanna," so petite was she, less than five feet tall in her shoes. But she was a small dynamo. Emily Margaret was twenty-seven when she arrived in Burma in 1898, and her fellow missionaries as well as the Burmese who loved her quickly realized that she had inherited much of Adoniram Judson's talent and skills. She excelled in the difficult Burmese languages and quickly put to good use her literary and musical talent. Emily's special work that first term was in kindergarten curriculum, and she developed culturally helpful materials in Burmese and trained competent kindergarten instructors for the mission schools.

Emily became principal of the Kemmendine Girls' School near Rangoon for the remainder of her first term. Her second term was spent in Moulmein where she was a mainstay of the Baptist Girls' High School and a pillar in Judson Church, working as a much loved teacher and leader. Emily's sudden illness at age thirty-nine was a shock to everyone. She first felt pain on February 9, 1911, and six days later was dead of cancer. Her last words were uttered very calmly and clearly: "God sends."[1] Emily's grave, with its gray marble marker, is in the courtyard of Moulmein's Judson Baptist Church.

Little Miss Hanna had seven younger brothers and sisters.[2] The *youngest* Hanna child, *also* a missionary, was Alexandar Carson, "A.C.," born in 1888 in Philadelphia. He lived a remarkably productive life until dying at age fifty-three. A.C. graduated from Colgate in 1910 and from Colgate Theological Seminary in 1913. He later received advanced degrees at the University of Chicago and Princeton. Also in 1913, A.C. married Hazel Ames, and they hoped to be appointed as missionaries to Burma. It was a bitter disappointment that in 1914—during the Judson Centennial, which celebrated one hundred years since the Judsons had begun mission work—there were not enough funds available to appoint those who were ready and willing to go. At that June meeting of the American Baptist Convention in Boston, however, was a couple from New York, Mr. and Mrs. Charles King. They heard about the Hannas and contacted the mission board. *They* would stand sponsor to the grandson of Judson. Mr. King actually put the Hannas on the payroll of his firm.[3]

The Hanna's first assignment was in Moulmein where A.C.'s famous grandfather had pioneered with such amazing effect. A.C. was placed in charge of the Burmese ministry there but after two years, felt drawn to work in remote Kentung, and they remained there three years. Then the condition of their health forced the young couple to move to Sagaing. They completed their first term in Sagaing, just across the Irrawady River from the spot where his grandfather had suffered in the death prison. When they returned from furlough in 1923, the Hannas were first placed in charge of the Henzada Burmese field but then asked to move to Insein—the Burma Theological Seminary in the suburbs of Rangoon. All his life Hanna had been a fine scholar and relished teaching. This was the most enjoyable and fulfilling period of his mission career. He not only led the seminary, but was also pastor of the oldest Rangoon church, Immanuel.

In 1931, the Hannas opened up work in Mogok, the famous ruby mine area above Mandalay. It bothered him that there was so little Christian literature available in the Burmese language, so he edited a monthly periodical to provide what they needed. No one was surprised that Hanna had an amazing command of the Burmese language. That seemed to be a family trait.

Their last years in Burma, the Hannas were once again in Rangoon, and again A.C. preached at Immanuel Church in the heart of the city. However, A.C.'s health was broken by furlough time in 1938, and he suffered with dangerously high blood pressure. They lived in Granville, Ohio, and A.C. gradually weakened, dying of a massive stroke in 1942. He had lived only fifty-three years, but devoted twenty-three of them to his beloved adopted country. From the very beginning he had felt strong ties to the people of the land that had so influenced his family for three generations. The Burmese were his people; Burma was his nation and his heritage. One of Hanna's sons recalls above all his father's deep integrity and his great love for Burma.

A.C.'s wife, Hazel Ames Hanna, was a true partner and had a gift for making any place they happened to move seem like home. She had a singularly sweet and gentle personality that influenced all around her. The extreme climatic conditions in Burma were difficult for her, however, because she was a diabetic most of her life. Hazel Ames Hanna died in 1949 in Granville, Ohio.

A.C. and Hazel Hanna were survived by four children. Three had been born in Burma, and their earliest memories were of that country.[4] One great-grandson of Adoniram Judson is still living. This most well-known of the A.C. Hanna children was second son, Stanley, born in 1920 in a house on the banks of the Irrawady River in Sagaing, just outside of Mandalay. As a little boy, Stanley remembers his father often pointing out the ancient watchtower rising above the trees across the river in Ava. The old tower had been in use in 1824 when Stanley's great-grandfather had been in Let Ma Yoon death prison, just a stone's throw away. History became very real and immediate in the heart of the little boy who heard so much about the daring exploits of his ancestor.

Clearly the brilliant Judson genes bred true, for when Stanley was just four, he realized that big sister, Helen, and big brother, Ames, could read all those strange marks in books, and why couldn't he? History repeated itself, and little Stanley got a Bible and taught himself to read those little black marks. Not knowing any better, he started right in, first chapter, first verse—in Genesis. By the time he reached age six, he had read to 2 Chronicles. When Stanley went to first grade at the school for missionary children in Taungyi, his mother became the "housemother" for all the young MKs. That early promise of brilliance was amply fulfilled in the life of Stanley Sweet Hanna, and throughout his eminent career, he never lost his childhood fascination with the history of his unique family.

Stanley came to the United States for school when he was fourteen. After undergraduate work at Denison University, he received a Ph.D. in physics from Johns Hopkins. For nine years he was instructor and then assistant professor of physics at Johns Hopkins; then he spent eight years as physicist and senior physicist at Argonne National Laboratory. Subsequently Hanna served twenty-seven years as distinguished professor of physics at Stanford University. He has been a major presence in nuclear physics for nearly half a century, known for an inner spark of innovative science that has come to be his legacy. His work on a national level has been greatly instrumental in guiding policies affecting the role of nuclear physics in relation to United States education and scientific needs. His work has been prolific, with close to two hundred articles published in national journals.[5] And in all his work, a key factor has been his keen and sincere personal interest in his students and their professional development. He has left a deep impact on his field. Stanley married Denison classmate Jane Martin in 1942, and they forged a talented partnership. The Hannas had two sons and a daughter.[6] Stanley Hanna traveled in dozens of countries but was drawn again and again to the land of his birth.

The footprints of Judson descendants grow dim and seem to fade away. Tracing the broader families of Sarah Boardman Judson and Ann Hasseltine Judson proved no easy task. Sarah's only living child from her first marriage, George Dana Boardman Jr., although married, never had children. Sarah herself came from a family that was considered large even in that day of big families, for she was the oldest of thirteen. However, efforts to locate great-nieces and nephews have proved elusive.

The descendants of Ann Hasseltine Judson's siblings proved nearly as difficult to locate. Biographies of the Judsons gave no clues, and books of genealogy seemed to have lost the trail of Ann's brothers and sisters after one generation, or two at most. Surely somewhere was some great-niece or nephew who had kept the family line alive. Ann had had three sisters and three brothers. Two brothers had died young, one at six months old, the other at age twenty. Only one of her three sisters had married, Rebecca (Becky) Hasseltine, who married Rev. Joseph Emerson. They had two sons, who in turn had children, but those children did not leave descendants, so the line ended there. The other Hasseltine sisters, Polly (always called Mary) and Abigail, never married.

On the other hand, Ann's younger brother Joseph had children, who in turn gave him grandchildren. Only one, however, had children into still another generation. This was Joseph's son Judson Adoniram Hasseltine, born in 1822, when his famous Aunt Ann was in America for a few months. J.A., as he came to be called, moved to South Carolina in 1839, and there the trail grew dim. Two years of digging for clues, of trying to trace Ann's family line, were both frustrating and fascinating. A handwritten list slipped into a loose file marked "Hasseltine" in Haverhill's archives was the beginning of some success. The name "J.A. Hasseltine" was on the penciled list, and it led to many months of letters, scores of phone calls, and numerous dead ends. Finally, a call to North Carolina brought a positive answer: "Yes, I am Lucy Witherspoon, and my great-grandfather was Judson Adoniram Hasseltine." Miss Witherspoon was in her nineties as was her brother, William. These were Ann's great-great-great-niece and nephew. William had a daughter and grandchildren, as well, so Ann's family line continues.[7]

In descendants and in impact, the Judsons live on. And it is not just in America that there is posterity. In Judson's adopted land, there are a vast host of spiritual descendants, true living links to those intrepid pioneers of two hundred years ago, with fascinating stories to explore.

Living Links

You are a letter from Christ…written not with ink but with the spirit of the living God, not on tablets of stone but on tablets of human hearts.
—2 Corinthians 3:3 NIV

ON THURSDAY, JULY 13, 1813, ANN AND ADONIRAM JUDSON ARRIVED IN Rangoon—and were destined to become the spiritual parents of generations yet to come. Either directly or indirectly, the majority of Burmese Christians are spiritual descendants of that vibrant young couple who committed their lives to the future of a people. Stories are handed down to the little ones in a small thatched cottage in remote Shan State. In a house on stilts by beautiful Inle Lake, a mother tells

The Nyein sisters, granddaughters of Daw Lone Ma and Ah Vong, the first Chinese-Burmese printer, grow up in the home of their grandmother Lone Ma. L to R: Daw Tin, Daw Dwe, Daw May, Daw Nge, ages 93-104. *Inset*: Only known lithograph of Daw Lone Ma. Both courtesy of Harriet Bain.

her children of the gospel her parents told her, and near a tropical jungle in south Burma, an elderly grandfather tells his grandson the wonderful news his own grandfather told him.

Among Burma's "living stones" are some remarkable stories of how the gospel changed the history of a family and even of an entire tribe. There is the tale of Ah Vong, who became one of the pillars of beginning Baptist work in Burma. His father, Lau Yin Phan, came from Canton, China, after Britain assumed control of southern Burma. Yin Phan married the daughter of the mayor of Mingun near Moulmein, people of Mon descent. The first child born to this couple was Ah Vong, who even as a child showed a keen intellect. His proud parents sent him to the best schools in Moulmein—which happened to be the Baptist mission schools. When in his teens he attended what was called the Free School. The first mention of Ah Vong in Baptist records is actually in a letter written by Sarah Judson to her childhood pastor's wife, Mrs. Lucius Bolles, in Massachusetts. On October 10, 1836, Sarah wrote: "An interesting young Chinese man from the Free School was baptized last Lord's day."[1] Little did Sarah know that Ah Vong would soon be one of those responsible for printing the first edition of the complete Burmese Bible her husband had spent so many years translating.

Ah Vong's life changed drastically when he became a Christian. His parents disowned him, and he found himself completely on his own. The mission printer, Cephas Bennett, and his wife took the promising young man in and never regretted their investment in his life. When the Bennetts went on furlough in 1840, Ah Vong went with them so he could learn typesetting. He proved an apt pupil, for in an account written a dozen years later by Mission Press, they noted that Ah Vong was ingenious and "able to meet any demand upon his skill in the preparation of type."[2] In those early years, the press was printing Christian literature in Burmese, English, and at least five tribal languages, so his skills were multifaceted.

Ah Vong became a church leader and prosperous businessman. His great-great-grandchildren learned from family records that Ah Vong actually donated the teak timber from which the first permanent church in Moulmein was built. Ah Vong's marriage consolidated two of the earliest Christian families of Burma, for he married Daw Lone Ma, who had been baptized by *Sayagyi* ("teacher") Judson when just twelve years old. Lone Ma's intriguing story was one of the highlights at the Judson Moulmein Centennial when she was eighty-five. In her testimony delivered for her by Pastor Ah Syoo (who was also her son), Daw Lone Ma related her childhood memories of Dr. Judson. Lone Ma's father used to take her and her younger brother to church in baskets slung over a pole on his shoulders. Dr. Judson always heard them recite their Bible lesson. The family moved to Ryan Road, just one block from the Judson compound. Her father was responsible for lighting the chapel for evening services, and those services were held every day. Lone Ma always went with her father and early came to saving faith. She requested baptism, but Judson felt she was very young. She must have convinced him of her clear understanding, however, for within a few weeks, he had agreed to baptize the twelve-year-old. Young Lone Ma soon began teaching younger children and even into her eighties was still a favorite Sunday school teacher. Lone Ma recalled for the Centennial celebration that special day of her baptism. The baptistry itself was a tank located by the bubbling stream that ran in the hollow of the Judson compound. The Christians gathered around singing as the townspeople flocked to observe this strange custom.

Daw Lone Ma also remembered Communion services with *Sayagyi* Judson: "Just before communion service," she related, "he would look at us with bright piercing eyes, and we felt that he was looking right down into our hearts, and when he suggested to us to make up our differences between each other, we would hurry out of the room to ask forgiveness of one another."[3] She called Judson an ideal pastor, ever watchful for the welfare of the flock and like a father to each one.

Ah Vong and Daw Lone Ma were successful in publishing, in business, and in raising an exceptional family—fourteen children in all. One son, L.T. Ah Pan, became a well-known builder and was responsible for the construction of many Baptist churches, schools, and hospitals. Their son L.T. Ah Pon was a Baptist doctor, first working in remote areas and then becoming one of the leading surgeons in Moulmein. It was he who discovered the tumor that took the life of Emily Margaret Hanna. Two other sons became Baptist leaders. Ah Seong was an influential pastor, and his brother Ah Syoo was first a school headmaster and then pastor of the Judson Baptist Church in Moulmein. In 1919, he was the first national to become president of the Burma Baptist Convention.

On the marble tablet of honor mounted near the entrance of Moulmein's Judson Church, Ah Vong is one of those names inscribed, along with that of Adoniram Judson and other missionary pioneers. Each subsequent generation in the Ah Vong family has been sprinkled with leaders who have been instrumental in spreading the gospel. In direct lineal descent are the four Nyein sisters, ranging in age from their early nineties to more than one hundred years old. All were educated in Baptist mission schools where aunts, uncles, and parents taught, and each sister in turn became a teacher. They feel a keen link with their heritage and consider themselves privileged to have learned that legacy firsthand from their grandmother Daw Lone Ma, who lived with them.

The Ah Vong family history became intermeshed with another family that is outstanding among Burmese Baptists. Pye Tha Htin was born in 1871 into a strongly Buddhist home. When thirteen, he was sent to the monastery to study, and he became a novice monk at fifteen. For four years he immersed himself in the intricacies of Buddhism. During this time, a prominent village leader became a Christian and started a new school. Pye Tha Htin was curious but leery of this strange new teaching. One day a young Christian teacher noticed Pye and said (in his hearing) to a student who was a believer and standing nearby, "Go ask that young monk where he goes after he dies." Hearing that question haunted the young monk for months. He finally asked the question of his kindly abbot, who frankly confessed, "I don't know."[4]

Young Pye was both confused and uncertain, and in this uncertainty, he decided he would study mathematics rather than become a monk. He began attending the new Christian school in the village. Within months, the truth of the living God had changed his life forever, and he was baptized, as he put it "on the 14th day of the new moon of Tha Din Kyut in the Burmese calendar year 1253 [1891]."[5] From there, Pye's life took an entirely new direction. His desire to learn more about God compelled him to the seminary in Rangoon where he found he "could not help being Christ's witness."[6] Pye began preaching in several places in Rangoon and on Sundays in the very shadow of the giant Shwe Dagon Pagoda. U Pye graduated from Insein (Baptist) Seminary in 1894 and became a pastor and evangelist.

Pye Tha Htin's abilities and commitment were so singular, however, that the seminary urged him, young as he was, to join the faculty. Only twenty-six in 1897, he was ordained and that same year became a seminary professor. His remarkable career spanned forty-three years, and he influenced the lives of hundreds of seminary students. He wrote numerous books on Christian theology, preparing vital material for use in the Burmese culture. U Pye was also the key leader in forming the Burma Baptist Churches Union. His impact on Christianity in Burma has been vast and enduring.

Pye Tha Htin and his talented wife, Ma Kin, also made another contribution to the future of Burma—a son named Hla Bu. This brilliant young man became the first Burman to earn a Ph.D. abroad. U Hla Bu received a doctorate in psychology from England and went on to become the first Burmese president of Judson College in Rangoon. There stands today, adjacent to the campus of the University of Rangoon (of which Judson College is now a part), the U Hla Bu Memorial Hall, a building for student activities and learning, honoring this first president and his contributions.

Two unique Baptist families, that of Ah Vong the printer and Pye Tha Htin the professor, became linked by marriage. Pye's son, U Hla Bu, married Ma Aye Tin, the great-granddaughter of Ah Vong, in a ceremony at Judson Church in Moulmein. That ceremony was solemized by Aye Tin's great-uncle Ah Syoo, the son of Ah Vong and Daw Lone Ma. The young couple had two daughters, one of whom is a professor in Rangoon, the other a prominent church leader in Missouri.[7]

Another eminent early convert also has descendants who are still a part of that first church in Moulmein. Dr. Shaw Loo (Saul) was the first Burmese to receive a medical degree in the United States. He returned to Burma to become a mainstay of Baptist medical work in Moulmein. Shaw Loo was a venerable seventy-four when he addressed the Judson Centennial audience in Moulmein in December 1913, and in flawless English he recalled his personal memories of Judson.[8]

One set of Shaw Loo's grandparents had been baptized by Dr. Judson in the early years, and his other grandmother, the daughter-in-law of a chief, was eighty years old when she believed and was baptized by Judson in 1829.[9] Shaw's parents were also baptized by the pioneer. As a small boy, Shaw Loo lived near the Judson family, and *Sayagyi* Judson was an important part of his childhood. His best friends were the missionary children who lived in the Judson compound, especially "Addy" Judson and his brother "Elly," all being close to the same age.

Dr. Shaw related his memories of *Sayagyi* Judson's daily work. He told of the *zayats* (worship rest houses) and schools Judson opened all over the city. He had watched as Dr. Judson visited these places early every morning to teach and preach. Shaw Loo vividly recalled the last time he saw Judson: "I remember seeing him placed on an ambulance about five or six o'clock one afternoon and carried by sailors from his house to the...jetty, where he was put in a boat and rowed to a ship anchored not far off in the river and then carried up into the ship. Many Christians, I among them followed him as far as the wharf and stood there looking with sorrowful eyes till we could not see the ship owing to the darkness of night that had fallen, and then only we returned to our homes."[10]

In this century, in the church founded by Judson and of which Dr. Shaw Loo was so many years a leader, the grandson of that eminent physician now worships. Victor Soe feels honored to be Shaw Loo's grandson. Eighty years old in 2001, Victor remembers being in the very first group baptized in the present church building, which was erected in 1937. In December 2002, Soe presided at the 175th

313

Anniversary Celebration of the church. Hundreds of Baptist leaders converged in Moulmein to mark the historic occasion. At the Centennial celebration there in 1913, no Judson descendant had been able to attend. The 175th anniversary, however, was highlighted by an address from Adoniram Judson's closest living descendant, Stanley Hanna.

Spiritual descendants of the Judsons are found throughout Myanmar and abroad. A prominent senior member of the Burmese delegation to the United Nations, Dr. Zaw T. Win, traces his Baptist ancestry back to U Khway and Daw Pu Le, his great-great-great-grandparents who were baptized by Judson nearly two centuries ago. Family histories in homes throughout Burma have a story to tell—a story linking them to the beginnings of Christian missions in their ancient country. The story is not over, for new chapters continue to be written. The years between the death of the Judsons and the twenty-first century are filled with accounts of a veritable army of missionaries who responded to the command to go and tell—and who faithfully joined with Burman believers in responding to the commission that still does not come to an end. The legacies of Adoniram, Ann, Sarah, and Emily continue.

A rare first page of Ann Judson's 1816 catechism. She also translated it into Siamese. Courtesy of the American Baptist Historical Society.

Ann—The Lasting Legacy

Beloved, in thy lonely grave,
How sadly I mourned
for thee,
All earthly dangers thou
didst brave, And now thou
art safe and free.
—Adoniram Judson, 1830

THE LEGACY OF ANN HASSEL-tine Judson is a powerful one, even into this millennium. One hundred years after the Judsons first sailed, historian James Hill called Ann Judson "the woman of the century."[1] The depth of her commitment was not common in *any* period. Her fidelity withstood the challenge of unimaginable suffering and emerged triumphant.[2]

The family and the community that shaped Ann Hasseltine were in some ways typical of the late eighteenth century. Bradford, Massachusetts, was a small town but possessed an unusual emphasis on education. This was not typical early New England thinking. Bradford Academy was a pioneer in women's education. Rebecca Hasseltine passed on to her gifted daughters an insatiable love of learning. So little about the lives and work of most women of that era was recorded; Rebecca Hasseltine would have made a fascinating study in character. Three of her daughters publicly distinguished themselves in an era when few women were considered "notable."

The oldest, Rebecca (called Becky), married Rev. Joseph Emerson, a well-known pastor, and was a community leader and educator. The second daughter, Abigail, was the eminent principal of Bradford Academy, and of course, Ann became America's premier woman missionary. The third sister, Mary, was the only daughter to remain at home, and she often wrote to Ann, calling her "Honey"—the family's pet name for their youngest daughter. In an 1821 letter, Mary noted that "Mother has not forgotten her beloved daughter Honey. Often says—Honey was her best child."3

As the youngest girl, Ann always managed to find a way to accomplish her goals and more than once had the adjectives "headstrong" and "determined" attached to her name. The spring she was sixteen, Ann's conversion marked a dramatic change in her life. The "Belle of Bradford" became the *committed* belle. There were no seminaries that accepted females, but not deterred, Ann obtained works by leading theologians and immersed herself in study. Her journal gives a glimpse of her concern for the "benighted heathen" who had never heard the gospel.

Twenty-year-old Ann met Adoniram Judson one fine June day in 1810, and her life forever changed. It could be no accident that two such exceptional young adults should meet and blend those talents in a way that would influence not only their own nation, but permanently impact another country far away. Ann and Adoniram were remarkably alike in outlook: headstrong, impulsive, and equally determined to persuade to his or her point of view. It must have led to some interesting and lively discussions. Ann freely admitted that she liked to have her own way. Adoniram confessed to the same. But this inbred determination was molded by Providence into the ability to withstand trials and suffering not even conceivable to the average American of that day, or *any* day.

There are few records of many of the difficulties that faced them. It is a loss to history that Ann had to burn their papers and diaries in Ava at the beginning of the war. For example, how must that first Christmas have felt? There is no record. They were isolated, with no friends, no way to communicate other than a few rudimentary Burmese sentences, and no one else in that land who had an inkling of what "Christmas" meant. There was no mail from home, no denominational support, and no way of knowing if and when they might *have* any.

Ann's writings revealed more of the emotional impact of these adversities than did Adoniram's. Her surviving writing records some of her early impressions of Burma: exotic, fascinating, frightening, and needy. The bright spirit of determination ingrained in both Judsons stood them in good stead for much worse to come. Health was a constant problem, with no doctor and no medicine. Every disease known to humanity seemed to have been their lot at one time or another. Adoniram had a terrible time with his eyes, throat, fevers, and stomach. Ann was struck by typhoid fever, dengue fever, cerebral spinal meningitis, and severe liver disease. Yet they persevered and their bond to one another grew still stronger. Together they faced a despotic emperor and tackled one of the world's most difficult languages. Repeatedly the two faced separation from each other, and that was far worse than the isolation. The loneliness must have been appalling, the sense of isolation overwhelming, but "looking back" was not in their vocabulary—in any language.

Ann must have agonized over her babies. Her suffering with that first stillborn little boy was never recorded. Writing of that period was so sanitized that pregnancy and childbirth were never discussed. Did they even name the baby boy born on the deck of the *Georgiana*? Ann did write her parents about the agony of little Roger William's sudden fever and death in 1816. And her last sentence before her own death was that they take care of little Maria when she was gone.

Some of the Judsons' impressions are recorded in excerpts from their journals published in the *Baptist Missionary Magazine*. Many bought the magazine regularly just to read the next exciting chapter in their saga. The magazine printed part of a letter Ann wrote her parents in 1819: "You can hardly conceive our joy my dear Parents and Sisters, on receiving a large parcel of letters from America. Six months had elapsed without an arrival from Bengal. We almost began to think we should never again hear from America. But our joy was great in proportion to the length of time we had waited. When I recognized the well-known hand of my sisters, I wept for joy, and could hardly compose myself so far as to be capable of reading them."[4]

Ann's epic letter written to Adoniram's brother after the prison months was a masterpiece of understatement and was read by hundreds of thousands of fascinated Americans and British, riveted by the unembellished account of nearly two years of suffering. This young woman who wrote in such a matter-of-fact way about the most agonizing experiences had a number of adjectives applied to her by Stacy Warburton, well-known American Baptist professor and historian. In just one sentence, he describes Ann Judson as: "beautiful, vivacious, winsome, loving, fearless, with tact and resourcefulness unsurpassed, an example to all future generations of nobility and faithfulness, devotion and strength."[5]

When Ann's liver disease became dangerous in 1821, there was no alternative but that she sail to a healthier climate and medical help. The few occasions when Ann was able to speak or to appear in public those few months in the United States made a profound impact on the missionary zeal of both Baptists and other denominations. Immediately upon her arrival back in Burma, Ann wrote of the joy of "going home," and it truly felt like home by this time. She could not have imagined the horror of what lay ahead.

Ann never knew Adoniram Brown Judson, of course, the first son of Adoniram to reach adulthood. Born in 1837, he grew up hearing stories of his father's heroic first wife. Years later, this son recalled the letter his father had written Ann on New Year's Day, 1811, in which he remarked that their next New Year's greeting might be exchanged in the "uncouth dialect of Hindustan or Burma." "Little did they think," wrote Judson's son, "that in a few short years her life was to end in the desolation of a Burmese hut, with no friend near but heathen converts, and that her last word would be a sigh in the strange language that both had learned to love. Such was to be the ending of one of the most heroic lives ever laid on the altar of sacred duty."[6]

A quarter of a century after Ann's death, the prestigious *Calcutta Review* gave the highest of praise to Ann: "The prison of Oung-pen-le, though the name be not euphonious, merits an immortality of renown, for never on earth was witnessed a more truly heroic example of the unconquerable strength of a Christian lady's love and fortitude, than was exhibited at Oung-pen-le by Ann Judson. What the mother and the wife must have endured, we will not endeavor to depict."[7]

For Judson himself to speak of the pain of losing Ann was close to impossible. He did write to his parents and sister, and to Ann's mother, Rebecca Hasseltine, telling of all he had learned of the circumstances surrounding her final days. To Rebecca he wrote: "Amid the desolation that death has made, I take up my pen once more to address the mother of my beloved Ann. I am sitting in the house she built, in the room where she breathed her last, and at a window from which I see the tree that stands at the head of her grave."[8] Shortly after her death, his grief found some relief in writing a poem about her, *The Solitary Lament*, which he later sent to Rebecca Hasseltine. A later stanza reveals a hint of his pain:

> O, bitter cup which God has given!
> Where can relief be found?
> Anon I lift my eyes to heaven,
> Anon in tears they're drowned.[9]

Adoniram's grief over the loss of Ann always remained in a sheltered recess of his heart, but his magnificent capacity to endure and to fulfill his calling never faltered.

The number of nineteenth-century women about whom biographies were written is small. Among those select few, Ann Judson is exceptional; more biographies, accounts, and sketches of her life have been written than of any other American woman of that century. When Harriet Chaplin Conant wrote a biography of Adoniram Judson, she made frequent references to the character of Ann as well. Conant spoke of several traits the two Judsons held in common: their hopeful temperaments and a heroic courage and fortitude in the face of death itself. In addition to their brilliant intellects, both had a healthy portion of practical good sense. This saving grace on Ann's part accounted for the preservation of Adoniram's life through the death prison months. Ann's love for him was singular in its importance to his achievements. Conant put it succinctly: "Ann's influence upon his happiness and upon the success of his great work can never be fully estimated."[10]

Ann had a remarkable talent for determining the right course of action and then pursuing it without hesitation. She pursued excellence with skill and unfaltering determination, whether it was in learning a complex language, founding a school, translating the Scripture, or bribing a government official to help keep her husband alive. Ann Judson, not hampered by the expectations of other missionaries, accomplished phenomenal work as a missionary wife, wrote missiologist Dana Robert.[11] She translated several tracts and the books of Daniel and Jonah, and her translation of the Gospel of Matthew in 1819 was the first-ever portion of Scripture written in Siamese. This required unusual linguistic skills in yet another complicated language. Ann ran a household, had two babies who lived a short time, directed a school, did evangelistic work, and kept her husband alive, becoming a hallmark of "the outstanding missionary wives in Burma." Robert declares, "Ann Judson was an evangelist, school teacher, pioneer Bible translator and savior of her husband Adoniram."[12] That one sentence would make a compelling epitaph.

Ann and Adoniram are remembered as founders of the Burmese church and the catalyst that led to the organization of Baptists in America into a powerful denomination, echoes author Sharon James. Ann was a woman who loved intensely: her husband, her little ones, the Burmese, and above all—God.[13] And Harriet Conant examined a little-explored facet of Ann's heart—the depth of her love for Adoniram. "She was Shakespeare's Cordelia," wrote Conant, "with all the unconscious loftiness, scantiness of outward profession, and serene but profound depths of feeling and affection....Her words told but little of her heart, but her heart wrote itself on her life."[14]

Over a period of nearly two centuries, tributes to Ann Judson are consistent and extensive. More modern students of missions do not fail to note her stubbornness or headstrong tendencies; she did not suffer fools gladly, but her amazing depth of fortitude and devotion were unquestionable. James Hill commented that Ann Judson's "queenly soul exhibits a character, which in some of its elements is not equaled in female biography." He noted her capacity for exertion and endurance and her infallible instincts. She was Judson's good genius, a woman of consummate tact and inventiveness, showing heroic resolution in the very face of death. Yet all her life, she seemed wholly unaware of being heroic. Hill concluded that the "renowned heroine" of Ava "introduced to the world a marked feature in the new Acts of the Apostles, which is the apostolate of women."[15]

And in the late twentieth century, Joan Brumberg studied Ann Judson's life in depth, concluding that "without doubt, it was Ann Judson whose perseverance, ingenuity and initiative kept the Baptist Mission alive."[16] It was a final measure of Ann Judson's self-assertion that she, not Adoniram, articulated the emotional realities of the Judsons' life in Burma. Because of what she recorded, today something of the spirit of that remarkable couple has been preserved.[17]

Very few portraits of Ann Judson exist, but her memory was indelibly imprinted on countless lives.[18] Ann remained fresh and real in the heart of Adoniram the remainder of his life. He married two more times, but the love he felt for Ann was always an intrinsic part of him, this man with a remarkable heart and capacity for love. Surely Ann Judson would have been exceptional in any generation. Her life still remains a profound influence. The legacy of the heroine of Ava resounds throughout the land and echoes still in the land of her birth. In an 1846 letter, Adoniram summed up Ann in a single word: *incomparable.*

Sarah—The Gentle Spirit

Love, sweetness, goodness in her person shined.
—John Milton, 1658

THE JUDSON LOVE STORY IS ACTUALLY THREE LOVE STORIES. ADONIRAM had been extraordinarily blessed in his marriage to Ann. He had loved her without reserve. But he was blessed again, with Sarah, the gentle spirit—Sarah Hall Boardman Judson who would never in a lifetime have thought of herself as exceptional, say nothing of heroic. Little is recorded of Sarah's early years, but there is enough to form a picture of a beautiful little girl who in adulthood more than fulfilled her early promise. Being the oldest of thirteen in a family where money was scarce meant that Sarah became her mother's trusted assistant and babysitter as well as teacher of the little ones who followed her one right after another. Sarah's mother, Abiah, was herself only sixteen years old when she married, so that child-mother soon had an eldest daughter who was a mother as much as a child.

All of the Judson babies were placed in this wicker basket at birth. Courtesy of the American Baptist Historical Society, Valley Forge, Pennsylvania.

One of Sarah's brothers recounted that his oldest sister could read from any book by the age of four. Sarah had an insatiable appetite for learning. Any time her mother could spare her to attend school, Sarah ranked at the top of her class. She became inured to toil and responsibility long before her teen years, however. The Halls moved to Salem, Massachusetts when Sarah was nine, and her chief responsibility remained caring for the little ones. Almost the only relic of her childhood is a tiny volume, written in childish script, giving glimpses into a young girl's heart: "My mother cannot spare me to attend school this winter, but I have begun this evening to pursue my studies at home." And the following spring she wrote, "My parents are not in a situation to send me to school this summer, so I must make every exertion in my power to improve at home."[1]

Throughout life Sarah was quiet and reserved, but she showed an amazing elasticity of spirit and an internal drive that sustained her in the most perilous of situations and ensured that she never gave up. She was writing polished poetry before she became a teenager. How she found time to study and write is a mystery. Perhaps it was late at night when the babies were tucked in bed. In a letter to a friend, she mentioned some of her studies: *Butler's Analogy, Paley's Evidence, Campbell's Philosophy of Rhetoric.* Heavy fare. In another letter, she concluded, "I am at home this winter, teaching my little brothers and so have more leisure to devote to my Latin."[2]

Sarah Hall's childhood was never carefree. Maybe those early years forged the steel in the soul of Sarah Boardman Judson, who later pioneered in jungles half a world away. One biographer felt that Sarah's keen mind had early been trained and disciplined in "that noblest of all schools—the school of adverse fortune."[3] While still young, Sarah was writing poetry and articles for religious journals. As a teenager, she professed faith and was baptized in Salem. Sarah read everything about missions that she could get her hands on, her journal full of references to America's pioneer missionaries. Ann Judson was her heroine. Less than a month after her baptism, Sarah wrote: "While I have this day had the privilege of worshipping the true God in solemnity, I have been pained by the thoughts of those who have never heard the sound of the gospel. When will the time come that the poor hea-then…shall own the living and true God? Dear Savior, haste to spread the knowledge of thy dying love to earth's remotest bounds."[4]

But as a modern sociologist puts it, Sarah Hall was "doomed by gender" to staying at home.[5] America was in the "neo-natal" stage of missions. *Single* women were not considered. This did not stop Sarah from caring. Her elegy to young martyr Colman caught the eye of George Boardman, and they married two years later. How amaz-ing Sarah must have found it, to be sailing for Burma to become a fel-low missionary with the famous Ann Judson.

That was not to be. When the Boardmans sailed, Burma was at war, so they went to India and studied Burmese until the war was over and they could join the Judsons. They and their little six-month-old girl arrived in South Burma in April 1827, to find Ann's grave and to be there with Adoniram Judson as he watched at the bedside of his dying child. Sarah composed a poem of tribute to the little Maria, innocent victim of war and disease. What an introduction that first week must have been to what would become Sarah's home for the rest of her life. She and George became the first missionaries in Moulmein, the new British capital of South Burma.

Gentle exterior. Steel on the inside. The next years would prove just how apt a description this was of Sarah. The Boardmans were in Moulmein only a few months before moving south to Tavoy to pioneer work among the wild Karens, but long enough to come perilously close to being murdered in their little wooden house that stood alone next to the jungle. They awoke one dawn to find all their belongings rifled, many articles missing, and knife slashes in the mosquito net-ting right by their heads. Death had been that near. The British com-mandant immediately placed two sentries by their house as guards. A few nights later, one of those guards was attacked by a tiger. Sarah wrote her pastor's wife, Mrs. Bolles, about the harrowing experience and told her that she sometimes longed for "some little, 'little' room, composed of such materials as would enable us to sleep in safety." But then she went on to say that she could put her trust in "the Great Shepherd of Israel, who never slumbers nor sleeps."[6]

That same inner strength sustained her again when she and George, who was already failing rapidly with tuberculosis, began their jungle ministry with the Karens. Sarah began schools for the children of Tavoy and had two more babies, while continuing to work as her husband's faithful coworker in their jungle evangelism. Little George Jr. was frail from the very beginning, as was Judson Wade, their third child. Then two-year-old Sarah sickened and died within days. Judson Wade lived only eight months.

There were more struggles to come. Rebel insurgents in Tavoy revolted against the British, and the lives of the handful of foreigners there hung in the balance. The horrors of those days haunted Sarah the rest of her life. They lived through it, only to have George grow weaker by the day. He insisted on making one last jungle trip, even though he had to be borne on a stretcher. He lay smiling as he watched new converts being baptized. And Sarah returned to Tavoy with the body of her young husband and grieved over his grave, placed there at the side of their two babies.

Judson was in central Burma when the news reached him of the untimely death of George Boardman. Boardman had been just thirty years old. Adoniram wrote that beautiful letter to Sarah, telling her how he had lived through the loss of Ann and urging her to stay on and not to return to America.[7] Her situation, however, was different from his own. Widowed women did not stay on alone. There was certainly no precedent. Sarah had the sole care of little George, and she struggled mightily over what to do. To just pack up and leave must have been exceedingly tempting. She was weary, grieving, and responsible for her frail little three-year-old. The dilemma of what to do hung over her head.

In June of that year, Judson wrote friends in Maine about several of the missionaries who were dangerously ill and who must leave in order to survive. There would be so few left to do the work. He added, "Mrs. Boardman also writes that she must go home" for the sake of George, but he further wrote, "I am not the one to speak against her going home for an obvious reason."[8] However, Sarah stayed. That inner mettle asserted itself yet again, and she remained in Tavoy, the revered "White Mamma" of the Karens, as she continued not only teaching, but maintaining Boardman's jungle ministry of preaching as well.

Sarah's courage was exceptional, although she would never have applied such an adjective to herself. Her son, George, forever remembered his mother's incredible fortitude. Sixty years later, when the well-known pastor of First Baptist Church Philadelphia was asked about his early years, certain memories were vivid. "I left my mother at six," George Jr. said, "and never saw her afterwards. There is another memory, perhaps as early. I remember going out with my mother to the Buddhist grove in which my father was buried, and I clambered upon the tomb and went to sleep. When I awoke, I found my mother weeping, which impressed the scene upon my mind."[9] George sent to Tavoy a monument of American granite for his father's grave. One side reads: "Sacred to the Memory of George Dana Boardman, American Missionary to Burmah. Born February 8, 1801, Died February 11, 1831. His epitaph is written in the adjoining forests." On the reverse is carved: "Ask in the Christian villages of yonder mountains—who taught you to abandon the worship of demons? Who raised you from vice to morality? Who brought you your Bibles, your Sabbaths, and your words of prayer? Let the reply be his eulogy."[10]

Sarah Boardman remained a widow for more than three years. The love story of Sarah and Adoniram was far different from that of Ann and Adoniram, yet this relationship was just as deep and fulfilling as his first marriage. No "paper trail" of their courtship remains. The only extant correspondence was Adoniram's letter of sympathy when Boardman died in 1831 and Sarah's letter to Adoniram after he had completed the Burmese Bible in 1834.[11] There are other hints of her esteem for him, however, such as the fact that she and George had named a son for Judson. And on Judson's part, he had admired the character of Sarah for years, for he had given Ann's "charmed watch" to Sarah after Ann's death back in 1827.[12] There must have been other letters exchanged between the two. Maybe one day those "other letters" will turn up.

There are some surviving letters from the period of their marriage. A few were written when one or the other had to "take to the sea" in order to regain health. Sarah frequently wrote describing her wonderful husband to her family in America, who had only heard of the renowned "Dr. Judson." In every letter to her parents and various siblings, Sarah talks about Adoniram. In a letter to her parents written just two days before their first child, Abby Ann, was born, Sarah exclaimed, "I am blest with a most affectionate partner, the very person whom of *all others* I would have chosen as the father of my child."[13] In 1836 she told her mother, "I have such a treasure in my husband that I feel as if I could ask for nothing more on earth. He is all I could ask for in sickness and in health. I had no attendant but him when Abby was born."[14]

By 1838, Sarah's ardor had not dimmed an iota. She told her parents: "How I wish you had been acquainted with my precious husband—all I could desire in a bosom companion is united in him....He is now fifty years old but does not look as if he were more than thirty-five, at least I think so. He is about common size and I have always thought him unusually well-looking. His hair is not grey or his brow wrinkled."[15] Throughout her family correspondence, she unfailingly commented on Judson and her love for him.

Possibly the single most difficult and ongoing trial of Sarah's forty-one years was her parting with young George. Her letters are full of references to her oldest child—the one she had kissed goodbye when he was only a frail six-year-old. He may have been 10,000 miles away, but he was achingly close in heart. Sarah's letters reveal her thoughts. Was he lonely? Was he warm in the cold American winter? Had he inherited his father's weak lungs? Was he too indulged? The underlying anxiety, never expressed but always apparent, was a mother's heart saying: "Do you know how hard it was to let you go? Can you understand I didn't want to?"

In later years, Sarah's youngest son, Edward, spoke lovingly of this mother he never knew. In writing Judson's biography, this son said of his mother's relationship with Adoniram: "He found in her a kindred spirit....She was the guiding spirit of the mission."[16] The "job description" for a pioneer missionary wife would surely have discouraged 99 percent of all applicants. Sarah Boardman Judson would have been in the remaining 1 percent. The task involved dangerous conditions, low pay, enervating climate, tropical diseases, full-time mothering, full-time translating, full-time teaching, and full-time wife. Sarah did it all, but a thread running through all her correspondence and in the memories of her children indicates that she never felt adequate. Of Judson's three wives, Sarah was by nature the most self-effacing. She never fully comprehended the tremendous contribution she was making. In an 1839 letter to one of her brothers, she laments, "Souls are perishing and I ought to be up and doing."[17]

Sarah loved her roles as wife and mother, and journals reveal she would frequently be sitting at her desk translating with the children playing all around her. Adoniram was the axis around which the family revolved and certainly at the center of her heart. In an 1838 letter to her parents, she says, "I have now three little ones, the oldest but a little over three years old. They are a great comfort to their fond papa. You know he lost his only two children by his former marriage."[18] In the same letter, she tries to explain the dilemma of missionary parents over caring for their children; they needed to be sent to America for both their health and education, but then both parent and child suffered the agony of early separation. There was no easy answer.

Sarah the mother was tender and loving. Sarah the translator was uniquely gifted. Languages and translating could be called the major task of both Sarah and Adoniram, but they were involved in so much work that the lines become blurred. Sarah wrote a number of hymns in Burmese that have been sung for more than a century and a half, and her fine translation of *Pilgrim's Progress* is still in use. Sarah conducted mothers' classes and prayer groups, preparing the materials for all of them. Her translation work involved three languages: Burmese, Karen, and Peguan. She and Ann Judson thus had another link; Ann had also learned Siamese and translated portions of the gospel into that language. That the two wives could both be so singularly brilliant in linguistics is amazing.

Sarah's nemesis was dysentery, which first struck her two days after arriving in Burma in 1827 and eventually killed her. Sailing for the cooler climate of America seemed her only hope, but Sarah's body gave out at St. Helena. Adoniram later sent back to that lonely island spot the inscription for her monument: "Sacred to the Memory of SARAH B. JUDSON, Member of the American Baptist Mission to Burma, Formerly wife of the Rev. George D. Boardman, of Tavoy, And lately wife of the Rev. Adoniram Judson, of Maulmain: Who died in this port Sept. 1, 1845, on her passage to the United States, in the 42nd year of her age, and the 21st of her Missionary life. She sleeps sweetly here on this rock of the ocean, away from the home of her youth, and far from the land where with heartfelt devotion she scattered the bright beams of truth."[19]

Sarah's "bright beams" diffused far and wide—in the changed lives she left behind in Burma, in the translations that continue to influence a nation, and through the lives of her children and her children's children. Judson commented numerous times after Sarah's death about his deep regret that her children had no portrait of their mother because her face had never been depicted on canvas.

But maybe there *is* such a portrait. The mystery lingers. In an obscure biographical file in the American Baptist Historical Library in Rochester, New York, is a picture, its source unknown. It is the photocopy of a young woman's portrait, painted in the style of the early 1800s, and under it is written in spidery script: "Sarah Boardman Judson." There is another photocopy of the same portrait and of an oval wicker baby basket right beside it. Under them is written in the same script: "Sarah Boardman Judson, basket her children was [sic] rocked in at Burmah." Possibly some relative of Sarah's sent these pictures to the historical society. There is a New York postmark on one of the photocopies. There is just no record of who sent them.[20] The baby basket is now in the archives at Valley Forge and is in quite good condition. All efforts to trace these clues to Hall relations have thus far come to a dead end. Could this actually be a portrait of Sarah Judson? The question begs an answer. If it is, where is that original portrait? It would be the only known likeness of a remarkable woman.

Missiologist Dana Robert called Sarah a pioneer missionary to the Karens who became their minister upon the death of her husband, doing so in such an unassuming way that not even high sticklers were offended.[21] The English of India summed up Sarah's personal loveliness and grace of manner by calling her "the most finished and faultless specimen of an American woman that they had ever known."[22] Shortly after Sarah died, Adoniram tried to pay her adequate tribute: "Her bereaved husband is the more desirous of bearing this testimony to her various attainments, her labors, and her worth, from the fact that her own unobtrusive and retiring disposition always led her to seek the shade."[23]

Sarah left behind the indelible mark of her gracious spirit and quiet courage to a distant nation that sorely needed it. Her legacy continues. She left behind children who never forgot the early influence of their remarkable mother and several of whom made remarkable contributions of their own.

Who would ever imagine that one man, no matter how distinguished and exceptional, could be blessed with not just two, but three unforgettable wives? Because there was Emily too.

Emily—
The Poetic Heart

And joy it give my inmost soul, that,
as thy love is mine,
Thou knowst, beyond a shade of
doubt, my constant heart is thine.
—Adoniram to Emily 1847

SO ALIKE, YET SO DIFFERENT—ANN, SARAH, then Emily, each of whom left her imprint on the land of her birth and on the country of her adoption. And bright young author Emily Chubbuck might have seemed the unlikeliest missionary heroine of the three. A twenty-one-year old Emily had expressed a desire to devote her life to missionary service, but her wise pastor had advised her to "await the openings of Providence."[1] She told a friend, "I have felt ever since I read the memoir of Ann H. Judson when I was a small child, that I must become a missionary. I fear it is but a childish fancy, and am making every effort to banish it from my mind; yet the more I seek to divert my thoughts from it, the more unhappy I am."[2] Providence did open for her eight years later.

Early biographer Asahel Kendrick considered that Emily's months in Philadelphia brought her into society in such a way as to override her reticence and replace it with self-confidence. He felt "the shy, timid, silent girl…would hardly be recognized in the genial, animated and often brilliant young lady of a little later date."[3] And friends could only wonder at the amazing blossoming of Emily Chubbuck under the loving aegis of Adoniram Judson. They were astounded at

Emily Judson preserved the recollections and memories of Adoniram Judson's final years of pioneer ministry. From *Life of Adoniram Judson,* by E. Judson.

the event of the next few months, for at the time Emily met Judson, she was close to receiving a proposal of marriage from an important literary figure.

It is only recently that private letters in the possession of a Judson descendant have come to light, revealing the intriguing story of Emily's rise to fame and of a romance that *nearly* was. Emily's clever letter in 1844 to literary critic N.P. Willis was the beginning of her fame. In a biography of Willis, the "birth of Fanny Forester" was summed up: "Probably the most prominent writer for the *Evening* and *Weekly Mirrors,* other than Willis himself, was Fanny Forester. In June 1844, a Miss Emily Chubbuck, a teacher of Utica, New York,...wrote a short sketch and sent it to *New Mirror* editors. They recognized her ability and solicited more contributions. For many weeks, her short, sentimental, chatty sketches appealed to readers. Very early, Willis commended her work to the publishers of *Graham's* and *Godey's.* As a direct result, she became one of the most popular contemporary writers of sketches for these magazines."[4]

Fanny Forester came to life, surely Galatea to Willis's Pygmalion. He became the foster father of her intellect, helping her with accurate criticism as well as praise, teaching her to appreciate herself and inspiring her to become self-confident.[5] Willis recognized that Emily wrote from her heart, the source of the power of her work. Of that heart he wrote, "You are gifted far beyond your own belief, but your heart is more gifted than your head. Your affections are in more need of room and wings than your imagination." Then Willis added a line that proved prophetically true: "I should bless God for your sake to hear that a poet and man-angel had taken you to a dell in the wilderness, never to be heard of more."[6] A man-angel indeed took her—to a "dell" far across the sea.

In spite of the wealth of correspondence between Emily and Willis those two years, there was, according to biographers, just one face-to-face meeting. They became friends via letters. A handful of Willis's letters are partially quoted in Emily's early biography. There is not one quote from a letter of Emily's to Willis. Her biographer even mentions his regret at having nothing from Emily's side of the correspondence. He wrote Willis after Emily's death, requesting permission to see her letters. And the mystery became apparent. First Willis replied that he would search for them in his "wilderness" of correspondence, and later he wrote regretfully that upon exploring the "wilderness," Emily's letters had disappeared. (More than a century later, when Emily's great-grandson read one of her letters to Adoniram Judson, that mystery was solved. Emily's letters to Judson revealed that Willis had known after all just how her letters had "disappeared.")[7]

In the meantime, Willis introduced Emily to America's leading literary circles, to Graham of *Graham's* magazine who quickly became a fan of hers, and to eminent literary critic Horace Binny Wallace who praised her abilities to all: "We regard her as possessing talents for narrative of a very high and rare order—talents which place her in the front rank of writers of dramatic fiction on either side of the water."[8]

Emily's first meeting with the newly widowed Willis was in New York City during a two-week period in May 1845, shortly before he left for Europe to take his little daughter, three-year-old Imogene, to her aunt. Their correspondence never abated in his months abroad. A century and a half later, N.P.'s letters to Emily were discovered in her family papers, and the evidence of his intentions was clearly stated. Unknown to Emily at the time, Willis had planned to propose to her upon his return to New York. His proposal never happened, for Providence intervened on a Christmas Day and someone else proposed first.

That morning was the beginning of the romance between Emily Chubbuck and Adoniram Judson, as farfetched as that must have appeared to all who only know them by reputation. Judson was true to character once again: Don't waste time. As Adoniram and Emily discussed the writing of Sarah's memoirs, their mutual respect quickly grew into deepening admiration, and admiration into love.[9] The flame never flickered, only growing brighter through their remaining years.

Discussing the need for a memoir of a previous wife does not seem a likely setting for romance. But Adoniram Judson was *never* a usual man. Public reaction was immediate. Adoniram Judson and

Fanny Forester? So different! So soon after his wife's death! But they were uncommonly alike, uncannily so for two from such different worlds, and indeed, different generations. Time appeared inexorable to the fifty-seven-year-old Judson; it was not his readiest commodity. He was lonely, and America was like a foreign country to him. His children needed a mother, and his capacious heart needed a soul companion. It was being "surprised by joy" for them that Christmas morning, and they received the best of gifts, true love.

"What will people say" was never an issue for Judson, although he was always considerate, weighing graciously the opinions and ideas of others, ever able to work cooperatively with his colleagues. His son Edward summed it up forty years later: "He was not dependent on happiness and well-being upon the opinion of others."[10] Judson realized it was different for Emily. As he wrote her: "I feel for you, for it is your first field. Whatever of strength or shield is mine, or I can draw down from heaven, is yours."[11] And it *was* different for Emily—she was so newly in the limelight that she cringed from the criticism when away from him. This is obvious in their love letters. When with him, she felt strong enough to withstand any remarks. Separated, the painful arrows of criticism struck her heart.

The "Watch" letter,[12] Adoniram's first to Emily, in which he follows up on his proposal to her, is the beginning of a fascinating collection of love letters written by one remarkable writer to another. The story they tell, sprinkled with allusions to moments and matters known only to the two of them, is engrossing. Their amazed joy in finding each other is almost palpable. Emily's pain about the "Willis" situation is obvious. She confesses to Judson that in her letters to Willis, written before she had met Adoniram, she had not exactly discouraged Willis's interest in her as he wrote regularly from England. She felt she could not fully commit to Adoniram while those letters still "existed" because they could potentially become an embarrassment to Judson if they fell into the wrong hands. Adoniram in turn wrote of his "nightmare"—that she might ultimately refuse him. Two weeks later, Emily wrote that Willis was returning her letters, which she intended to show to her "good Dr. Judson."[13]

A gap in dates of their letters occurred then; the two met again in New York for several days, and in following correspondence, Judson expressed thankfulness that the "nightmare" was over. Emily had shared Willis's letters with him, and that issue was put behind them. A strange twist in the story comes to light well over a century later. Clearly, Emily destroyed her letters to Willis after he had returned them to her, for there is not one of them among the hundreds of letters she preserved and which were passed down in the family. However, she couldn't bring herself to destroy Willis's letters to her; she saved all fifty of them, including the ones that reveal his feelings upon returning to America and learning that Emily was in love with Judson. He had swallowed all pride, this New York literary giant, confessing his love for her and his intention to propose. However, Willis must not have suffered the pangs of unrequited love too long, for he himself married just four months later.

Before Emily and Adoniram sailed to Burma, Willis met Judson and wrote Emily of his impressions of the greatness of the man and how truly he deemed him worthy of "Fanny Forester." And a June 1846 letter from Emily to a friend reveals that she and Willis did indeed meet more than that one time in 1845. Just about two weeks before the Judsons sailed, while they were in New York, Emily wrote: "Willis called twice. The last day we had a private interview....He is a noble fellow, & he and the Doct. are completely charmed with each other. I am glad of it for each deserves the other's good opinion." [14]

If the letters of Emily, Adoniram, and N.P. Willis are another story within a story, the love letters of Emily and Adoniram are Exhibit A in the art of letter writing. They reveal the gamut of two unique personalities, playfulness and wit as well as deep spiritual values and wells of wisdom. In one note, Emily confided: "How he [Judson] came to pick me out to fall in love with is the greatest mystery,...but I know that as far as any man on earth has power to make me happy, Doctor Judson will do it. And I can't conceive of any situation in which I could be happier....[W]hen I pledge my heart and hand to my good doctor, I also take upon myself *another vow*;...the small remnant of my life shall be devoted to doing good." [15]

The two saw each other for just a few days on a handful of occasions between the time they parted in Philadelphia in late January and their wedding in June, but those beautiful letters trace the growth and strengthening of that most unlikely of love matches.

That pastor of Emily's youth, who advised her to await God's opening, later performed their wedding ceremony and Emily became one of the "matchless Mrs. Judsons."[16]

Well-known Baptist minister George Tooze wrote of Emily: "She was, to be sure, a remarkable woman. Talented, sensitive, possessed of a remarkable sense of humor, exhibiting a positive vitality, sustained by a profound faith, she explored depths of life, depths of which few of us would want to descend. Yet having descended to depths of suffering, she also ascended to heights of faith, heights attained…by very few of those who had considered her faith so weak and her life so 'worldly.'"[17]

Emily Judson had only four years in Burma and four more back in America before her death, but it was she who revealed and articulated the heart and ministry of the final years of the "Father of American Missions". She joined the ranks of two other remarkable women who left their marks on a distant land and on a leading denomination.

The Matchless Mrs. Judsons

Missions history has no parallel for the extraordinary trio who graced the title Mrs. Adoniram Judson. God uniquely touched the life of each, and each made an unequivocal response—a commitment to "mission for life."

The matchless Mrs. Judsons had much in common. None lived long, but each was memorable. Ann died at thirty-six; Sarah was forty-one and Emily, thirty-six. Not one of the unions was a marriage of convenience. Each woman had a unique place in Adoniram's heart, and each loved him with singular devotion. One writer examined the exceptional relationship of each to Judson: "He [Judson] was a center of a family group to which no parallel can be found in ancient or modern history. Ann, Sarah, and Emily shared in his labors, rose to his height, and deserve to shine beside him. A reversal, or any change whatever in the order, would have made the whole result impossible. No one of the three could possibly have taken the place or have done the work of either of the others....To the first he owed his life when the foundations of his monumental work were hardly laid. Another surpassed him in a fine discrimination of words, sympathized with him in his great work of translation, helped him turn his problematic beginnings into phenomenal growth, and called him 'a complete assemblage of all that a woman could wish to love and honor.' The other had more than talent, even genius...With grace, elegance...and unapproachable nicety of language, she gives us an estimate of him,...and a clear reflection of his habits, spirit and style of oratory which illumine the brightest pages of any biography of him."[18]

All three women loved Adoniram intensely. Ann loved him fiercely, unreservedly, even to the point of giving her life for him. They were equals in calling, in spirit, in commitment. Those two were equal parts of the whole in courage and depth, and purely a matched pair in abilities. The contribution of one to the beginning of American missions would not have been successful without the other.

Sarah idolized Judson, loving him with deep passion and tenderness. She unabashedly looked to him for spiritual guidance and saw in him the ideal role model. There could be no higher tribute than to live day in and day out with a person, to know his every mood and response, and to steadfastly see him as the superlative example of what living in close relationship with Christ should be like.

Emily idolized Adoniram as well, and in a unique way. She was inspired by his unswerving faith, the depth of his relationship with God, the very passion of his commitment. Without doubt it was the keen descriptive skills of Emily Judson that communicated to those at home and to subsequent generations the essence of the man who was the Apostle of Burma.

The matchless Mrs. Judsons each possessed attributes uniquely her own. Ann was "her own woman," assertive in a time when that trait was rarely noted (or applauded) in women. She saved Judson's life during the prison years, not once but several times. Ann Judson was a woman born *before* her time, who carved her contributions permanently into the history *of* her time. She was Adoniram's contemporary, his equal in skill and fidelity. Never one to crumble under pressure, Ann matched him in practical good sense. Biographer Conant spoke of her "majestic consistency,"[19] stating that the influence of Ann Judson "spreads like a vital element through the whole history of the Burman mission.[20]

On the other hand, Sarah was all that was gentle and non-assertive, yet when the occasion demanded, she stepped forward to preach and lead. Sarah was quietly brilliant. She never felt quite capable enough, but her actions and achievements reveal a high degree of self-motivation. The few written records Sarah left reveal the insecurity she always felt about her own abilities. As Adoniram told her parents, she always sought the shade. Of the three, Sarah no doubt most closely represented the nineteenth century's conception of ideal Christian womanhood. Adoring wife, devoted mother, powerful translator, writer of elegant poetry, she excelled in all she did.

And there was Emily, brilliant of mind and spirit—a magician with words. Her reserved exterior concealed an astute observer of the human condition, a master of description and discernment as she quietly listened and observed.[21] Judson's biographer Wayland contrasted her frail and failing body with her incredible power of mind. He wrote a friend concerning the dying Emily: "Though sinking steadily into the grave, she was able to accomplish more than most women in perfect health."[22]

And Adoniram Judson unconditionally loved all three women. His love for everything that was Ann did not diminish because he married Sarah in 1834 and loved her for all the goodness and blessing that she was. And his adoration for Sarah remained unchanged even as he loved Emily without reservation in later years. It is nearly too unusual to comprehend. Kendrick called it "a beautiful tribute...to the native largeness of his soul."[23]

A summary description of this highly unusual man who in turn loved three highly unusual women comes from Warburton: "He had a boundless love for each of his wives, and…each loved him with a full devotion. Ann's effervescent nature, deeply joyous, richly loving, fascinatingly attractive, drew him to her with a perfect union of spirit that had little need for words. Sarah was quiet,…lacking the inspiring qualities of Ann, but by her exquisite womanhood winning from Judson a love that matched her own. Emily, with less of missionary zeal,…poured out her love like a torrent, with a bright happiness and a marvelous devotedness that was equaled only by Judson's full, joyous love in return. It was Ann's high privilege to dare the unknown for his sake and Christ's to share the pioneering of the early years, and to save Judson for his great achievements by the gift of her own life. After the dark years of loneliness, Sarah gave him the comfort and delight of a home, and drew forth once more that bright, youthful spirit that was so largely the real Judson. To Emily it was due in rich measure that the ending of his day of life was so happy and peaceful, and that so vivid and human a picture of him has been given to us, a picture that no one but Emily could have painted."[24]

For all their similarities and differences, the matchless Mrs. Judsons shared one common bond above all—their love for that most uncommon of men, Adoniram Judson. To succeeding generations, they left a legacy of courage and a path to follow. And their husband stood alone in the forefront of American foreign missions—without doubt, more than just a memory.

More Than a Memory

If you have succeeded without suffering, it is because those who have gone before you have suffered without succeeding.
—Edward Judson, 1914

1845 engraving of 57-year-old Adoniram Judson, made during his return visit to his homeland. From *To the Golden Shore.*

LEGENDS ALWAYS SEEM LARGER THAN life. The legend that is Adoniram Judson comes from a host of sources but very little from his own writing. He would doubtless have been appalled to know that he became an icon. Edward revealed what Adoniram had felt about his own work: "My father's life, when viewed from his own standpoint, and even that of his contemporaries, must often have looked like failure."[1]

Yet even before his death, Judson had become a household word in his own country.[2] He and William Carey have been placed in a class of their own, due, according to historian W.O. Carver, "[partly] to the circumstances of their service and partly to the heroic mold of the personality of the men." Neither stood alone in his service or could have achieved such greatness without the help of others; both were great in humility and in the power of their devotion to a great cause. Judson was a pioneer whose efforts were marked by obstacles, danger, and suffering. The spirit in which he endured them all made him one of the most popular of all heroes of the church.[3]

Adoniram Judson had a "genius for generalship."[4] A "private" would not have survived those thirty-eight years in the trenches.

Judson's earliest biographer, Wayland, studied his life in great detail and found Adoniram's "will" of particular interest; "He was endowed with a will of the very highest order. It was capable of controlling his physical nature, so that his body would do or suffer whatever it was commanded. It subjected the material to the spiritual in a degree very rarely attained."[5] Wayland was awed by Judson's faith: "It may be supposed that the faith of such a man was in a high degree simple and confiding. In this respect I have rarely seen it equaled. It seemed to place him in direct communication to God."[6]

To view such a unique personality objectively is difficult. Judson would have been the first to say how human he was, how riddled with flaws. And just as surely he was criticized, sometimes justly, other times without merit. No one was ever as censorious of Judson as he was of himself. Certainly he did not suffer fools gladly. In the early years, he and Ann often made unilateral decisions that others sometimes regarded as imperious. Both were forceful and had had only one another to turn to during those lonely early years. Judson's oldest son commented that Judson as a young man was "disposed to carry things with a high hand....Traits which are accepted and admired in conquerors who slay their tens of thousands are deplored in those who risk life and forgo fame to carry the gospel to the heathen....There is always hesitation on the dangerous border of an unknown field till some zealous, or reckless, soul comes in sight to compel the forward step which leads to success or failure."[7] Strong character traits in Judson mellowed through the years, enriching the impact of his great ministry.

Judson's character has been the subject of much speculation in the century and a half since his death. Just what attributes and abilities distinguished the man? Carver called him "a man of childlike openness, faith, frankness, simplicity and loyalty."[8] Conant felt that Judson inherited his "warmth and exquisite tenderness of heart," from his mother and these tempered well the force of will and self-confidence he got from his father. "Slothfulness" was not in his vocabulary.[9] She concluded: "It was the strength, not the weakness of his character, his power of grasping a sublime idea, and of living or dying to actualize it, that gave the subject of missions such a spell-like influence over his mind."[10]

Judson's oldest and youngest sons' view of their father's character and personality is intriguing. Adoniram Brown reflected on his father as a young skeptic, proud of his own knowledge. Following his shattering experience when his deist friend had so suddenly died, Judson began an unprecedented soul search and gave himself unreservedly to the God he had earlier doubted. "He gave his heart to the Saviour and perceived that the ambition to please God was more delightful than all the other forms of ambition....His ardent and restless nature in after years led him into many situations which can only be understood by recognizing the fact that his was in absolute and complete surrender to the Divine will. With him it was only a step, and a short one, between seeing a duty and doing it. It may have given him the appearance of being impulsive, but he moved so quickly that there was little time to wonder how it would appear to others."[11]

Youngest son Edward felt that Judson was "possessed with a consuming zeal to be made holy,"[12] and Edward quoted his stepmother Emily on this trait. Emily declared, "I was first attracted by the freshness, the "originality," if I may so call it, of his goodness."[13] Emily drew a vivid picture of Judson's personality. Of his character, she talked of harmonizing and recognizing its singularly diverse elements, "its delicacy with its strength, its almost unparalleled tenderness with its uncompromising sternness,...its frank, genial socialness with its tendency to asceticism, (and) the simplicity of its devotion...(with) its constant aspiration after holiness."[14] The gifted pen of his wife who knew him so well defined the essence of the man.

Wayland found Adoniram "incapable of doing a thing by halves."[15] "Difficulties did not discourage him. Obstacles did not embarrass him."[16] Judson showed extraordinary emotional balance, especially when the equation of the horrors of the death prison is figured in. Because of the depth of his faith, those grieving years following Ava and the death of Ann ultimately became a time of healing. A century later, a scholar wrote that much of Judson's depth of understanding of God was wrought out in the crucible of his life's experiences, that he and Ann discovered that "their theology had to grow to meet such hard actualities of life."[17] Adoniram bore the scars of death prison on his ankles and wrists—not in his heart.

A hallmark of Judson's philosophy was his commitment to the principle of his call as a "Mission for Life."[18] Judson declared, "The motto of every missionary, whether preacher, printer, or schoolmaster, ought to be 'Devoted for life.'" In a letter, Judson recalled that a missionary friend just a few days earlier had been asked how long he intended to stay in Burma and the answer was Judson's as well, "until all Burmah worship the eternal God." Judson then signed the letter, your 'devoted for life' A Judson."[19]

Judson's philosophy of training national workers was miles ahead of his time. From the very first, Judson began training Burmese to reach their own people, spending countless hours teaching and training leaders and taking them along on jungle preaching tours. His view of single women in mission service was groundbreaking as well. In numerous letters, he referred to their effective work and pointed to several needs that could best be met by single women. No chauvinist, this nineteenth-century man, one more visionary than many men two centuries later.

The essence of the man who was Judson is likely best found in two small books, both bound in cracked leather. The first is Adoniram's personal journal. In it he entered, with little comment, the most significant events in his life, beginning with the birth of his parents and then his own birth. He pinpointed the day of his conversion with a December 2, 1808, entry—just four words: "Made a solemn decision." The final entry in this journal, which marks the highlights of an extraordinary life is dated January 24, 1849: "Finished the English Burmese Dictionary."[20]

The second little book was passed down to Judson's youngest grandson, A.C. Hanna, who called it "one of my most treasured possessions."[21] Missionary Hanna was the only grandson who could properly appreciate the notebook, written mostly in Burmese. This was Judson's prayer journal. Hanna concluded: "Here, it seems to me, is to be found the secret of the success which finally attended the founding of the Burmese Mission....Judson's main trust was in prayer; that was his chief reliance."[22]

Although much of Judson's writing was destroyed, enough remains to hint at unplumbed depths and give insight into the legacy of the man who was in large part the catalyst in the formation of a denomination. The Apostle of Burma. Judson would not have wanted to be so honored, but nothing seemed to stem the acclaim. Destiny? Providence? Both were played out in his life, his achievements so singular and his legacy so lasting, that the designation seems inevitable. During his nine months back in America, Judson was introduced to President Polk as the "greatest ecclesiastical character now living."[23]

From the vantage point of history, it is easier to get a clear picture of the impact Judson continues to make into the twenty-first century. His single most notable achievement is the translation of the Bible into the heart language of the people. He was a master of linguistics. Edward noted that his father "had a very strong relish for literature and linguistic research. One can not fail to observe the poetic genius, original and quoted, scattered through his correspondence."[24] Judson once told Emily that, when making his translation of the Bible, "he felt an almost overpowering sense of the awfulness of his work, and an ever-present conviction that every word was as from the lips of God."[25]

Further, his Burmese grammar had to be considered among the most remarkable achievements in the field of philology, a jewel in its brevity and completeness.[26] Such a work of art was it that a century and a half later, all Burmese grammars are still based on Judson's original work. His secret was in his approach. He was determined not only to "know" the language, but to "live" it. Judson somehow divorced his mind from the specific forms of his own culture and remolded his thinking around the forms of this new and strange speech, becoming a Burman to the Burmans.[27] Adoniram achieved this not just in the language but in thinking and empathy. It was one of the secrets of his success.

Emily explained how Adoniram would sift through texts and ideas on his morning walks: "He preached with great fervour and earnestness; but besides this, there was a touching simplicity in the matter of language….His figures…were drawn from immediately surrounding objects. Of these, in accordance with eastern taste, he made great use. He often remarked that 'Christ was the model preacher' and that 'he' never preached 'great sermons.'"[28]

The Burmese Bible, grammar, and dictionary were all crowning accomplishments, but Judson also wrote the first hymn ever composed in Burmese. One of his compositions, "The Golden Land of Heaven," opens with the famous line so often associated with Judson: "I long to reach the golden shore."[29] "Come Holy Spirit, Dove Divine," his best known hymn, is in nearly every contemporary American hymnal.

The grieving period following prison and Ann's death was the one period of Judson's life that seems out of character with the whole of who he was. It is difficult to get a true picture of those years because much of what has been accepted as "fact" is not fact at all but is based on the fictionalized account of Judson's life, *Splendor of God*, by Honore Morrow. Judson's grandson, T. C. Hanna, did an in-depth study of her account, comparing it with known facts. He concluded that her book "is cumbered with historical and biographical inaccuracies which extend beyond the license commonly allowed a historical novel."[30] Morrow even put words in Adoniram's mouth about Roger's death, saying that his soul had "merged" with God's and that if God willed he might be "born again." Hanna calls this bald paganism and even Buddhistic in its phrasing.[31] It is also pure fiction, somewhat like a colony of termites in the timber of Judson history.

Prison had been suffering enough for a lifetime. Then Ann died and the darkness nearly overwhelmed Judson.[32] Small wonder Judson never wanted to talk about the prison years. He once told Emily, "O, I dare not tell you half the horrors I have seen and felt. They haunt me, when I am ill and sad, even now, and the simplest relation of them would do no good to either of our dreams."[33]

Having suffered so greatly himself, Judson was noted for his remarkable gift for comforting people.[34] Emily once wrote that

345

Adoniram could succeed where others failed "for he has a combined dignity and winningness of manner, which has great power over the natives."[35]

Praises for Judson's translation skills are legion. From throughout Asia came unanimous agreement that his Bible translation was by far the most superior work of its kind. Missionary Russell Brown told an interesting footnote to the story of Judson's translation. In the 1950s, Burma's prime minister U Nu, himself a Buddhist, attended a tea held by the Burma Christian Council. Discussion arose about the possible need for a new colloquial translation of the Bible in Burmese. U Nu declared, "Oh no, a new translation of the Bible is not necessary. Judson's translation captures the language and idiom of Burmese perfectly and is very clear and understandable."[36] Amazing tribute— over a hundred years after Judson had done his monumental work.

And the legacy is both deep and far-reaching. One historian called the conversion of Luther Rice and the Judsons to the Baptist faith as "one of the watersheds of Baptist history,"[37] and "as the catalyst through which Baptist involvement in world missions would have its morning hour."[38]

The focal point of the 1914 Judson Centennial in Boston was Edward Judson's message, focusing on his father's life. Edward stressed, "The difficulties of my father's life have been an inspiration to me. In hours of gloom I have been nerved to continued endeavor by the obstacles that lay across his path." Edward centered on his father's character and commitment: "No small part of my father's achievement was his character,...and then his becoming a Baptist occasioned the organization of the American Baptist Foreign Mission Society."[39]

Fifty years later, Warburton wrote: "[Judson] inspired a great fellowship of churches to organize for the spreading of the gospel to earth's remotest bound,...he gave to the number of earth's great souls three queenly women who bore his name,...(and) he established principles of Christian service that still make successful missions everywhere."[40] The story of Adoniram Judson is in some areas a hagiographic account, for it is difficult not to idealize such an exceptional

person. One historian summed it up well: Adoniram Judson is surpassed by no missionary since the Apostle Paul in self-devotion and
scholarship, in labor and perils, in saintliness and humility, in the
result of his toil on the future of an empire and its multitudinous people."[41] Judson died as he had lived, with his eyes fixed on heaven. He
had often looked death squarely in the face; that last day he knew
that heaven was opening. Ann's last words had been in Burmese; so
were Adoniram's as he said, "It is done. I am going."[42] Wayland stated it superbly: "The record of his deeds is beyond the reach of both
fire and flood."[43]

The death of Judson in 1850 was the end of an era in Burma and
the beginning of another one. The Judsons had established a world-
wide standard of excellence in mission building. Upon their arrival in
1813, Burma had no believers. After one century there were 65,000
church members and at least that many more believers. A veritable
army of national leaders and missionaries followed in their footsteps,
some of them ordinary but committed, others extraordinary and committed. One died just two months after arriving, another labored for
sixty-three years, but every one of the hundreds made a contribution.

By his sixty-first year, Judson must have echoed Habakkuk's
prophecy: "Look at the nations...and be utterly amazed." Yet
scarcely could Judson the visionary have "envisioned" the startling
statistics that greeted the new millennium, for by the year 2000, the
United States—not surprisingly—had more Baptists than any other
nation, and India, with its 1 billion people, had the second largest
number. But little Burma, just 49 million people—had the third
largest number of Baptists of *any* nation. *Operation World* estimates
an astounding 3,370,000 Protestants in Burma, with nearly 2 million of them Baptists.[44]

Conceivably, an "event" is history. Significant events are "historic."
The going of the Judsons to Burma falls in the "historic" category, for
the far-reaching impact of that event continues. They were the catalyst for the beginning of a national Baptist life in America and the
leavening for the rise of the church in Burma. It was no *accident*
of history that took the Judsons to a remote land. They were God's

chosen people in God's time, used by Him to change a nation. All four were remarkable for their passion for a people not their own, who *became* their own.

There was a changeless immediacy to their Great Commission, and its urgency is just as real in this century. The challenge of that commission becomes a personal summons to every believer. How often did Judson feel a hand touching his sleeve and turn to look into a face imploring, "Are you Jesus Christ's man?" Every Christian who stands next to any need still feels a touch on the arm: "Are you Jesus Christ's man?" The old story is as new as the heart needs of the present. How many times did the Judsons "bless God and take courage"? Their theme is our challenge.

The Church in Burma since 1850

THE CHURCH IN BURMA/MYANMAR CONTINUES TO THRIVE IN SPITE OF great difficulties. The primary goal of evangelism, established two centuries ago, has never changed, but the means of achieving that goal have shifted. New emphasis was given to schools training Christian leaders. Medical work, agricultural outreach, industrial schools, and translation and publication of Christian material kept expanding as the work grew.[1]

For the Baptist Mission, the period following Judson's death until the end of America's Civil War was a time of uncertainty and change. Financial problems following the Civil War inevitably affected the work in Burma. Then came a period of consolidation and development with the formation of the Burma Baptist Mission Convention in October 1865,[2] which went on record as being in favor of an indigenous church in Burma—surely the fruition of one of Judson's goals.

With the end of the Third Anglo-Burmese War in 1885, the remainder of Burma came under British rule and the last Burmese monarch was deposed.[3] This was a major factor in enabling Baptists to plant strong work in all Burma.[4] Work among the Karens was the most dramatic, and the effects nothing short of spectacular. Christians from the tribes themselves went out evangelizing. In the second half of the nineteenth century, tribal evangelism extended throughout Burma. It was not easy to gain access to the hill peoples, especially those living on the borders of China and Siam (Thailand), but the gospel slowly began to reach the Kachins, Chins, Lahus, and Shans. Baptists then reached across the plains of Lower Burma, into the mountains of Upper Burma, and to the borders of China.[5]

Education also played a vital role in disseminating the gospel message and solidifying its foundation, reflecting a shift from the early missionaries' emphasis to "concentrate on preaching" and a recognition of the importance of preparing future leaders. Formal theological training began as early as 1836 in Tavoy, and in 1845 a Karen theological school was begun in Moulmein, later moving to Rangoon.[6] The early center for education was Moulmein, and schools were strengthened still more when the women's societies in America began sending missionaries in 1871. From then until the Centennial, thirty-nine high schools were established and scores of primary schools,[7] with Judson College as one of the showpieces. When it began in 1872 as Rangoon College, it was a middle and high school; then with the addition of a bachelor's degree in 1920, it became Judson College and a constituent part of the University of Rangoon. Quickly becoming known for its excellence and the caliber of its graduates, who moved into various positions of prominence, Judson College also came full circle with the selection in 1938 of U Hla Bu as its first national president. He remained its leader until war forced the college to close in 1942.[8]

One of the early missionary kids, Susan Haswell, was the initiator of Burma's medical missions. A teacher and a visionary, Haswell emphasized health care for women and children. Through her ardent appeals, Dr. Ellen Mitchell came in 1879 as Burma's first missionary physician and for the next twenty-two years, used a hillside house in Moulmein as a hospital.[9] Haswell also began the leprosy work that continues today at the Christian Leprosy Hospital in Moulmein, whose purpose reads, "We treat. God heals."[10]

No one element influenced the spread of the gospel more than did translation and publications, which did not stop those first one hundred years.[11] The standard had been peerlessly set by Judson. In the years following his death, six of the unwritten native languages and several of the dialects were set down in writing.[12]

With observances conducted in America, Rangoon, Moulmein, and Mandalay, the centennial celebration of missions in Burma took place on both sides of the globe. At that time, a remarkable 78 percent of the 900 Burmese churches were self-supporting[13] and 200 missionaries rejoiced with hundreds of Burmese believers at the celebration.[14] At this point and for a number of years to follow, the Baptist mission in Burma was recognized as the most successful in the world.[15]

Following World War I, however, revolutionary changes in politics affected Christian missions.[16] Since 1885, Burma had been a British province. This changed dramatically in 1937 when Britain handed over to Burma its own internal affairs but maintained control of foreign policy. Just prior to the cataclysmic changes brought on by the devastation of World War II, Burma Baptists had 200,000 baptized believers.[17] Then World War II began, and everything changed; the Japanese entered Rangoon in March 1942 and controlled the country by May. Thousands of believers suffered, many died, and church buildings were destroyed or taken over by the Japanese. Missiologist Leslie Dunstan said, it was "as though a tremendous tornado had swept across the land, bringing destruction, confusion and devastation."[18] When in 1945 Britain and the United States began retaking Burma, further havoc was wreaked. World War II—a war neither of their making nor their choosing—cost the Burmese dearly. The years leading up to the Japanese invasion had been a time of Burma growing and taking its rightful place among nations, but now they were thrust into the center of world events with no going back.[19]

Missionaries were able to return to Burma in July 1945. In spite of the horrors of war, the membership of the churches had increased, and having lived through a time of agony, the church found itself stronger than ever. At that first convention meeting, a new mood prevailed; Burma's Christians had clearly earned the right to lead in the advances of Christ's kingdom among their own people.[20]

Following independence from Britain in 1948, civil war broke out in Burma with the Communists and the Karens opposing the central government. By 1951, there were more casualties in Burma's *civil* war than the United States had suffered through all of World War II. In the years that followed, however, the government of Burma gradually became stronger. Churches thrived and grew as well.

In spite of wars, upheaval, and repression, Burma remains a sterling example of a work built on a solid foundation. Government changes led to the removal of all missionaries by 1966, but the

351

Burman church has continued to grow, reaching out to a nation sorely in need of hope. Today Burma is controlled by a military dictatorship, but the core strength of the church remains. Even in the glaring light of a fragmented twenty-first-century world, Judson's example endures. God's work in this ancient land has not diminished. More than ten years after missionaries left, a singular event occurred in Myitkyina in the mountains of northern Burma. In 1977, more than 90,000 Baptists gathered in Myitkyina, and some 6,200 converts were baptized in a nearby river, one of the largest single baptismal services ever held in the history of church.[21]

Life has not been easy for the Burmese people, including the great majority of believers. Government policy and economic realities make it hard. The country has a middle class, but it is really only a class in education and heritage. They are painfully poor. Many Christians fall into this category. According to a volunteer educator in Myanmar, the culture evidences two extremes—urban jumble and rural innocence. The vast majority in both categories suffer deprivation. Life could be said to be "barefoot," both for comfort and from necessity. Human rights organizations list Myanmar as one of the most repressed nations on earth.

Burmese believers are clearly a strong people surviving a grim situation, but such conditions cannot remain static. Education is one of the basic problems. Universities essentially shut down after student protests in 1988. That meant an entire student generation lost the opportunity to study.

Among those hardest hit by the nation's woes is the community of faith. Often Christians are deliberately targeted, especially the ethnic minorities, where the percentage of Christians is impressively high. Burma is in some respects a great deal like it was when Ann and Adoniram arrived in 1813. Then it was one of the poorest lands in Asia.[22] It still is. The Burma of 1813 was controlled by an emperor who held life and death in his hands. The present government exercises essentially the same authority. There is one striking contrast, however. Now there is hope, and along with thousands of pagodas, the spires of churches dot the landscape.

The hope that is alive in Myanmar is evident in the lives of believers. Although the number of Christians is especially high among the tribal groups, 50,000 are to be found among the strongly Buddhist majority of Burma—the Bhama people.[23] Among the tribal groups, the Karens are at least 40 percent Christian, the Kachins 90 percent, and the Chins 95 percent.[24] Significantly, one estimate of missionaries sent out by various groups of believers in Burma exceeds an amazing 2,000.[25]

The largest Baptist organization in the nation is the Myanmar Baptist Convention, and there are various independent Baptist entities, but all can be traced to the same roots. Numerous groups abroad encourage the Christians of Burma; some make short visits to give specialized training and others give assistance to Burmese students in higher education. Many Americans who spent early years in Burma as the children of missionaries never forgot their early ties and maintain their contacts with Burma, lending assistance and encouragement.

Anyone meeting Baptist Christians from Burma will notice their spirit and genuine feelings of love and gratitude for those who came long ago to bring the gospel. Burmese Christians stand on their own feet. They appreciate prayer, concern, and encouragement from abroad, yet their message is clear: We thank you for caring, but whatever happens, we are committed to bringing the gospel to our nation. We will not falter. One pastor put it this way to a visiting American friend: "The bones of your fathers are here in our land! Your ancestors gave their lives for us. Please, you must not forget what they have done. We must continue their work together."[26]

The Judson legacy continues as both inspiration and challenge to the believers of Burma as well as to America's community of faith. Throughout his life, Adoniram Judson was often asked, "What hope do you see for the years ahead?" Judson invariably responded with a never-changing affirmation of confidence, "The future is as bright as the promises of God."

N O T E S

CHAPTER 1

1. Francis Wayland, *A Memoir of the Life and Labors of the Rev. Adoniram Judson,* 2 vols. (Boston: Phillips, Sampson and Company, 1853), 1:170.

2. Edward Judson, *The Life of Adoniram Judson* (New York: American Baptist Publication Society, 1883), 3.

3. Courtney Anderson, *To the Golden Shore,* 1st ed. (Boston: Brown and Company, 1956), 12.

4. Ibid., 10–17.

5. Ibid., 14–15.

6. Ibid., 15.

7. Wayland, 1:17.

8. J. Mervin Hull, *Judson the Pioneer* (Philadelphia: American Baptist Publication Society, 1903), 2.

9. E. Judson, 6.

10. Wayland, 1:14.

11. Anderson, 26.

12. Ibid., 27.

13. Ibid., 29.

14. Ibid., 30.

15. The same fall that Adoniram Judson entered Rhode Island College, its name was changed to Brown University.

16. Anderson, 31.

CHAPTER 2

1. Stacy R. Warburton, *Eastward: The Story of Adoniram Judson* (New York: Round Table Press, 1937), 7. Brown University in 1804 consisted of two professors, a three-hundred-square-foot campus, and two buildings. The curriculum was prescribed, and there were no electives. Tuition and room were twenty dollars a year, with a modest charge for food. By contrast, Brown University at the beginning of the 21st century boasted a vast campus, more than 550 full-time faculty, and annual total student fees exceeding $32,000. Yet two centuries ago, even as now, it ranked with the best universities in the land.

2. Ibid., 8.

3. Courtney Anderson, *To the Golden Shore,* First ed. (Boston: Brown and Company, 1956), 31.

4. Warburton, 9.

5. Sharon James, *My Heart in His Hands* (Durham, England: Evangelical Press, 1998), 209.

6. Henry Gouger, *Personal Narrative of Two Years' Imprisonment in Burmah, 1824–1826* (London: John Murray, 1860), 179.

7. Anderson, 42.

8. Edward Judson, *The Life of Adoniram Judson* (Philadelphia: American Baptist Publication Society, 1883), 11–13.

9. Warburton, 14–16.

10. Adoniram Judson, Personal Journal, 1788–1849, American Baptist Historical Society Library, Rochester, N.Y.

11. Ibid.

12. Ibid., 19.

13. A. Judson, Journal.

14. A. Judson, Journal.

15. Anderson, 59.

16. Ibid., 63.

17. Ibid., 67.

CHAPTER 3

1. Walter N. Wyeth, *Ann H. Judson: A Memorial* (Cincinnati: privately printed, 1888), 11.

2. Gordon Langley Hall, *Golden Boats from Burma* (Philadelphia: Macrae Smith Co., 1961), 20.

3. Courtney Anderson, *To the Golden Shore*, 1st ed. (Boston: Brown and Company, 1956), 73.

4. Hall, 23.

5. James D. Knowles, *Memoir of Mrs. Ann H. Judson, Late Missionary to Burmah*, 1st ed. (Boston: Lincoln and Edmands, 1829), 12–13.

6. Ibid., 14.

7. Ibid.

8. Ibid., 77.

9. Ibid., 17.

10. Ibid., 18–19.

11. Ibid., 31.

12. Ibid., 39.

13. Stacy R. Warburton, *Eastward: The Story of Adoniram Judson* (New York: Round Table Press, 1937), 29.

14. Anderson, 83.

15. Knowles, 37.

16. Ibid., 42.

17. Hall, 32.

18. Edwin Dwight, *Memoir of Henry Obookiah a Native of Owhyee and a Member of the Foreign Mission School* (New Haven: privately printed, 1818), 22.

19. Hall, 36.

20. Frances Wayland, *A Memoir of the Life and Labors of the Rev. Adoniram Judson*, 2 vols. (Boston: Phillips, Sampson and Company, 1853), 1:74.

21. Ibid., 1:36.

22. Sharon James, *My Heart in His Hands* (Durham, England: Evangelical Press, 1999), 39.

CHAPTER 4

1. Courtney Anderson, *To the Golden Shore,* 1st ed. (Boston: Brown and Company, 1956), 108.
2. Stacy R. Warburton, *Eastward: The Story of Adoniram Judson* (New York: Round Table Press, 1937), 41. Tabernacle Church was founded in 1629.
3. Anderson, 112.
4. Warburton, 40.
5. Ibid., 43.
6. Gordon Langley Hall, *Golden Boats from Burma* (Philadelphia: Macrae Smith Co., 1961), 47–48.
7. Ibid., 51.
8. Winifred Matthews, *Dauntless Women: Stories of Pioneer Wives* (New York: Friendship Press, 1947), 5.
9. Warburton, 45.
10. James D. Knowles, *Memoir of Mrs. Ann H. Judson, Late Missionary to Burmah,* 1st ed. (Boston: Lincoln and Edmands, 1829), 46–48.
11. Ibid., 51.
12. Adoniram Brown Judson, "How Judson Became a Baptist Missionary," pamphlet (Philadelphia: American Baptist Publication Society, 1913), 12.
13. Hall, 58.
14. Warburton, 47.
15. Hall, 58.
16. Knowles, 52–54.
17. Warburton, 55.
18. Anderson, 140.
19. Ibid., 141.
20. Francis Wayland, *A Memoir of the Life and Labors of the Rev. Adoniram Judson,* 2 vols. (Boston: Phillips, Sampson and Company, 1853), 1:105–6.
21. Edward Judson, *The Life of Adoniram Judson* (New York: American Baptist Publication Society, 1883), 42–43.
22. Knowles, 74.
23. Warburton, 51.
24. Anderson, 145–46.
25. Knowles, 74. In fact, the Baptist press in India printed several editions of Judson's powerful message on baptism. There are also extant records dating back to 1813–1814, made by Judson and sent to the English mission in Calcutta, listing all their expenditures for their first year in Burma. The originals are in the archives of the Baptist Missionary Society in London, England, and copies are in the Southern Baptist Historical Archives, Nashville, Tennessee.

CHAPTER 5

1. Stacy R. Warburton, *Eastward: The Story of Adoniram Judson* (New York: Round Table Press, 1937), 56.

2. Ibid., 56–58.

3. Ann Hasseltine Judson, *An Account of the American Baptist Mission to the Burman Empire, in a Series of Letters Addressed to a Gentleman in London* (Washington, D.C.: Mission Press, Columbian Office, 1823), 21.

4. James D. Knowles, *Memoir of Mrs. Ann H. Judson, Late Missionary to Burmah,* 1st ed. (Boston: Lincoln and Edmands, 1829), 61.

5. The Isle of France is modern Mauritius, an island east of Madagascar, off the coast of Africa.

6. Knowles, 77.

7. Ibid., 79–80.

8. Francis Wayland, *A Memoir of the Life and labors of the Rev. Adoniram Judson,* 2 vols. (Boston: Phillips, Sampson and Company, 1853), 1:119–20.

9. A. H. Judson, 23–24.

10. Courtney Anderson, *To the Golden Shore,* 1st ed. (Boston: Brown and Company, 1956), 166.

11. Ibid.

12. A. H. Judson, 28.

13. Edward Judson, *The Life of Adoniram Judson* (New York: American Baptist Publication Society, 1883), 52–53.

14. Knowles, 102.

15. "Letter from Ann Hasseltine Judson to Her Parents," *The Latter Day Luminary* 2 (1821): 39.

16. Warburton, 64.

17. Knowles, 102.

18. Harriet Chapman Conant, *The Earnest Man: The Character and Labors of Adoniram Judson* (Boston: Phillips, Sampson and Company, 1856), 151–52.

19. Anderson, 179.

20. Knowles, 108.

21. Gordon Langley Hall, *Golden Boats from Burma* (Philadelphia: Macrae Smith Co., 1961), 10.

22. A. H. Judson, 30.

23. Anderson, 175.

24. Knowles, 110.

25. Ibid., 120.

26. Ibid., 106–7.

27. Ibid., 107.

28. Warburton, 68.

29. Ibid.

CHAPTER 6

1. James D. Knowles, *Memoir of Mrs. Ann H. Judson, Late Missionary to Burmah,* 1st ed. (Boston: Lincoln and Edmands, 1829), 112–13.

2. Gordon Langley Hall, *Golden Boats from Burma* (Philadelphia: Macrae Smith Co., 1961), 93.

3. Francis Wayland, *A Memoir of the Life and Labors of the Rev. Adoniram Judson,* 2 vols. (Boston: Phillips, Sampson and Company, 1853), 1:170.

4. Ann Hasseltine Judson, *An Account of the American Baptist Mission to the Burman Empire, in a Series of Letters Addressed to a Gentleman in London* (Washington, D.C.: Mission Press, 1823), 11.

5. Knowles, 118. The Judsons realized that no other country on earth was so bound by Buddhism. It taught that the soul may pass through countless forms of existence. It might be in the body of a beast or a reptile, a prime reason for the Buddhist precept that taking the life of any living thing was the worst of sins. Buddhism advocated piling up "merit," which accounted for the tens of thousands of pagodas. (Building a pagoda was a prime method of obtaining merit.) The ultimate goal of Buddhism was the state of Nigban where there is no existence. Only by accruing sufficient worthiness could one aspire to such "nothingness."

6. Stacy R. Warburton, *Eastward: The Story of Adoniram Judson* (New York: Round Table Press, 1937), 69.

7. Courtney Anderson, *To the Golden Shore,* 1st ed. (Boston: Brown and Company, 1956), 183.

8. Bill Leonard, *Baptist Ways: A History* (Valley Forge, Pa.: Judson Press, 2003), 165. Leonard states: "The willingness to use the word *denomination* to describe this new society was an important step for Baptists in the new nation. It brought together various associations, individuals, and churches concerned about the foreign missionary task."

9. A. H. Judson, 53–54.

10. Edward Judson, *The Life of Adoniram Judson* (New York: American Baptist Publication Society, 1883), 55.

11. Warburton, 74–75.

12. Knowles, 118.

13. Ibid., 123.

14. Ibid., 123–24.

15. E. Judson, 96–97.

16. Knowles, 122–24.

17. Anderson, 205.

18. Ibid., 206.

19. Ibid., 209.

20. Knowles, 141.

21. Anderson, 213.

CHAPTER 7

1. Edward Judson, *The Life of Adoniram Judson* (New York: American Baptist Publication Society, 1883), 84.

2. Ann Hasseltine Judson, *An Account of the American Baptist Mission to the Burman Empire, in a Series of Letters Addressed to a Gentleman in London* (Washington D.C.: Mission Press, Columbian Office, 1823), 93.

3. Courtney Anderson, *To the Golden Shore,* 1st. ed. (Boston: Brown and Company, 1956). 199–201.

4. A. H. Judson, 81.

5. *Baptist Missionary Magazine, 1817–1850.* 2 (January 1819), 14–15.

6. Anderson, 231.

7. *Baptist Missionary Magazine* (January 1819): 135.

8. Anderson, 231. In the archives of Andover Newton Seminary is a November 1820 letter written by Ann Judson to her friend Mrs. Carleton in Boston, explaining the whole sad experience surrounding Edward's death and asking Carleton to share with his parents, who were friends of Carletons, the faith and courage Edward had exhibited in his dying days.

9. E. Judson, 85.

10. Ibid., 87–88.

11. Ibid., 122.

12. James D. Knowles, *Memoir of Mrs. Ann H. Judson, Late Missionary to Burmah,* 1st ed. (Boston: Lincoln and Edmands, 1829), 144.

13. Ibid.

14. Anderson, 222.

15. Knowles, 148.

16. E. Judson, 130.

17. A. H. Judson, 174.

18. Anderson, 228.

19. *Baptist Missionary Magazine, 1817–1850, 2* (March 1820): 290.

20. A. H. Judson, 176.

CHAPTER 8

1. Ann Hasseltine Judson, *An Account of the American Baptist Mission to the Burman Empire, in a Series of Letters Addressed to a Gentleman in London* (Washington D.C.: Mission Press, Columbian Office, 1823), 190.

2. James D. Knowles, *Memoir of Mrs. Ann H. Judson, Late Missionary to Burmah,* 1st ed. (Boston: Lincoln and Edmands, 1829), 155.

3. Edward Judson, *The Life of Adoniram Judson* (New York: American Baptist Publication Society, 1883), 137–38.

4. A. H. Judson, 202.

5. Stacy R. Warburton, *Eastward: The Story of Adoniram Judson* (New York: Round Table Press, 1937), 79.

6. Courtney Anderson, *To the Golden Shore,* 1st ed. (Boston: Brown and Company, 1956), 240–41.

7. A. H. Judson, 220.

8. Warburton, 80. The capital was still in Amarapura in January 1820, but Bagidaw had begun work on his new palace in Old Ava, which would again become the seat of government.

9. Gordon Langley Hall, *Golden Boats from Burma* (Philadelphia: Macrae Smith Co., 1961), 141–42.

10. Warburton, 80.

11. Ibid., 80–81. There is no known record of what happened to the gold-bound volumes of the Bible.

12. Knowles, 168.

13. E. Judson, 170.

14. Anderson, 266.

15. Ibid., 266–67.

CHAPTER 9

1. Gordon Langley Hall, *Golden Boats from Burma* (Philadelphia: Macrae Smith Co., 1961), 164.

2. *Baptist Missionary Magazine, 1817–1850*, 3 (January 1822) :254.

3. James D. Knowles, *Memoir of Mrs. Ann H. Judson, Late Missionary to Burmah*, 1st ed. (Boston: Lincoln and Edmands, 1829), 180.

4. Knowles, 181.

5. Sharon James, *My Heart in His Hands* (Durham, England: Evangelical Press, 1999), 119.

6. *Baptist Missionary Magazine*, 121.

7. Knowles, 184.

8. *Baptist Missionary Magazine, 1817–1850*. 3 (November 1822), 458.

9. Ibid., 4 (January 1823), 22–23.

10. Courtney Anderson, *To the Golden Shore*, 1st ed. (Boston: Brown and Company, 1956), 274–75.

11. Ibid., 276–77.

12. *Baptist Missionary Magazine*, 4 (November 1823), 207.

13. Ibid., 210.

14. Knowles, 189.

15. Ibid., 190–91.

16. Peale's superb painting of Ann, done in rich oils, was passed down in her family and finally arrived at the renowned Peabody Essex Museum in Salem, Massachusetts, where it is now displayed.

17. *Baptist Missionary Magazine*, 4 (July 1824) :376.

18. Letter from Ann Hasseltine Judson to Mrs. Baldwin, November 2, 1822. Andover Newton Seminary, Franklin Trask Library Archives, Correspondence: 1811–1853.

19. Stacy R. Warburton, *Eastward: The Story of Adoniram Judson* (New York: Round Table Press, 1937), 85–86.

CHAPTER 10

1. Sharon James, *My Heart in His Hands* (Durham, England: Evangelical Press, 1999), 139–40.

2. James D. Knowles, *Memoir of Mrs. Ann H. Judson, Late Missionary to Burmah,* 1st ed. (Boston: Lincoln and Edmands, 1829), 218–19.

3. Tan Chung Lee, "A Tale of Two Royal Cities," *Pyinsa Rupa* (July–September 1997), 10. Ava had been the capital of Burma two previous times. It is just eight miles south of the present-day city of Mandalay and was referred to as the "City of Gems." It is actually an island city created by the Myitha Chaung (canal), which has been cut to join the Irrawady with the Myitnge River, its tributary.

4. Edward Judson, *The Life of Adoniram Judson* (New York: American Baptist Publication Society, 1883), 215. Price had been able, from his acquaintance with neighbors around him, to collect a group of a dozen to twenty individuals for Sunday services.

5. Ibid., 216.

6. Henry Gouger, *A Personal Narration of Two Years' Imprisonment in Burmah* (London: John Murray, 1860), 44–45. (Preserves many memories of the Judsons during the war years.)

7. Ibid., 107. Bandoola was inordinately proud of his fleet of war boats shaped like giant canoes and gilded from bow to stern, glittering brightly in the Burmese sun. Some of them were as much as a hundred feet long and staffed with scores of muscular oarsmen.

8. J. Clements, *The Life of the Rev. Adoniram Judson, the Heroic Pioneer Missionary to the Tropics of the Orient* (New York: Derby and Miller, 1857). See Clements, 136–42, for an account of the escape of the Houghs and Wades from Rangoon.

9. Knowles, 224.

10. Courtney Anderson, *To the Golden Shore*, 1st ed. (Boston: Brown and Company, 1956), 302–3.

CHAPTER 11

1. Courtney Anderson, *To the Golden Shores*, 1st ed. (Boston: Brown and Company, 1956), 302.

2. James D. Knowles, *Memoir of Mrs. Ann H. Judson, Late Missionary to Burmah,* 1st ed. (Boston: Lincoln and Edmands, 1829), 232.

3. Gordon Langley Hall, *Golden Boats from Burma* (Philadelphia: Macrae Smith Co., 1961), 202–4.

4. Henry Gouger, *A Personal Narration of Two Years' Imprisonment in Burmah* (London: John Murray, 1860), 169.

5. Knowles, 234.

6. Anderson, 315.

CHAPTER 12

1. Courtney Anderson, *To the Golden Shore,* 1st ed. (Boston: Brown and Company, 1956), 364.

2. Both Judsons became quite inventive. Ann frequently wrote notes on a hard, baked cake, similar to a biscuit, and placed it in his dish of rice. Adoniram would send her messages on pieces of tile, the scratched message only visible when Ann dried the tiles in the sun.

3. James D. Knowles, *Memoir of Mrs. Ann H. Judson, Late Missionary to Burmah,* 1st ed. (Boston: Lincoln and Edmands, 1829), 238–39.

4. Edward Judson, *The Life of Adoniram Judson* (New York: American Baptist Publication Society, 1883), 223. Twenty-five years later a family member commented that Judson's "predilection for neatness, uniformity and order mounted, indeed, to a passion. Then he had an innate sort of refinement about him, which would subject him to annoyance when a less sensitive person would only be amused—a most inconvenient qualification for a missionary."

5. Francis Wayland, *A Memoir of the Life and Labors of the Rev. Adoniram Judson,* 2 vols. (Boston: Phillips, Sampson and Company, 1853), 1:383–84. The full text of Judson's poem reads, "Our Father God, who art in heaven, All hallowed be thy name, Thy kingdom come; thy will be done, In earth and heaven the same. Give us, this day, our daily bread; And, as we those forgive Who sin against us, so may we Forgiving grace receive. Into temptation lead us not; From evil set us free; This kingdom, power, and glory, Lord, Ever belong to thee. Prison, Ava, March 1825."

6. Henry Gouger, *A Personal Narration of Two Years' Imprisonment in Burmah* (London: John Murray, 1860), 175. Judson particularly remembered William Cowper's translation of Guyon's verse: "No bliss I seek, but to fulfil, In life, in death, Thy lovely will; No succour in my woes I want, Except what Thou art pleased to grant. Our days are number'd—let us spare, Our anxious hearts a needless care: 'Tis Thine to number out our days, And ours to give them to Thy praise."

7. Knowles, 240.

8. Gouger, 212–13.

9. Ibid., 228–29.

10. Wayland, 378–79.

11. It was at this point that the courageous Ann tried something new. She appealed to Bandula directly but her efforts yielded no helpful results.

12. Wayland, 387–88.

13. Letter from Emily Judson to Mr. Stevens, June 27, 1852. American Baptist Archives.

14. Excerpt from Adoniram Judson's journal, January 18, 1820 in *Baptist Missionary Magazine,* 1817–1850 3 (January 1821): 3:28.

15. Stacy R. Warburton. *Eastward: The Story of Adoniram Judson.* (New York: Round Table Press, 1937), 103–5.

16. Knowles, 241–43.

17. Ibid., 243–44.

18. Ibid.

19. Ibid., 244.

CHAPTER 13

1. James D. Knowles, *Memoir of Mrs. Ann H. Judson, Late Missionary to Burmah,* 1st ed. (Boston: Lincoln and Edmands, 1829), 245.
2. Ibid.
3. Henry Gouger, *A Personal Narration of Two Years' Imprisonment in Burmah* (London: John Murray, 1860), 244–45.
4. Courtney Anderson, *To the Golden Shore,* 1st ed. (Boston: Brown and Company, 1956), 343.
5. Knowles, 246.
6. *Baptist Missionary Magazine, 1817–1850* 7 (March 7, 1827): 73.
7. Knowles, 250.
8. Anderson, 349–50.
9. Ibid., 351–52.
10. Adoniram Judson, Personal Journal, 1788–1849, American Baptist Historical Society Library, Rochester, N.Y.
11. Adoniram Judson, "Deposition: First Anglo-Burmese War" (1826), 234. Jonathan Price was also involved in the diplomatic process during part of this time. He appeared to relish the role of negotiator.
12. Anderson, 355–56.
13. Knowles, 253–54.
14. Edward Judson, *The Life of Adoniram Judson* (New York: American Baptist Publication Society, 1883), 276.
15. Walter N. Wyeth, *Ann H. Judson: A Memorial* (Cincinnati: privately published, 1888), 194–95.
16. Francis Wayland, *A Memoir of the Life and Labors of the Rev. Adoniram Judson,* 2 vols. (Boston: Phillips, Sampson, and Company, 1853), 1:377.
17. Anderson, 359.
18. Ibid., 356–61.
19. John L. Christian, "Americans and the First Anglo-Burmese War," *The Pacific Review* V, 4 (1936): 319–20. English journals later reported that Price was restored to favor in the Burmese court and that he had received a title. He died near Ava almost exactly two years later.
20. Anderson, 361.
21. A. Judson, Journal.

CHAPTER 14

1. James D. Knowles, *Memoir of Mrs. Ann H. Judson, Late Missionary to Burmah,* 1st ed. (Boston: Lincoln and Edmands, 1829), 259.
2. Ibid., 260.
3. Edward Judson, *The Life of Adoniram Judson* (New York: American Baptist Publication Society, 1883), 277–79.
4. "Adoniram Judson, the Apostle of Burma," in *Calcutta Review XXVII* (1850): 437.
5. John L. Christian, "Americans and the First Anglo-Burmese War," in *The Pacific*

Review V, 4 (1936): 322. In a later communication from the British government headquarters in India the authorities stated: "Mr. Judson's good offices and the influence of his personal character contributed in an eminent degree to bring about the pacification which ensued."

6. Ibid., 322.

7. Knowles, 260.

8. See E. Judson, 280–81. In his biography of his father's life, Edward Judson recounted a story told by a British officer, Lieutenant Calder, who encountered the Judsons during their journey downriver in 1826. Calder had been descending the Irrawady in a canoe manned by Burmans when he was attacked in the night, robbed, and severely beaten. He lay there waiting for some friendly boat to pass his way. At long last a rowboat was seen approaching: Signals of distress were made, and a skiff came to his assistance. Calder recalled: "We were taken on board. My eyes first rested on the thin, attenuated form of a lady—a white lady! The first white woman I had seen for more than a year! She was standing on the little deck of the row-boat, leaning on the arm of a sickly-looking gentleman with an intellectual cast of countenance, in whom I at once recognized the husband or the brother. I have said that I had not beheld a white female for many months; and now the soothing accents of female words fell upon my ears like a household hymn of my youth. My wound was tenderly dressed, my head bound up, and I was laid upon a sofa bed….With what delight did I drink in the mild, gentle sounds of that sweet woman's voice, as she pressed me to recruit my strength….She was seated in a large sort of swinging chair, of American construction, in which her slight, emaciated, but graceful form appeared almost ethereal. Yet, with much of heaven, there were still the breathings of earthly feeling about her, for at her feet rested a babe, a little, wan baby, on which her eyes often turned with all a mother's love; and gazing frequently upon her delicate features, with a fond yet fearful glance, was that meek missionary, her husband. Her face was pale, very pale, with that expression of deep and serious thought which speaks of the strong and vigorous mind within the frail and perishing body; her brown hair was braided over a placid and holy brow; but her hands—those small, lily hands—were quite beautiful; beautiful they were, and very wan; for ah, they told of disease—of death—death in all its transparent grace—when the sickly blood shines through the clear skin, even as the bright poison lights up the Venetian glass which it is about to shatter. That lady was Mrs. Judson, whose long captivity and severe hardships amongst the Burmese have since been detailed in her published journals.

"I remained two days with them; two delightful days they were to me. Mrs. Judson's powers of conversation were of the first order, and the many affecting anecdotes that she gave us of their long and cruel bondage, their struggles in the cause of religion, and their adventures during a long residence at the court of Ava, gained a heightened interest from the beautiful, energetic simplicity of her language, as well as from the certainty I felt that so fragile a flower as she in very truth was, had but a brief season to linger on earth."

9. Sharon James, *My Heart in His Hands* (Durham, England: Evangelical Press, 1999), 189.

10. E. Judson, 289.
11. Knowles, 267–68.
12. Ibid., 271.
13. E. Judson, 290.
14. Ibid.
15. Knowles, 268.

CHAPTER 15

1. Edward Judson, *The Life of Adoniram Judson* (New York: American Baptist Publication Society, 1883), 294.
2. Ibid., 294–97.
3. James D. Knowles, *Memoir of Mrs. Ann H. Judson, Late Missionary to Burmah*, 1st ed. (Boston: Lincoln and Edmands, 1829), 272–73.
4. Ibid., 274.
5. Courtney Anderson, *To the Golden Shore*, 1st ed. (Boston: Brown and Company, 1956), 383.
6. E. Judson, 20–21.
7. Sharon James, *My Heart in His Hands* (Durham, England: Evangelical Press, 1999), 197.
8. Stacy R. Warburton, *Eastward: The Story of Adoniram Judson* (New York: Round Table Press, 1937), 116–19.
9. Ibid.
10. Ibid.

CHAPTER 16

1. Stacy R. Warburton, *Eastward: The Story of Adoniram Judson* (New York: Round Table Press, 1937), 121.
2. Courtney Anderson, *To the Golden Shore*, 1st ed. (Boston: Brown and Company, 1956), 294.
3. Warburton, 125–26.
4. Adoniram Judson, Personal Journal, 1788–1849, American Baptist Historical Society Library, Rochester, N.Y..
5. Anderson, 397–99.
6. Francis Wayland, *A Memoir of the Life and Labors of the Rev. Adoniram Judson*, 2 vols. (Boston: Phillips, Sampson and Company, 1853), 1: 528–29.
7. Warburton, 130.
8. Judson wrote an account of Boardman's death to the *American Baptist Magazine* in December 1831: "One of the brightest luminaries of Burmah is extinguished—dear brother Boardman has gone to his eternal rest. He fell gloriously at the head of his troops, in the arms of victory—thirty-eight wild Karens having been brought into the camp of King Jesus, since the beginning of the year....Disabled by mortal

wounds, he was obliged, through the whole of his last expedition, to be carried on a litter; but his presence was a host….Such a death, next to that of martyrdom, must be glorious in the eyes of Heaven" (p. 373).

9. Letter from Adoniram Judson to Sarah Boardman, March 4, 1831, American Baptist Historical Society Library, Rochester, N.Y..

10. Warburton, 132.

11. J. Clement, *The Life of the Rev. Adoniram Judson, the Heroic Pioneer Missionary to the Tropics of the Orient* (New York: Derby and Miller, 1857), 213.

12. Don Hughes, "Advice to Candidates for Missionary Labor, 1832–1834," *Europe* (August 1998): 3.

13. James Langdon Hill, *The Immortal Seven* (Philadelphia: American Baptist Publication Society, 1913), 91.

14. Wayland, 455.

15. Ibid., 471–72.

16. Anderson, 408.

17. Personal testimony of Daw Lone Ma, written for family and church, 1913. *Sayagyi* is a title for an honored teacher.

CHAPTER 17

1. Adoniram Judson, Personal Journal. 1788–1849. American Baptist Historical Society Library, Rochester, N.Y..

2. Francis Wayland, *A Memoir of the Life and Labors of the Rev. Adoniram Judson,* 2 vols. (Boston: Phillips, Sampson and Company, 1853), 2:75–76.

3. Letter from Sarah Boardman to Adoniram Judson, February 17, 1834. American Baptist Historical Society Library, Rochester, N.Y..

4. A. Judson, Personal Journal.

5. Edward Judson, *The Life of Adoniram Judson* (New York: American Baptist Publication Society, 1883), 400.

6. Courtney Anderson, *To the Golden Shore,* 1st ed. (Boston: Brown and Company, 1956), 413–14.

7. Wayland, 210.

8. Walter N. Wyeth, *Sarah B. Judson: A Memorial.* (Philadelphia: privately published, 1890), 174.

9. Ibid., 11.

10. Joan Jacobs Brumberg, *Mission for Life: The Story of the Family of Adoniram Judson* (New York: The Free Press, 1980), 112.

11. Arabella Stuart (Mrs. Arabella M. Willson), *The Three Mrs. Judsons.* Gary W. Long, ed. Missionary Series (Springfield, Mo.: Particular Baptist Press, 1999), 201.

12. Ibid.

13. Wayland, 207.

14. Anderson, 415. Their house was similar to that of the other mission houses in the city, rather like an expanded native hut. They had three large rooms and two small ones, with a separate cookhouse.

15. A. Judson, Journal.
16. Wyeth, 125.
17. Anderson, 416.
18. Stacy R. Warburton, *Eastward: The Story of Adoniram Judson* (New York: Round Table Press, 1937), 145.
19. Anderson, 416–18.
20. Wayland, 106.
21. Anderson, 420.
22. Ibid.
23. E. Judson, 420.
24. Warren P. Mild, *Howard Malcom and the Great Mission Advance* (Valley Forge, Pa.: American Baptist Churches U.S.A., 1988), 44. Howard Malcom was pastor of Federal Street Church in Boston, later becoming president of Georgetown College, then of Bucknell University. He was an experienced and flexible traveler, and his reports upon returning home gave Baptists in America fresh inspiration.
25. Ibid., 27.
26. Brumberg, 115.
27. E. Judson, 421.
28. Warburton, 172.
29. Anderson, 422–23.
30. Letter from Sarah Boardman Judson to Adoniram Judson, 1839, American Baptist Historical Society Library, Rochester, N.Y..
31. Anderson, 423.
32. Ibid.
33. Wyeth, 134.
34. Warburton, 166.
35. Ibid., 176.

CHAPTER 18

1. Stacy R. Warburton, *Eastward: The Story of Adoniram Judson* (New York: Round Table Press, 1937), 176–77.
2. Edward Judson, *The Life of Adoniram Judson* (New York: American Baptist Publication Society, 1883), 433–44.
3. Ibid., 444.
4. Judson had taken along his two able Burmese assistants so that he could continue the work of the dictionary. He had hastily written the board that the dictionary was at such a point that, unless he was able to work on it himself, his past three years of intense labor would be lost. He had never wanted to work on it at all but was convinced it was vital. It developed that he put the assistants on a ship returning to Burma from Port Louis, thinking he himself could return shortly, but Sarah's condition worsened.
5. Courtney Anderson, *To the Golden Shore*, 1st ed. (Boston: Brown and Company, 1956), 437.
6. Francis Wayland, *A Memoir of the Life and Labors of the Rev. Adoniram Judson,*

2 vols. (Boston: Phillips, Sampson and Company, 1853), 2:199.

7. Ibid., 2:199–200.

8. Anderson, 433.

9. Ibid., 433–34.

10. E. Judson, 456. Sarah's youngest son, Edward, some fifty years later, paid her tribute by quoting the poem in its entirety in his biography of his father.

11. Anderson, 440.

12. E. Judson, 456.

13. Ibid., overleaf. St. Helena is an island in the South Atlantic Ocean, about midway between South America and Africa.

14. Wayland, 2:203.

15. Anderson, 441.

16. E. Judson, 459.

17. Warburton, 185.

18. Anderson, 446–47.

19. Warburton, 188.

20. Joan Jacobs Brumberg, *Mission for Life: The Story of the Family of Adoniram Judson* (New York: The Free Press, 1980), 228.

21. Ibid., 11.

22. Warburton, 193–94.

23. E. Judson, 460–61.

24. Warburton, 192.

25. Ibid., 196.

26. Wayland, 2: 234–35.

27. Ibid., 215.

CHAPTER 19

1. William R. Estep, *Whole Gospel, Whole World* (Nashville: Broadman Press, 1994), 47.

2. Joan Jacobs Brumberg, *Mission for Life: The Story of the Family of Adoniram Judson* (New York: The Free Press, 1980), 108.

3. "Emily Judson," a series of articles in *Mid-York Weekly News* (1951), 4. American Baptist Historical Society Library, Rochester, N.Y.

4. A. C. Kendrick, *The Life and Letters of Mrs. Emily C. Judson* (New York: Sheldon and Co., 1860), 15.

5. Ibid., 16.

6. Ibid., 19.

7. Edward Judson, *The Life of Adoniram Judson* (New York: American Baptist Publication Society, 1883), 476–77.

8. Ibid., 477.

9. William Dean became one of America's first missionaries to China. This was the same William Dean who in 1835 was knifed on the little boat with six-year-old George Dana Boardman Jr., when pirates attacked them off the coast of Singapore. There is some correspondence between William Dean and the Judsons in the archives

of the American Baptist Historical Society at Valley Forge, Pennsylvania.

10. Kendrick, 34.

11. Ibid., 43.

12. Kendrick, 38.

13. "Emily Judson," 15.

14. Brumberg, 121.

15. Letter from Emily Chubbuck to Walter Chubbuck, March 22, 1840. Wisconsin Historical Society Archives, Madison, Wisconsin.

16. "Emily Judson," 44.

17. Kendrick, 55.

18. Brumberg, 119.

19. Kendrick, 57.

20. E. Judson, 478.

21. Kendrick, 105.

22. Ibid., 108.

23. Winifred Hervey, *The Story of Baptist Missions in Foreign Lands* (St. Louis: Chancy R. Barns, 1885), 314.

24. Kendrick, 416–417.

25. Cecil B. Hartley, *The Three Mrs. Judsons: The Celebrated Female Missionaries* (Philadelphia: G. G. Evans, 1860), 284.

26. Letter from Adoniram Judson to Emily Chubbuck, February 25, 1846. In possession of a Judson descendant.

CHAPTER 20

1. A. C. Kendrick, *The Life and Letters of Mrs. Emily C. Judson* (New York: Sheldon and Co., 1860), 142–43.

2. Ibid., 143.

3. Ibid., 158.

4. Ibid., 188. Emily learned that Adoniram's effect in a personal setting was even more profound. In describing this effect, she later wrote that Judson's "spirit was intensely, unconquerably youthful. He seemed to have quaffed the elixir that keeps the heart always young—to have drawn his very life-blood from the 'deep heart of existence' which 'beats forever like a boy's.'"

5. A. Judson, Journal.

6. Letter from Emily Chubbuck to Anna Maria Anable, January 6, 1846. In possession of a Judson descendant.

7. Letter from Adoniram Judson to Emily Chubbuck, February 19, 1846. In possession of a Judson descendant.

8. Kendrick, 154.

9. Letter from Adoniram Judson to Emily Chubbuck, January 20, 1846. In possession of a Judson descendant.

10. Letter from Emily Chubbuck to Cynthia Sheldon, January 24, 1846. In possession of a Judson descendant.

11. Letter from Emily Chubbuck to Adoniram Judson, January 25, 1846. In posses-

sion of a Judson descendant.

12. Letter from Adoniram Judson to Emily Chubbuck, January 26, 1846. In possession of a Judson descendant.

13. Ibid.

14. Louise Manly, *History of Judson College* (Atlanta: Foote and Davies, 1913), 140.

15. Letter from Adoniram Judson to Emily Chubbuck, April 18, 1846. In possession of a Judson descendant.

16. Letter from Adoniram Judson to Emily Chubbuck, January 30, 1846. In possession of a Judson descendant.

17. Letter from Adoniram Judson to Emily Chubbuck, April 11, 1846. In possession of a Judson descendant.

18. Letter from Emily Chubbuck to Adoniram Judson, February 7, 1846. In possession of a Judson descendant.

19. Courtney Anderson, *To the Golden Shore*, 1st ed. (Boston: Brown and Company, 1956), 461.

20. Letter from Emily Chubbuck to Anna Maria Anable, May 8, 1846. In possession of a Judson descendant.

21. Anderson, 458.

22. Letter from Adoniram Judson to Emily Chubbuck, May 16, 1846. In possession of a Judson descendant.

23. Letter from Adoniram Judson to Emily Chubbuck, April 15, 1846. In possession of a Judson descendant.

CHAPTER 21

1. A. C. Kendrick, *The Life and Letters of Mrs. Emily C. Judson* (New York: Sheldon and Co., 1860), 229.

2. Letter from Emily Chubbuck Judson to Lavinia Chubbuck, July 10, 1846. In possession of a Judson descendant.

3. Letter from Emily Chubbuck Judson to Cynthia Sheldon, 1846. In possession of a Judson descendant.

4. Courtney Anderson, *To the Golden Shore*, 1st ed. (Boston: Brown and Company, 1956), 468.

5. Francis Wayland, *A Memoir of the Life and Labors of the Rev. Adoniram Judson*, 2 vols. (Boston: Phillips, Sampson and Company, 1853), 2:262.

6. Kendrick, 238–39.

7. Ibid., 245.

8. Edward Judson, *The Life of Adoniram Judson* (New York: American Baptist Publication Society, 1883), 497.

9. Ibid.

10. Ibid., 298.

11. Kendrick, 247–48.

12. Ibid., 251.

13. Ibid., 270–71.

14. Ibid., 271–72.

15. Ibid.
16. Anderson, 483.
17. Kendrick, 276–77.
18. Letter from Emily Chubbuck Judson to Kate Chubbuck, October 4, 1847. In possession of a Judson descendant.
19. Kendrick, 282–83.
20. Wayland, 2:284.
21. Kendrick, 284.
22. E. Judson, 503.
23. Arabella Stuart, *The Three Mrs. Judsons*, Missionary Series, Gary W. Long, ed. (Springfield, Mo.: Particular Baptist Press, 1999), 250–51.
24. Anderson, 489.
25. George H. Tooze, *Judson Treasures of the First Baptist Church, Malden, with a Short Biography of the Life of Emily Chubbuck Judson* (Malden, Mass.: First Baptist Church, Malden, 1979), 43.
26. E. Judson, 513.
27. Ibid., 512–13.
28. Letter from Emily Chubbuck Judson to Anna Maria Anable, December 24, 1847. "My Bird" was included in Clarence Stedman Edmund's *An American Anthology 1787–1900*, a collection of the one hundred best poems of the nineteenth century.
29. E. Judson, 523–24.
30. Ibid., 522.
31. Wayland, 2:312.
32. Kendrick, 291–92.
33. Ibid., 289.
34. Stacy R. Warburton, *Eastward: The Story of Adoniram Judson* (New York: Round Table Press, 1937), 218.
35. Wayland, 2:338.
36. E. Judson, 517.
37. Ibid., 517–22.
38. Warburton, 220–21. One hundred fifty years later, Judson's nineteenth-century edition is still the basis of all Burma's current dictionaries. In fact, within recent years, Judson's own Burmese-English dictionary itself has been reprinted.
39. Kendrick, 293–94.
40. Ibid., 294–95.
41. Anderson, 494.
42. Warburton, 222–23.
43. Wayland, 2:319.
44. Kendrick, 299.

CHAPTER 22
1. A. C. Kendrick, *The Life and Letters of Mrs. Emily C. Judson* (New York: Sheldon and Co., 1860), 306.

2. Ibid., 307.

3. Ibid.

4. Ibid., 322.

5. Stacy R. Warburton, *Eastward: The Story of Adoniram Judson* (New York: Round Table Press, 1937), 222.

6. Francis Wayland, *A Memoir of the Life and Labors of the Rev. Adoniram Judson,* 2 vols. (Boston: Phillips, Sampson and Company, 1853), 2:328–29.

7. Ibid.

8. Edward Judson, *The Life of Adoniram Judson* (New York: American Baptist Publication Society, 1883), 530–33.

9. Ibid., 532.

10. Ibid., 533–34.

11. Warburton, 224.

12. E. Judson, 537.

13. Ibid., 539.

14. Kendrick, 333.

15. Wayland, 2:333.

16. Warburton, 227.

17. Ibid.

18. Ibid., 228. Judson was overjoyed when Emily read to him a paragraph from an account printed in Germany of Judson's efforts at Ava. They had been read by some Turkish Jews and it had won them to Christ. When he heard this news, Adoniram recalled his early plans for a Jewish mission and exclaimed, "I never was deeply interested in any object, I never prayed sincerely and earnestly for anything, but it came; at some time—no matter at how distant a day—somehow, in some shape, probably the last I should have devised—it came. And yet I have always had so little faith!"

19. Kendrick, 335.

20. Courtney Anderson, *To the Golden Shore,* 1st ed. (Boston: Brown and Company, 1956), 500.

21. Kendrick, 335.

22. Anderson, 503.

23. Ibid., 504.

24. Ibid.

25. Warburton, 230.

26. E. Judson, 542. A marble tablet hangs on the wall of the auditorium of First Baptist Church of Malden, Massachusetts that reads: "Rev. Adoniram Judson, America's First Foreign Missionary, 1788–1850, Malden, His Birthplace, The Ocean, His Sepulchre, Converted Burmans and the Burman Bible, His Monument, His Record Is On High."

27. Warburton, 229.

28. Wayland, 2:334.

29. Mrs. Margaret Shipman, a great-granddaughter of Adoniram and Emily, had two letters that had been in her family through the intervening years. In 1974, she gave them to the First Baptist Church of Malden, Massachusetts. George Tooze, pastor of First Baptist Church Malden from 1977 until 1983, included these two letters

in a short biography of Emily Judson that he wrote in 1979.

30. George H. Tooze, *Judson Treasures of the First Baptist Church, Malden, with a Short Biography of the Life of Emily Chubbuck Judson* (Malden, Mass.: First Baptist Church, Malden, 1979), 61.

31. Ibid.

32. Ibid.

33. Kendrick, 337.

34. Ibid., 334.

35. Ibid., 348.

36. Ibid., 349.

37. In December, Emily received a visit from the Lord Bishop of Calcutta, who had greatly admired Judson. She later wrote thanking him for the honor of his visit and the tribute he had paid Judson. She then sent him a memento—an engraving made from the portrait of Judson done by H. C. Pratt in 1845. The twin of that engraving was cherished by Emily herself in a little velvet-lined frame so used and loved that the hinges of the cover had fallen off. This little frame is in the American Baptist Historical Society Library in Rochester, New York. There is no record of how the archives acquired it.

38. Kendrick, 358.

39. Ibid., 363.

40. Ibid., 407.

41. Ibid., 410.

42. Ibid., 425–26.

CHAPTER 23

1. Tan Chung Lee, "A Luxury Cruise up the River Ayeyarwady," *Pyinsa Rupa* (January–March, 1997), 22.

2. *Judson Centennial Celebration in Burma, 1813–1913* (Rangoon: American Baptist Mission Press, 1913), 16.

3. S. Mydans, "Freed Burmese Democracy Leader Proclaims 'New Dawn,'" *New York Times*, May 7, 2002.

4. B. R. Pearn, *A History of Rangoon* (Rangoon: American Baptist Mission Press, 1939), 83.

5. Shwe Wa Maung, Erville Sowards, and Genevieve Sowards, *Burma Baptist Chronicles* (Rangoon: Burma Baptist Convention, 1963), 18–19.

6. The Judson legacy in Rangoon makes for a memorable walk, moving from one historic Baptist spot to others nearby. Walking from Immanuel Baptist Church down Barr Street (Mahabandoola Garden Street) and turning west to 33rd Street, just two blocks away, one reaches the spot where the mission once stood. From that point, it is easy to follow the route of that 1819 baptismal group, over the bridge now spanning the railroad yards, and to the left up to Scot's Kirk, less than half a mile from the mission house site. Even in the midst of honking horns and buses belching diesel smoke, it is a moving experience to stand on the hill and look down upon the spot where U Naw was baptized.

CHAPTER 24

1. Michael Clark and Joe Cumming, eds., *Myanmar (Burma)* (Melbourne: Lonely Planet Publications, 2000), 37.

2. James D. Knowles, *Memoir of Mrs. Ann H. Judson, Late Missionary to Burmah,* 1st ed. (Boston: Lincoln and Edmands, 1829), 218.

3. Wilhelm Klein, *Burma: Insight Guides* (Singapore: Houghton Mifflin, 1996), 199.

4. Ann Hasseltine Judson, *An Account of the American Baptist Mission to the Burman Empire, in a Series of Letters Addressed to a Gentleman in London* (Washington, D.C.: Mission Press, 1823), 100.

5. Clark and Cummings, 237.

6. Klein, 8–9.

7. Clark and Cummings, 241.

8. Tan Chung Lee, "A Tale of Two Royal Cities," *Pyinsa Rupa* (July–September 1997), 10–11. Most of Burma's ancient capitals were square, but Ava was shaped like a stylized lion seated on its hindquarters.

9. Klein, 181. King Bagyidaw's chief queen, Nanmadaw Me Nu, had ordered the monastery built for her "favorite" royal abbot.

10. The inscription can clearly be read on extant photographs of the memorial stone.

11. The story of the manuscript pillow came down through the years, recounted differently by various writers, each version leaving some unanswered questions. Judson's youngest grandson, A. C. Hanna, himself a missionary in Burma, related the true account as his mother, Emily Frances Judson Hanna, had described it to him many times. Although Judson had not been able to take the pillow with him on that dreadful march, it had been miraculously preserved. The account is found in chapters 17 and 20.

12. In 2002, Judson Baptist Church at Aungbinle repaired the 1988 earthquake damage and painted the soft golden brick of the building a vivid red.

CHAPTER 25

1. N. Greenwood, *Guide to Burma* (Guilford, Conn.: The Globe Pequot Press, Inc., 1996), 201.

2. See Daw Lone Ma's story in chapters 16 and 31.

3. Michael Cumming and Joe Clark, *Myanmar (Burma)* (Melbourne: Lonely Planet Publications, 2000), 409–10.

4. A plinth stone is one of a continuous course of stones supporting a wall.

5. In the Ann Hasseltine Judson (1812–1826) biographical file in the Valley Forge archives of the American Baptist Historical Society is a short account of this incident, written by missionary Sarah L. Smith in 1914.

CHAPTER 26

1. Ann's ever-so-great-grandfather and his brother John were pioneer settlers of Bradford, Massachusetts, and the Hasseltine name is an important part of the town's history.

2. Across the street is Bell Park, looking much as it did when the child Adoniram played among its trees. The Congregational church where his father was pastor once stood nearby.

3. See chapter 22, note 26, for the tribute.

4. J. M. Hull, "American Reminders of Judson," *Baptist Missionary Magazine* (December, 1903), 762–69.

5. W. T. Davis, *History of the Town of Plymouth* (Philadelphia: J. W. Lewis & Co., 1885), 80.

6. Small wonder that several biographies note that Rev. Judson became quite an extensive landowner and was never afterward dependent on his minister's salary. The land he purchased was not only prime real estate but also a remarkable piece of early American history.

7. Judson family history touches on the very beginnings of America's history and Plymouth's as well, for Adoniram's mother, Abigail, was a descendant of Peter Brown, who arrived on the Mayflower. The Judson family plot is on Plymouth's Burial Hill, just yards from the site of the 1621 fort. In addition to the graves of Adoniram's mother and sister, a memorial stone has been placed there in honor of Adoniram Judson Sr., Adoniram Jr., his wives Ann, Sarah, and Emily, and Ann and Adoniram's babies.

8. The other building is Hardy House, which was the home of Eliphant Pearson, the academy's first principal.

9. Ronald H. Brown, *The Judson Family Connection.* Manuscript, 1983. American Baptist Historical Society, Valley Forge, Pa.

CHAPTER 27

1. Joan Jacobs Brumberg, *Mission for Life: The Story of the Family of Adoniram Judson* (New York: The Free Press, 1980), 145.

2. John Codman, "The Captain's Story" (1895), American Baptist Historical Society Archives, Valley Forge, Pa.

3. See chapter 17 for the account of six-year-old George Boardman's traumatic encounter with pirates.

4. J. I. Mortensen, *The Career of the Rev. G. D. Boardman,* (unpublished dissertation, 1966), 14–15.

5. Letter from Sarah Boardman Judson to Harriet Hall, November 9, 1839, American Baptist Historical Society Archives, Valley Forge, Pa.

6. Mortensen, 20.

7. Ibid., 21.

8. From the George Dana Boardman Jr. biographical file in the American Baptist Historical Society Archives, Valley Forge, Pa.

9. Mortensen, 31.

10. Ibid., 38–65.

11. Mitchell Bronk, "George Dana Boardman," (unpublished article in the Rochester Library of the American Baptist Historical Society, 1948), 5.
12. Ibid., 7.
13. Ibid., 8.
14. Ibid., 9.
15. Francis Wayland, *Memoir of the Life and Labors of the Rev. Adoniram Judson,* 2 vols. (Boston: Phillips, Sampson and Company, 1853), 7:105.
16. Ibid., 110.
17. Ibid., 120.
18. Ibid., 193–94.
19. A. A. Judson, *From Night to Morn* (Cincinnati: N. Watkin, 1894), 17.
20. Letter from Abigail (Abby) Ann Judson to Adoniram Judson, August 9, 1848. American Baptist Historical Society Archives, Valley Forge, Pennsylvania.
21. Abigail A. Judson, 12.
22. Ibid., 7.
23. Brumberg, 167.
24. Ibid., 168.
25. A. A. Judson, 12.
26. Obituary in *Minneapolis Journal* (December 12, 1902).

CHAPTER 28

1. Adoniram Brown Judson, "Early Recollections of Burma," *Brown University Alumni Monthly* (1915), 2.
2. Ibid.
3. Howard A. Haggard and Fred Groce, *Judson Centennial: 1813–1914.* (Philadelphia: American Baptist Publication Society, 1914), 152.
4. Letter from Adoniram Brown Judson to Emily Judson, March 19, 1853, American Baptist Historical Society Archives, Valley Forge, Pa.
5. In 1865, Adoniram Brown took his first medical degree from Jefferson Medical College in Philadelphia, and then later earned another from the College of Physicians and Surgeons in New York.
6. *Dictionary of American Biography* (New York: Scribner's, 1960), 235.
7. Ibid., 236.
8. T. A. T. Hanna, *Watchman-Examiner* (October 12, 1916), 4A.
9. Charles Hatch Sears, *Edward Judson: Interpreter of God* (Philadelphia: Griffith and Rowland, 1917), 14. Adoniram Brown Judson suffered from diabetes many years, but lived to be seventy-nine.
10. Letter from Adoniram Judson to Emily Chubbuck, March 28, 1846. In possession of a Judson descendant.
11. Letter from Adoniram Judson to Emily Chubbuck, April 7, 1846. In possession of a Judson descendant. The sailing to Burma was delayed, so Adoniram went again on July 4 to see the boys one last time. Each goodbye must have been wrenching for both father and sons.

12. Letter from Emily Chubbuck Judson to Anna Maria Anable, 1851. In possession of a Judson descendant.

13. Letter from Elnathan Judson to Emily Chubbuck Judson, October 15, 1853. In possession of a Judson descendant.

14. From biographical file on Elnathan Judson, Class of 1862, at Union Seminary, New York. Elnathan graduated in the spring of 1862 and was declared "insane" just a year and a half later. No record can be found of what happened during those eighteen months.

15. Quoted from the obituary of Elnathan Judson. From the Judson files in the American Baptist Historical Society Library, Rochester, N.Y.

16. Joan Jacobs Brumberg, *Mission for Life: The Story of the Family of Adoniram Judson* (New York: The Free Press, 1980), 177–78.

17. Ibid. Abby Ann had suffered a serious fall that led to cataracts on both eyes, which made caring for Elnathan doubly difficult.

18. Brumberg, 177–78.

19. From the Judson manuscript collections, American Baptist Historical Society Library, Rochester, N.Y.

20. Letter from Emily Chubbuck Judson to Anna Maria Anable, December 23, 1849. In possession of a Judson descendant.

21. Letter from Henry Hall Judson to Emily Chubbuck Judson, February 1, 1853. In possession of a Judson descendant.

22. Ibid. Henry Hall Judson always signed his letters to Emily, "Your affectionate sonny, Henry."

23. From the biographical file on Henry Hall Judson at Williams College.

24. From the archives of the U.S. Department of the Army.

25. From the biographical file on Henry Hall Judson at Williams College.

26. From the archives of the U.S. Department of the Army.

27. This tribute was discovered in the Edward Judson file in the American Baptist Historical Society Library, Rochester, N.Y.

28. Letter from hospital chaplain to the family of Henry Hall Judson, 1918. In possession of a Judson descendant.

29. From the U.S. Department of the Army archives, Washington, D.C.

CHAPTER 29

1. Howard W. Haggard and Fred Groce, *Judson Centennial, 1814–1914* (Philadelphia: American Baptist Publication Society, 1914), 154.

2. James M. Bruce, "In Memoriam: Edward Judson," in *Watchman-Examiner* (November 12, 1914), 1493.

3. Charles Hatch Sears, *Edward Judson: Interpreter of God* (Philadelphia: Griffith and Rowland, 1917), vii–viii.

4. *Judson Centennial Celebration in Burma, 1813–1913* (Rangoon: Mission Press, 1913), 32.

5. Ibid., 44.

6. George H. Tooze, *Judson Treasures of the First Baptist Church, Malden, with a Short Biography of the Life of Emily Chubbuck Judson* (Malden, Mass.: First Baptist Church, Malden, 1979), 14.

7. Edward Judson, *The Life of Adoniram Judson* (New York: American Baptist Publication Society, 1883), 523–24.

8. From personal speech notes prepared by Edward Judson for delivery at the Malden Judson Centennial, 1888. In the Edward Judson file, American Baptist Historical Society Library, Rochester, New York.

9. Sears, 19.

10. Ibid.

11. Letter from Edward Judson to Emily Chubbuck Judson, November 27, 1852. American Baptist Historical Society Archives, Valley Forge, Pa.

12. Letter from Edward Judson to Emily Chubbuck Judson, February 8, 1853. American Baptist Historical Society Archives, Valley Forge, Pa.

13. Letter from Edward Judson to Emily Chubbuck Judson, 1853. American Baptist Historical Society Archives, Valley Forge, Pa.

14. Sears, 22.

15. Ibid., 23.

16. Ibid., 27.

17. Ibid., 45.

18. E. Judson, v, from the dedication.

19. Scars, 56–59.

20. *Judson Centennial, 1814–1914*, 158.

21. Ibid., 154.

22. Ibid., 155.

23. Bruce, 1493–95.

24. Letter from Emily Chubbuck Judson to Anna Maria Anable, December 24, 1847. In possession of a Judson descendant.

25. Letter from Emily Chubbuck Judson to her parents, Charles and Lavinia Chubbuck, and sister, Kate, January 13, 1848. In possession of a Judson descendant.

26. Tooze, 14.

27. Letter from Emily Chubbuck Judson to Catherine Chubbuck, March 19, 1848. In possession of a Judson descendant.

28. Letter from Emily Chubbuck Judson to Anna Maria Anable, June 2, 1849. In possession of a Judson descendant.

29. Joan Jacobs Brumberg, *Mission for Life: The Story of the Family of Adoniram Judson* (New York: The Free Press, 1980), 147.

CHAPTER 30

1. L. Hughes, *Emily Margaret Hanna* (Boston: Women's Baptist Foreign Missionary Society, 1911).

2. Emily Frances had eight children over a span of seventeen years. The following are notes collected on this third generation of Judsons—and the few offspring who comprise the fourth generation.

The second Hanna child was Thomas Carson, born in 1872. After university he pursued another degree in theology from Yale and was at the same time a pastor. A very singular event occurred in his life when he was just twenty-five. April 15, 1897, affected his entire life. Actually, the day came close to ending his life tragically early. T.C. had a traumatic fall from his horse and struck his head with tremendous force. He had a case of total amnesia. His was the first such case of complete amnesia to be directly observed and recorded, and it fascinated the medical world with its just-emerging practice of psychiatry, particularly since one result of T.C.'s amnesia was the development of two distinct personalities. Dr. Boris Sidis of Harvard and Simon Goodhart of Yale did a thorough study of T.C.'s symptoms and recovery and wrote a book, *Multiple Personality*, largely based on this study.

T.C.'s amnesia was so profound and so rare that he lost all skills, and became like a baby in a twenty-five-year-old body. He could not control his muscles, talk, or walk. He had no idea of time, didn't know what food was, and even had to be forced to swallow reflexively. Everything had to be relearned. His first word relearned was *apple,* and he thought all food was "apple." Cause and effect fascinated him. He would point to others, then to himself and say, "People?" He had no concept of growth and thought people came alive as grown adults. (See *Multiple Personality* [New York: Appleton and Co., 1905], 206–9.)

T.C.'s profound intellect and talents again became obvious; he learned with remarkable speed but developed two distinct personalities. Over a period of a couple months the two finally merged, and amazingly, he never afterward appeared to show any ill effects from his near-death trauma. He became a well-known pastor in Pennsylvania and a frequent writer for Baptist publications.

T.C. married Anna Barnes Cook, and they had three children—the fourth generation of Judsons: Margaret, who died unmarried at age thirty-seven; Marjorie, who lived to be eighty-five; and T.C. Hanna Jr., who died before his fiftieth birthday. T.C. Jr. and his wife had a daughter who had two daughters, but the trail has grown dim on this family line. (See Ron Brown, *The Judson Family Connection* [Valley Forge: American Baptist Historical Society. manuscript, 1983], 32.)

The third child of Emily Frances was another son, and he received the auspicious name of Adoniram Judson. "Jud," as he was called, was a soldier in the Spanish-American War and became a journalist and editor. Jud and his wife had two sons and a daughter. The daughter had a son, but efforts to trace that family line have failed. (See Brown, 33–34.) Emily Frances' fourth child was another son, Arthur Ledlie, a graduate of Bucknell. He too was a journalist. Arthur never married. His younger sister, Miriam, was born in 1879 and outlived all her siblings. Miriam married but never had children. She was the family historian who kept records and collected Judson/Hanna memorabilia. (See Brown, 33–34.) Emily's sixth child was Anabel, born in 1881. She also attended Bucknell and worked with the Salvation Army in India. She married but had no children. There were two more sons. Edward Judson, named for Emily's brother "Eddy," was born in 1885 and was a proof-reader. He and his wife had four daughters, but none of those had children. (See Brown, 35.)

3. "A Commendable Example," in *Watchman-Examiner,* Vol. 2, no. 42 (1914), 1374.

4. Helen was the firstborn and married a Canadian. Her three sons still live in Canada. Next was George Ames Carson, always called "Ames." He was a major in the Marine Corps before attending Crozer Seminary, but he later became an insurance salesman. He and his wife had five children. The third and youngest child of A.C. and Helen was given the name Margaret but was called "Patty." Patty never married; she became a social worker and lived in Iowa.

5. Calvin Class and Leslie Cohen, *Variations in Nuclear Themes* (Princeton, N.J.: World Scientific, 1994), xv–xviii.

6. Two of the children are living. Daughter Sue has three children, and the Hannas' son David has a son of his own. Thus the Judson legacy lives on to the seventh generation.

7. William Witherspoon had a daughter who had twins, so that family also survived to the seventh generation. Witherspoon contributed an interesting footnote about his great-grandfather. Hasseltine's birth name was Adoniram Judson, but people seemed to think he was deliberately assuming the initials "A.J." for Andrew Jackson. Therefore, he decided to reverse the order and be known for himself—Judson Adoniram Hasseltine. Thus the name "J.A." Hasseltine.

CHAPTER 31

1. Letter from Sarah Boardman Judson to Mrs. Lucius Bolles, October 10, 1836. American Baptist Historical Society Archives, Valley Forge, Pa.

2. Shwe Wa Maung, Erville Sowards, and Genevieve Sowards, *Burma Baptist Chronicles,* 1st ed. (Rangoon: Burma Baptist Convention, 1963), 339.

3. From the personal testimony of Daw Lone Ma (1913), 2. See chapter 25 for more about the Ah Vong family.

4. Testimony of Pye Tha Htin. Bain family papers.

5. Ibid., 4.

6. Ibid., 5.

7. Harriet Bain lives in Rolla, Missouri, and is a Women's Missionary Union leader there. Joan Myint is a professor of economics in Rangoon.

8. Shaw was Bucknell Unversity's first ever student from Burma. Bucknell now has a scholarship fund for Burmese students, which is named for Dr. Shaw Loo.

9. Maung, 65.

10. *Judson Centennial Celebration in Burma, 1813–1913* (Rangoon: Mission Press, 1913), 95–97.

CHAPTER 32

1. James Langdon Hill, *The Immortal Seven* (Philadelphia: American Baptist Publication Society, 1913), 32.

2. Ibid.

3. Letter from Mary Hasseltine to Ann Hasseltine Judson, January 12, 1821, American Baptist Historical Society Archives, Valley Forge, Pa.

4. Letter from Ann Hasseltine Judson to her parents, July 1820. In *Baptist Missionary Magazine, 1817–1850,* 2:382.

5. Stacy R. Warburton, *Eastward: The Story of Adoniram Judson* (New York: Round Table Press, 1937), 115.

6. Adoniram Brown Judson, "How Judson Became a Baptist Missionary," pamphlet (Philadelphia: American Baptist Publication Society, 1913), 9–10.

7. "Adoniram Judson, the Apostle of Burma," in *Calcutta Review,* 27 (1850): 436.

8. Francis Wayland, *A Memoir of the Life and Labors of the Rev. Adoniram Judson,* 2 vols. (Boston: Phillips, Sampson and Company, 1853), 1:421.

9. Ibid., 1:476.

10. Harriet Chapman Conant, *The Earnest Man: The Character and Labors of Adoniram Judson* (Boston: Phillips, Sampson and Co., 1856), 84.

11. Dana L. Robert, *Women in Mission: A Social History of Their Thought and Practice* (Macon, Ga.: Mercer University Press, 1996), 45.

12. Dana L. Robert, "Evangelist or Homemaker," in *International Bulletin of Missionary Research* 17, no. 1 (1993): 4–5.

13. Sharon James, *My Heart in His Hands* (Durham, England: Evangelical Press, 1999), 201–4.

14. Conant, 341.

15. Hill, 30–33.

16. Joan Jacobs Brumberg, *Mission for Life* (New York: The Free Press, 1980) 95.

17. Ibid., 103.

18. The earliest painting of Ann, a miniature of her at twenty-one by Nathaniel Rogers in 1811 that is held in the Valley Forge archives of American Baptist Historical Society is remarkably well-preserved. All subsequent early engravings and lithographs were based on this original miniature. There is also evidently a missing portrait, for in 1823, Ann wrote to Francis Wayland that a "Miss Peale" had painted her "likeness" but it was "not very good." There is a reference to a painting (likely a miniature) of Ann Hasseltine Judson in *The Peale Family: Creation of a Legacy 1770–1870,* ed. Lillian B. Miller (235). This painting of Ann by Anna Claypoole Peale was exhibited at the Boston Athenaeum in 1828 but is now listed as "unlocated."

CHAPTER 33

1. Emily Chubbuck Judson, *Memoir of Sarah B. Judson, Member of the Mission to Burma* (New York: privately published, 1848), 8.

2. Ibid., 16–17.

3. Arabella Stuart, *The Three Mrs. Judsons.* Missionary Series, ed. Gary W. Long (Springfield, Mo.: Particular Baptist Press, 1999), 123.

4. E. C. Judson, 21.

5. Joan Jacobs Brumberg, *Mission for Life: The Story of the Family of Adoniram Judson* (New York: The Free Press, 1980), 69.

6. Walter N. Wyeth, *Sarah B. Judson: A Memorial* (Philadelphia: privately published, 1890), 50.

7. See the account of the letter in chapter 16.

8. Letter from Adoniram Judson to Mrs. Chaplin, June 7, 1831. American Baptist Historical Society Archives, Valley Forge, Pa.

9. Laurens, "Men I Meet: George Dana Boardman," in *The Standard* (1893). Article included in the George D. Boardman Jr. file, American Baptist Historical Society Library, Rochester, N.Y.

10. Wyeth, 95–96.

11. See account of the letter in chapter 17.

12. See chapter 20 for Adoniram's letter about the watch.

13. Letter from Sarah Boardman Judson to her parents, October 28, 1835, American Baptist Historical Society Archives, Valley Forge, Pa.

14. Letter from Sarah Boardman Judson to her parents, April, 1836, American Baptist Historical Society Archives, Valley Forge, Pa.

15. Letter from Sarah Boardman Judson to her parents, November 21, 1838, American Baptist Historical Society Archives, Valley Forge, Pa.

16. Edward Judson, *The Life of Adoniram Judson* (New York: American Baptist Publication Society, 1883), 399–400.

17. Letter from Sarah Boardman Judson to her parents, November 21, 1839, American Baptist Historical Society Archives, Valley Forge, Pa.

18. Letter from Sarah Boardman Judson to her parents, November 30, 1838, American Baptist Historical Society Archives, Valley Forge, Pa.

19. Wyeth, 169.

20. An accompanying list of family items mentions books, dishes, miscellany, and the painting of a tree by Mrs. Joseph (Mabel) Hall. Sarah's maiden name was Hall.

21. Dana L. Robert, "Evangelist or Homemaker," *International Bulletin of Missionary Research* 17, no. 1 (1993): 5.

22. James Langdon Hill, *The Immortal Seven* (Philadelphia: American Baptist Publication Society, 1913), 66.

23. E. Judson, 453–54.

CHAPTER 34

1. A. C. Kendrick, *The Life and Letters of Mrs. Emily C. Judson* (New York and Boston: Sheldon and Co., 1860), 207.

2. Ibid., 38.

3. Ibid., 127

4. Cortland P. Auser, *Nathaniel Parker Willis* (New York: Twayne Publishers, 1969), 63. Chapter 19 tells the story of Emily's first contact with N. P. Willis.

5. Kendrick, 122.

6. Emily Chubbuck Judson, 1817–1854. (Letter written by N. P. Willis to Emily Chubbuck, November 16, 1844, in possession of Judson family descendant.)

7. Kendrick, 109.

8. Ibid, 137.

9. An 1846 letter in the Valley Forge archives, from Anna Maria Anable to Emily, was evidently written the first week of January. It has recently been brought to light by Dr. George Tooze. This letter makes reference to one received from Emily that same day, in which she has just revealed to Anna Maria that she is in love with Adoniram. Anna Maria replies: "I see clearly that you love your dear old Dr. . . .I did think once that Willis had a hold on you that no one could loosen but your 'noble-minded holy old man' has done it, I see, and it seems to me that he is sent from God and we should not say a word." Later in the letter, Anna Maria writes: "In the meantime write me all about the Dr.—all that he says to you and what your plans are—for I feel quite confident as to how the whole will terminate. It seems as if this would be one of the heavenly matches."

10. Edward Judson, *The Life of Adoniram Judson* (New York: American Baptist Publication Society, 1883), 485.

11. Adoniram Judson and Emily Chubbuck Judson, 1846–1854. (Letter from Adoniram Judson to Emily Chubbuck, April 7, 1846, in possession of Judson family descendant)

12. See chapter 20 for Adoniram's letter to Emily.

13. In letters to Emily on April 2, 1846, and on April 6, Willis wrote: "I will bring all your letters as you request." In one of the letters he requested of her. "Please burn my letters to you," and ended by asking, "Gratify me by burning this explanatory letter." (N. P. Willis's letters, have been donated to the American Baptists archives at Valley Forge, Pa.)

14. Judson (Letter from Emily Chubbuck Judson to Anna Maria Anable, June 1846, in possession of Judson descendant.)

15. Letter written by Emily Chubbuck to Anna Maria Anable, February 13, 1846, in possession of Judson descendant

16. In a March 6, 1846 letter from Hamilton N.Y., Emily writes Anna Maria about Dr. Kendrick's response to news of their impending marriage: "The old man sits and laughs more heartily than I ever heard him before. He says he has always believed I would be a missionary." (Letter in possession of Judson descendant.)

17. George H. Tooze, *Judson Treasures of the First Baptist Church, Malden, with a Short Biography of the Life of Emily Chubbuck-Judson* (Malden, Mass.: First Baptist Church, Malden, 1979), 63. George Tooze was pastor of First Baptist Church, Malden, Adoniram Judson's birthplace, from 1877–1983.

18. James Langdon Hill, *The Immortal Seven* (Philadelphia: American Baptist Publication Society, 1913), 31.

19. Mrs. H.C. Conant, *The Earnest Man: The Character and Labors of Adoniram Judson* (Boston and New York: Phillips, Sampson and Co., 1856), 82.

20. Ibid., 84.

21. Emily scrutinized herself as well. In a March 5, 1851, letter to Anna Maria Anable (in the possession of a Judson descendant), she said: "Do you recall how we used to laugh about my coming home, an old woman, and how 'missionaryish' I should be. Well darling, I am very old (she was thirty-three) and very missionaryish."

22. A. C. Kendrick, *The Life and Letters of Mrs. Emily C. Judson* (New York and Boston: Sheldon and Co., 1860), 370.

23. Ibid., 146.

24. Stacy R. Warburton, *Eastward: The Story of Adoniram Judson* (New York: Round Table Press, 1937), 208.

CHAPTER 35

1. Edward Judson, sermon preparation notes for the 1888 Malden Judson Centennial. Held in the American Baptist Historical Society Library, Rochester, N.Y.

2. Joan Jacobs Brumberg, *Mission for Life: The Story of the Family of Adoniram Judson* (New York: The Free Press, 1980), 7.

3. W. O. Carver, "The Significance of Adoniram Judson," *Review and Expositor* 10, no. 4 (1913): 475–76.

4. James Langdon Hill, *The Immortal Seven* (Philadelphia: American Baptist Publication Society, 1913), 59.

5. Francis Wayland, *A Memoir of the Life and Labors of the Rev. Adoniram Judson*, 2 vols. (Boston: Phillips, Sampson and Co., 1853), 2:377.

6. Ibid., 2:380.

7. Adoniram Brown Judson, "How Judson Became a Baptist Missionary," pamphlet (Philadelphia: American Baptist Publication Society, 1913), 15–16.

8. Carver, 484.

9. Mrs. H. C. Conant, *The Earnest Man*, 10–12.

10. Ibid., 42.

11. A. B. Judson, 8–10.

12. Edward Judson, *The Life of Adoniram Judson* (New York: American Baptist Publication Society, 1883), 311.

13. Ibid, 314.

14. Ibid., 311.

15. Wayland, 1:446.

16. Ibid., 2:376.

17. Russell Brown, "The Life and Work of Adoniram Judson," in *Andover Newton Quarterly* 2 (January 1962), 17.

18. So keenly did it permeate all Adoniram stood for that Brumberg titled her book about Judson and nineteenth-century American evangelism *Mission for Life*.

19. Conant, 452.

20. Adoniram Judson, Personal Journal (1788–1849).

21. A. C. Hanna, "Judson's Prayer Life," in *Watchman-Examiner* (January 19, 1939), 68–69.

22. Ibid., 68.

23. Brumberg, 11.

24. E. Judson, 321.

25 Ibid., 413.

26 Conant, 153.

27 Ibid., 153–54.

28 Wayland, 390–91.

29. *Judson Centennial Celebration in Burma, 1813–1913*, 91.

30. T. Carson Hanna, "What Price Missions?" in *Watchman-Examiner* (June 26, 1930), 811.

31. Ibid.

32. Letter from Adoniram Judson to Mrs. Chaplin, June 7, 1831, American Baptist Historical Society Archives, Valley Forge, Pa. Judson tried self-denial and asceticism to a degree few ever do, even spending a symbolic period of forty days alone on the edge of the jungle. Judson alluded to this "space of forty days" in this letter to his friend, Mrs. Chaplin. In seeking to explain the process of grief through which he had been those four years, Judson commented that "the conviction is daily strengthening in my mind, that this world was designed as a state of discipline, not of rest."

33. Walter N. Wyeth, *Ann H. Judson: A Memorial* (Cincinnati: privately published, 1888), 156.

34. E. Judson, 324.

35. Letter from Emily Chubbuck Judson to Anna Maria Anable, October 21, 1849. In possession of a Judson descendant.

36. Brown, 24.

37. James A. Rogers, *Richard Furman: Life and Legacy* (Macon, Ga. Mercer University Press, 1985), 141.

38. Ibid., 138.

39. *Judson Centennial 1814–1914* (Philadelphia: American Baptist Publication Society, 1914), 154–58.

40. Warburton, 231.

41. William H. Brackney, "The Legacy of Adoniram Judson," *International Bulletin of Missionary Research* 1, no. 22 (1998), 7.

42. E. Judson, 546.

43. Wayland, 1:4.

44. Patrick Johnstone, *Operation World* (Richmond, Va.: International Mission Board, 2001), 462.

APPENDIX

1. Robert G. Torbet, *Venture of Faith* (Philadelphia: Judson Press, 1955), 122.

2. Shwe Wa Maung, Erville Sowards, and Genevieve Sowards, *Burma Baptist Chronicles*, 1st ed. (Rangoon: Burma Baptist Convention, 1963), 254.

3. Ibid, 136.

4. Torbet, 207.

5. Ibid., 252.

6. Maung, 222-24.

7. Ibid., 135, 269.

8. Ibid., 219.

9. Torbet, 224-25.

10. The grave and monument of Susan Haswell are in front of the hospital chapel, mute testimony to her fifty-nine years of service.

11. The Baptist Press moved from Moulmein to Rangoon in 1862 and was an essential part of Burmese Baptist work.

12. Genevieve Sowards, "Our Baptist Heritage in Burma," *Burma News*. Rangoon: Baptist Press, 1962, 5.

13. Torbet, 222.

14. In 1913 alone there were 3,600 baptisms, and by 1924 there were 1,100 churches with more than 86,000 members. By this time, Burmese Baptists had a college, two seminaries, two women's training schools, sixty-four secondary and high schools and 825 primary schools.

15. "In the Footsteps of Adoniram Judson," editorial in *Watchman-Examiner* April 16, 1925, 404.

16. Torbet, 461.

17. Ibid., 462.

18. J. Leslie Dunstan, "The Church in Burma Yesterday and Today," *Andover Newton Quarterly* Old Series LIV, New Series 2, no. 1 (1962): 34-36.

19. Ibid., 36.

20. Ibid., 36.

21. John R. W. Stott, "The Christian Church in Burma," *Christianity Today*, February 2, 1979, 31.

22. Arabella Stuart, *The Three Mrs. Judsons*, Missionary Series, Gary W. Long, ed. (Springfield, Mo.: Particular Baptist Press, 1999), xix.

23. Patrick Johnstone, Operation World (Richmond, Va. International Mission Board, 2001), 464.

24. Keith Tennis, *Burma News* October 1997, 2.

25. Johnstone, 463.

26. Tennis, 5.

BIBLIOGRAPHY

"Adoniram Judson, The Apostle of Burma." *Calcutta Review* 27 (1850): 423–55.

"Adoniram Judson's Great Confession." *Baptist Leader,* November 1958, 6–9.

Allen, Jonathan. "Sermon Delivered at Haverhill, February 5, 1812, on the Occasion of Two Young Ladies Being about to Embark as Wives of Messieurs Judson and Newell, Going as Missionaries to India." Haverhill, Mass., 1812.

Anderson, Courtney. *To the Golden Shore.* 1st ed. Boston: Brown and Company, 1956.

———. "Why I Wrote a Life of Adoniram Judson." *Missions Magazine* March 1962, 16–18.

Anderson, Rufus. *Memoir of Catherine Brown—A Cherokee Indian of the Cherokee Nation.* 2nd ed. New York: Crocker and Brewster, 1825.

Andover Newton Seminary Archives. Judson correspondence: 1811–1853.

Auser, Cortland P. *Nathaniel Parker Willis.* New York: Twayne Publishers, 1969.

Bain, Harriet Hla Bu. Family Documents, 1828 to present.

Beaver, Pierce R. *American Protestant Women in World Mission Endeavors.* Grand Rapids: Eerdmans, 1968.

Boardman, George Dana, Jr. Manuscript Collection, RG1016, American Baptist Samuel Colgate Historical Library, Rochester, New York.

Brackney, William H. "The Legacy of Adoniram Judson." *International Bulletin of Missionary Research.* 1, no. 22 (1998): 122–27.

Brown, Ron. *The Judson Family Connection.* Valley Forge, Pa.: American Baptist Historical Society, 1983.

Bruce, James M. "In Memoriam: Edward Judson." *Watchman-Examiner,* November 12, 1914, 1493–95.

Brumberg, Joan Jacobs. *Mission for Life: The Story of the Family of Adoniram Judson.* New York: The Free Press, 1980.

Carver, W. O. "The Significance of Adoniram Judson." *Review and Expositor* 10, no. 4 (1913): 475–84.

Christian, John L. "Americans and the First Anglo-Burmese War." *The Pacific Review* 5, no. 4 (1936): 312–24.

Chubbuck, Emily. Documents and family letters from Manuscript Collection, RG1099, American Baptist Samuel Colgate Library, Rochester, NY, and official correspondence, Board of International Ministries, American Baptist Historical Society, Valley Forge, PA.

Clement, J. *The Life of the Rev. Adoniram Judson: The Heroic Pioneer Missionary to the Tropics of the Orient.* New York: Derby and Miller, 1857.

Codman, John. "The Captain's Story." Typescript from *The Standard* (September 14, 1895), American Baptist Historical Society, Valley Forge, PA.

Conant, Harriet Chaplin. *The Earnest Man: The Character and Labors of Adoniram Judson.* Boston: Phillips, Sampson and Co., 1856.

Crain, L. A. "The Judson Memorials." *Burma News,* 75, no. 5 (1962): 8–9.

Cumming, Michael, and Joe Clark, eds. *Myanmar (Burma).* Melbourne: Lonely Planet Publications, 2000.

Dean, William. "Reminiscence" (1893). American Baptist Samuel Colgate Library, Rochester, N.Y.

Dunstan, J. Leslie. "The Church in Burma Yesterday and Today." *Andover Newton Quarterly,* Old Series 54, New Series 2, no. 1 (1962): 34–51.

Dwight, Edwin. *Memoir of Henry Obookiah A Native of Owhyee and a Member of the Foreign Mission School.* New Haven: privately published, 1818.

Estep, William R. *Whole Gospel, Whole World.* Nashville: Broadman Press, 1994.

Gammell, William. *History of American Baptist Missions.* Boston: Gould, Kendall and Lincoln, 1849.

Gouger, Henry. *A Personal Narration of Two Years' Imprisonment in Burmah.* London: John Murray, 1860.

Greenwood, Nicholas. *Guide to Burma,* 2nd ed. The Globe Pequot Press, Inc., 1996.

Haggard, Howard W., and Fred Groce. "Judson Centennial: 1813–1914." Philadelphia: American Baptist Publication Society, 1914.

Hall, Gordon Langley. *Golden Boats from Burma.* Philadelphia: Macrae Smith Co., 1961.

Hanna, T. A. T. *Watchman-Examiner,* October 12, 1916.

Hanna, T. Carson. "What Price Missions?" *Watchman-Examiner,* June 26, 1930, 811–12.

Hartley, Cecil B. *The Three Mrs. Judsons: The Celebrated Female Missionaries.* Philadelphia: G. G. Evans, 1860.

Hervey, Winfred. *The Story of Baptist Missions in Foreign Lands.* St. Louis: Chancy R. Barns, 1885.

Hill, James Langdon. *The Immortal Seven.* Philadelphia: American Baptist Publication Society, 1913.

Howard, Randolph L. *It Began in Burma.* Philadelphia: Judson Press, 1942.

Hubbard, Ethel Daniels. *Ann of Ava.* New York: Books for Libraries Press, 1913.

Hull, J. Mervin. "American Reminders of Judson." *Baptist Missionary Magazine,* December 1903, 762–65.

Johnstone, Patrick, and Jason Mandryk. *Operation World, 21st Century Edition.* Richmond, Va.: International Mission Board, 2001.

Judson, Abigail Ann. Official correspondence, Board of International Ministries, American Baptist Historical Society, Valley Forge, PA.

———. *From Night to Morn.* Cincinnati: N. Watkin, 1894.

Judson, Adoniram. Personal Journal, 1788–1849, and correspondence. American Baptist Samuel Colgate Library, Rochester, New York.

———. "Advice to Candidates for Missionary Labor (1832)." *Europe,* August 1998, 3–5.

Judson, Adoniram Brown. Official correspondence, Board of International Ministries, American Baptist Historical Society, Valley Forge, PA.

———. "Early Recollections of Burma." *Brown University Alumni Monthly* (1915).

————. "How Judson Became a Baptist Missionary." Philadelphia: American Baptist Publication Society, 1913.

Judson, Ann Hasseltine. *An Account of the American Baptist Mission to the Burman Empire, in a Series of Letters Addressed to a Gentleman in London.* Washington, D.C.: Mission Press, Columbian Office, 1823.

Judson Centennial Celebration in Burma, 1813–1913. Rangoon: Mission Press, 1913.

"Judson Centennial, 1814–1914." Philadelphia: American Baptist Publication Society, 1914.

Judson Centennial: Malden, Massachusetts, 1888. Malden, Mass.: Mystic Side Press, 1888.

The Life of Adoniram Judson, 1st ed. New York: American Baptist Publication Society, 1883.

————. Official correspondence, Board of International Ministries, American Baptist Historical Society, Valley Forge, PA.

Judson, Emily Chubbuck. Manuscript Collection RG1099, American Baptist Samuel Colgate Library, Rochester, N.Y., and official correspondence, Board of International Ministries, American Baptist Historical Society, Valley Forge, Pa.

————. *Memoir of Sarah B. Judson, Member of the Mission to Burmah.* New York and Cincinnati: privately published, 1848.

Judson, Elnathan. Official correspondence, Board of International Ministries, American Baptist Historical Society, Valley Forge, Pa., and personnel records from Union Theological Seminary, N. Y.

Judson, Henry Hall. Official correspondence, Board of International Ministries, American Baptist Historical Society, Valley Forge, Pa., and personnel files from the Department of the Army Archives, Washington, D.C.

Judson, Sarah Boardman. Manuscript Collection RG1093, American Baptist Samuel Colgate Library, Rochester NY, and official correspondence, Board of International Ministries, American Baptist Historical Society, Valley Forge, Pa.

Kendrick, A. C. *The Life and Letters of Mrs. Emily C. Judson.* New York: Sheldon and Co., 1860.

Klein, Wilhelm. *Burma: Insight Guides.* Singapore: Houghton Mifflin, 1996.

Knowles, James D. *Memoir of Mrs. Ann H. Judson, Late Missionary to Burmah,* 1st ed. Boston: Lincoln and Edmands, 1829.

Laurens. "Men I Meet: George Dana Boardman." *The Standard* (1893).

Lee, Tan Chung. "A Tale of Two Royal Cities." *Pyinsa Rupa,* July–September 1997, 9–13.

Leonard, Bill J. *Baptist Ways: A History.* Valley Forge, Pa.: Judson Press, 2003.

"The Magnetism of Adoniram Judson." *Andover Newton Quarterly,* Old Series 54, New Series 2, no. 1 (1962): 3–4.

Manly, Louise. *History of Judson College.* Atlanta: Foote and Davies, 1913.

Maung, Shwe Wa, Erville Sowards, and Genevieve Sowards. *Burma Baptist Chronicles,* 1st ed. Rangoon: Burma Baptist Convention, 1963.

Mild, Warren P. *Howard Malcom and the Great Mission Advance.* Valley Forge, Pa.: Board of International Ministries, ABC/USA. 1988

Mortensen, Joseph Ide. "The Career of the Rev. G. D. Boardman." Boston: unpublished dissertation, 1966.

Myanmar (Burma): Lonely Planet Travel Survival Kit. Melbourne, Australia: Lonely Planet Publications, 1996.

Pearn, B. R. *A History of Rangoon.* Rangoon: American Baptist Mission Press, 1939.

Robert, Dana L. "Evangelist or Homemaker." *International Bulletin of Missionary Research* 17, no. 1 (1993): 4–8.

———. *Women in Mission: A Social History of Their Thought and Practice.* Macon, Ga.: Mercer University Press, 1996.

Rogers, James A. *Richard Furman: Life and Legacy.* Macon, Ga.: Mercer University Press, 1996.

Seagrave, Gordon S. *Burma Surgeon.* New York: Norton and Co., 1943.

Sears, Charles Hatch. *Edward Judson: Interpreter of God.* Philadelphia: Griffith and Rowland, 1917.

Sowards, Genevieve. "Our Baptist Heritage in Burma." *Burma News,* April 1962, 5–9.

Stott, John R. W. "The Christian Church in Burma." *Christianity Today,* February 2, 1979, 30–31.

Tooze, George H. *Judson Treasures of the First Baptist Church, Malden, with a Short Biography of the Life of Emily Chubbuck Judson.* Malden, Mass.: First Baptist Church, Malden, 1979.

Torbet, Robert G. *Venture of Faith.* Philadelphia: Judson Press, 1955.

Warburton, Stacy R. *Eastward: The Story of Adoniram Judson.* New York: Round Table Press, 1937.

Wayland, Francis. *A Memoir of the Life and Labors of the Rev. Adoniram Judson,* 2 vols. Boston: Phillips, Sampson and Company, 1853.

Willson, Arabella Stuart. *The Lives of Mrs. Ann H. Judson and Mrs. Sarah B. Judson, with a Biographical Sketch of Mrs. Emily C. Judson, Missionaries to Burma.* Buffalo, N.Y.: privately published, 1854.

———. *The Three Mrs. Judsons.* Missionary Series, edited by Gary W. Long. Springfield, Mo.: Particular Baptist Press, 1999.

Wyeth, Walter N. *Ann H. Judson: A Memorial.* Cincinnati: privately published, 1888.

———. *Emily C. Judson: A Memorial.* Philadelphia: privately published, 1890.

———. *Sarah B. Judson: A Memorial.* Philadelphia: privately published, 1890.

I N D E X

CHRONOLOGY

1788 – August 9. Adoniram Judson born at Malden, Massachusetts

1789 – December 22. Ann Hasseltine born at Bradford, Massachusetts

1803 – November 3. Sarah Hall born at Alstead, New Hampshire

1804 – August 17. Adoniram enters Brown University

1807 – April 30. Adoniram graduates from Brown

1808 – October 12. Adomiram enters Andover Seminary

1808 – December 2. Adoniram makes a solemn dedication to God

1810 – February. Adoniram resolves to become a missionary

1810 – June 28. Adoniram petitions General Association to form a missionary society *and* meets Ann

1810 – July 28. Adoniram proposes to Ann

1812 – February 5. Adoniram and Ann marry

1812 – February 6. Adoniram ordained at Tabernacle Church, Salem, Massachusetts

1812 – February 19. Adoniram and Ann embark for Calcutta

1812 – June 17. Adoniram and Ann arrive in Calcutta

1812 – September 6. Adoniram and Ann baptized in Calcutta

1813 – July. Ann gives birth at sea to stillborn son

1813 – July 13. Adoniram and Ann arrive in Rangoon

1815 – September 5. Receive news of formation of American Baptist Board of Foreign Missions in 1814

1815 – September 11. Roger Williams Judson born in Rangoon

1816 – May 4. Roger Williams Judson dies

1817 – August 22. Emily Chubbuck born at Eaton, New York

1819 – June 27. Maung Nau, first Burman convert, is baptized

1823 – July 12. Adoniram completes translation of New Testament into Burmese

1824 – January 23. Adoniram and Ann arrive in Ava

1824 – June 8. Adoniram fettered in prison

1825 – January 26. Maria Elizabeth Butterworth Judson born in Ava

1825 – May 2. Adoniram removed to Aungbinle prison

1825 – December 31. Adoniram released from prison and put under charge of Governor of the North Gate

1826 – February 21. Adoniram and Ann leave Ava

1826 – July 2. Adoniram and Ann arrive in Amherst

1826 – July 5. Adoniram leaves to translate Treaty of Yandabo

1826 – October 24. Ann Hasseltine Judson dies in Amherst

1827 – April 24. Maria Elizabeth Butterworth Judson dies in Amherst

1827 – August 10. Adoniram joins George and Sarah Boardman in mission in Moulmein

1831 – February 11. George Boardman dies in Tavoy

1834 – January 31. Adoniram finishes translation of Old Testament

1834 – April 10. Adoniram marries Sarah Hall Boardman in Tavoy

1835 – October 31. Abigail Ann Judson born in Moulmein

1837 – April 7. Adoniram Brown Judson born in Moulmein

1839 – December 31. Henry Judson born in Moulmein

1841 – March 8. Luther Judson stillborn in Moulmein

1841 – July 30. Henry Judson dies at Serampore

1842 – July 8. Henry Hall Judson born at Moulmein

1843 – December 18. Charles Judson born at Moulmein

1844 – December 27. Edward Judson born at Moulmein

1845 – August 5. Charles Judson dies at Moulmein

1845 – September 1. Sarah Hall Boardman Judson dies at St. Helena

1846 – June 2. Adoniram marries Emily Chubbuck

1846 – July 11. Adoniram and Emily sail for Burma

1847 – December 24. Emily Frances Judson born in Moulmein

1850 – April 12. Adoniram Judson dies at sea

1851 – April 23. Charlie Judson stillborn in Moulmein

1854 – June 1. Emily Chubbuck Judson dies in Hamilton, New York

the Judson Family Tree

Sarah Hall (1803-1845) –m– George Dana Boardman (1801-1831)

- Sarah (1826-1829)
- George Dana (1828-1903)
- Judson Wade (1830)

Ann Hasseltine (1789-1826) –m– 1812 Adoniram Judson (1788-1850)

- Stillborn boy (1813)
- Roger Williams (1815-1816)
- Maria Elizabeth (1825-1827)

Sarah Boardman (1803-1845) –m– 1834 Adoniram Judson (1788-1850)

- Abby Ann (1835-1902)
- Adoniram Brown (1837-1916) –m– Ann Haughtwont
- Elnathan (1838-1896)
- Henry (1839-1841)
- Luther (Stillborn 1841)
- Henry Hall (1842-1918) –m– Emily Holland
- Charles (1843-1845)
- Edward (1844-1914) –m– Antoinette Barstow
  - Sarah Elizabeth (1877-1952)
  - Margaret (1880-1963)

Emily Chubbuck (1817-1854) –m– 1846 Adoniram Judson (1788-1850)

- Emily Frances (1847-1911)
- Charlie (Stillborn 1850)

Emily Frances –m– 1870 Thomas Alexander Thomson Hanna

- Emily Margaret (1871-1911)
- Thomas Carson (1872-1934)
  - Margaret (b. 1899)
  - Marjorie (b. 1901)
  - Thomas (b. 1905)
- Adoniram Judson (1875-1928)
  - Kenneth (b. 1899)
  - Ruth (b. 1901)
  - Malcolm (b. 1904)
- Arthur Ledlie (1877-1928)
- Miriam (1880-1958)
- Anabel (1881-1937)
- Edward Judson (1885-1948)
  - Marie (b. 1908)
  - Emily (b. 1911)
  - Dorothy (b. 1914)
  - Betty (b. 1918)
- Alexander Carson (1888-1942)
  - Helen (1916-1944)
  - George Ames (1917-1985)
  - Stanley (b. 1920)
  - Margaret (Patty) (b. 1928)